Microsoft®
Training &
            Certification

2073A: Programming a Microsoft SQL Server 2000 Database

Project Lead: Rich Rose
Instructional Designers: Rich Rose, Cheryl Hoople, Marilyn McGill
Instructional Software Design Engineers: Karl Dehmer, Carl Raebler, Rick Byham
Technical Lead: Karl Dehmer
Subject Matter Experts: Karl Dehmer, Carl Raebler, Rick Byham
Graphic Artist: Kirsten Larson (Independent Contractor)
Editing Manager: Lynette Skinner
Editor: Wendy Cleary
Copy Editor: Edward McKillop (S&T Consulting)
Production Manager: Miracle Davis
Production Coordinator: Jenny Boe
Production Support: Lori Walker (S&T Consulting)
Test Manager: Sid Benavente
Courseware Testing: TestingTesting123
Classroom Automation: Lorrin Smith-Bates
Creative Director, Media/Sim Services: David Mahlmann
Web Development Lead: Lisa Pease
CD Build Specialist: Julie Challenger
Online Support: David Myka (S&T Consulting)
Localization Manager: Rick Terek
Operations Coordinator: John Williams
Manufacturing Support: Laura King; Kathy Hershey
Lead Product Manager, Release Management: Bo Galford
Lead Product Manager, Data Base: Margo Crandall
Group Manager, Courseware Infrastructure: David Bramble
Group Product Manager, Content Development: Dean Murray
General Manager: Robert Stewart

Course Number: 2073A
Part Number: X09-89603
Released: 9/2000

END-USER LICENSE AGREEMENT FOR MICROSOFT OFFICIAL CURRICULUM COURSEWARE –STUDENT EDITION

PLEASE READ THIS END-USER LICENSE AGREEMENT ("EULA") CAREFULLY. BY USING THE MATERIALS AND/OR USING OR INSTALLING THE SOFTWARE THAT ACCOMPANIES THIS EULA (COLLECTIVELY, THE "LICENSED CONTENT"), YOU AGREE TO THE TERMS OF THIS EULA. IF YOU DO NOT AGREE, DO NOT USE THE LICENSED CONTENT.

1.   **GENERAL.** This EULA is a legal agreement between you (either an individual or a single entity) and Microsoft Corporation ("Microsoft"). This EULA governs the Licensed Content, which includes computer software (including online and electronic documentation), training materials, and any other associated media and printed materials. This EULA applies to updates, supplements, add-on components, and Internet-based services components of the Licensed Content that Microsoft may provide or make available to you unless Microsoft provides other terms with the update, supplement, add-on component, or Internet-based services component. Microsoft reserves the right to discontinue any Internet-based services provided to you or made available to you through the use of the Licensed Content. This EULA also governs any product support services relating to the Licensed Content except as may be included in another agreement between you and Microsoft. An amendment or addendum to this EULA may accompany the Licensed Content.

2.   **GENERAL GRANT OF LICENSE.** Microsoft grants you the following rights, conditioned on your compliance with all the terms and conditions of this EULA. Microsoft grants you a limited, non-exclusive, royalty-free license to install and use the Licensed Content solely in conjunction with your participation as a student in an Authorized Training Session (as defined below). You may install and use one copy of the software on a single computer, device, workstation, terminal, or other digital electronic or analog device ("Device"). You may make a second copy of the software and install it on a portable Device for the exclusive use of the person who is the primary user of the first copy of the software. A license for the software may not be shared for use by multiple end users. An "Authorized Training Session" means a training session conducted at a Microsoft Certified Technical Education Center, an IT Academy, via a Microsoft Certified Partner, or such other entity as Microsoft may designate from time to time in writing, by a Microsoft Certified Trainer (for more information on these entities, please visit www.microsoft.com). WITHOUT LIMITING THE FOREGOING, COPYING OR REPRODUCTION OF THE LICENSED CONTENT TO ANY SERVER OR LOCATION FOR FURTHER REPRODUCTION OR REDISTRIBUTION IS EXPRESSLY PROHIBITED.

3.   **DESCRIPTION OF OTHER RIGHTS AND LICENSE LIMITATIONS**

       3.1   *Use of Documentation and Printed Training Materials.*

              3.1.1   The documents and related graphics included in the Licensed Content may include technical inaccuracies or typographical errors. Changes are periodically made to the content. Microsoft may make improvements and/or changes in any of the components of the Licensed Content at any time without notice. The names of companies, products, people, characters and/or data mentioned in the Licensed Content may be fictitious and are in no way intended to represent any real individual, company, product or event, unless otherwise noted.

              3.1.2   Microsoft grants you the right to reproduce portions of documents (such as student workbooks, white papers, press releases, datasheets and FAQs) (the "Documents") provided with the Licensed Content. You may not print any book (either electronic or print version) in its entirety. If you choose to reproduce Documents, you agree that: (a) use of such printed Documents will be solely in conjunction with your personal training use; (b) the Documents will not republished or posted on any network computer or broadcast in any media; (c) any reproduction will include either the Document's original copyright notice or a copyright notice to Microsoft's benefit substantially in the format provided below; and (d) to comply with all terms and conditions of this EULA. In addition, no modifications may made to any Document.

              Form of Notice:

              © 2000. Reprinted with permission by Microsoft Corporation. All rights reserved.

              Microsoft and Windows are either registered trademarks or trademarks of Microsoft Corporation in the US and/or other countries. Other product and company names mentioned herein may be the trademarks of their respective owners.

       3.2   *Use of Media Elements.* The Licensed Content may include certain photographs, clip art, animations, sounds, music, and video clips (together "Media Elements"). You may not modify these Media Elements.

       3.3   *Use of Sample Code.* In the event that the Licensed Content includes sample code in source or object format ("Sample Code"), Microsoft grants you a limited, non-exclusive, royalty-free license to use, copy and modify the Sample Code; if you elect to exercise the foregoing rights, you agree to comply with all other terms and conditions of this EULA, including without limitation Sections 3.4, 3.5, and 6.

       3.4   *Permitted Modifications.* In the event that you exercise any rights provided under this EULA to create modifications of the Licensed Content, you agree that any such modifications: (a) will not be used for providing training where a fee is charged in public or private classes; (b) indemnify, hold harmless, and defend Microsoft from and against any claims or lawsuits, including attorneys' fees, which arise from or result from your use of any modified version of the Licensed Content; and (c) not to transfer or assign any rights to any modified version of the Licensed Content to any third party without the express written permission of Microsoft.

3.5   *Reproduction/Redistribution Licensed Content.* Except as expressly provided in this EULA, you may not reproduce or distribute the Licensed Content or any portion thereof (including any permitted modifications) to any third parties without the express written permission of Microsoft.

4.   **RESERVATION OF RIGHTS AND OWNERSHIP.** Microsoft reserves all rights not expressly granted to you in this EULA. The Licensed Content is protected by copyright and other intellectual property laws and treaties. Microsoft or its suppliers own the title, copyright, and other intellectual property rights in the Licensed Content. You may not remove or obscure any copyright, trademark or patent notices that appear on the Licensed Content, or any components thereof, as delivered to you. **The Licensed Content is licensed, not sold.**

5.   **LIMITATIONS ON REVERSE ENGINEERING, DECOMPILATION, AND DISASSEMBLY.** You may not reverse engineer, decompile, or disassemble the Software or Media Elements, except and only to the extent that such activity is expressly permitted by applicable law notwithstanding this limitation.

6.   **LIMITATIONS ON SALE, RENTAL, ETC. AND CERTAIN ASSIGNMENTS.** You may not provide commercial hosting services with, sell, rent, lease, lend, sublicense, or assign copies of the Licensed Content, or any portion thereof (including any permitted modifications thereof) on a stand-alone basis or as part of any collection, product or service.

7.   **CONSENT TO USE OF DATA.** You agree that Microsoft and its affiliates may collect and use technical information gathered as part of the product support services provided to you, if any, related to the Licensed Content. Microsoft may use this information solely to improve our products or to provide customized services or technologies to you and will not disclose this information in a form that personally identifies you.

8.   **LINKS TO THIRD PARTY SITES.** You may link to third party sites through the use of the Licensed Content. The third party sites are not under the control of Microsoft, and Microsoft is not responsible for the contents of any third party sites, any links contained in third party sites, or any changes or updates to third party sites. Microsoft is not responsible for webcasting or any other form of transmission received from any third party sites. Microsoft is providing these links to third party sites to you only as a convenience, and the inclusion of any link does not imply an endorsement by Microsoft of the third party site.

9.   **ADDITIONAL LICENSED CONTENT/SERVICES.** This EULA applies to updates, supplements, add-on components, or Internet-based services components, of the Licensed Content that Microsoft may provide to you or make available to you after the date you obtain your initial copy of the Licensed Content, unless we provide other terms along with the update, supplement, add-on component, or Internet-based services component. Microsoft reserves the right to discontinue any Internet-based services provided to you or made available to you through the use of the Licensed Content.

10.   **U.S. GOVERNMENT LICENSE RIGHTS**. All software provided to the U.S. Government pursuant to solicitations issued on or after December 1, 1995 is provided with the commercial license rights and restrictions described elsewhere herein. All software provided to the U.S. Government pursuant to solicitations issued prior to December 1, 1995 is provided with "Restricted Rights" as provided for in FAR, 48 CFR 52.227-14 (JUNE 1987) or DFAR, 48 CFR 252.227-7013 (OCT 1988), as applicable.

11.   **EXPORT RESTRICTIONS.** You acknowledge that the Licensed Content is subject to U.S. export jurisdiction. You agree to comply with all applicable international and national laws that apply to the Licensed Content, including the U.S. Export Administration Regulations, as well as end-user, end-use, and destination restrictions issued by U.S. and other governments. For additional information see <http://www.microsoft.com/exporting/>.

12.   **TRANSFER.** The initial user of the Licensed Content may make a one-time permanent transfer of this EULA and Licensed Content to another end user, provided the initial user retains no copies of the Licensed Content. The transfer may not be an indirect transfer, such as a consignment. Prior to the transfer, the end user receiving the Licensed Content must agree to all the EULA terms.

13.   **"NOT FOR RESALE" LICENSED CONTENT.** Licensed Content identified as "Not For Resale" or "NFR," may not be sold or otherwise transferred for value, or used for any purpose other than demonstration, test or evaluation.

14.   **TERMINATION.** Without prejudice to any other rights, Microsoft may terminate this EULA if you fail to comply with the terms and conditions of this EULA. In such event, you must destroy all copies of the Licensed Content and all of its component parts.

15.   **DISCLAIMER OF WARRANTIES.** **TO THE MAXIMUM EXTENT PERMITTED BY APPLICABLE LAW, MICROSOFT AND ITS SUPPLIERS PROVIDE THE LICENSED CONTENT AND SUPPORT SERVICES (IF ANY)** *AS IS AND WITH ALL FAULTS,* **AND MICROSOFT AND ITS SUPPLIERS HEREBY DISCLAIM ALL OTHER WARRANTIES AND CONDITIONS, WHETHER EXPRESS, IMPLIED OR STATUTORY, INCLUDING, BUT NOT LIMITED TO, ANY (IF ANY) IMPLIED WARRANTIES, DUTIES OR CONDITIONS OF MERCHANTABILITY, OF FITNESS FOR A PARTICULAR PURPOSE, OF RELIABILITY OR AVAILABILITY, OF ACCURACY OR COMPLETENESS OF RESPONSES, OF RESULTS, OF WORKMANLIKE EFFORT, OF LACK OF VIRUSES, AND OF LACK OF NEGLIGENCE, ALL WITH REGARD TO THE LICENSED CONTENT, AND THE PROVISION OF OR FAILURE TO PROVIDE SUPPORT OR OTHER SERVICES, INFORMATION, SOFTWARE, AND RELATED CONTENT THROUGH THE LICENSED CONTENT, OR OTHERWISE ARISING OUT OF THE USE OF THE LICENSED CONTENT. ALSO, THERE IS NO WARRANTY OR CONDITION OF TITLE, QUIET ENJOYMENT, QUIET POSSESSION, CORRESPONDENCE TO DESCRIPTION OR NON-INFRINGEMENT WITH REGARD TO THE LICENSED CONTENT. THE ENTIRE RISK AS TO THE QUALITY, OR ARISING OUT OF THE USE OR PERFORMANCE OF THE LICENSED CONTENT, AND ANY SUPPORT SERVICES, REMAINS WITH YOU.**

16.   **EXCLUSION OF INCIDENTAL, CONSEQUENTIAL AND CERTAIN OTHER DAMAGES. TO THE MAXIMUM EXTENT PERMITTED BY APPLICABLE LAW, IN NO EVENT SHALL MICROSOFT OR ITS SUPPLIERS BE LIABLE FOR ANY SPECIAL, INCIDENTAL, PUNITIVE, INDIRECT, OR CONSEQUENTIAL DAMAGES WHATSOEVER (INCLUDING, BUT NOT**

LIMITED TO, DAMAGES FOR LOSS OF PROFITS OR CONFIDENTIAL OR OTHER INFORMATION, FOR BUSINESS INTERRUPTION, FOR PERSONAL INJURY, FOR LOSS OF PRIVACY, FOR FAILURE TO MEET ANY DUTY INCLUDING OF GOOD FAITH OR OF REASONABLE CARE, FOR NEGLIGENCE, AND FOR ANY OTHER PECUNIARY OR OTHER LOSS WHATSOEVER) ARISING OUT OF OR IN ANY WAY RELATED TO THE USE OF OR INABILITY TO USE THE LICENSED CONTENT, THE PROVISION OF OR FAILURE TO PROVIDE SUPPORT OR OTHER SERVICES, INFORMATION, SOFTWARE, AND RELATED CONTENT THROUGH THE LICENSED CONTENT, OR OTHERWISE ARISING OUT OF THE USE OF THE LICENSED CONTENT, OR OTHERWISE UNDER OR IN CONNECTION WITH ANY PROVISION OF THIS EULA, EVEN IN THE EVENT OF THE FAULT, TORT (INCLUDING NEGLIGENCE), MISREPRESENTATION, STRICT LIABILITY, BREACH OF CONTRACT OR BREACH OF WARRANTY OF MICROSOFT OR ANY SUPPLIER, AND EVEN IF MICROSOFT OR ANY SUPPLIER HAS BEEN ADVISED OF THE POSSIBILITY OF SUCH DAMAGES. BECAUSE SOME STATES/JURISDICTIONS DO NOT ALLOW THE EXCLUSION OR LIMITATION OF LIABILITY FOR CONSEQUENTIAL OR INCIDENTAL DAMAGES, THE ABOVE LIMITATION MAY NOT APPLY TO YOU.

17. **LIMITATION OF LIABILITY AND REMEDIES.** NOTWITHSTANDING ANY DAMAGES THAT YOU MIGHT INCUR FOR ANY REASON WHATSOEVER (INCLUDING, WITHOUT LIMITATION, ALL DAMAGES REFERENCED HEREIN AND ALL DIRECT OR GENERAL DAMAGES IN CONTRACT OR ANYTHING ELSE), THE ENTIRE LIABILITY OF MICROSOFT AND ANY OF ITS SUPPLIERS UNDER ANY PROVISION OF THIS EULA AND YOUR EXCLUSIVE REMEDY HEREUNDER SHALL BE LIMITED TO THE GREATER OF THE ACTUAL DAMAGES YOU INCUR IN REASONABLE RELIANCE ON THE LICENSED CONTENT UP TO THE AMOUNT ACTUALLY PAID BY YOU FOR THE LICENSED CONTENT OR US$5.00. THE FOREGOING LIMITATIONS, EXCLUSIONS AND DISCLAIMERS SHALL APPLY TO THE MAXIMUM EXTENT PERMITTED BY APPLICABLE LAW, EVEN IF ANY REMEDY FAILS ITS ESSENTIAL PURPOSE.

18. **APPLICABLE LAW.** If you acquired this Licensed Content in the United States, this EULA is governed by the laws of the State of Washington. If you acquired this Licensed Content in Canada, unless expressly prohibited by local law, this EULA is governed by the laws in force in the Province of Ontario, Canada; and, in respect of any dispute which may arise hereunder, you consent to the jurisdiction of the federal and provincial courts sitting in Toronto, Ontario. If you acquired this Licensed Content in the European Union, Iceland, Norway, or Switzerland, then local law applies. If you acquired this Licensed Content in any other country, then local law may apply.

19. **ENTIRE AGREEMENT; SEVERABILITY.** This EULA (including any addendum or amendment to this EULA which is included with the Licensed Content) are the entire agreement between you and Microsoft relating to the Licensed Content and the support services (if any) and they supersede all prior or contemporaneous oral or written communications, proposals and representations with respect to the Licensed Content or any other subject matter covered by this EULA. To the extent the terms of any Microsoft policies or programs for support services conflict with the terms of this EULA, the terms of this EULA shall control. If any provision of this EULA is held to be void, invalid, unenforceable or illegal, the other provisions shall continue in full force and effect.

Should you have any questions concerning this EULA, or if you desire to contact Microsoft for any reason, please use the address information enclosed in this Licensed Content to contact the Microsoft subsidiary serving your country or visit Microsoft on the World Wide Web at http://www.microsoft.com.

Si vous avez acquis votre Contenu Sous Licence Microsoft au CANADA :

DÉNI DE GARANTIES. Dans la mesure maximale permise par les lois applicables, le Contenu Sous Licence et les services de soutien technique (le cas échéant) sont fournis *TELS QUELS ET AVEC TOUS LES DÉFAUTS* par Microsoft et ses fournisseurs, lesquels par les présentes dénient toutes autres garanties et conditions expresses, implicites ou en vertu de la loi, notamment, mais sans limitation, (le cas échéant) les garanties, devoirs ou conditions implicites de qualité marchande, d'adaptation à une fin usage particulière, de fiabilité ou de disponibilité, d'exactitude ou d'exhaustivité des réponses, des résultats, des efforts déployés selon les règles de l'art, d'absence de virus et d'absence de négligence, le tout à l'égard du Contenu Sous Licence et de la prestation des services de soutien technique ou de l'omission de la 'une telle prestation des services de soutien technique ou à l'égard de la fourniture ou de l'omission de la fourniture de tous autres services, renseignements, Contenus Sous Licence, et contenu qui s'y rapporte grâce au Contenu Sous Licence ou provenant autrement de l'utilisation du Contenu Sous Licence. PAR AILLEURS, IL N'Y A AUCUNE GARANTIE OU CONDITION QUANT AU TITRE DE PROPRIÉTÉ, À LA JOUISSANCE OU LA POSSESSION PAISIBLE, À LA CONCORDANCE À UNE DESCRIPTION NI QUANT À UNE ABSENCE DE CONTREFAÇON CONCERNANT LE CONTENU SOUS LICENCE.

EXCLUSION DES DOMMAGES ACCESSOIRES, INDIRECTS ET DE CERTAINS AUTRES DOMMAGES. DANS LA MESURE MAXIMALE PERMISE PAR LES LOIS APPLICABLES, EN AUCUN CAS MICROSOFT OU SES FOURNISSEURS NE SERONT RESPONSABLES DES DOMMAGES SPÉCIAUX, CONSÉCUTIFS, ACCESSOIRES OU INDIRECTS DE QUELQUE NATURE QUE CE SOIT (NOTAMMENT, LES DOMMAGES À L'ÉGARD DU MANQUE À GAGNER OU DE LA DIVULGATION DE RENSEIGNEMENTS CONFIDENTIELS OU AUTRES, DE LA PERTE D'EXPLOITATION, DE BLESSURES CORPORELLES, DE LA VIOLATION DE LA VIE PRIVÉE, DE L'OMISSION DE REMPLIR TOUT DEVOIR, Y COMPRIS D'AGIR DE BONNE FOI OU D'EXERCER UN SOIN RAISONNABLE, DE LA NÉGLIGENCE ET DE TOUTE AUTRE PERTE PÉCUNIAIRE OU AUTRE PERTE

DE QUELQUE NATURE QUE CE SOIT) SE RAPPORTANT DE QUELQUE MANIÈRE QUE CE SOIT À L'UTILISATION DU CONTENU SOUS LICENCE OU À L'INCAPACITÉ DE S'EN SERVIR, À LA PRESTATION OU À L'OMISSION DE LA 'UNE TELLE PRESTATION DE SERVICES DE SOUTIEN TECHNIQUE OU À LA FOURNITURE OU À L'OMISSION DE LA FOURNITURE DE TOUS AUTRES SERVICES, RENSEIGNEMENTS, CONTENUS SOUS LICENCE, ET CONTENU QUI S'Y RAPPORTE GRÂCE AU CONTENU SOUS LICENCE OU PROVENANT AUTREMENT DE L'UTILISATION DU CONTENU SOUS LICENCE OU AUTREMENT AUX TERMES DE TOUTE DISPOSITION DE LA U PRÉSENTE CONVENTION EULA OU RELATIVEMENT À UNE TELLE DISPOSITION, MÊME EN CAS DE FAUTE, DE DÉLIT CIVIL (Y COMPRIS LA NÉGLIGENCE), DE RESPONSABILITÉ STRICTE, DE VIOLATION DE CONTRAT OU DE VIOLATION DE GARANTIE DE MICROSOFT OU DE TOUT FOURNISSEUR ET MÊME SI MICROSOFT OU TOUT FOURNISSEUR A ÉTÉ AVISÉ DE LA POSSIBILITÉ DE TELS DOMMAGES.

LIMITATION DE RESPONSABILITÉ ET RECOURS. MALGRÉ LES DOMMAGES QUE VOUS PUISSIEZ SUBIR POUR QUELQUE MOTIF QUE CE SOIT (NOTAMMENT, MAIS SANS LIMITATION, TOUS LES DOMMAGES SUSMENTIONNÉS ET TOUS LES DOMMAGES DIRECTS OU GÉNÉRAUX OU AUTRES), LA SEULE RESPONSABILITÉ 'OBLIGATION INTÉGRALE DE MICROSOFT ET DE L'UN OU L'AUTRE DE SES FOURNISSEURS AUX TERMES DE TOUTE DISPOSITION DEU LA PRÉSENTE CONVENTION EULA ET VOTRE RECOURS EXCLUSIF À L'ÉGARD DE TOUT CE QUI PRÉCÈDE SE LIMITE AU PLUS ÉLEVÉ ENTRE LES MONTANTS SUIVANTS : LE MONTANT QUE VOUS AVEZ RÉELLEMENT PAYÉ POUR LE CONTENU SOUS LICENCE OU 5,00 $US. LES LIMITES, EXCLUSIONS ET DÉNIS QUI PRÉCÈDENT (Y COMPRIS LES CLAUSES CI-DESSUS), S'APPLIQUENT DANS LA MESURE MAXIMALE PERMISE PAR LES LOIS APPLICABLES, MÊME SI TOUT RECOURS N'ATTEINT PAS SON BUT ESSENTIEL.

À moins que cela ne soit prohibé par le droit local applicable, la présente Convention est régie par les lois de la province d'Ontario, Canada. Vous consentez Chacune des parties à la présente reconnaît irrévocablement à la compétence des tribunaux fédéraux et provinciaux siégeant à Toronto, dans de la province d'Ontario et consent à instituer tout litige qui pourrait découler de la présente auprès des tribunaux situés dans le district judiciaire de York, province d'Ontario.

Au cas où vous auriez des questions concernant cette licence ou que vous désiriez vous mettre en rapport avec Microsoft pour quelque raison que ce soit, veuillez utiliser l'information contenue dans le Contenu Sous Licence pour contacter la filiale de succursale Microsoft desservant votre pays, dont l'adresse est fournie dans ce produit, ou visitez écrivez à : Microsoft sur le World Wide Web à http://www.microsoft.com

Contents

About This Course

This section provides you with a brief description of the course, audience, suggested prerequisites, and course objectives.

Description

This five-day course provides students with the technical skills required to program a database by using Microsoft® SQL Server™ 2000.

Course 2073A is a major revision of course 833, *Implementing a Database on Microsoft SQL Server 7.0.* This course incorporates new features of SQL Server 2000. The course omits some of the content on querying. The deleted content will be offered in a separate two-day course, course 2071, *Querying Microsoft SQL Server 2000 with Transact-SQL.* The course adds content from course 2013, *Optimizing Microsoft SQL Server 7.0.* The course contains a new module on user-defined functions.

Audience

This course is designed for those who are responsible for implementing database objects and programming SQL Server databases by using Transact-SQL.

Student Prerequisites

This course requires that students meet the following prerequisites:

Experience using the Microsoft Windows® 2000 operating system to:

Connect clients running Windows 2000 to networks and the Internet.

Configure the Windows 2000 environment.

Create and manage user accounts.

Manage access to resources by using groups.

Configure and manage disks and partitions, including disk striping and mirroring.

Manage data by using NTFS.

Implement Windows 2000 security.

Optimize performance in Windows 2000.

> For students who do not meet these prerequisites, the following courses provide students with the necessary knowledge and skills:

Course 2051, *Microsoft Windows 2000 Network and Operating System Essentials*

Course 2052, *Supporting Microsoft Windows 2000 Professional and Server*

An understanding of basic relational database concepts, including:

Logical and physical database design.

Data integrity concepts.

Relationships between tables and columns (primary key and foreign key, one-to-one, one-to-many, many-to-many).

How data is stored in tables (rows and columns).

For students who do not meet these prerequisites, the following course provides students with the necessary knowledge and skills:

Course 1609, *Designing Data Services and Data Models*

Knowledge of basic Transact-SQL syntax (SELECT, UPDATE, and INSERT statements).

For students who do not meet these prerequisites, the following course provides students with the necessary knowledge and skills:

Course 2071A, *Querying Microsoft SQL Server 2000 with Transact-SQL*

Familiarity with the role of the database administrator.

Course Objectives

After completing this course, students will be able to:

Describe the elements of SQL Server.

Design a SQL Server enterprise application architecture.

Describe the conceptual basis of programming in Transact-SQL.

Create and manage databases and their related components.

Implement data integrity by using the IDENTITY column property, constraints, defaults, rules, and unique identifiers.

Plan for the use of indexes.

Create and maintain indexes.

Create, use, and maintain data views.

Design, create, and use stored procedures.

Implement user-defined functions.

Create and implement triggers.

Program across multiple servers by using distributed queries, distributed transactions, and partitioned views.

Optimize query performance.

Analyze queries.

Manage transactions and locks to ensure data concurrency and recoverability.

Student Materials Compact Disc Contents

The Student Materials compact disc contains the following files and folders:

Default.htm. This file opens the Student Materials Web page. It provides you with resources pertaining to this course, including additional reading, review and lab answers, lab files, multimedia presentations, and course-related Web sites.

Readme.txt. This file contains a description of the compact disc contents and setup instructions in ASCII format (non-Microsoft Word document).

AddRead. This folder contains additional reading pertaining to this course.

Answers. This folder contains answers to any questions in the modules and hands-on labs.

Appendix. This folder contains Appendix files for this course.

Fonts. This folder contains fonts that are required to view the PowerPoint presentation and Web-based materials.

Labfiles. This folder contains files that are used in the hands-on labs. These files may be used to prepare the student computers for the hands-on labs.

Media. This folder contains files that are used in multimedia presentations for this course.

Mplayer. This folder contains files that are required to install Microsoft Windows Media™ Player.

Pptview. This folder contains the PowerPoint Viewer, which is used to display the PowerPoint presentations that accompany the additional reading.

Webfiles. This folder contains the files that are required to view the Student Materials Web page.

Wordview. This folder contains the Word Viewer that is used to view any Word document (.doc) files that are included on the compact disc.

Document Conventions

The following conventions are used in course materials to distinguish elements of the text.

Convention	Use
◆	Indicates an introductory page. This symbol appears next to a topic heading when additional information on the topic is covered on the page or pages that follow it.
bold	Represents commands, command options, and syntax that must be typed exactly as shown. It also indicates commands on menus and buttons, dialog box titles and options, and icon and menu names.
italic	In syntax statements or descriptive text, indicates argument names or placeholders for variable information. Italic is also used for introducing new terms, for book titles, and for emphasis in the text.
Title Capitals	Indicate domain names, user names, computer names, directory names, and folder and file names, except when specifically referring to case-sensitive names. Unless otherwise indicated, you can use lowercase letters when you type a directory name or file name in a dialog box or at a command prompt.
ALL CAPITALS	Indicate the names of keys, key sequences, and key combinations —for example, ALT+SPACEBAR.
`monospace`	Represents code samples or examples of screen text.
[ ]	In syntax statements, enclose optional items. For example, [*filename*] in command syntax indicates that you can choose to type a file name with the command. Type only the information within the brackets, not the brackets themselves.
{ }	In syntax statements, enclose required items. Type only the information within the braces, not the braces themselves.
|	In syntax statements, separates an either/or choice.
►	Indicates a procedure with sequential steps.
...	In syntax statements, specifies that the preceding item may be repeated.
. . .	Represents an omitted portion of a code sample.

Microsoft®
Training &
Certification

Introduction

Contents

Microsoft®

Project Lead: Rich Rose
Instructional Designers: Rich Rose, Cheryl Hoople, Marilyn McGill
Instructional Software Design Engineers: Karl Dehmer, Carl Raebler, Rick Byham
Technical Lead: Karl Dehmer
Subject Matter Experts: Karl Dehmer, Carl Raebler, Rick Byham
Graphic Artist: Kirsten Larson (Independent Contractor)
Editing Manager: Lynette Skinner
Editor: Wendy Cleary
Copy Editor: Edward McKillop (S&T Consulting)
Production Manager: Miracle Davis
Production Coordinator: Jenny Boe
Production Support: Lori Walker (S&T Consulting)
Test Manager: Sid Benavente
Courseware Testing: TestingTesting123
Classroom Automation: Lorrin Smith-Bates
Creative Director, Media/Sim Services: David Mahlmann
Web Development Lead: Lisa Pease
CD Build Specialist: Julie Challenger
Online Support: David Myka (S&T Consulting)
Localization Manager: Rick Terek
Operations Coordinator: John Williams
Manufacturing Support: Laura King; Kathy Hershey
Lead Product Manager, Release Management: Bo Galford
Lead Product Manager, Data Base: Margo Crandall
Group Manager, Courseware Infrastructure: David Bramble
Group Product Manager, Content Development: Dean Murray
General Manager: Robert Stewart

Introduction

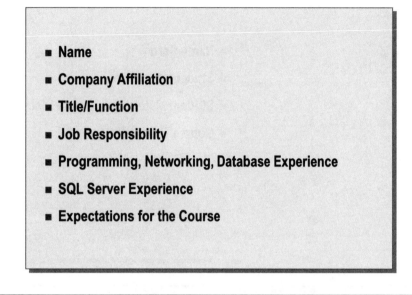

- Name
- Company Affiliation
- Title/Function
- Job Responsibility
- Programming, Networking, Database Experience
- SQL Server Experience
- Expectations for the Course

Course Materials

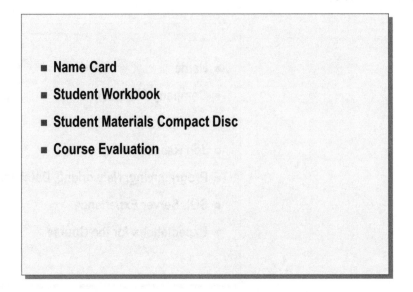

The following materials are included with your kit:

- *Name card.* Write your name on both sides of the name card.

- *Student workbook.* The student workbook contains the material covered in class, in addition to the hands-on lab exercises.

- *Student Materials compact disc.* The Student Materials compact disc contains the Web page that provides you with links to resources pertaining to this course, including additional readings, review and lab answers, lab files, multimedia presentations, and course-related Web sites.

Note To open the Web page, insert the Student Materials compact disc into the CD-ROM drive, and then in the root directory of the compact disc, double-click **Default.htm**.

- *Course evaluation.* To provide feedback on the course, training facility, and instructor, you will have the opportunity to complete an online evaluation near the end of the course.

To provide additional comments or inquire about the Microsoft Certified Professional program, send e-mail to mcphelp@microsoft.com.

Prerequisites

- **Experience Using Microsoft Windows 2000**
- **Understanding of Basic Relational Database Concepts**
- **Knowledge of Basic Transact-SQL Syntax**
- **Familiarity with the Role of the Database Administrator**

This course requires that you meet the following prerequisites:

- Experience using the Microsoft® Windows® 2000 operating system to:
  - Connect clients running Windows 2000 to networks and the Internet.
  - Configure the Windows 2000 environment.
  - Create and manage user accounts.
  - Manage access to resources by using groups.
  - Configure and manage disks and partitions, including disk striping and mirroring.
  - Manage data by using NTFS.
  - Implement Windows 2000 security.
  - Optimize performance in Windows 2000.

  For students who do not meet these prerequisites, the following courses provide students with the necessary knowledge and skills:

  - Course 2051, *Microsoft Windows 2000 Network and Operating System Essentials*
  - Course 2052, *Supporting Microsoft Windows 2000 Professional and Server*

- An understanding of basic relational database concepts, including:

    - Logical and physical database design.

    - Data integrity concepts.

    - Relationships between tables and columns (primary key and foreign key, one-to-one, one-to-many, many-to-many).

    - How data is stored in tables (rows and columns).

    For students who do not meet these prerequisites, the following course provides students with the necessary knowledge and skills:

    - Course 1609, *Designing Data Services and Data Models*

- Knowledge of basic Transact-SQL syntax (SELECT, UPDATE, and INSERT statements).

    For students who do not meet these prerequisites, the following course provides students with the necessary knowledge and skills:

    - Course 2071A, *Querying Microsoft SQL Server 2000 with Transact-SQL*

- Familiarity with the role of the database administrator.

Course Outline

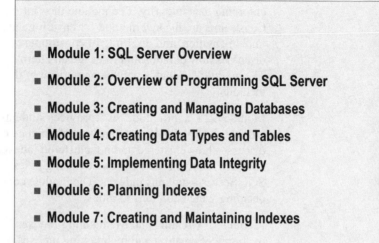

- Module 1: SQL Server Overview
- Module 2: Overview of Programming SQL Server
- Module 3: Creating and Managing Databases
- Module 4: Creating Data Types and Tables
- Module 5: Implementing Data Integrity
- Module 6: Planning Indexes
- Module 7: Creating and Maintaining Indexes

Module 1, "SQL Server Overview," provides a high-level overview of Microsoft SQL Server™ 2000 platforms, architecture, components, and security. It also identifies and defines key SQL Server terminology and concepts. This module discusses how well SQL Server integrates with Windows 2000 and other Microsoft server applications. It concludes with an overview of SQL Server administration and SQL Server database implementation, as well as application design options.

Module 2, "Overview of Programming SQL Server," provides students with an overview of enterprise-level application architecture and Transact-SQL as a programming language. Transact-SQL is a data definition, manipulation, and control language. Students are assumed to be familiar with ANSI-SQL and basic programming concepts, such as functions, operators, variables, and control-of-flow statements. Students will also learn the different ways to execute Transact-SQL.

Module 3, "Creating and Managing Databases," describes how to create a database, set database options, create filegroups, and manage a database and the transaction log. It reviews disk space allocation and how the transaction log records data modifications.

Module 4, "Creating Data Types and Tables," describes how to create data types and tables and generate Transact-SQL scripts containing statements that create a database and its objects.

Module 5, "Implementing Data Integrity," shows how centrally managed data integrity is a benefit of relational databases. This module begins with an introduction to data integrity concepts, including the methods available for enforcing data integrity. The module then introduces a section on constraints. Constraints are the key method for ensuring data integrity. The creation, implementation, and disabling of constraints are discussed. This module also discusses how defaults and rules are an alternate way to enforce data integrity. The module concludes with a comparison of the different data integrity methods.

Module 6, "Planning Indexes," provides students with an overview of planning indexes. It explains how database performance can be improved with indexes. It discusses how clustered and nonclustered indexes are stored in SQL Server and how SQL Server retrieves rows by using indexes. It also explores how SQL Server maintains indexes. The module concludes with guidelines for deciding which columns to index.

Module 7, "Creating and Maintaining Indexes," provides students with an overview of creating and maintaining indexes by using the CREATE INDEX options. It describes how maintenance procedures physically change the indexes. The module discusses maintenance tools and describes the use of statistics in SQL Server. It also describes ways to verify that indexes are used and explains how to tell whether they perform optimally. The module concludes with a discussion of when to use the Index Tuning Wizard.

Course Outline *(continued)*

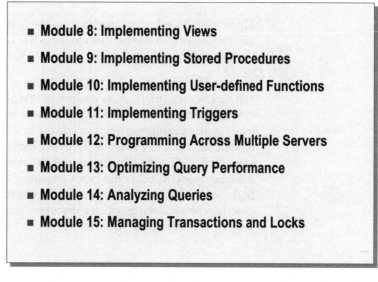

- ■ **Module 8: Implementing Views**
- ■ **Module 9: Implementing Stored Procedures**
- ■ **Module 10: Implementing User-defined Functions**
- ■ **Module 11: Implementing Triggers**
- ■ **Module 12: Programming Across Multiple Servers**
- ■ **Module 13: Optimizing Query Performance**
- ■ **Module 14: Analyzing Queries**
- ■ **Module 15: Managing Transactions and Locks**

Module 8, "Implementing Views," shows how views provide the ability to store a predefined query as an object in the database for later use. They offer a convenient way to hide sensitive data or the complexities of a database design and to provide a set of information without requiring the user to write or execute Transact-SQL statements. The module also defines views and their advantages. The module then describes creating views and provides examples of projections and joins. These examples illustrate how to include computed columns and built-in functions in the view definitions. The module then covers restrictions on modifying data through views. The last section discusses how views can improve performance.

Module 9, "Implementing Stored Procedures," describes how to use stored procedures to improve application design and performance by encapsulating business rules. It discusses ways to process common queries and data modifications. The module provides numerous examples and demonstrations of stored procedures.

Module 10, "Implementing User-defined Functions," discusses the implementation of user-defined functions. It explains the three types of user-defined functions and the general syntax for creating and altering them, and provides an example of each type.

Module 11, "Implementing Triggers," shows that triggers are useful tools for database implementers who want to have certain actions performed whenever data is inserted, updated, or deleted from a specific table. They are especially useful tools to cascade changes throughout other tables in the database, while preserving complex referential integrity.

Module 12, "Programming Across Multiple Servers," provides students with information on how to design security for a multi-server environment. It also explains the construction of distributed queries, distributed transactions, and partitioned views.

Module 13, "Optimizing Query Performance," provides students with an in-depth look at how the query optimizer works, how to obtain query plan information, and how to implement indexing strategies.

Module 14, "Analyzing Queries," describes how the query optimizer evaluates and processes queries that contain the AND operator, the OR operator, and join operations.

Module 15, "Managing Transactions and Locks," introduces how transactions and locks ensure transaction integrity while allowing for concurrent use. The module continues with a discussion of how transactions are executed and rolled back. A short animation helps to convey how transaction processing works. The module next describes how SQL Server locks maintain data consistency and concurrency. The module then introduces resources that can be locked, the different types of locks, and lock compatibility. A discussion follows on SQL Server dynamic locking based on schema and query. The final section describes some locking options, discusses deadlocks, and explains how to display information on active locks.

Setup

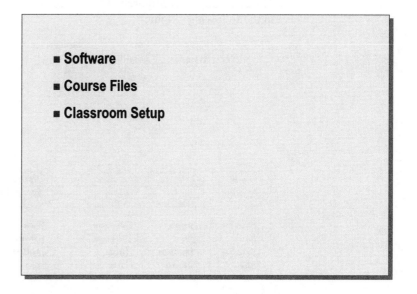

- Software
- Course Files
- Classroom Setup

The classroom environment is set up with software and a path to course files that you will use in class. You should also take note of the classroom configuration in which you will be performing the lab exercises.

Software

The following software will be used in the classroom:

- Microsoft Windows 2000 Advanced Server
- Microsoft SQL Server 2000, Enterprise Edition

Course Files

There are files associated with the labs in this course. The lab files are located in the C:\Moc\2073A\Labfiles on the student computers.

Classroom Setup

The classroom is configured in the single domain/workgroup model, as shown in the following graphic.

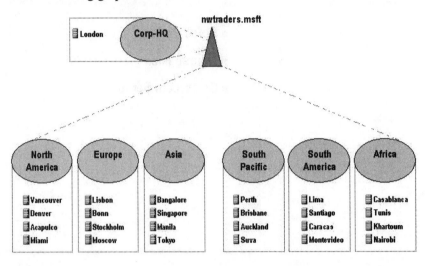

Each student computer in the classroom has Windows 2000 Advanced Server installed as a stand-alone server in a workgroup.

The organization of the classroom is meant to simulate that of a worldwide trading firm named Northwind Traders. Its fictitious domain name is nwtraders.msft. The primary DNS server for nwtraders.msft is the instructor computer, which has an Internet Protocol (IP) address of 192.168.*x*.200 (where *x* is the assigned classroom number). The name of the instructor computer is London.

The following table provides the user name, computer name, and IP address for each student computer in the fictitious **nwtraders.msft** domain. Find the user name for your computer, and make a note of it.

User name	Computer name	IP address
SQLAdmin1	Vancouver	192.168.*x*.1
SQLAdmin2	Denver	192.168.*x*.2
SQLAdmin3	Perth	192.168.*x*.3
SQLAdmin4	Brisbane	192.168.*x*.4
SQLAdmin5	Lisbon	192.168.*x*.5
SQLAdmin6	Bonn	192.168.*x*.6
SQLAdmin7	Lima	192.168.*x*.7
SQLAdmin8	Santiago	192.168.*x*.8
SQLAdmin9	Bangalore	192.168.*x*.9
SQLAdmin10	Singapore	192.168.*x*.10
SQLAdmin11	Casablanca	192.168.*x*.11
SQLAdmin12	Tunis	192.168.*x*.12
SQLAdmin13	Acapulco	192.168.*x*.13
SQLAdmin14	Miami	192.168.*x*.14
SQLAdmin15	Auckland	192.168.*x*.15
SQLAdmin16	Suva	192.168.*x*.16
SQLAdmin17	Stockholm	192.168.*x*.17
SQLAdmin18	Moscow	192.168.*x*.18
SQLAdmin19	Caracas	192.168.*x*.19
SQLAdmin20	Montevideo	192.168.*x*.20
SQLAdmin21	Manila	192.168.*x*.21
SQLAdmin22	Tokyo	192.168.*x*.22
SQLAdmin23	Khartoum	192.168.*x*.23
SQLAdmin24	Nairobi	192.168.*x*.24

Microsoft Official Curriculum

- **Microsoft Certified Systems Engineer (MCSE)**

- **Microsoft Certified Database Administrator (MCDBA)**

- **Microsoft Certified Solution Developer (MCSD)**

- **Microsoft Certified Professional + Site Building (MCP + Site Building)**

- **Microsoft Certified Professional**

- **Microsoft Certified Trainer (MCT)**

MOC is hands-on, facilitated classroom and Web-based training. Microsoft develops skills-based training courses to educate computer professionals who develop, support, and implement solutions by using Microsoft products, solutions, and technologies. MOC courses are available for the following products and solutions:

- Windows operating systems
- Microsoft Office
- Microsoft BackOffice® Small Business Server
- SQL Server
- Microsoft Exchange
- Microsoft BackOffice Server Infrastructure and Solutions
- Microsoft FrontPage®
- Microsoft Systems Management Server
- Knowledge Management Solutions

MOC has a curriculum path for each product and solution. For more information on the curriculum paths, see the Microsoft Official Curriculum Web page at http://www.microsoft.com/traincert/moc/

The Microsoft Official Curriculum Web page provides information about MOC courses. In addition, you can find recommended curriculum paths for individuals who are entering the Information Technology (IT) industry, who are continuing training on Microsoft products and solutions, or who currently support non-Microsoft products.

Microsoft Certified Professional Program

- **Microsoft Certified Systems Engineer (MCSE)**

- **Microsoft Certified Database Administrator (MCDBA)**

- **Microsoft Certified Solution Developer (MCSD)**

- **Microsoft Certified Professional + Site Building (MCP + Site Building)**

- **Microsoft Certified Professional**

- **Microsoft Certified Trainer (MCT)**

The Microsoft Certified Professional program is a leading certification program that validates your experience and skills to keep you competitive in today's changing business environment. The following table describes each certification in more detail.

Certification	Description
MCSA on Microsoft Windows 2000	The Microsoft Certified Systems Administrator (MCSA) certification is designed for professionals who implement, manage, and troubleshoot existing network and system environments based on Microsoft Windows 2000 platforms, including the Windows .NET Server family. Implementation responsibilities include installing and configuring parts of the systems. Management responsibilities include administering and supporting the systems.
MCSE on Microsoft Windows 2000	The Microsoft Certified Systems Engineer (MCSE) credential is the premier certification for professionals who analyze the business requirements and design and implement the infrastructure for business solutions based on the Microsoft Windows 2000 platform and Microsoft server software, including the Windows .NET Server family. Implementation responsibilities include installing, configuring, and troubleshooting network systems.
MCSD	The Microsoft Certified Solution Developer (MCSD) credential is the premier certification for professionals who design and develop leading-edge business solutions with Microsoft development tools, technologies, platforms, and the Microsoft Windows DNA architecture. The types of applications MCSDs can develop include desktop applications and multi-user, Web-based, N-tier, and transaction-based applications. The credential covers job tasks ranging from analyzing business requirements to maintaining solutions.
MCDBA on Microsoft SQL Server 2000	The Microsoft Certified Database Administrator (MCDBA) credential is the premier certification for professionals who implement and administer Microsoft SQL Server databases. The certification is appropriate for individuals who derive physical database designs, develop logical data models, create physical databases, create data services by using Transact-SQL, manage and maintain databases, configure and manage security, monitor and optimize databases, and install and configure SQL Server.

(*continued*)

Certification	Description
MCP	The Microsoft Certified Professional (MCP) credential is for individuals who have the skills to successfully implement a Microsoft product or technology as part of a business solution in an organization. Hands-on experience with the product is necessary to successfully achieve certification.
MCT	Microsoft Certified Trainers (MCTs) demonstrate the instructional and technical skills that qualify them to deliver Microsoft Official Curriculum through Microsoft Certified Technical Education Centers (Microsoft CTECs).

Certification Requirements

The certification requirements differ for each certification category and are specific to the products and job functions addressed by the certification. To become a Microsoft Certified Professional, you must pass rigorous certification exams that provide a valid and reliable measure of technical proficiency and expertise.

For More Information   See the Microsoft Training and Certification Web site at http://www.microsoft.com/traincert/.

You can also send e-mail to mcphelp@microsoft.com if you have specific certification questions.

Acquiring the Skills Tested by an MCP Exam

Microsoft Official Curriculum (MOC) and MSDN® Training Curriculum can help you develop the skills that you need to do your job. They also complement the experience that you gain while working with Microsoft products and technologies. However, no one-to-one correlation exists between MOC and MSDN Training courses and MCP exams. Microsoft does not expect or intend for the courses to be the sole preparation method for passing MCP exams. Practical product knowledge and experience is also necessary to pass the MCP exams.

To help prepare for the MCP exams, use the preparation guides that are available for each exam. Each Exam Preparation Guide contains exam-specific information, such as a list of the topics on which you will be tested. These guides are available on the Microsoft Training and Certification Web site at http://www.microsoft.com/traincert/.

Facilities

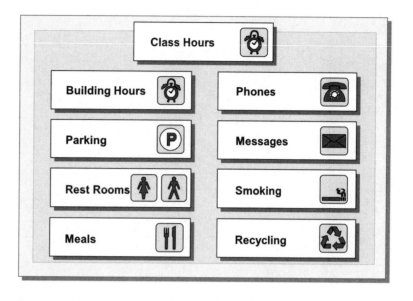

Microsoft®
Training &
Certification

Module 1: SQL Server Overview

Contents

Microsoft®

Project Lead: Rich Rose
Instructional Designers: Rich Rose, Cheryl Hoople, Marilyn McGill
Instructional Software Design Engineers: Karl Dehmer, Carl Raebler, Rick Byham
Technical Lead: Karl Dehmer
Subject Matter Experts: Karl Dehmer, Carl Raebler, Rick Byham
Graphic Artist: Kirsten Larson (Independent Contractor)
Editing Manager: Lynette Skinner
Editor: Wendy Cleary
Copy Editor: Edward McKillop (S&T Consulting)
Production Manager: Miracle Davis
Production Coordinator: Jenny Boe
Production Support: Lori Walker (S&T Consulting)
Test Manager: Sid Benavente
Courseware Testing: TestingTesting123
Classroom Automation: Lorrin Smith-Bates
Creative Director, Media/Sim Services: David Mahlmann
Web Development Lead: Lisa Pease
CD Build Specialist: Julie Challenger
Online Support: David Myka (S&T Consulting)
Localization Manager: Rick Terek
Operations Coordinator: John Williams
Manufacturing Support: Laura King; Kathy Hershey
Lead Product Manager, Release Management: Bo Galford
Lead Product Manager, Data Base: Margo Crandall
Group Manager, Courseware Infrastructure: David Bramble
Group Product Manager, Content Development: Dean Murray
General Manager: Robert Stewart

Overview

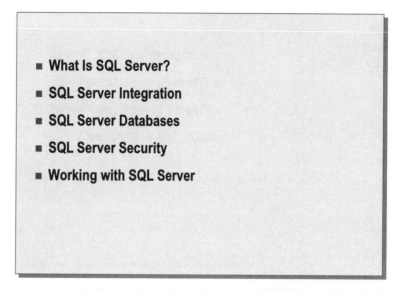

- **What Is SQL Server?**
- **SQL Server Integration**
- **SQL Server Databases**
- **SQL Server Security**
- **Working with SQL Server**

This module provides a high-level overview of Microsoft® SQL Server™ 2000 platforms, architecture, components, and security. It also identifies and defines key SQL Server terminology and concepts. This module discusses how SQL Server integrates with Microsoft Windows® 2000 and other Microsoft server applications. It concludes with an overview of SQL Server database administration and implementation activities, as well as SQL Server application design options.

After completing this module, you will be able to:

- Describe SQL Server 2000 and its supported operating system platforms.
- Describe SQL Server integration with Windows 2000 and other server applications.
- Describe SQL Server databases.
- Describe SQL Server security.
- Describe SQL Server administration and implementation activities, as well as SQL Server application design options.

◆ What Is SQL Server?

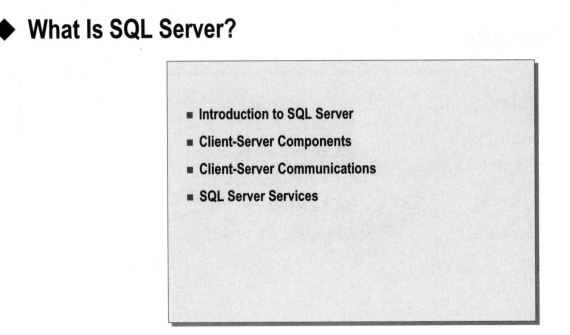

- Introduction to SQL Server
- Client-Server Components
- Client-Server Communications
- SQL Server Services

You use SQL Server to manage two types of databases—online transaction processing (OLTP) databases, and online analytical processing (OLAP) databases. Typically, separate clients access the databases by communicating over a network.

You can scale SQL Server up to terabyte-size databases and down to small business servers and portable computers. You can scale SQL Server out to multiple servers by using Windows Clustering in Windows 2000.

Introduction to SQL Server

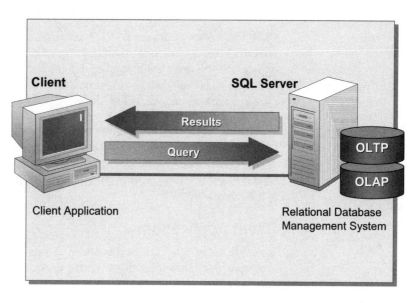

You can use SQL Server to perform transaction processing, store and analyze data, and build new applications.

SQL Server is a family of products and technologies that meets the data storage requirements of OLTP and OLAP environments. SQL Server is a relational database management system (RDBMS) that:

- Manages data storage for transactions and analysis.

- Responds to requests from client applications.

- Uses Transact-SQL, Extensible Markup Language (XML), multidimensional expressions (MDX), or SQL Distributed Management Objects (SQL-DMO) to send requests between a client and SQL Server.

Note This course focuses on activities associated with OLTP databases and Transact-SQL.

Relational Database Management System

The RDBMS of SQL Server is responsible for:

- Maintaining the relationships among data in a database.

- Ensuring that data is stored correctly and that the rules defining the relationships among data are not violated.

- Recovering all data to a point of known consistency, in the event of a system failure.

Data Storage Models

SQL Server manages OLTP and OLAP databases.

OLTP Databases   Data in an OLTP database is generally organized into relational tables to reduce redundant information and to increase the speed of updates. SQL Server enables a large number of users to perform transactions and simultaneously change real-time data in OLTP databases. Examples of OLTP databases include airline ticketing and banking transaction systems.

OLAP Databases   OLAP technology organizes and summarizes large amounts of data so that an analyst can evaluate data quickly and in real time. SQL Server 2000 Analysis Services organizes this data to support a wide array of enterprise solutions, from corporate reporting and analysis to data modeling and decision support.

Client Applications

Users do not access SQL Server and Analysis Services directly; instead, they use separate client applications written to access the data. These applications access SQL Server by using:

Transact-SQL   This query language, a version of Structured Query Language (SQL), is the primary database query and programming language that SQL Server uses.

XML   This format returns data from queries and stored procedures by using URLs or templates over Hypertext Transfer Protocol (HTTP). You also can use XML to insert, delete, and update values in a database.

MDX   The MDX syntax defines multidimensional objects and queries and manipulates multidimensional data in OLAP databases.

OLE DB and ODBC APIs   Client applications use OLE DB and Open Database Connectivity (ODBC), application programming interfaces (APIs) to send commands to a database. Commands that you send through these APIs use the Transact-SQL language.

ActiveX Data Objects and ActiveX Data Objects (Multidimensional)

Microsoft ActiveX® Data Objects (ADO) and ActiveX Data Objects (Multidimensional) (ADO MD) wrap OLE DB for use in languages such Microsoft Visual Basic®, Visual Basic for Applications, Active Server Pages, and Microsoft Internet Explorer Visual Basic Scripting. You use ADO to access data in OLTP databases. You use ADO MD to access data in Analysis Services data cubes.

English Query   This application provides an Automation API that lets users resolve natural-language questions instead of writing complex Transact-SQL or MDX statements about information in a database. For example, users are able to ask the question, "What are the total sales for Region 5?"

Client-Server Components

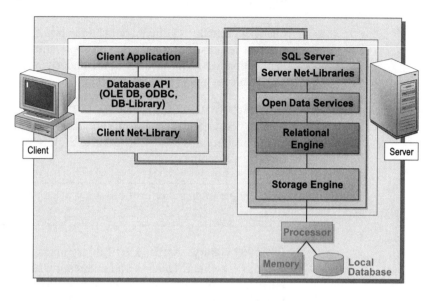

SQL Server consists of client and server components that store and retrieve data. SQL Server uses layered communication architecture to isolate applications from the underlying network and protocols. This architecture allows you to deploy the same application in different network environments.

Client-Server Architecture

SQL Server uses client-server architecture to separate the workload into tasks that run on server computers and those that run on client computers:

- The client is responsible for business logic and presenting data to the user. The client typically runs on one or more computers, but it also can run on the server computer along with SQL Server.

- SQL Server manages databases and allocates the available server resources—such as memory, network bandwidth, and disk operations— among multiple requests.

Client-server architecture allows you to design and deploy applications to enhance a variety of environments. Client programming interfaces provide the means for applications to run on separate client computers and communicate to the server over a network.

Note   In this course, the term client by itself refers to a client application.

Client Components

The client components in the communication architecture include:

Client Application   A client application ends Transact-SQL statements and receives result sets. You develop an application by using a database API. The application has no knowledge of the underlying network protocols used to communicate with SQL Server.

Database API   Database API (OLE DB, ODBC) uses a provider, driver, or DLL to pass Transact-SQL statements and receive result sets. This is an interface that an application uses to send requests to SQL Server and to process results that SQL Server returns.

Note   Some Internet applications are written to HTTP rather than a database API.

Client Net-Library   A client Net-Library manages network connections and routing on a client. This is a communication software component that packages the database requests and results for transmission by the appropriate network protocol.

Server Components

The server components in the communication architecture include:

Server Net-Libraries   SQL Server can monitor multiple Net-Libraries concurrently. The client Net-Library must match one of the server Net-Libraries to communicate successfully. SQL Server supports network protocols such as TCP/IP, Named Pipes, NWLink, IPX/SPX, VIA ServerNet II SAN, VIA GigaNet SAN, Banyan VINES, and AppleTalk.

Open Data Services   Open Data Services makes data services appear to a client as SQL Server by providing a network interface for handling network protocol processes and server routines. This is a component of SQL Server that handles network connections, passing client requests to SQL Server for processing and returning any results and replies to SQL Server clients. Open Data Services automatically listens on all server Net-Libraries that are installed on the server.

Relational Engine   The relational engine parses Transact-SQL statements, optimizes and executes execution plans, processes data definition language (DDL) and other statements, and enforces security.

Storage Engine   The storage engine manages database files and the use of space in the files, builds and reads data from physical pages, manages data buffers and physical input/output (I/O), controls concurrency, performs logging and recovery operations, and implements utility functions such as Database Consistency Checker (DBCC), backup, and restore.

Client-Server Communication Process

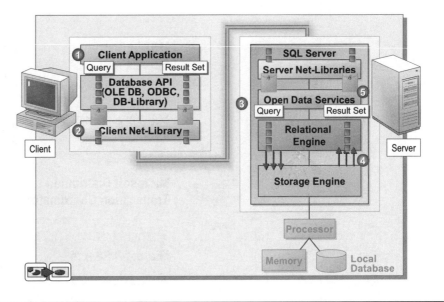

Clients and servers typically communicate over a network. The following sequence uses a query to illustrate the typical client-server communication process using a database API:

1. A client application submits a query. The client calls the database API and passes the query. The database API uses a provider, driver, or DLL to encapsulate the query in one or more Tabular Data Stream (TDS) packets and pass packets to the client Net-Library.

2. The client Net-Library packages the TDS packets into network protocol packets. The client Net-Library calls a Windows interprocess communication (IPC) API to send the network protocol packets to a server Net-Library by using the network protocol stack of the operating system. The appropriate server Net-Library extracts the TDS packets from the network protocol packets and passes the TDS packets to Open Data Services.

3. Open Data Services extracts the query from the TDS packets and passes the query to the relational engine. The relational engine then compiles the query into an optimized execution plan. It executes the execution plan. The relational engine communicates with the storage engine by using the OLE DB interface.

4. The storage engine transfers data from a database to data buffers and then passes rowsets containing data to the relational engine. The relational engine combines the rowsets into the final result set and passes the result set to Open Data Services.

5. Open Data Services packages the result set and returns it to the client application by using a server Net-Library, the network protocol stack, the client Net-Library, and the database API. The result set can also be returned in XML format.

SQL Server Services

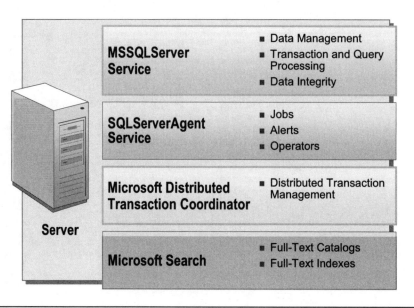

The SQL Server services include MSSQLServer service, SQLServerAgent service, Microsoft Distributed Transaction Coordinator (MS DTC), and Microsoft Search. Although these SQL Server services usually run as services on Windows 2000, they also can run as applications.

Four SQL Server Services

SQL Server includes four services, which are installed by default with a new installation: MSSQLServer service, SQLServerAgent service, Microsoft Distributed Transaction Coordinator, and Microsoft Search.

MSSQLServer Service

MSSQLServer service is the database engine. It is the component that processes all Transact-SQL statements and manages all files that comprise the databases on the server. MSSQLServer service:

- Allocates computer resources among multiple concurrent users.

- Prevents logic problems, such as timing requests from users who want to update the same data at the same time.

- Ensures data consistency and integrity.

SQLServerAgent Service

SQLServerAgent service works in conjunction with SQL Server to create and manage alerts, local or *multiserver* jobs, and operators. Consider the following about SQLServerAgent service:

- Alerts provide information about the status of a process, such as when a job is complete or when an error occurs.

- SQLServerAgent service includes a job creation and scheduling engine that automates tasks.

- SQLServerAgent service can send e-mail messages, page an operator, or start another application when an alert occurs. For example, you can set an alert to occur when a database or transaction log is almost full or when a database backup is successful.

Microsoft Distributed Transaction Coordinator

MS DTC allows clients to include several different sources of data in one transaction. MS DTC coordinates the proper completion of distributed transactions to ensure that all updates on all servers are permanent—or, in the case of errors, that all modifications are cancelled.

Microsoft Search

Microsoft Search is a full-text engine that runs as a service in Windows 2000. Full-text support involves the ability to issue queries against character data and the creation and maintenance of the indexes that facilitate these queries.

Multiple Instances of SQL Server

Multiple instances of the SQL Server may run concurrently on the same computer.

Each instance of SQL Server has its own set of system and user databases that are not shared between instances. Each instance operates as if it were on a separate server. Applications can connect to each SQL Server database engine instance on a computer in nearly the same way that they connect to SQL Server database engines running on different computers.

When you specify only the computer name, you work with the default instance. You must specify the *computer_name\instance_name* to connect to a named instance.

◆ SQL Server Integration

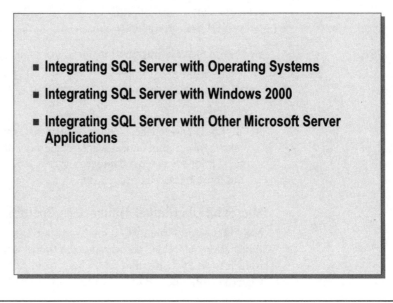

- **Integrating SQL Server with Operating Systems**
- **Integrating SQL Server with Windows 2000**
- **Integrating SQL Server with Other Microsoft Server Applications**

SQL Server includes client and server components that integrate with various Microsoft operating systems, including Windows 2000, and other Microsoft server applications. Internet browsers and third-party client applications running on various operating systems also can access SQL Server.

Integrating SQL Server with Operating Systems

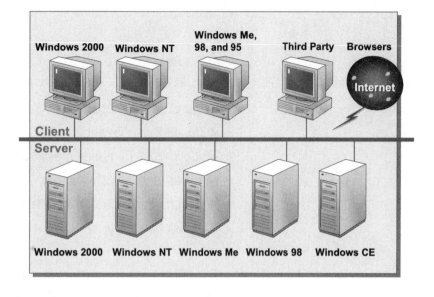

SQL Server includes client and server components that run on various operating systems.

Client Components

The client components from all SQL Server 2000 editions, except SQL Server Windows CE Edition, run on all editions of Windows 2000, versions of Microsoft Windows NT®, on Microsoft Windows Millennium Edition (Me), Microsoft Windows 98, and Microsoft Windows 95.

All client components from SQL Server 2000 CE edition run exclusively on the Windows CE operating system.

Server Components

The various editions of SQL Server allow it to run on all editions of Windows 2000, versions of Windows NT, Windows Me, Windows 98, and Windows CE. Specific versions of the operating systems and editions of SQL Server limit server components. Microsoft Windows NT Server 4.0, Service Pack 5 (SP5) or later must be installed as a minimum requirement for all SQL Server 2000 editions. Only the server components, such as the database engine and the Analysis server, are limited to specific versions of the operating systems. For example, although the database engine for Microsoft SQL Server 2000 Enterprise Edition does not run on Microsoft Windows 2000 Professional, Microsoft Windows NT Workstation, Windows Me, or Windows 98, you can use the SQL Server 2000 Enterprise Edition compact disc to install the client software on any of these operating systems.

Windows NT 4.0 Terminal Server does not support SQL Server 2000.

Internet Browsers and Third-Party Applications

Internet browsers and third-party client applications running on various operating systems also can access SQL Server.

Integrating SQL Server with Windows 2000

- **Active Directory**
- **Security**
- **Multiprocessor Support**
- **Microsoft Event Viewer**
- **Windows 2000 Component Services**
- **Windows 2000 System Monitor**
- **Microsoft Internet Information Services**
- **Windows Clustering**

SQL Server is fully integrated with Windows 2000 and takes advantage of many of its features.

Active Directory Servers and their attributes are registered automatically in the Active Directory™ directory service on server startup. Users can search and locate a particular server through Active Directory Search. For example, a user might use the directory to locate all of the servers running one or more instances of SQL Server with a particular database name installed on them.

Security SQL Server is integrated with the security system in Windows 2000. This integration allows a single user name and password to access both SQL Server and Windows 2000. SQL Server also uses encryption features in Windows 2000 for network security, including Kerberos support. SQL Server provides its own security for clients that need to access SQL Server without authentication by Windows 2000.

Multiprocessor Support SQL Server supports the symmetric multiprocessing (SMP) capabilities of Windows 2000. SQL Server automatically takes advantage of any additional processors that are added to the server computer.

Microsoft Event Viewer SQL Server writes messages to the Windows 2000 application, security, and system event logs, providing a consistent mechanism for viewing and tracking problems.

Windows 2000 Component Services Component Services is based on extensions of the Component Object Model (COM) and Microsoft Transaction Server. It provides improved threading, improved security, transaction management, object pooling, queued components, application administration, and application packaging. For example, software developers can use Component Services to visually configure routine component and application behavior, such as security and participation in transactions, and to integrate components into COM+ applications.

Windows 2000 System Monitor   SQL Server sends performance metrics to the Windows 2000 System Monitor, enabling you to monitor the system performance of SQL Server.

Microsoft Internet Information Services   SQL Server uses Microsoft Internet Information Services (IIS) so that Internet browsers can access a SQL Server database by using the HTTP protocol.

Windows Clustering   Windows Clustering, a component of Windows 2000 Advanced Server, supports the connection of two servers, or nodes, into a cluster for greater availability and better manageability of data and applications. SQL Server works in conjunction with Windows Clustering to switch automatically to the secondary node if the primary node fails.

Integrating SQL Server with Other Microsoft Server Applications

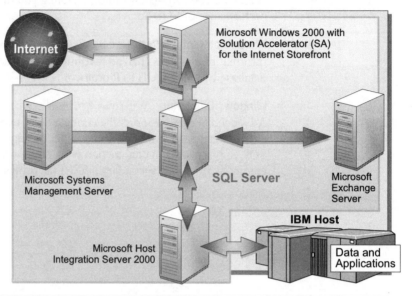

SQL Server integrates well with other Microsoft server applications. Microsoft provides a group of server applications that work together to help you build business solutions. The following table describes some commonly used server applications that work with or use SQL Server.

Server application	Description
Microsoft Windows 2000 Server with Solution Accelerator (SA) for the Internet Storefront	Provides secure, fast, manageable Internet connectivity. Includes an extensible, multilevel enterprise firewall and scalable high-performance Web cache.
Microsoft Exchange Server	Allows SQL Server to send e-mail messages by using Exchange Server or other Messaging Application Programming Interface (MAPI)-compliant providers.
	SQL Server can send messages when an error occurs or a scheduled task (such as a database backup) succeeds or fails. It also can respond to queries embedded in messages.
Microsoft Host Integration Server 2000	Links IBM environments running the Systems Network Architecture (SNA) protocol with PC-based networks.
	You can integrate SQL Server with IBM mainframe or AS/400 applications and data by using Microsoft Host Integration Server 2000.
Microsoft Systems Management Server	Manages computer software, hardware, and inventory and uses SQL Server to store its databases.

◆ SQL Server Databases

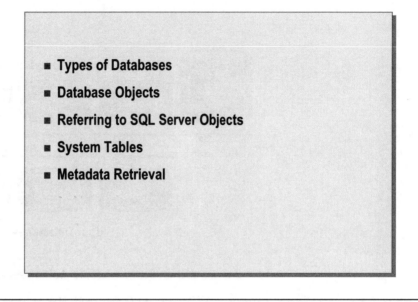

- Types of Databases
- Database Objects
- Referring to SQL Server Objects
- System Tables
- Metadata Retrieval

An understanding of SQL Server database structure will help you develop and implement your database effectively.

Types of Databases

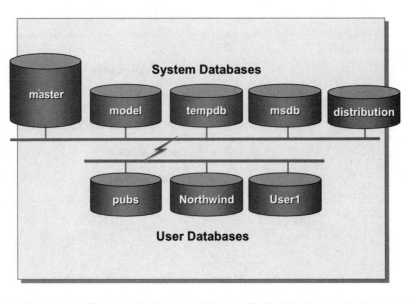

Each SQL Server has two types of databases: *system databases* and *user databases*. System databases store information about SQL Server as a whole. SQL Server uses system databases to operate and manage the system. User databases are databases that users create.

When SQL Server is installed, SQL Server Setup creates system databases and sample user databases. The Distribution Database is installed when you configure SQL Server for replication activities. The following table describes each database.

Database	Description
master	Controls the user databases and operation of SQL Server as a whole by keeping track of information such as user accounts, configurable environment variables, and system error messages
model	Provides a template or prototype for new user databases
tempdb	Provides a storage area for temporary tables and other temporary working storage needs
msdb	Provides a storage area for scheduling information and job history
distribution	Stores history and transaction data used in replication
pubs	Provides a sample database as a learning tool
Northwind	Provides a sample database as a learning tool
User1	Identifies a user-defined database

Database Objects

A database is a collection of data, tables, and other objects. Database objects help you structure data and define data integrity mechanisms. The following table describes SQL Server database objects.

Database object	Description
Table	Defines a collection of rows that have associated columns.
Data type	Defines the data values allowed for a column or variable.
	SQL Server provides system-supplied data types. Users create user-defined data types.
Constraint	Defines rules regarding the values allowed in columns and is the standard mechanism for enforcing data integrity.
Default	Defines a value that is stored in a column if no other value is supplied.
Rule	Contains information that defines valid values that are stored in a column or data type.
Index	Is a storage structure that provides fast access for data retrieval and can enforce data integrity.
	In a clustered index, the logical or indexed order of the key values is the same as the physical, stored order of the corresponding rows that exist in the table.
	In a nonclustered index, the logical order of the index does not match the physical, stored order of the rows in the table.

(continued)

Database object	Description
View	Provides a way to look at data from one or more tables or views in a database.
User-defined function	Can return either a scalar value or a table. Functions are used to encapsulate frequently performed logic. Any code that must perform the logic incorporated in a function can call the function rather than having to repeat all of the function logic.
Stored procedure	Is a named collection of precompiled Transact-SQL statements that execute together.
Trigger	Is a special form of a stored procedure that is executed automatically when a user modifies data in a table or a view.

Referring to SQL Server Objects

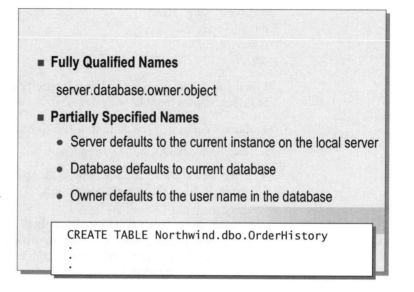

- **Fully Qualified Names**

  server.database.owner.object

- **Partially Specified Names**

  - Server defaults to the current instance on the local server

  - Database defaults to current database

  - Owner defaults to the user name in the database

```
CREATE TABLE Northwind.dbo.OrderHistory
  .
  .
  .
```

You can refer to SQL Server objects in several ways. You can specify the full name of the object (its fully qualified name), or specify only part of the name of the object name and allow SQL Server to determine the rest of the name from the context in which you are working.

Fully Qualified Names

The complete name of a SQL Server object includes four identifiers—the server name, database name, owner name, and object name in the following format:

server.database.owner.object

An object name that specifies all four parts is known as a fully qualified name. Each object that you create in SQL Server must have a unique, fully qualified name. For example, you can have two tables named **Orders** in the same database as long as they belong to different owners. Also, column names must be unique within a table or view.

Partially Specified Names

When referencing an object, you do not always have to specify the server, database, and owner. Intermediate identifiers can be omitted as long as their positions are indicated by periods.

The following list contains valid formats for object names:

server.database.owner.object
database.owner.object
database..object
owner.object
object

When you create an object and do not specify the different parts of the name, SQL Server uses the following defaults:

- Server defaults to the current instance on the local server.

- Database defaults to the current database.

- Owner defaults to the user name in the specified database associated with the login ID of the current connection.

A user that is a member of a role can explicitly specify the role as the object owner. A user that is a member of the **db_owner** or **db_ddladmin** role in a database should specify the **dbo** user account as the owner of an object. This practice is recommended.

Example

The following example creates an **OrderHistory** table in the **Northwind** database.

```
CREATE TABLE Northwind.dbo.OrderHistory
(OrderID int,
ProductID int,
UnitPrice money,
Quantity int,
Discount decimal)
```

Most object references use three-part names and default to the local server. Four-part names are generally used for distributed queries or remote stored procedure calls.

SQL Server supports a three-part naming convention when referring to the current server. The SQL-92 standard also supports a three-part naming convention. The terms used in both naming conventions are different. The following table describes the relationships between SQL Server names and SQL-92-standard names.

SQL Server name	SQL-92 name
Database	catalog
Owner	schema
Object	object

System Tables

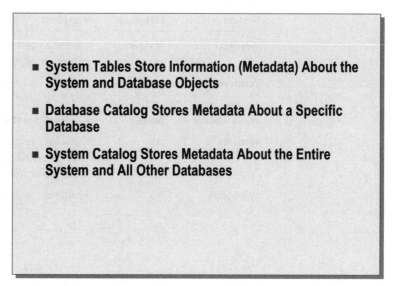

- **System Tables Store Information (Metadata) About the System and Database Objects**

- **Database Catalog Stores Metadata About a Specific Database**

- **System Catalog Stores Metadata About the Entire System and All Other Databases**

SQL Server stores information, called metadata, about the system and objects in databases for an instance of SQL Server. *Metadata* is information about data.

Metadata includes information about the properties of data, such as the type of data in a column (numeric, text, and so on), or the length of a column. It can also be information about the structure of data or information that specifies the design of objects.

System Tables   The information about data in system tables includes configuration information and definitions of all of the databases and database objects in the instance of SQL Server. Users should not directly modify any system table.

Database Catalog   Each database (including **master**) contains a collection of system tables that store metadata about that specific database. This collection of system tables is the database catalog. It contains the definition of all of the objects in the database, as well as permissions.

System Catalog   The system catalog, found only in the **master** database, is a collection of system tables that stores metadata about the entire system and all other databases.

Most system tables begin with the **sys** prefix. The following table identifies several frequently used system tables and views.

System table	Database	Function
syslogins	**master**	Contains one row for each login account that can connect to SQL Server
sysmessages	**master**	Contains one row for each system error or warning that SQL Server can return
sysdatabases	**master**	Contains one row for each database on SQL Server
sysusers	All	Contains one row for each Windows 2000 user, Windows 2000 group, SQL Server user, or SQL Server role in a database
sysobjects	All	Contains one row for each object in a database

Metadata Retrieval

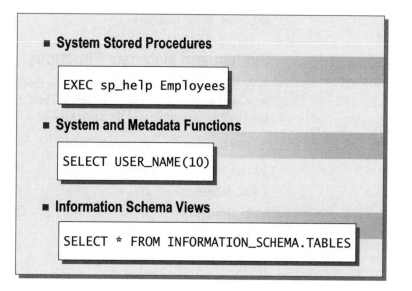

- **System Stored Procedures**

  ```
  EXEC sp_help Employees
  ```

- **System and Metadata Functions**

  ```
  SELECT USER_NAME(10)
  ```

- **Information Schema Views**

  ```
  SELECT * FROM INFORMATION_SCHEMA.TABLES
  ```

When you write applications that retrieve metadata from system tables, you should use system stored procedures, system functions, or system-supplied information schema views.

You can query a system table in the same way that you do any other database table to retrieve information about the system. However, you should not write scripts that directly query system tables, because if the system tables change in future product versions, your scripts may fail or may not provide accurate information.

Warning You should not alter system tables directly. Changing a system table may make it impossible for SQL Server to recover properly in the event of a system failure.

System Stored Procedures

To make it easier for you to gather information about the state of the server and database objects, SQL Server provides a collection of prewritten queries called system stored procedures.

The names of most system stored procedures begin with the **sp_** prefix. The following table describes three commonly used system stored procedures.

System stored procedure	Description
sp_help [*object_name*]	Provides information on the specified database object
sp_helpdb [*database_name*]	Provides information on the specified database
sp_helpindex [*table_name*]	Provides information on the index for the specified table

Example

The following example executes a system stored procedure to get information on the **Employees** table.

```
EXEC sp_help Employees
```

System and Metadata Functions

System and metadata functions provide a method for querying system tables from within Transact-SQL statements. The following table describes commonly used system functions and the corresponding information returned.

System function	Parameter passed	Results
DB_ID	Name	Returns the database ID
USER_NAME	ID	Returns the user's name
COL_LENGTH	Column	Returns the column width
STATS_DATE	Index	Returns the date when statistics for the specified index were last updated
DATALENGTH	Data type	Returns the actual length of an expression of any data type

Example 1

The following example uses a system function in a query to retrieve the user name for a user ID of 10.

```
SELECT USER_NAME(10)
```

Information Schema Views

Information schema views provide an internal, system table-independent view of the SQL Server metadata. These views conform to the ANSI SQL standard definition for the information schema.

Each information schema view contains metadata for all data objects stored in that particular database. The following table describes commonly used information schema views.

Information schema view	Description
INFORMATION_SCHEMA.TABLES	List of tables in the database
INFORMATION_SCHEMA.COLUMNS	Information on columns defined in the database
INFORMATION_SCHEMA.TABLES_PRIVILEGES	Security information for tables in the database

Example 2

The following example queries an information schema view to retrieve a list of tables in a database.

```
SELECT * FROM INFORMATION_SCHEMA.TABLES
```

◆ SQL Server Security

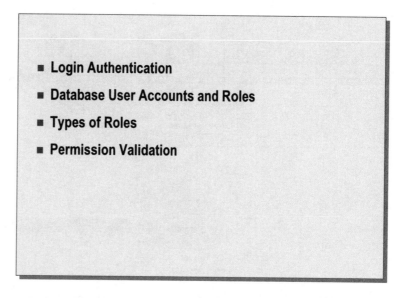

- Login Authentication
- Database User Accounts and Roles
- Types of Roles
- Permission Validation

SQL Server validates users at two levels of security—login authentication, and permissions validation on database user accounts and roles.

Authentication identifies the user who is using a login account and verifies the user's the ability to connect with SQL Server. If authentication is successful, the user connects to SQL Server.

The user then must have permission to access databases on the server. The database administrator assigns database-specific permissions to user accounts and roles in order to access databases on the server. Permissions control the activities that the user is allowed to perform in the SQL Server database.

Login Authentication

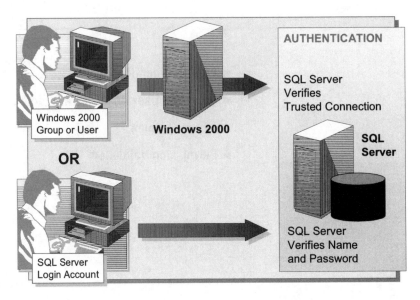

A user must have a login account to connect to SQL Server. SQL Server recognizes two login authentication mechanisms—Windows Authentication and SQL Server Authentication—each of which has a different type of login account.

Windows Authentication

When using Windows Authentication, a Windows 2000 account or group controls user access to SQL Server. A user does not provide a SQL Server login account when connecting. A SQL Server system administrator must define either the Windows 2000 account or the Windows 2000 group as a valid SQL Server login account.

SQL Server Authentication

When using SQL Server Authentication, a SQL Server system administrator defines a SQL Server login account and password. Users must supply both SQL Server logins and passwords when they connect to SQL Server.

Authentication Mode

When SQL Server is running on Windows 2000, a system administrator can specify that it run in one of two authentication modes:

Windows Authentication Mode   Only Windows 2000 authentication is allowed. Users cannot specify a SQL Server login account.

Mixed Mode   Users can connect to SQL Server with Windows Authentication or SQL Server Authentication.

Database User Accounts and Roles

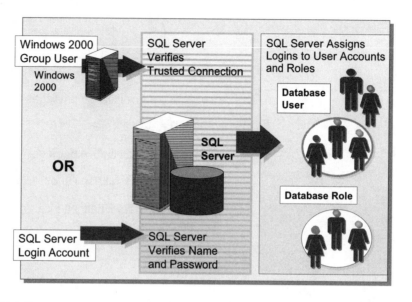

After users have been authenticated by Windows 2000 or SQL Server and have been allowed to log in to SQL Server, they must have accounts in a database. User accounts and roles identify a user within a database and control ownership of objects and permissions to execute statements.

Database User Accounts

The user accounts that apply security permissions are Windows 2000 users or groups or SQL Server login accounts. User accounts are specific to a database.

Roles

Roles enable you to assemble users into a single unit to which you can apply permissions. SQL Server provides predefined server and database roles for common administrative functions so that you can easily grant a selection of administrative permissions to a particular user. You also can create your own user-defined database roles. In SQL Server, users can belong to multiple roles.

Types of Roles

- **Fixed Server Roles**
  - Group administrative privileges at the server level
- **Fixed Database Roles**
  - Group administrative privileges at the database level
- **User-defined Database Roles**
  - Represent work defined by a group of employees within an organization

SQL Server enables three types of roles to help manage permissions: fixed server roles, fixed database roles, and user-defined database roles.

Fixed Server Role

Fixed server roles provide groupings of administrative privileges at the server level. They are managed independently of user databases at the server level. The following table describes the fixed server roles in SQL Server 2000.

Role	Permission
Database creators (**dbcreator**)	Create and alter databases
Disk administrators (**diskadmin**)	Manage disk files
Process administrators (**processadmin**)	Manage SQL Server processes
Security administrators (**securityadmin**)	Manage and audit server logins
Server administrators (**serveradmin**)	Configure server-wide settings
Setup administrators (**setupadmin**)	Install replication
System administrators (**sysadmin**)	Perform any activity
Bulk administrators (**bulkadmin**)	Execute BULK INSERT statement

Fixed Database Roles

Fixed database roles provide groupings of administrative privileges at the database level. The following table describes the fixed database roles in SQL Server 2000.

Role	Permission
public	Maintain all default permissions for users in a database
db_owner	Perform any database role activity
db_accessadmin	Add or remove database users, groups, and roles
db_ddladmin	Add, modify, or drop database objects
db_securityadmin	Assign statement and object permissions
db_backupoperator	Back up databases
db_datareader	Read data from any table
db_datawriter	Add, change, or delete data from all tables
db_denydatareader	Cannot read data from any table
db_denydatawriter	Cannot change data in any table

User-defined Database Roles

You also can create your own database roles to represent work performed by a group of employees in your organization. You do not have to grant and revoke permissions from each person. If the function of a role changes, you easily can change the permissions for the role and have the changes apply automatically to all members of the role.

Permission Validation

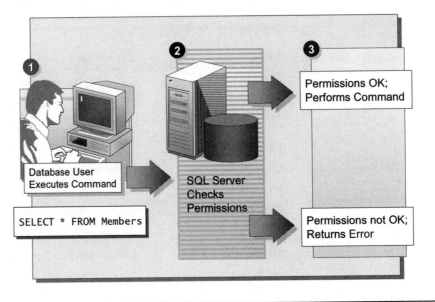

Within each database, you assign permissions to user accounts and roles to perform (or restrict) certain actions. SQL Server accepts commands after a user has successfully accessed a database.

SQL Server takes the following steps when validating permissions:

1. When the user performs an action, such as executing a Transact-SQL statement or choosing a menu option, the client sends Transact-SQL statements to SQL Server.

2. When SQL Server receives a Transact-SQL statement, it checks that the user has permission to execute the statement.

3. SQL Server then performs one of two actions:

    *   If the user does not have the proper permissions, SQL Server returns an error.

    *   If the user has the proper permissions, SQL Server performs the action.

◆ Working with SQL Server

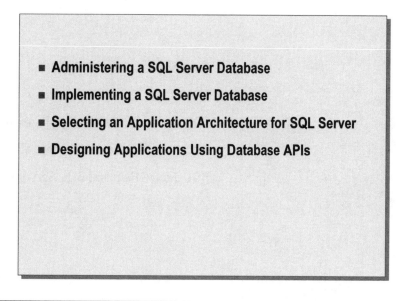

- **Administering a SQL Server Database**
- **Implementing a SQL Server Database**
- **Selecting an Application Architecture for SQL Server**
- **Designing Applications Using Database APIs**

Working with SQL Server involves administering and implementing a SQL Server database and developing applications.

When you work with SQL Server, you can use graphical tools that SQL Server provides, or you can use scripts. For example, when you need to create a database, you can use scripts or a graphical tool. Because generally you only create a particular database once, you would most likely use a graphical tool. However, when backing up the database, you would most likely use a script, because backing up is a task that must be done repeatedly.

Administering a SQL Server Database

- **Common Administrative Tasks**

- **SQL Server Enterprise Manager**

- **SQL Server Administration Tools and Wizards**

- **SQL Server Command Prompt Management Tools**

- **SQL Server Help and SQL Server Books Online**

SQL Server provides graphical and command prompt tools and utilities to administer SQL Server. It also includes different types of Help to assist you.

Common Administrative Tasks

Administering a SQL Server database involves:

- Installing, configuring, and securing SQL Server.

- Building databases.

  Tasks include allocating disk space to the database and log, transferring data into and out of the database, defining and implementing database security, creating automated jobs for repetitive tasks, and setting up replication to publish data to multiple sites.

- Managing ongoing activities, such as importing and exporting data, backing up and restoring the database and log, and monitoring and tuning the database.

SQL Server includes tools and wizards for administering and managing the server, designing and creating databases, and querying data. It also provides online Help.

SQL Server Enterprise Manager

SQL Server provides an administrative client, SQL Server Enterprise Manager, which is a Microsoft Management Console (MMC) snap-in. MMC is a shared user interface for the management of Microsoft server applications.

SQL Server Administration Tools and Wizards

SQL Server provides a number of administrative tools and wizards that assist with particular aspects of its administration. The following table describes SQL Server tools and wizards.

Graphical tool	Purpose
Client Network Utility	Utility for managing the client configuration for network libraries
SQL Server Network Utility	Utility for managing the server configuration for network libraries
SQL Profiler	Utility for capturing a continuous record of server activity and providing auditing capability
SQL Query Analyzer	Graphical query tool for analyzing the plan of a query, viewing statistics information, and managing multiple queries in different windows simultaneously
SQL Server Service Manager	Graphical utility for starting, stopping, and pausing SQL Server services
SQL Server Setup	Application for installing and configuring SQL Server
SQL Server wizards	Collection of tools that guide users through complex tasks

SQL Server Command Prompt Management Tools

SQL Server command prompt management tools allow you to enter Transact-SQL statements and execute script files. The following table describes the most frequently used command prompt utilities that are provided with SQL Server. Each file is an executable application.

Utility	Description
osql	Utility that uses Open Database Connectivity (ODBC) to communicate with SQL Server—primarily used to execute batch files containing one or more SQL statements
bcp	Batch utility used to import and export data to and from SQL Server—copies data to or from a data file in a user-specified format

SQL Server Help and SQL Server Books Online

SQL Server offers different types of Help to assist you. The following table describes each type of Help that SQL Server provides.

Type of Help	Description
Tool Help	SQL Server tools generally provide context-sensitive help on the application interface. Click the **Help** button or a command on the **Help** menu.
Transact-SQL Help	When using SQL Query Analyzer, select a statement name and then press SHIFT+F1.
SQL Server documentation set	SQL Server Books Online provides online access to SQL Server documentation.

Implementing a SQL Server Database

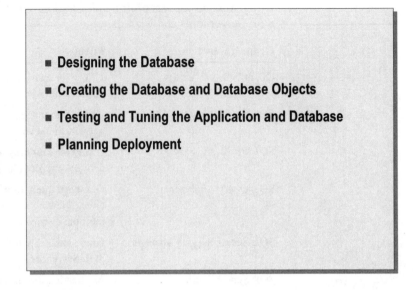

- Designing the Database
- Creating the Database and Database Objects
- Testing and Tuning the Application and Database
- Planning Deployment

Implementing a SQL Server database means planning, creating, and maintaining a number of interrelated components.

The nature and complexity of a database application, as well as the process of planning it, can vary greatly. For example, a database can be relatively simple, designed for use by a single person, or it can be large and complex, designed to handle all the banking transactions for hundreds of thousands of clients.

Regardless of the size and complexity of the database, implementing it usually involves:

- Designing the database so that your application uses hardware optimally and allows for future growth; identifying and modeling database objects and application logic; and specifying the types of information for each object and type of relationship.

- Creating the database and database objects, including tables, data integrity mechanisms, data entry and retrieval objects (often stored procedures), appropriate indexes, and security.

- Testing and tuning the application and database.

  When you design a database, you want to ensure that the database performs important functions correctly and quickly. In conjunction with correct database design, the correct use of indexes, RAID, and filegroups are essential to achieving good performance.

- Planning deployment, which includes analyzing the workload and recommending an optimal index configuration for your SQL Server database.

Selecting an Application Architecture for SQL Server

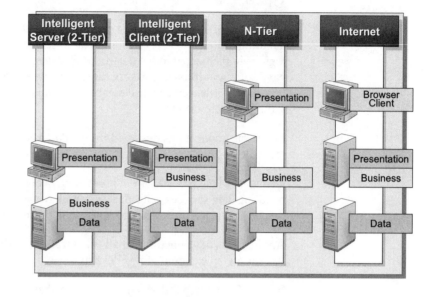

Planning a database design requires knowledge of the business functions that you want to model and the database concepts and features that you use to represent those business functions.

Before you design an application for SQL Server, it is important to take time designing a database to model the business accurately. A well-designed database requires fewer changes and generally performs more efficiently. The architecture that you select affects how you develop, deploy, and manage your software application.

Software Architecture

You can use one of several application architectures to implement client/server applications. However, selecting a layered application approach affords flexibility and a choice of management options. You can divide software applications into three logical layers, which can physically reside on one or more servers.

Logical layer	Description
Presentation	Includes the logic for presenting the data and application to users. This layer is almost always implemented on a client computer.
Business	Includes the application logic and business rules. (SQL Server can be involved with this layer.)
Data	Includes database definition, data integrity logic, stored procedures, and other operations that are closely associated with the data. (SQL Server is involved primarily with this layer.)

Architectural Design

Typical application deployment options include:

Intelligent Server (2-Tier)   Most processing occurs on the server, with the client handling presentation services. In many instances, most of the business services logic is implemented in the database. This design is useful when clients do not have sufficient resources to process the business logic. However, the server can become a bottleneck because database and business services compete for the same hardware resources.

Corporate applications designed from a database-centric point of view are an example of this design.

Intelligent Client (2-Tier)   Most processing occurs on the client, with the server handling data services. This design is widely used. However, network traffic can be heavy and transactions longer, which can affect performance.

Applications developed for small organizations with products such as Microsoft Access are an example of this design.

N-Tier   Processing is divided among a database server, an application server, and clients. This approach separates logic from data services, and you easily can add more application servers or database servers as needed. However, the potential for complexity increases, and this approach may be slower for small applications.

Multitiered enterprise applications and applications developed with transaction processing monitors are examples of this design.

Internet   Processing is divided into three layers, with the business and presentation services residing on the Web server and the clients using Internet browsers. SQL Server uses XML support for presentation of data to browsers. SQL Server can support any client that has a browser, and software does not need to be maintained on the client.

An example of this design is a Web site that uses several Web servers to manage connections to clients and a single SQL Server database that services requests for data.

You can access SQL Server over HTTP by using a URL. This allows you to directly access database objects and execute template files. This is not recommended for environments that must be highly secure and in which performance is critical.

Designing Applications Using Database APIs

You can develop a database application that accesses SQL Server through an API. A database API contains two parts:

- Transact-SQL language statements passed to the database.

- A set of functions or object-oriented interfaces and methods used to send the Transact-SQL statements to the database and process the results returned by the database.

Examples of relational database applications include data entry applications for airline ticketing and banking transaction systems.

OLE DB

OLE DB is a Component Object Model (COM)-based API. This API is a library of COM interfaces that enables universal access to diverse data sources.

SQL Server includes a native OLE DB provider. The provider supports applications written by using OLE DB, or other APIs that use OLE DB, such as ADO. Through the native provider, SQL Server also supports objects or components using OLE DB, such as ActiveX, ADO, or Microsoft .NET Enterprise Servers.

ADO

This database API defines how to write an application to connect to a database by using OLE DB and how to pass Transact-SQL commands to a database.

ADO is an application-level interface that uses OLE DB. Because ADO uses OLE DB as its foundation, it benefits from the data access infrastructure that OLE DB provides, yet it shields the application developer from the necessity of programming COM interfaces. Developers can use ADO for general-purpose access programs in business applications (Accounting, Human Resources, and Customer Management), and can use OLE DB for tool, utility, or system-level development (development tools and database utilities).

Lab A: SQL Server Overview

Objectives

After completing this lab, you will be able to:

- View the contents, use the index, and search for information in Microsoft® SQL Server™ Books Online, as well as save the location of information on the **Favorites** tab.

- Create a **Northwind** database diagram.

Prerequisites

None.

Lab Setup

None.

For More Information

If you require help with executing files, search SQL Query Analyzer Help for "Execute a query".

Other resources that you can use include:

- The **Northwind** database schema.

- SQL Server Books Online.

Scenario

The organization of the classroom is meant to simulate a worldwide trading firm named Northwind Traders. Its fictitious domain name is nwtraders.msft. The primary DNS server for nwtraders.msft is the instructor computer, which has an Internet Protocol (IP) address of 192.168.x.200 (where x is the assigned classroom number). The name of the instructor computer is London.

The following table provides the user name, computer name, and the IP address for each student computer in the fictitious nwtraders.msft domain. Find the user name for your computer and make a note of it.

User name	Computer name	IP address
SQLAdmin1	Vancouver	192.168.x.1
SQLAdmin2	Denver	192.168.x.2
SQLAdmin3	Perth	192.168.x.3
SQLAdmin4	Brisbane	192.168.x.4
SQLAdmin5	Lisbon	192.168.x.5
SQLAdmin6	Bonn	192.168.x.6
SQLAdmin7	Lima	192.168.x.7
SQLAdmin8	Santiago	192.168.x.8
SQLAdmin9	Bangalore	192.168.x.9
SQLAdmin10	Singapore	192.168.x.10
SQLAdmin11	Casablanca	192.168.x.11
SQLAdmin12	Tunis	192.168.x.12
SQLAdmin13	Acapulco	192.168.x.13
SQLAdmin14	Miami	192.168.x.14
SQLAdmin15	Auckland	192.168.x.15
SQLAdmin16	Suva	192.168.x.16
SQLAdmin17	Stockholm	192.168.x.17
SQLAdmin18	Moscow	192.168.x.18
SQLAdmin19	Caracas	192.168.x.19
SQLAdmin20	Montevideo	192.168.x.20
SQLAdmin21	Manila	192.168.x.21
SQLAdmin22	Tokyo	192.168.x.22
SQLAdmin23	Khartoum	192.168.x.23
SQLAdmin24	Nairobi	192.168.x.24

Estimated time to complete this lab: 30 minutes

Exercise 1
Using SQL Server Books Online

In this exercise, you will use SQL Server Books Online to retrieve information on SQL Server.

▶ **To view the contents of Getting Started in SQL Server Books Online**

In this procedure, you will view the contents of SQL Server Books Online and familiarize yourself with conventions used in the documentation.

1. Log on to the **NWTraders** classroom domain by using the information in the following table.

Option	Value
User name	**SQLAdmin***x* (where *x* corresponds to your computer name as designated in the nwtraders.msft classroom domain)
Password	**password**

2. On the taskbar, click the **Start** button, point to **Programs**, point to **Microsoft SQL Server**, and then click **Books Online**.

   Note that you can also access SQL Server Books Online directly from the SQL Server 2000 compact disc. Insert the SQL Server 2000 compact disc into the CD-ROM drive, and when the **Microsoft SQL Server** dialog box appears, click **Browse Books Online**.

3. In the console tree, review the organization of SQL Server Books Online.

4. On the **Contents** tab, in the **Active Subset** list, click **Entire Collection**, and then review the contents of **Getting Started**.

5. In the console tree, expand **Getting Started with SQL Server Books Online**, and then click **Documentation Conventions**. Review the information in the details pane.

6. In the console tree, expand **Using SQL Server Books Online**, and then click **Finding a Topic**. Review the information in the details pane.

7. In the console tree, expand **Finding a Topic**, and then click **Using the Search tab**. Review the information in the details pane.

▶ **To use the SQL Server Books Online index to obtain information on the Northwind sample database**

In this procedure, you will use the SQL Server Books Online index to view information on the **Northwind** sample database quickly.

1. Click the **Index** tab, and then type **Northwind**

2. Double-click **Northwind sample database**.

3. In the **Topics Found** dialog box, double-click **Northwind sample database**. Review the information in the details pane.

4. Click the **Favorites** tab, and then click **Add**.

   Click the **Contents** tab, and then in the console tree, expand **Northwind sample database** and notice the available topics.

▶ **To search SQL Server Books Online for a word or phrase**

In this procedure, you will use SQL Server Books Online to search for information about the architecture of SQL Server.

1. Click the **Search** tab, type **sql NEAR architecture** and then click **List Topics**.

    Notice the number of topics that are found.

2. On the **Search** tab, clear the **Match similar words** check box, select the **Search titles only** check box, and then click **List Topics**.

    Notice that only two topics are found.

3. Double-click **Fundamentals of SQL Server Architecture**.

4. Click the details pane, and then press CTRL+F.

5. In the **Find** box, type **oltp** and then click **Find Next**.

    Notice that the search finds the first instance of oltp.

6. Close SQL Server Books Online.

Exercise 2
Creating a Database Diagram

In this exercise, you will use the Create Database Diagram Wizard to generate a diagram for the **Northwind** database automatically. You will then use Query Designer to build a query.

▶ **To create a database diagram**

In this procedure, you will create a database diagram of the **Northwind** database by using the Create Database Diagram Wizard.

1. On the taskbar, click the **Start** button, point to **Programs**, point to **Microsoft SQL Server**, and then click **Enterprise Manager**.

2. In the console tree, expand **Microsoft SQL Servers**, expand **SQL Server Group**, and then expand your server.

3. Expand **Databases**, and then expand **Northwind**.

4. Right-click **Diagrams**, and then click **New Database Diagram**.

   The **Welcome to the Create Database Diagram Wizard** dialog box appears.

5. Using the Create Database Diagram wizard, add the following tables to the diagram:

   - **Categories**
   - **CustomerCustomerDemo**
   - **CustomerDemographics**
   - **Customers**
   - **Employees**
   - **EmployeeTerritories**
   - **Order Details**
   - **Orders**
   - **Products**
   - **Region**
   - **Shippers**
   - **Suppliers**
   - **Territories**

6. On the toolbar, click **Zoom**, and then click **100%**.

7. On the toolbar, click **Save**.

8. In the **Save As** dialog box, type **Northwind** and then click **OK**.

▶ **To build a query by using Query Designer**

In this procedure, you will use Query Designer to build a query joining the **Products** and **Categories** tables.

1. In the diagram, right-click **Products**, point to **Task**, and then click **Open Table**.

   This opens a separate window and displays all rows in the **Products** table.

2. On the toolbar, click **Show/Hide Diagram Pane**.

   This will display the table diagram of the **Products** table.

3. Right-click an open area of the diagram pane, and then click **Add Table**.

4. Double-click **Categories**, and then click **Close**.

   This will add the **Categories** table to the diagram pane and display the relationship between the **Categories** and **Products** tables.

5. On the toolbar, click **Show/Hide SQL Pane**.

   This will display the Transact-SQL script that has been created for you.

6. In the **Products** table, select the **ProductName** and **UnitPrice** check boxes, and in the **Categories** table, select the **CategoryName** check box.

7. In the **Products** table, click **UnitPrice**, and then on the toolbar, click **Sort descending**.

   Notice the modifications that occur to the Transact-SQL script.

8. In the SQL pane, delete the asterisk and comma in the SELECT statement.

9. On the toolbar, click **Run**.

   What is the highest-priced product?

   _____

   _____

Note Query Designer is running as a Microsoft Management Console (MMC) snap-in. Note that you now have three active MMC windows—SQL Server Enterprise Manager, Database Designer, and Query Designer.

Review

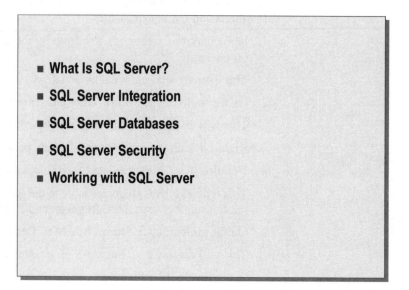

- **What Is SQL Server?**
- **SQL Server Integration**
- **SQL Server Databases**
- **SQL Server Security**
- **Working with SQL Server**

1. You have created a new login account within SQL Server for a Windows 2000 group. You want the members of this group to be able to use SQL Server. What additional security tasks must you perform?

   _____

   _____

2. You want to view metadata about objects in a SQL Server database. What methods would you use?

   _____

   _____

3. You want to reference two tables that reside in different databases on the same server. From the **Inventory** database, you want to reference a table in the **Sales** database. How would you reference the table in the **Sales** database in a query?

   _____

   _____

Microsoft®
Training &
    Certification

Module 2: Overview of Programming SQL Server

Contents

Microsoft®

Project Lead: Rich Rose
Instructional Designers: Rich Rose, Cheryl Hoople, Marilyn McGill
Instructional Software Design Engineers: Karl Dehmer, Carl Raebler, Rick Byham
Technical Lead: Karl Dehmer
Subject Matter Experts: Karl Dehmer, Carl Raebler, Rick Byham
Graphic Artist: Kirsten Larson (Independent Contractor)
Editing Manager: Lynette Skinner
Editor: Wendy Cleary
Copy Editor: Edward McKillop (S&T Consulting)
Production Manager: Miracle Davis
Production Coordinator: Jenny Boe
Production Support: Lori Walker (S&T Consulting)
Test Manager: Sid Benavente
Courseware Testing: TestingTesting123
Classroom Automation: Lorrin Smith-Bates
Creative Director, Media/Sim Services: David Mahlmann
Web Development Lead: Lisa Pease
CD Build Specialist: Julie Challenger
Online Support: David Myka (S&T Consulting)
Localization Manager: Rick Terek
Operations Coordinator: John Williams
Manufacturing Support: Laura King; Kathy Hershey
Lead Product Manager, Release Management: Bo Galford
Lead Product Manager, Data Base: Margo Crandall
Group Manager, Courseware Infrastructure: David Bramble
Group Product Manager, Content Development: Dean Murray
General Manager: Robert Stewart

Overview

- **Designing Enterprise Application Architecture**
- **SQL Server Programming Tools**
- **The Transact-SQL Programming Language**
- **Elements of Transact-SQL**
- **Additional Language Elements**
- **Ways to Execute Transact-SQL Statements**

After completing this module, you will be able to:

- Describe the concepts of enterprise-level application architecture.
- Describe the primary Microsoft® SQL Server™ 2000 programming tools.
- Explain the difference between the two primary programming tools in SQL Server.
- Describe the basic elements of Transact-SQL.
- Describe the use of local variables, operators, functions, control of flow statements, and comments.
- Describe the various ways to execute Transact-SQL statements.

◆ Designing Enterprise Application Architecture

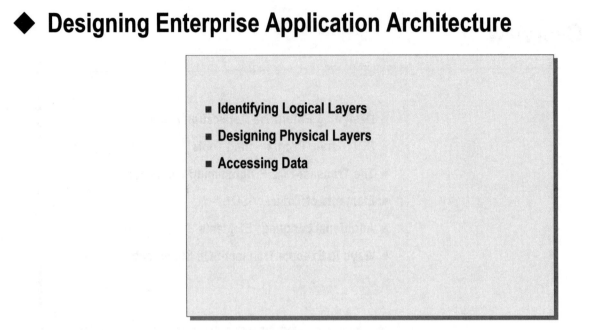

- Identifying Logical Layers
- Designing Physical Layers
- Accessing Data

SQL Server is often part of a distributed application. The design of a
SQL Server implementation for an enterprise solution depends on your choice
of architecture and how you intend to dsistribute logic across applications.

Identifying Logical Layers

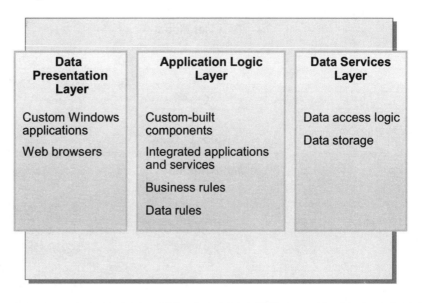

Enterprise application architecture contains logical layers. The layers represent data presentation, application logic, and data services.

Data Presentation Layer

The data presentation layer is also referred to as user services and allows users to browse and manipulate data. The two main types of client applications are custom Microsoft Windows® applications and Web browsers. The data presentation layer uses the services that the application logic layer provides.

Application Logic Layer

This layer contains the application logic that defines rules and processes. It allows for scalability; instead of many clients directly accessing a database (with each client requiring a separate connection), clients can connect to business services that, in turn, connect to the data servers. Business services can be custom-built components or integrated applications and services, such as Web services. The application logic layer can also contain components that make use of transaction services, messaging services, or object and connection management services.

Data Services Layer

Data services include data access logic and data storage. These services can include SQL Server stored procedures to manage data traffic and integrity on the database server.

Designing Physical Layers

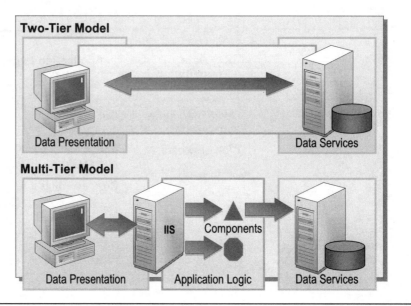

You can physically place logical layers in a distributed environment in a variety of ways. Although all logical layers can exist on one computer, it is typical to distribute the logical layers in a *two-tier* or *multi-tier model*. This allows you to implement logic, business rules, and processing where they are most effective.

Using a Two-Tier Model

If you use this model, you can locate the presentation and application logic on the client and the data services on a server. Alternatively, you can locate the application logic in stored procedures on the server. You can also have a mixed solution in which the application logic is divided between the client and the server.

Two-tier designs are less common than multi-tier designs, due to the growing popularity of Internet applications. They are not as scalable and may not be as easy to maintain as multi-tier designs are.

Using a Multi-Tier Model

The multi-tier model, also known as three-tier or *n*-tier, allows you to distribute logic across applications. Business rules can be separate from the client or the database. When this model is applied to the Internet, you can divide presentation services between a browser client and a Microsoft Internet Information Services (IIS) Web server; the Web server formats the Web pages that the browser displays.

The multi-tier model is scalable for large client bases and many applications, and you can spread the workload among many computers. A multi-tier model is easy to manage because you can isolate a change to one business rule without affecting others. Also, an update to an Active Server Page (ASP) on a Web server automatically updates all clients.

Accessing Data

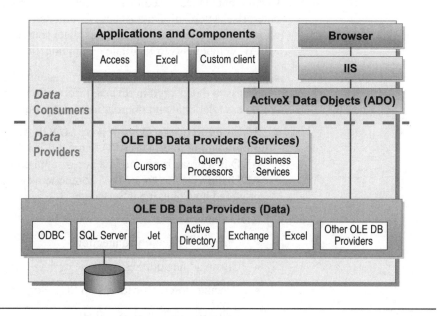

Microsoft technologies allow you to access enterprise data by using a wide range of pre-built clients or custom clients that use a data access-programming interface.

Using Pre-Built Clients

You can use pre-built client applications to access data on SQL Server. The data retrieval logic is part of the client application.

Microsoft Office 2000 includes Microsoft Access and Microsoft Excel. When part of a multi-tier solution, you use these applications primarily for presentation services. However, you can also use them for application logic and data services. These applications allow users to browse server-side data and perform ad hoc queries. You can use them to retrieve SQL Server data or as a client in a multi-tier design. You can also use Office 2000 as a development environment for building data access applications.

Access and Excel are examples of pre-built clients that offer a range of functionality. You can also use pre-built clients that only offer presentation services, such as a browser that communicates with IIS.

Building Custom Clients

You can build custom clients by using a data access programming interface and a development environment, such as Microsoft Visual Studio® version 6.0 Enterprise Edition.

Providing Universal Data Access

Custom clients may need to access many different data sources in the enterprise. Microsoft Data Access Components (MDAC) is an interface that allows communication with different data sources. You can use the following MDAC components to facilitate communication:

■ *OLE DB*. A set of Component Services interfaces that provides uniform access to data stored in diverse information sources. OLE DB enables you to access relational and nonrelational data sources.

■ *Microsoft ActiveX® Data Objects (ADO)*. An easy-to-use application programming interface (API) to any OLE DB data provider. You can use ADO in a broad range of data access application scenarios. OLE DB and ADO allow you to create data components that use the integrated services provided by Component Services.

ADO allows you to:

- Open and maintain connections.

- Create ad hoc queries.

- Execute stored procedures on SQL Server.

- Retrieve results and use cursors.

- Cache query results on the client.

- Update rows in the database.

- Close connections.

SQL Server Programming Tools

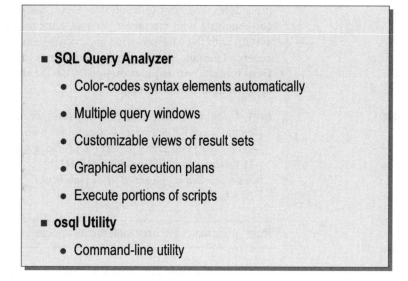

- ■ **SQL Query Analyzer**
  - • Color-codes syntax elements automatically
  - • Multiple query windows
  - • Customizable views of result sets
  - • Graphical execution plans
  - • Execute portions of scripts
- ■ **osql Utility**
  - • Command-line utility

SQL Server 2000 offers several programming tools, including SQL Query Analyzer and the **osql** utility. SQL Query Analyzer is a Windows-based application, and **osql** is a utility that you can run from a command prompt.

SQL Query Analyzer

You can use SQL Query Analyzer to view query statements and results at the same time. You also can use it for writing, modifying, and saving Transact-SQL scripts.

SQL Query Analyzer provides the following features:

- ■ Customized marking of syntax elements. As you write a query, SQL Query Analyzer highlights keywords, character strings, and other language elements; you can customize how they appear.

- ■ Multiple query windows, each with its own connection.

- ■ Customizable views of result sets. You can view results in default result set form or in a grid so that you can manipulate them as you would a table.

- ■ Graphical execution plans that describe how SQL Server executes the query. You can view the optimized plan of execution and verify your syntax.

- ■ The ability to execute portions of a script. You can select portions of a script, and SQL Server will execute only those portions.

osql Utility

The **osql** utility allows you to write Transact-SQL statements, system procedures, and script files. It uses Open Database Connectivity (ODBC) to communicate with the server. You start the utility directly from the operating system with the case-sensitive arguments listed below. Once started, **osql** accepts Transact-SQL statements and sends them to SQL Server interactively. **Osql** formats and displays the results on the screen. Use the QUIT or EXIT commands to exit from **osql**.

Syntax

osql -U *login_id* [-e] [-E] [-p] [-n] [-d *db_name*] [-q "*query*"] [-Q "*query*"]
    [-c *cmd_end*] [-h *headers*] [-w *column_width*] [-s *col_separator*]
    [-t *time_out*] [-m *error_level*] [-L] [-?] [-r {0 | 1}]
    [-H *wksta_name*] [-P *password*] [-R]
    [-S *server_name*] [-i *input_file*] [-o *output_file*] [-a *packet_size*]
    [-b] [-O] [-l *time_out*]

Note   Parameters in **osql** statements are case sensitive.

The following table describes the most commonly used arguments.

Argument	Description
-U *login_id*	Is the user login ID. Login IDs are case sensitive. If neither the **-U** or **-P** option is used, SQL Server uses the currently logged in user account and will not prompt for a password.
-E	Uses a trusted connection instead of requesting a password.
-?	Displays the syntax summary of **osql** switches.
-P *password*	Is a user-specified password. If the **-P** option is not used, **osql** prompts for a password. If the **-P** option is used at the end of the command prompt without any password, **osql** uses the default password (NULL). Passwords are case sensitive. If neither the **-U** or **-P** option is used, SQL Server uses the currently logged in user account and will not prompt for a password.
-S *server_name*	Specifies the SQL Server to which to connect. *server_name* is the name of the server computer on the network. This option is required if you execute **osql** from a remote computer on the network.
-i *input_file*	Identifies the file that contains a batch of Transact-SQL statements or stored procedures. You can use the less than (<) symbol instead of **-i**.
-o *output_file*	Identifies the file that receives output from **osql**. You can use the greater than (>) symbol in place of **-o**. If the input file is Unicode, the output file will be Unicode if you specify **-o**. If the input file is not Unicode, the output file is OEM.
-b	Specifies that **osql** exits and returns a Microsoft MS-DOS® ERRORLEVEL value when an error occurs. The value returned to the DOS ERRORLEVEL variable is 1 when the SQL Server error message has a severity of 10 or greater; otherwise, the value returned is 0. MS-DOS batch files can test the value of DOS ERRORLEVEL and handle the error appropriately.

The Transact-SQL Programming Language

- **SQL Server Implementation of Entry-Level ANSI ISO Standard**

- **Can Be Run on Any Entry-Level Compliant Product**

- **Contains Additional Unique Functionality**

Transact-SQL is the SQL Server implementation of the entry-level ANSI-SQL International Standards Organization (ISO) standard. The ANSI-SQL compliant language elements of Transact-SQL can be executed from any entry-level ANSI-SQL compliant product. Transact-SQL also contains additional language elements that are unique to it.

Important   It is recommended that you write scripts that include only ANSI-SQL standard statements to increase the compatibility and portability of your database.

◆ Elements of Transact-SQL

- ■ **Data Control Language Statements**
- ■ **Data Definition Language Statements**
- ■ **Data Manipulation Language Statements**
- ■ **SQL Server Object Names**
- ■ **Naming Guidelines**

As you write and execute Transact-SQL statements, you will use different languages statements, which are used to determine who can see or modify the data, create objects in the database, and query and modify the data. You should follow the rules for naming SQL Server objects, and become familiar with the naming guidelines for database objects.

Data Control Language Statements

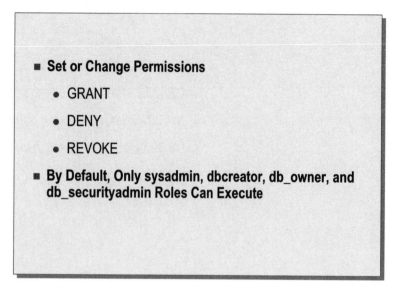

- **Set or Change Permissions**
  - GRANT
  - DENY
  - REVOKE
- **By Default, Only sysadmin, dbcreator, db_owner, and db_securityadmin Roles Can Execute**

You use Data Control Language (DCL) statements to change the permissions associated with a database user or role. The following table describes the DCL statements.

Statement	Description
GRANT	Creates an entry in the security system that allows a user to work with data or execute certain Transact-SQL statements.
DENY	Creates an entry in the security system that denies a permission from a security account, and prevents the user, group, or role from inheriting the permission through its group and role memberships.
REVOKE	Removes a previously granted or denied permission.

By default, only members of the **sysadmin**, **dbcreator**, **db_owner**, or **db_securityadmin** role can execute DCL statements.

Example

This example grants the **public** role permission to query the **Products** table.

```
USE Northwind
GRANT SELECT ON Products TO public
```

Data Definition Language Statements

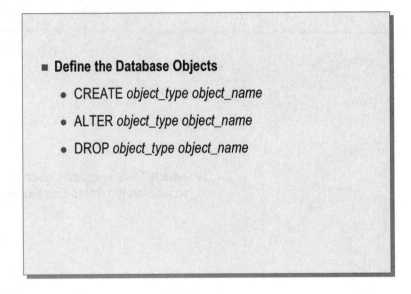

- **Define the Database Objects**
  - CREATE *object_type object_name*
  - ALTER *object_type object_name*
  - DROP *object_type object_name*

Data Definition Language (DDL) statements define the database by creating databases, tables, and user-defined data types. You also use DDL statements to manage your database objects. Some DDL statements include:

- CREATE *object_type object_name*.
- ALTER *object_type object_name*.
- DROP *object_type object_name*.

By default, only members of the **sysadmin**, **dbcreator**, **db_owner**, or **db_ddladmin** role can execute DDL statements. In general, it is recommended that no other accounts be allowed to create database objects. If users create their own objects in databases, then each object owner is required to grant the proper permissions to each user of those objects. This causes an administrative burden and should be avoided. Restricting statement permissions to these roles also avoids problems with object ownership that can occur when an object owner has been dropped from a database, or when the owner of a stored procedure or view does not own the underlying tables.

If multiple user accounts create objects, the **sysadmin** and **db_owner** roles can use the SETUSER function to impersonate other users or the **sp_changeobjectowner** system stored procedure to change the owner of an object.

Example

The following script creates a table called **Client** in the **ClassNorthwind** database. It includes **CustomerID**, **Company**, **Contact**, and **Phone** columns.

```
USE ClassNorthwind
CREATE TABLE Client
(CustomerID int, Company varchar(40),Contact varchar(30),
Phone char(12) )
```

Data Manipulation Language Statements

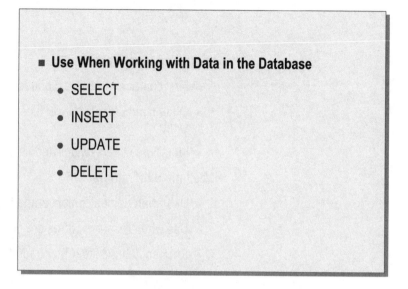

- **Use When Working with Data in the Database**
  - SELECT
  - INSERT
  - UPDATE
  - DELETE

DML statements work with the data in the database. By using DML statements, you can change data or retrieve information. DML statements include:

- SELECT.
- INSERT.
- UPDATE.
- DELETE.

By default, only members of the **sysadmin**, **dbcreator**, **db_owner**, **db_datawriter**, and **db_datareader** roles can execute DML statements.

Example

This example retrieves the category ID, product name, product ID, and unit price of the products in the **Northwind** database.

```
SELECT CategoryID, ProductName, CategoryID, ProductID,
UnitPrice
FROM Northwind..Products
```

SQL Server Object Names

- **Standard Identifiers**
  - First character must be alphabetic
  - Other characters can include letters, numerals, or symbols
  - Identifiers starting with symbols have special uses
- **Delimited Identifiers**
  - Use when names contain embedded spaces
  - Use when reserved words are portions of names
  - Enclose in brackets ([ ]) or quotation marks (" ")

SQL Server provides a series of standard naming rules for object identifiers and a method of using delimiters for identifiers that are not standard. It is recommended that you name objects by using the standard identifier characters, if possible.

Standard Identifiers

Standard identifiers can contain from one to 128 characters, including letters, symbols (_, @, or #), and numbers. No embedded spaces are allowed in standard identifiers. You should observe the following rules for using identifiers:

- The first character must be an alphabetic character of a–z or A–Z.

- After the first character, identifiers can include letters, numerals, or the @, $, #, or _ symbol.

- Identifier names starting with a symbol have special uses:

  - An identifier beginning with the at sign (@)denotes a local variable or parameter.

  - An identifier beginning with a number sign (#) denotes a temporary table or procedure.

  - An identifier beginning with a double-number sign (##) denotes a global temporary object.

Note Names for temporary objects should not exceed 116 characters, including the number sign (#) or double-number sign (##), because SQL Server gives temporary objects an internal numeric suffix.

Delimited Identifiers

If an identifier complies with all of the rules for the format of identifiers, you can use it with or without delimiters. If an identifier does not comply with one or more of the rules for the format of identifiers, it must always be delimited.

You can use delimited identifiers in the following situations:

- When names contain embedded spaces
- When reserved words are used for object names or portions of object names

You must enclose delimited identifiers in brackets or quotation marks when you use them in Transact-SQL statements.

- Bracketed identifiers are delimited by square brackets ([ ]):

```
SELECT * FROM [Blanks In Table Name]
```

Note You can always use bracketed delimiters, regardless of the status of the SET QUOTED_IDENTIFIER option.

- Quoted identifiers are delimited by quotation marks (""):

```
SELECT * FROM "Blanks in Table Name"
```

You can use quoted identifiers only if the SET QUOTED_IDENTIFIER option is on.

Naming Guidelines

- **Use Meaningful Names Where Possible**

- **Keep Names Short**

- **Use a Clear and Simple Naming Convention**

- **Chose an Identifier That Distinguishes Types of Objects**
  - Views
  - Stored procedures

- **Keep Object Names and User Names Unique**

Guidelines for naming database objects are important for identifying the type of object and to promote ease in troubleshooting or debugging. When naming database objects, you should:

- Use meaningful names where possible.

  For example, for a column that contains the name of customers, you could name the column **Chr_Name_Of_Customer**. A prefix of **Chr** in the column name denotes a **character** data type.

- Keep names short.

  For example, although the column name **Chr_Name_Of_Customer** is meaningful, you could shorten the column name to **Name** or **Chr_Name**.

- Use a clear and simple naming convention.

  Decide what works best for your situation, and be consistent. Avoid naming conventions that are too complex, because they can become difficult to remember. For example, you can remove vowels if an object name must resemble a keyword (such as a backup stored procedure named **Bckup**).

- Chose an identifier that distinguishes the type of object, especially when using views and stored procedures.

  System administrators often mistake views for tables, an oversight that can cause unexpected problems. For example, if you create a view that joins two tables, you could name that view, **SoldView**.

- Keep object names and user names unique.

  For example, avoid creating a **Sales** table and a **sales** role in the same database.

◆ Additional Language Elements

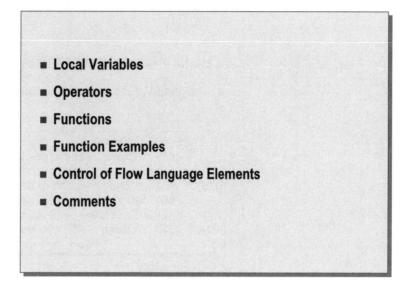

- **Local Variables**
- **Operators**
- **Functions**
- **Function Examples**
- **Control of Flow Language Elements**
- **Comments**

Some additional elements of the Transact-SQL language include local variables, operators, functions, control of flow statements, and comments.

Local Variables

- **User-defined with DECLARE Statement**
- **Assigned Values with SET or Select Statement**

```
DECLARE @vLastName        char(20),
     @vFirstName varchar(11)
SET @vLastName = 'Dodsworth'
SELECT @vFirstName = FirstName
     FROM Northwind..Employees
     WHERE LastName = @vLastName
PRINT @vFirstName + ' ' + @vLastName
GO
```

Variables are language elements with assigned values. You can use local variables in Transact-SQL.

You define a local variable in a DECLARE statement and then assign it an initial value with either the SET or SELECT statement. Use the SET statement when the desired value is known. Use the SELECT statement when you must look up the desired value in a table. After you establish the value of the variable, you can use it in the statement, batch, or procedure in which it was declared. A batch is a set of Transact-SQL statements that are submitted together and executed as a group. A local variable is shown with one at sign (@) preceding its name.

Syntax

DECLARE {@local_variable data_type} [,...*n*]

SET @*local_variable_name* = *expression*

Example

The following example declares two variables. It uses the SET statement to establish the value of the @vLastName variable and the SELECT statement to look up the value of the @vFirstName variable. It then prints both variables.

```
DECLARE @vLastName      char(20),
     @vFirstName   varchar(11)
SET @vLastName = 'Dodsworth'
SELECT @vFirstName = FirstName
   FROM Northwind..Employees
   WHERE LastName = @vLastName
PRINT @vFirstName + ' ' + @vLastNameGO
```

Result

Anne Dodsworth

Operators

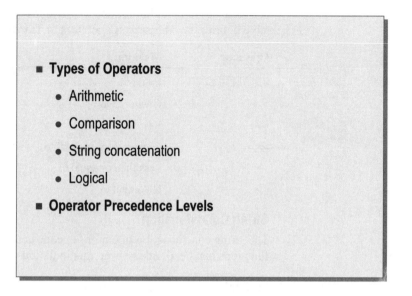

Operators are symbols that perform mathematical computations, string concatenations, and comparisons between columns, constants, and variables. You can combine them and use them in search conditions. When you combine them, the order in which SQL Server processes the operators is based on a predefined precedence.

Partial Syntax

{constant | column_name | function | (subquery)}
  [{arithmetic_operator | string_operator |
    AND | OR | NOT}
    {constant | column_name | function | (subquery)}...]

Types of Operators

SQL Server supports four types of operators: arithmetic, comparison, string concatenation, and logical.

Arithmetic

Arithmetic operators perform computations with numeric columns or constants. Transact-SQL supports multiplicative operators, including multiplication (*), division (/), and modulo (%)—the integer remainder after integer division—and the addition (+) and subtraction (-) additive operators.

Comparison

Comparison operators compare two expressions. You can make comparisons between variables, columns, and expressions of similar type. The following table defines the comparison operators in Transact-SQL.

Operator	Meaning
=	Equal to
>	Greater than
<	Less than
>=	Greater than or equal to
<=	Less than or equal to
<>	Not equal to

String Concatenation

The string concatenation operator (+) concatenates string values. String functions handle all other string manipulation.

Logical

The logical operators AND, OR, and NOT connect search conditions in WHERE clauses.

Operator Precedence Levels

If you use multiple operators (logical or arithmetic) to combine expressions, SQL Server processes the operators in order of their precedence, which may affect the resulting value. The following table shows the precedence level of operators (levels go from highest to lowest).

Type	Operator	Symbol
Grouping	Primary grouping	( )
Arithmetic	Multiplicative	* / %
Arithmetic	Additive	- +
Other	String concatenation	+
Logical	NOT	NOT
Logical	AND	AND
Logical	OR	OR

SQL Server handles the most deeply nested expression first. In addition, if all arithmetic operators in an expression share the same level of precedence, the order is from left to right.

Functions

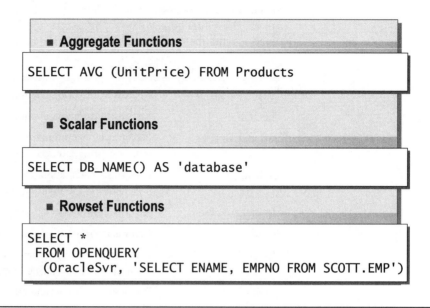

- **Aggregate Functions**

```
SELECT AVG (UnitPrice) FROM Products
```

- **Scalar Functions**

```
SELECT DB_NAME() AS 'database'
```

- **Rowset Functions**

```
SELECT *
 FROM OPENQUERY
   (OracleSvr, 'SELECT ENAME, EMPNO FROM SCOTT.EMP')
```

Transact-SQL provides many functions that return information. Functions take input parameters and return values that can be used in expressions. The Transact-SQL programming language provides three types of functions, aggregate, scalar, and rowset.

Aggregate Functions

Aggregate functions operate on a collection of values but return a single, summarizing value.

Example 1

This example determines the average of the **UnitPrice** column for all products in the **Products** table.

```
SELECT AVG(UnitPrice) FROM Products
```

Result

Products
28.8663

```
(1 row(s) affected)
```

Scalar Functions

Scalar functions operate on a single value and then return a single value. You can use these functions wherever an expression is valid. You can group scalar functions into the categories in the following table.

Function category	Description
Configuration	Returns information about the current configuration
Cursor	Returns information about cursors
Date and Time	Performs an operation on a date and time input value and returns a string, numeric, or date and time value
Mathematical	Performs a calculation based on input values provided as parameters to the function and then returns a numeric value
Metadata	Returns information about the database and database objects
Security	Returns information about users and roles
String	Performs an operation on a string (**char** or **varchar**) input value and returns a string or numeric value
System	Performs operations and returns information about values, objects, and settings in SQL Server
System Statistical	Returns statistical information about the system
Text and Image	Performs an operation on a text or image input value or column and returns information about the value

Example 2

This metadata function example returns the name of the database currently in use.

```
SELECT DB_NAME() AS 'database'
```

Result

Database

```
Northwind
```

```
(1 row(s) affected)
```

Rowset Functions

Rowset functions can be used like table references in a Transact-SQL statement.

Example 3

This example performs a distributed query to retrieve information from the **EMP** table.

```
SELECT *
FROM OPENQUERY(OracleSvr, 'SELECT ENAME, EMPNO FROM
SCOTT.EMP')
```

Function Examples

```
SELECT 'ANSI:' AS Region,
       CONVERT(varchar(30), GETDATE(), 102) AS Style
UNION
SELECT 'European:', CONVERT(varchar(30), GETDATE(), 113)
UNION
SELECT 'Japanese:', CONVERT(varchar(30), GETDATE(), 111)
```

Result

Region	Style
ANSI:	2000.03.22
European:	22 Mar 2000 14:20:00:010
Japanese:	2000/03/22

You commonly use functions when converting date data from the format of one country to that of another.

Note To change date formats, you should use the CONVERT function with the style option to determine the date format that will be returned.

Example 1

This example demonstrates how you can convert dates to different styles.

```
SELECT 'ANSI:' AS Region,
    CONVERT (varchar(30), GETDATE(), 102) AS Style
UNION
SELECT 'European:', CONVERT(varchar(30), GETDATE(), 113)
UNION
SELECT 'Japanese:', CONVERT(varchar(30), GETDATE(), 111)
```

Result

Region	Style
ANSI:	2000.03.22
European:	22 Mar 2000 14:20:00:010
Japanese:	2000/03/22

Example 2

This example uses the DATEFORMAT option of the SET statement to format dates for the duration of a connection. This setting is used only in the interpretation of character strings as they are converted to date values and has no effect on the display of date values.

```
SET DATEFORMAT dmy
GO
DECLARE @vdate datetime
SET @vdate = '29/11/00'
SELECT @vdate
```

Result

```
2000-11-29 00:00:00.000

(1 row(s) affected)
```

Example 3

This example returns the current user name and the application that the user is using for the current session or connection. The user in this example is a member of the **sysadmin** role.

```
USE Northwind
SELECT user_name(), app_name()
```

Result

```
dbo           MS SQL Query Analyzer

(1 row(s) affected)
```

Example 4

This example determines whether the **FirstName** column in the **Employees** table of the **Northwind** database allows null values.

A result of zero (false) means that null values are not allowed, and a result of one (true) means that null values are allowed. Notice that the OBJECT_ID function is embedded in the COLUMNPROPERTY function. This allows you to retrieve the **object id** of the **Employees** table.

```
USE Northwind
SELECT COLUMNPROPERTY(OBJECT_ID('Employees'), 'FirstName',
    'AllowsNull')
```

Result

```
0

(1 row(s) affected)
```

Control of Flow Language Elements

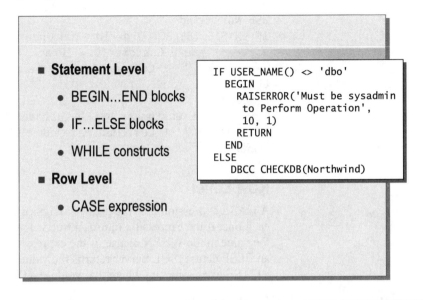

- ■ **Statement Level**
  - ● BEGIN...END blocks
  - ● IF...ELSE blocks
  - ● WHILE constructs
- ■ **Row Level**
  - ● CASE expression

```
IF USER_NAME() <> 'dbo'
   BEGIN
     RAISERROR('Must be sysadmin
     to Perform Operation',
     10, 1)
     RETURN
   END
ELSE
   DBCC CHECKDB(Northwind)
```

Transact-SQL contains several language elements that control the flow of logic in a statement. It also contains the CASE expression that allows you to use conditional logic on one row at a time in a SELECT or UPDATE statement.

Statement Level

The following language elements enable you to control the flow of logic in a script:

BEGIN...END Blocks   These elements enclose a series of Transact-SQL statements so that SQL Server treats them as a unit.

IF...ELSE Blocks   These elements specify that SQL Server should execute the first alternative if a certain condition is true. Otherwise, SQL Server should execute the second alternative.

WHILE Constructs   These elements execute a statement repeatedly as long as the specified condition is true. BREAK and CONTINUE statements control the operation of the statements inside a WHILE loop.

Example 1

This example determines whether a customer has any orders before deleting the customer from the customer list.

```
USE Northwind
IF EXISTS (SELECT OrderID FROM Orders
        WHERE CustomerID = 'Frank')
    PRINT '*** Customer cannot be deleted ***'
ELSE
  BEGIN
    DELETE Customers WHERE CustomerID = 'Frank'
    PRINT '*** Customer deleted ***'
  END
```

Row Level

A CASE expression lists predicates, assigns a value for each, and then tests each one. If the expression returns a true value, the CASE expression returns the value in the WHEN clause. If the expression is false, and you have specified an ELSE clause, SQL Server returns the value in the ELSE clause. You can use a CASE expression anywhere that you use an expression.

Syntax

CASE *expression*
    {WHEN *expression* THEN *result*} [,...*n*]
  [ELSE *result*]
  END

Example

The following example reviews the inventory status of products in the **Products** table and returns messages based on the quantities available and quantities back ordered, and whether the product has been discontinued.

```
SELECT ProductID, 'Product Inventory Status' =
  CASE
  WHEN (UnitsInStock < UnitsOnOrder AND Discontinued = 0)
     THEN 'Negative Inventory - Order Now!'
  WHEN ((UnitsInStock-UnitsOnOrder) < ReorderLevel AND
         Discontinued = 0)
     THEN 'Reorder level reached- Place Order'
  WHEN (Discontinued = 1) THEN '***Discontinued***'
  ELSE 'In Stock'
    END
FROM Northwind..Products
```

Result

ProductID	Product Inventory Status
1	In Stock
2	Negative Inventory - Order Now!
3	Negative Inventory - Order Now!
4	In Stock
5	***Discontinued***
6	In Stock
7	In Stock
8	In Stock
9	***Discontinued***
10	In Stock
11	Negative Inventory - Order Now!
12	In Stock
13	Reorder level reached - Place Order
.	
.	
.	

```
(77 row(s) affected)
```

Comments

```
■ In-Line Comments

SELECT ProductName,
(UnitsInStock + UnitsOnOrder) AS Max -- Calculates inventory
, SupplierID
FROM Products

■ Block Comments

/*
** This code retrieves all rows of the products table
** and displays the unit price, the unit price increased
** by 10 percent, and the name of the product.
*/
SELECT UnitPrice, (UnitPrice * 1.1), ProductName
FROM Products
```

Comments are non-executing strings of text placed in statements to describe the action that the statement is performing or to disable one or more lines of the statement. You can use comments in one of two ways—in line with a statement, or as a block.

In-Line Comments

You can create in-line comments by using two hyphens (--) to set a comment apart from a statement. Transact-SQL ignores text to the right of the comment characters. You can also use this commenting character to disable lines of a statement.

Example 1

This example uses an in-line comment to explain what a calculation is doing.

```
SELECT ProductName
,(UnitsInStock + UnitsOnOrder) AS Max -- Calculates inventory
  , SupplierID
FROM Products
```

Example 2

This example uses a second set of in-line comments, as represented by the second set of hyphens (--), to prevent the execution of a section (SupplierID) of a statement.

```
SELECT ProductName
,(UnitsInStock + UnitsOnOrder) AS Max -- Calculates inventory
-- , SupplierID
FROM Products
```

Block Comments

You can create multiple line blocks of comments by placing one comment character (/*) at the start of the comment text, typing your comments, and then concluding the comment with a closing comment character (*/).

Use this character designator to create one or more lines of comments or comment headers—descriptive text that documents the statements that follow it. Comment headers often include the author's name, creation and last modification dates of the script, version information, and a description of the action that the statement performs.

Note You cannot place the GO statement inside of block comments.

Example 3

This example shows a comment header that spans several lines. The two asterisks (**) preceding each line improve readability.

```
/*
** This code retrieves all rows of the products table
** and displays the unit price, the unit price increased
** by 10 percent, and the name of the product.
*/
SELECT UnitPrice, (UnitPrice * 1.1), ProductName
FROM Products
```

Note You should place comments throughout a script to describe the actions that the statements are performing. This is especially important if others must also review or implement the script.

Example 4

This section of a script is commented to prevent it from executing. This can be helpful when debugging or troubleshooting a script file.

```
/*
DECLARE @v1 int
SET @v1 = 0
WHILE @v1 < 100
   BEGIN
   SELECT @v1 = (@v1 + 1)
   SELECT @v1
   END
*/
```

◆ Ways to Execute Transact-SQL Statements

- ■ Dynamically Constructing Statements
- ■ Using Batches
- ■ Using Scripts
- ■ Using Transactions
- ■ Using XML

You can execute Transact-SQL statements by dynamically constructing statements, and by using batches, scripts, and transactions. You can also use Extensible Markup Language (XML) to present data to Web pages.

Dynamically Constructing Statements

- **Use EXECUTE with String Literals and Variables**

- **Use When You Must Assign Value of Variable at Execution Time**

- **Any Variables and Temporary Tables Last Only During Execution**

```
DECLARE @dbname varchar(30), @tblname varchar(30)
SET @dbname = 'Northwind'
SET @tblname = 'Products'

EXECUTE
('USE ' + @dbname + ' SELECT * FROM '+ @tblname)
```

You can build statements dynamically so that they are constructed at the same time that SQL Server executes a script.

To build a statement dynamically, use the EXECUTE statement with a series of string literals and variables that are resolved at execution time.

Dynamically constructed statements are useful when you want SQL Server to assign the value of the variable when it executes the statement. For example, you can create a dynamic statement that performs the same action on a series of database objects.

Syntax

EXECUTE ({@*str_var* | *'tsql_string'*} + [{@*str_var* | *'tsql_string'*}...])}

You set options dynamically, and variables and temporary tables that you create dynamically last only as long as it takes for SQL Server to execute the statement.

Consider the following facts about the EXECUTE statement:

- The EXECUTE statement executes statements composed of character strings in a Transact-SQL batch. Because these are string literals, be sure that you add spaces in the appropriate places to ensure proper concatenation.

- The EXECUTE statement can include a string literal, a string local variable, or a concatenation of both.

- All items in the EXECUTE string must consist of character data; you must convert all numeric data before you use the EXECUTE statement.

- You cannot use functions to build the string for execution.

- You can create any valid Transact-SQL statements dynamically, including functions.

- You can nest EXECUTE statements.

Example 1

This example demonstrates how you can use a dynamically executed statement to specify a database context other than the one you are currently in, and then use it to select all of the columns and rows from a specified table. In this example, the change of the database context to the **Northwind** database lasts only for the duration of the query. The current database context is unchanged.

By using a stored procedure, the user could pass the database and table information into the statement as parameters, and then query a specific table in a database.

```
DECLARE @dbname varchar(30), @tablename varchar(30)
SET @dbname = 'Northwind'
SET @tablename = 'Products'

EXECUTE
  ('USE ' + @dbname +
   ' SELECT ProductName FROM ' + @tablename)
```

Result

ProductName
Chai
Chang
Aniseed Syrup

Example 2

This example demonstrates how you can use a dynamically executed statement to change a database option for the duration of the statement. The following statement does not return a count of the number of rows affected.

```
EXECUTE ('SET NOCOUNT ON '+ 'SELECT LastName, ReportsTo
   FROM Employees WHERE ReportsTo IS NULL')
```

Result

LastName	ReportsTo
Fuller	NULL

Using Batches

- **One or More Transact-SQL Statements Submitted Together**
- **Define a Batch by Using the GO Statement**
- **How SQL Server Processes Batches**
- **You Cannot Combine Some Statements in a Batch**
  - CREATE PROCEDURE
  - CREATE VIEW
  - CREATE TRIGGER
  - CREATE RULE
  - CREATE DEFAULT

You can also submit one or more statements in a batch.

One or More Transact-SQL Statements Submitted Together

Batches can be run interactively or as part of a script. A script can include more than one batch of Transact-SQL statements.

Define a Batch by Using the GO Statement

Use a GO statement to signal the end of a batch. GO is not a universally accepted Transact-SQL statement; only SQL Query Analyzer and the **osql** utility accept it. Applications based on the ODBC or OLE DB APIs generate a syntax error if they attempt to execute a GO statement.

How SQL Server Processes Batches

SQL Server optimizes, compiles, and executes the statements in a batch together. However, the statements do not necessarily execute as a recoverable unit of work.

The scope of user-defined variables is limited to a batch, so a variable cannot be referenced after a GO statement.

Note If a syntax error exists in a batch, none of the statements in that batch executes. Execution begins with the next batch.

You Cannot Combine Some Statements in a Batch

SQL Server must execute certain object creation statements in their own batches in a script, because of the way that the objects are defined. Each of the following statements is defined by including an object definition header followed by the AS keyword (indicating that one or more statements follow). The object definitions are delimited by the GO statement; SQL Server recognizes the end of the object definition when it reaches the GO statement:

- CREATE PROCEDURE
- CREATE VIEW
- CREATE TRIGGER
- CREATE RULE
- CREATE DEFAULT

Example 1

If you want to use more than one of the non-combinable statements, you must submit multiple batches, as the following script indicates.

```
CREATE DATABASE ...
CREATE TABLE ...
GO

CREATE VIEW1 ...
GO
CREATE VIEW2 ...
GO
```

Example 2

The following example is a batch that fails. To execute it correctly, insert a GO statement before each CREATE TRIGGER statement.

```
CREATE DATABASE ...
CREATE TABLE ...
CREATE TRIGGER ...
CREATE TRIGGER ...
GO
```

Example 3

The following example shows how to group the statements of Example 2 so that they execute correctly.

```
CREATE DATABASE ...
CREATE TABLE ...
GO

CREATE TRIGGER ...
GO

CREATE TRIGGER ...
GO
```

Using Scripts

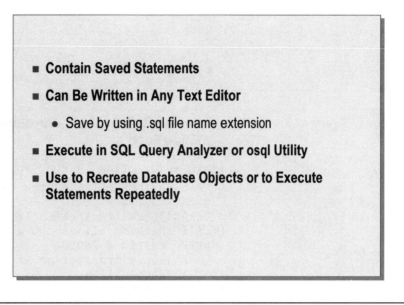

- **Contain Saved Statements**
- **Can Be Written in Any Text Editor**
  - Save by using .sql file name extension
- **Execute in SQL Query Analyzer or osql Utility**
- **Use to Recreate Database Objects or to Execute Statements Repeatedly**

Scripts are one of the most common ways to execute Transact-SQL statements. A script is one or more Transact-SQL statements that are saved as a file.

You can write and save scripts in SQL Query Analyzer or in any text editor, such as Notepad. Save the script file by using the .sql file name extension.

You can open and execute the script file in SQL Query Analyzer or the **osql** utility (or another query tool).

Saved scripts are very useful when recreating databases or data objects, or when you must use a set of statements repeatedly.

Format Transact-SQL statements to be legible to others. Use indenting to indicate levels of relationships.

Using Transactions

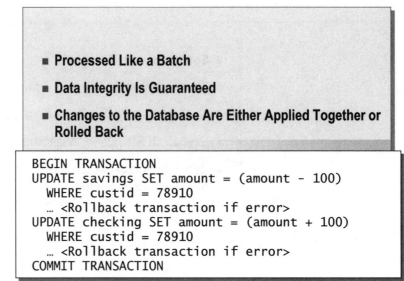

- **Processed Like a Batch**

- **Data Integrity Is Guaranteed**

- **Changes to the Database Are Either Applied Together or Rolled Back**

```
BEGIN TRANSACTION
UPDATE savings SET amount = (amount - 100)
  WHERE custid = 78910
  … <Rollback transaction if error>
UPDATE checking SET amount = (amount + 100)
  WHERE custid = 78910
  … <Rollback transaction if error>
COMMIT TRANSACTION
```

Transactions, like batches, are groups of statements that are submitted as a set. However, SQL Server handles transactions as a single unit of work, and the transaction succeeds or fails as a whole. This process maintains data integrity. Transactions can span multiple batches.

Preface a transaction with a BEGIN TRANSACTION statement, and terminate it with a COMMIT TRANSACTION or ROLLBACK TRANSACTION statement.

When a transaction is committed, SQL Server makes the changes to that transaction permanent. When a transaction is rolled back, SQL Server returns any rows affected by the transaction to their pretransaction states.

Partial Syntax

BEGIN TRANSACTION

COMMIT / ROLLBACK TRANSACTION

Example

In the following example, $100 is debited from the savings account of customer number 78910, and $100 is credited to the customer's checking account. The customer transferred $100 from savings to checking.

```
BEGIN TRANSACTION
UPDATE savings
   SET balance = (amount - 100)
   WHERE custid = 78910
IF @@ERROR <> 0
   BEGIN
      RAISERROR ('Transaction not completed due to
                   savings account problem.', 16, -1)
      ROLLBACK TRANSACTION
   END
UPDATE checking
   SET balance = (amount + 100)
   WHERE custid = 78910
IF @@ERROR <> 0
   BEGIN
      RAISERROR ('Transaction not completed due to
                   checking account problem.', 16, -1)
      ROLLBACK TRANSACTION
   END
COMMIT TRANSACTION
```

Using XML

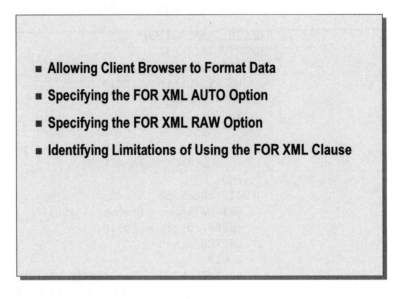

- Allowing Client Browser to Format Data
- Specifying the FOR XML AUTO Option
- Specifying the FOR XML RAW Option
- Identifying Limitations of Using the FOR XML Clause

XML is a programming language that Web developers can use to present data from a SQL Server database to Web pages.

Allowing Client Browser to Format Data

When using the FOR XML clause in the SELECT statement, SQL Server:

- Returns the results of a query as a character string.

- Returns the attributes of the data, such as column and table names, as tags. A client browser can then use these tags to format the returned data.

Specifying the FOR XML AUTO Option

You can specify the FOR XML AUTO option to return query results in a standardized format.

Each table in the FROM clause for which at least one column is listed in the SELECT clause is represented as an XML element. An element includes both data and attributes that describe the data.

Example 1

This example selects three columns from two joined tables. Notice that the results combine all of the columns into a single text string.

```
SELECT Orders.OrderID, Shippers.CompanyName, Orders.CustomerID
FROM Orders JOIN Shippers
ON Orders.shipvia = Shippers.ShipperID
WHERE OrderID < 10250
FOR XML AUTO
```

Result

```
XML_F52E2B61-18A1-11d1-B105-00805F49916B
--------------------------------------------
<Orders OrderID="10248" CustomerID="VINET">
  <Shippers CompanyName="Federal Shipping"/>
</Orders>
<Orders OrderID="10249" CustomerID="TOMSP">
  <Shippers CompanyName="Speedy Express"/>
</Orders>
```

Note   SQL Server reorders the result set to group columns by table name.

Specifying the FOR XML RAW Option

In some cases, Web developers do not want the automatic formatting. You can specify the RAW option to transform each row in the result set into an XML element with a generic identifier row as the element tag.

Example 2

Compare the result from this example with that of Example 1. This example returns the same data, but the formatting is more generic. Notice that the tables are not named, and the columns are not grouped by table name.

```
SELECT Orders.OrderID, Shippers.CompanyName, Orders.CustomerID
FROM Orders JOIN Shippers
ON Orders.shipvia = Shippers.ShipperID
WHERE OrderID < 10250
FOR XML RAW
```

Result

```
XML_F52E2B61-18A1-11d1-B105-00805F49916B
----------------------------------------
<row OrderID="10248"
  CompanyName="Federal Shipping"
  CustomerID="VINET"/>
<row OrderID="10249"
  CompanyName="Speedy Express"
  CustomerID="TOMSP"/>
```

Identifying Limitations of Using the FOR XML Clause

A SELECT statement that contains the FOR XML clause reformats the output for the SQL Server client. Because of these changes, you cannot use a query output in XML format as an input for further SQL Server processing.

You cannot use XML formatted output in:

- A nested SELECT statement.
- A SELECT INTO statement.
- A COMPUTE BY clause.
- Stored procedures that are called in an INSERT statement.
- A view definition or a user-defined function that returns a rowset.

Recommended Practices

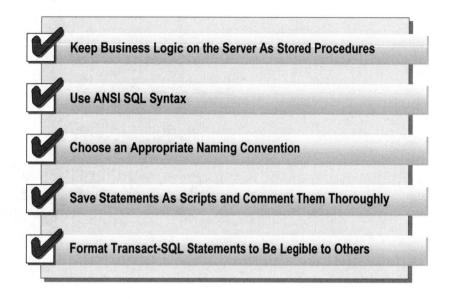

Keep Business Logic on the Server As Stored Procedures

Use ANSI SQL Syntax

Choose an Appropriate Naming Convention

Save Statements As Scripts and Comment Them Thoroughly

Format Transact-SQL Statements to Be Legible to Others

The following recommended practices should help you to create clean scripts in Transact-SQL:

- Keep business logic on the server as stored procedures.

- Use ANSI SQL syntax when possible to ensure that your scripts are as compatible and portable as possible.

- Choose an appropriate naming convention, and name items consistently.

- Save statements as scripts, and comment them thoroughly.

- Format Transact-SQL statements to be legible to others. Use indenting to indicate levels of relationships.

Additional information on the following topics is available in SQL Server Books Online.

Topic	Search on
Transact-SQL variables	variables
Functions	functions
Transact-SQL tips	transact-sql
Transact-SQL conventions	transact-sql
SQL syntax recommendations	"sql syntax"
Preparing statements	"preparing statements"
osql utility	osql
Reserved keywords	keywords
Ad hoc batch caching	"OLE DB", ODBC
Using XML	"SELECT (T-SQL)"

Lab A: Overview of Transact-SQL

Objectives

After completing this lab, you will be able to:

- Write basic SELECT statements that return ordered and limited result sets.
- Modify and execute a script.
- Execute a script by using the **osql** utility.
- Use system functions to retrieve system information.

Prerequisites

Before working on this lab, you must have:

- Script files for this lab, which are located in C:\Moc\2073A\Labfiles\L02.
- Answer files for this lab, which are located in C:\Moc\2073A\Labfiles\L02\Answers.

For More Information

If you require help in executing files, search SQL Query Analyzer Help for "Execute a query".

Other resources that you can use include:

- The **Northwind** database schema.
- Microsoft SQL Server Books Online.

Scenario

The organization of the classroom is meant to simulate that of a worldwide trading firm named Northwind Traders. Its fictitious domain name is nwtraders.msft. The primary DNS server for nwtraders.msft is the instructor computer, which has an Internet Protocol (IP) address of 192.168.x.200 (where x is the assigned classroom number). The name of the instructor computer is London.

The following table provides the user name, computer name, and IP address for each student computer in the fictitious nwtraders.msft domain. Find the user name for your computer, and make a note of it.

User name	Computer name	IP address
SQLAdmin1	Vancouver	192.168.x.1
SQLAdmin2	Denver	192.168.x.2
SQLAdmin3	Perth	192.168.x.3
SQLAdmin4	Brisbane	192.168.x.4
SQLAdmin5	Lisbon	192.168.x.5
SQLAdmin6	Bonn	192.168.x.6
SQLAdmin7	Lima	192.168.x.7
SQLAdmin8	Santiago	192.168.x.8
SQLAdmin9	Bangalore	192.168.x.9
SQLAdmin10	Singapore	192.168.x.10
SQLAdmin11	Casablanca	192.168.x.11
SQLAdmin12	Tunis	192.168.x.12
SQLAdmin13	Acapulco	192.168.x.13
SQLAdmin14	Miami	192.168.x.14
SQLAdmin15	Auckland	192.168.x.15
SQLAdmin16	Suva	192.168.x.16
SQLAdmin17	Stockholm	192.168.x.17
SQLAdmin18	Moscow	192.168.x.18
SQLAdmin19	Caracas	192.168.x.19
SQLAdmin20	Montevideo	192.168.x.20
SQLAdmin21	Manila	192.168.x.21
SQLAdmin22	Tokyo	192.168.x.22
SQLAdmin23	Khartoum	192.168.x.23
SQLAdmin24	Nairobi	192.168.x.24

Estimated time to complete this lab: 30 minutes

Exercise 1
Writing Basic SELECT Statements

In this exercise, you will write various statements that return rows from the **Products** table in the **Northwind** database.

▶ To write a SELECT statement that returns ordered data

In this procedure, you will write a statement that returns all of the rows and columns from the **Products** table and sorts the results in ascending order by the **ProductName** column. C:\Moc\2073A\Labfiles\L02\Answers\Basica.sql is a completed script for this procedure.

1. Log on to the **NWTraders** classroom domain by using the information in the following table.

Option	Value
User name	**SQLAdmin**x (where x corresponds to your computer name as designated in the **nwtraders.msft** classroom domain)
Password	**password**

2. Open SQL Query Analyzer and, if requested, log in to the (local) server with Windows authentication.

   You have permission to log in to and administer SQL Server because you are logged as **SQLAdmin**x, which is a member of the Microsoft Windows 2000 local group, Administrators. All members of this group are automatically mapped to the SQL Server **sysadmin** role.

3. In the **DB** list, click **Northwind**.

4. Write a SELECT statement that returns all of the rows and columns from the **Products** table and sorts the results in ascending order by the **ProductName** column.

   You can execute the **sp_help** system stored procedure on the **Products** table to find the correct column names.

5. On the toolbar, click **Execute mode**, and then click **Results in grid**.

6. Execute the statement again.

▶ To write a SELECT statement that returns limited data

In this procedure, you will write a statement that retrieves products from a specific category.

- Write a SELECT statement that retrieves all products in category (**CategoryID**) 4 from the **Products** table.

  You can execute the **sp_help** system stored procedure on the **Products** table to find the correct column names.

Tip For more information about the SELECT statement (as well as any Transact-SQL statement and system table), select the SELECT keyword in the query window, and then press SHIFT+F1 to open SQL Server Books Online. Double-click **SELECT: clauses**.

Exercise 2
Modifying a Script File

In this exercise, you will modify, save, and execute a simple script file.

▶ **To modify a script file**

In this procedure, you will execute a script that contains errors. By using the error information that SQL Server returns, you will make changes to the script so that it executes correctly. Then, you will save and execute the script.

1. Open C:\Moc\2073A\Labfiles\L02\Sample_Script.sql, review it, and then execute it.

    You will receive errors when you run this file. These errors are intentional. C:\Moc\2073A\Labfiles\L02\Answers\Sample_Script.sql is a completed script for this procedure.

2. Place comments around the script name and description so that they do not execute.

3. Add a statement that specifies that the script be executed in the context of the **Northwind** database.

4. Include end of batch markers (GO statements) in the proper areas of the script. Only two additional batch markers are necessary.

5. Save the script, and then execute it.

► **To execute a script file by using osql**

In this procedure, you will execute a script file by using the **osql** utility.

1. Open a command prompt window.

2. Type the following command to execute
    C:\Moc\2073A\Labfiles\L02\Sample_Script2.sql. Make sure that the path is
    correct.

```
osql /Usa /P /i
"c:\moc\2073A\labfiles\L02\Sample_Script2.sql"
```

Note   Write this command in one line.

Exercise 3
Using System Functions

In this exercise, you will gather system information by using system functions.

▶ **To determine the server process ID**

In this procedure, you will observe current server activity and determine the activity that your session is generating.

1. Execute the **sp_who** system stored procedure.

   SQL Server displays all activity that is occurring on the server.

2. To determine which activity is yours, execute the following statement:

   ```
   SELECT @@spid
   ```

   SQL Server returns the server process ID (spid) number of your process in the results.

3. Execute the **sp_who** system stored procedure again, using your spid number as an additional parameter. (In the following statement, *n* represents your spid number.)

   ```
   EXEC sp_who n
   ```

   SQL Server displays the activity related to your spid.

▶ **To retrieve environmental information**

In this procedure, you will determine the version of SQL Server that you are running, and you will retrieve connection, database context, and server information. You will perform these tasks by using system functions.

1. Execute the following statement:

   ```
   SELECT @@version
   ```

2. Execute the following statement:

   ```
   SELECT USER_NAME(), DB_NAME(), @@servername
   ```

▶ **To retrieve metadata**

In this procedure, you will execute several queries to return the metadata from specific database objects by using information schema views. Remember that **INFORMATION_SCHEMA** is a predefined database user who is the owner of the information schema views.

1. Execute the following statement to return a list of all of the user-defined tables in a database:

```
USE Northwind
SELECT * FROM INFORMATION_SCHEMA.TABLES
   WHERE TABLE_TYPE = 'BASE TABLE'
```

2. Execute the following statement to return the primary key and foreign key columns for the **Orders** table:

```
SELECT * FROM INFORMATION_SCHEMA.KEY_COLUMN_USAGE
   WHERE TABLE_NAME = 'Orders'
```

What column has a primary key defined on it?

_____

_____

Review

- Designing Enterprise Application Architecture
- SQL Server Programming Tools
- The Transact-SQL Programming Language
- Elements of Transact-SQL
- Additional Language Elements
- Ways to Execute Transact-SQL Statements

1. You are designing a multi-tier application with a Web interface. This application must update a database table frequently. How and where should you implement the logic to perform the update?

2. Explain the difference between a batch and a script.

3. What advantage does a transaction have over a batch or script?

4. If you want to include conditional logic in a script, what type of language element would you use? Give as many examples of the language element keywords as you can.

Microsoft®
Training &
Certification

Module 3:
Creating and Managing Databases

Contents

Microsoft®

Project Lead: Rich Rose
Instructional Designers: Rich Rose, Cheryl Hoople, Marilyn McGill
Instructional Software Design Engineers: Karl Dehmer, Carl Raebler, Rick Byham
Technical Lead: Karl Dehmer
Subject Matter Experts: Karl Dehmer, Carl Raebler, Rick Byham
Graphic Artist: Kirsten Larson (Independent Contractor)
Editing Manager: Lynette Skinner
Editor: Wendy Cleary
Copy Editor: Edward McKillop (S&T Consulting)
Production Manager: Miracle Davis
Production Coordinator: Jenny Boe
Production Support: Lori Walker (S&T Consulting)
Test Manager: Sid Benavente
Courseware Testing: TestingTesting123
Classroom Automation: Lorrin Smith-Bates
Creative Director, Media/Sim Services: David Mahlmann
Web Development Lead: Lisa Pease
CD Build Specialist: Julie Challenger
Online Support: David Myka (S&T Consulting)
Localization Manager: Rick Terek
Operations Coordinator: John Williams
Manufacturing Support: Laura King; Kathy Hershey
Lead Product Manager, Release Management: Bo Galford
Lead Product Manager, Data Base: Margo Crandall
Group Manager, Courseware Infrastructure: David Bramble
Group Product Manager, Content Development: Dean Murray
General Manager: Robert Stewart

Overview

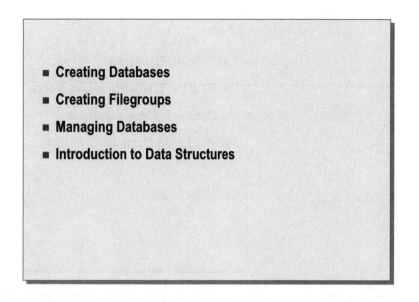

- Creating Databases
- Creating Filegroups
- Managing Databases
- Introduction to Data Structures

This module describes how to create a database, set database options, create filegroups, and manage a database and the transaction log. It also describes how Microsoft® SQL Server™ 2000 stores data.

After completing this module, you will be able to:

- Create a database.
- Create a filegroup.
- Manage a database.
- Describe data structures.

◆ Creating Databases

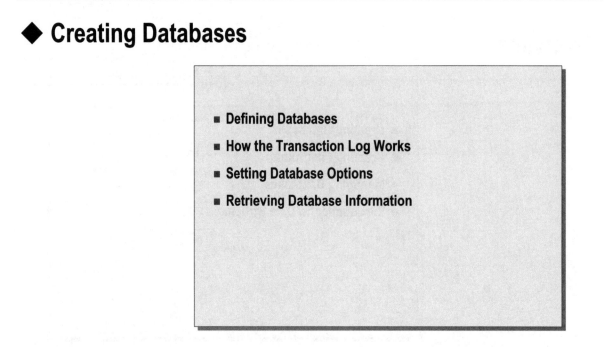

- Defining Databases
- How the Transaction Log Works
- Setting Database Options
- Retrieving Database Information

This section describes how to create databases, specify database options, and retrieve database information. It also describes how the transaction log works.

Defining Databases

■ **Creating a Database Defines:**

- The name of the database
- The size of the database
- The files where the database will reside

```
CREATE DATABASE Sample
ON
  PRIMARY ( NAME=SampleData,
  FILENAME='c:\Program Files\..\..\Data\Sample.mdf',
  SIZE=10MB,
  MAXSIZE=15MB,
  FILEGROWTH=20%)
LOG ON
  ( NAME=SampleLog,
  FILENAME= 'c:\Program Files\..\..\Data\Sample.ldf',
  SIZE=3MB,
  MAXSIZE=5MB,
  FILEGROWTH=1MB)
COLLATE SQL_Latin1_General_Cp1_CI_AS
```

You can define a database by using SQL Server Enterprise Manager or the CREATE DATABASE statement in SQL Query Analyzer. The process of defining a database also creates a transaction log for that database.

Information about each database in SQL Server is stored in the **sysdatabases** table in the **master** database. Therefore, you must use the **master** database to define a database when you use Transact-SQL.

Defining a database is a process of specifying the name of the database and designating the size and location of the database files. When the new database is created, it is a duplicate of the **model** database. Any options or settings in the **model** database are copied into the new database.

Important You should back up the **master** database each time that you create, modify, or drop a database.

Syntax

```
CREATE DATABASE database_name
  [ON
    { [PRIMARY] (NAME = logical_file_name,
        FILENAME = 'os_file_name'
        [, SIZE = size]
        [, MAXSIZE = {max_size | UNLIMITED}]
        [, FILEGROWTH = growth_increment] )
    } [,...n]
  ]
  [LOG ON
    { (NAME = logical_file_name,
        FILENAME = 'os_file_name'
        [, SIZE = size]
        [, MAXSIZE = {max_size | UNLIMITED}]
        [, FILEGROWTH = growth_increment] )
    } [,...n]
  ]
  [COLLATE collation_name]
```

When you create a database, you can set the following parameters:

PRIMARY   This parameter specifies the files in the primary filegroup. The primary filegroup contains all of the database system tables. It also contains all objects not assigned to user filegroups. Every database has one primary data file. The primary data file is the starting point of the database and points to the rest of the files in the database. The recommended file name extension for primary data files is .mdf. If you do not specify the PRIMARY keyword, the first file listed in the statement becomes the primary file.

FILENAME   This parameter specifies the operating system file name and path for the file. The path in the os_file_name must specify a folder on the server on which SQL Server is installed.

SIZE   This parameter specifies the size of the data or log file. You can specify sizes in megabytes (MB)—the default value—or kilobytes (KB). The minimum size is 512 KB for both the data and log file. The size specified for the primary data file must be at least as large as the primary file of the **model** database. When adding a data file or log file, the default value is 1 MB.

MAXSIZE   This parameter specifies the maximum size to which the file can grow. You can specify sizes in megabytes—the default value—or kilobytes. If you do not specify a size, the file grows until the disk is full.

FILEGROWTH   This parameter specifies the growth increment of the file. The FILEGROWTH setting for a file cannot exceed the MAXSIZE setting. A value of 0 indicates no growth. The value can be specified in megabytes—the default—in kilobytes, or as a percentage (%). The default value if FILEGROWTH is not specified is 10 percent, and the minimum value is 64 KB (one extent). The specified size is rounded to the nearest 64 KB.

COLLATION   This parameter specifies the default collation for the database. Collation includes the rules governing the use of characters for either a language or an alphabet.

Example

The following example creates a database called **Sample** with a 10-MB primary data file and a 3-MB log file in a default instance of SQL Server.

```
CREATE DATABASE Sample
ON
  PRIMARY ( NAME=SampleData,
  FILENAME='c:\Program Files\
    Microsoft SQL Server\MSSQL\Data\Sample.mdf',
  SIZE=10MB,
  MAXSIZE=15MB,
  FILEGROWTH=20%)
LOG ON
  ( NAME=SampleLog,
  FILENAME='c:\Program Files\
    Microsoft SQL Server\MSSQL\Data\Sample.ldf',
  SIZE=3MB,
  MAXSIZE=5MB,
  FILEGROWTH=1MB)
COLLATE SQL_Latin1_General_Cp1_CI_AS
```

How the Transaction Log Works

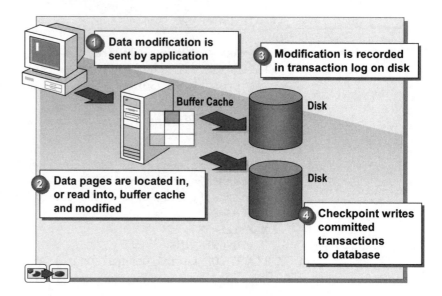

SQL Server records every transaction in a transaction log to maintain database consistency and to aid in recovery. The log is a storage area that automatically tracks changes to a database. SQL Server records modifications in the log on disk as the modifications are executed, before they are written in the database.

The logging process is as follows:

1. A data modification is sent by the application.

2. When a modification is executed, the affected data pages are loaded from disk into the *buffer cache*, provided that the pages are not already in the buffer cache from a previous query.

3. Each data modification statement is recorded in the log as it is made. The change is always recorded in the log and written to disk before that change is made in the database. This type of log is called a *write-ahead* log.

4. On a recurring basis, the checkpoint process writes all completed transactions to the database on the disk.

If the system fails, the automatic recovery process uses the transaction log to roll forward all committed transactions and roll back any incomplete transactions.

Transaction markers in the log are used during automatic recovery to determine the starting and ending points of a transaction. A transaction is considered complete when the BEGIN TRANSACTION marker has an associated COMMIT TRANSACTION marker. Data pages are written to the disk when a checkpoint occurs.

Setting Database Options

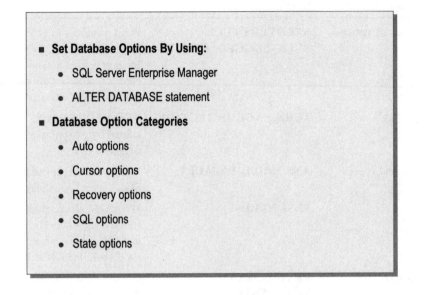

- ■ **Set Database Options By Using:**
  - SQL Server Enterprise Manager
  - ALTER DATABASE statement
- ■ **Database Option Categories**
  - Auto options
  - Cursor options
  - Recovery options
  - SQL options
  - State options

After you have created a database, you can set the database options by using SQL Server Enterprise Manager or the ALTER DATABASE statement.

You can configure a number of database options, but you are able to set them for only one database at a time. To affect options in all new databases, change the **model** database.

The following table lists some of the more frequently used options.

Database option category	Database option	Description
Auto options	**AUTO_CREATE_STATISTICS**	Automatically creates any missing statistics needed by a query for optimization. The default is ON.
	AUTO_UPDATE_STATISTICS	Automatically updates out-of-date statistics required by a query for optimization. The default is ON.
Cursor options	**CURSOR_CLOSE_ON_COMMIT**	Automatically closes open cursors when a transaction is committed. The default is OFF, and cursors remain open.
	CURSOR_DEFAULT LOCAL | GLOBAL	CURSOR_DEFAULT_LOCAL limits the scope of the cursor. It is local to the batch, stored procedure, or trigger in which the cursor was created. CURSOR_DEFAULT_GLOBAL is the default setting; the scope of the cursor is global to the connection.

(continued)

Database option category	Database option	Description
Recovery options	**RECOVERY FULL | BULK_LOGGED | SIMPLE**	FULL provides full recoverability from media failure; it is the default. BULK_LOGGED uses less log space because logging is minimal, but it has greater risk of exposure. SIMPLE recovers the database only to the last full database backup or last differential backup.
	TORN_PAGE_DETECTION	Allows SQL Server to detect incomplete I/O operations caused by power failures or other system outages. The default is ON.
SQL options	**ANSI_NULL_DEFAULT**	Allows the user to control the database default nullability. SQL Server 2000 defaults to NOT NULL.
	ANSI_NULLS	When ON, all comparisons to a null value evaluate to NULL (unknown). When OFF, comparisons of non-Unicode values to a null value evaluate to TRUE if both values are NULL. By default, the ANSI_NULLS database option is OFF.
State options	**READ_ONLY | READ_WRITE**	Defines a database as read-only—use to set security for decision-support databases—or returns database to read/write operations.
	SINGLE_USER | RESTRICTED_USER | MULTI_USER	**SINGLE_USER** allows one user at a time to connect to the database. All other user connections are broken. **RESTRICTED_USER** allows only members of the **db_owner** fixed database role and **dbcreator** and **sysadmin** fixed server roles to connect to the database. **MULTI_USER** allows all users with the appropriate permissions to connect to the database. **MULTI_USER** is the default setting.

Retrieving Database Information

- **Determine Database Properties by Using the DATABASEPROPERTYEX Function**

- **Use System Stored Procedures to Display Information About Databases and Database Parameters**
  - **sp_helpdb**
  - **sp_helpdb** *database_name*
  - **sp_spaceused** [*objname*]

You can determine database properties by using the DATABASEPROPERTYEX function.

Syntax

SELECT DATABASEPROPERTYEX (*database*, *property*)

The following table lists some of the database properties.

Collation	IsFulltextEnabled
IsAnsiNullDefault	IsInStandBy
IsAnsiNullsEnabled	IsNullConcat
IsAnsiPaddingEnabled	IsQuotedIdentifiersEnabled
IsAnsiWarningsEnabled	IsRecursiveTriggersEnabled
IsArithmeticAbortEnabled	Recovery
IsAutoCreateStatistics	Status
IsAutoShrink	Updateability
IsAutoUpdateStatistics	UserAccess
IsCloseCursorsOnCommitEnabled	Version

The following table lists commonly-used system stored procedures that display information about databases and database parameters.

System stored procedure	Description
sp_helpdb	Reports on all databases on a server. Provides database name, size, owner, ID, creation date, and options.
sp_helpdb *database_name*	Reports on a specified database only. Provides database name, size, owner, ID, creation date, and options. Also lists files for data and log.
sp_spaceused [*objname*]	Summarizes the storage space that a database, or database object uses.

Creating Filegroups

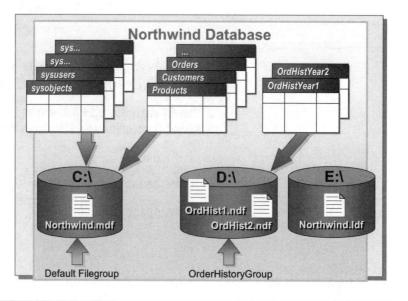

If your hardware setup includes multiple disk drives, you can locate specific objects and files on individual disks, grouping your database files into filegroups. *Filegroups* are named collections of files. SQL Server includes one filegroup as a default. You can create additional filegroups by using either the CREATE DATABASE or ALTER DATABASE statement.

With filegroups, you can locate specific objects on a specific file. In the illustration, the OrdHist1.ndf and OrdHist2.ndf files are placed on separate disk to separate files that are heavily queried from those that are heavily modified and to reduce disk drive contention.

System administrators also can back up and restore individual files or filegroups instead of backing up or restoring an entire database. Backing up files or filegroups is necessary on large databases to have an effective back up and restore strategy.

Considerations When Using Filegroups

Use of filegroups is an advanced database design technique. You must understand your database structure, data, transactions, and queries thoroughly to determine the best way to place tables and indexes on specific filegroups. In many cases, using the striping capabilities of RAID systems provides much of the same performance gain that you might achieve by using filegroups without the added administrative burden of defining and managing them.

Note Log files are not part of a filegroup. Log space is managed separately from data space.

Types of Filegroups

SQL Server offers the following two types of filegroups:

- The primary filegroup, which contains the system tables in the primary data file.

- User-defined filegroups, which are any filegroups that are specified by using the FILEGROUP keyword.

Designating the Default Filegroup

When you create a database, the primary filegroup automatically becomes the default filegroup. The default filegroup receives all new tables, indexes, and files for which a filegroup is not specified. If your database contains more than one filegroup, it is recommended that you change the default to be one of your user-defined filegroups. This prevents the primary filegroup, which contains the system tables, from being unexpectedly filled by a user table.

Sizing the Primary Default Filegroup

If the default filegroup remains the primary filegroup, sizing this filegroup correctly is important. If the filegroup runs out of space, you are not able to add any new information to the system tables. If a user-defined filegroup runs out of space, only the user files that are specifically allocated to that filegroup are affected.

Example

The following example creates a user-defined filegroup in the **Northwind** database and adds a secondary data file to the user-defined filegroup.

```
ALTER DATABASE Northwind
ADD FILEGROUP OrderHistoryGroup
GO

ALTER DATABASE Northwind
ADD FILE
  ( NAME = 'OrdHistYear1',
  FILENAME = 'c:\ Program Files\
    Microsoft SQL Server\MSSQL\Data\OrdHist1.ndf,
  SIZE = 5MB),
TO FILEGROUP OrderHistoryGroup
GO
```

Viewing Filegroup Information

Information about filegroups is available by using functions, such as FILE_NAME, FILE_ID, FILE_PROPERTY, FILEGROUP_NAME, FILEGROUP_ID, and FILEGROUP_PROPERTY. The system stored procedures in the following table also display information about filegroups.

System stored procedure	Description
sp_helpfile [[@**filename** =] '*name*']	Returns the physical names and attributes of files associated with the current database. Use this system stored procedure to determine the names of files to attach to, or detach from, the server.
sp_helpfilegroup [*filegroup_name*]	Returns the names and attributes of filegroups associated with the current database.

◆ Managing Databases

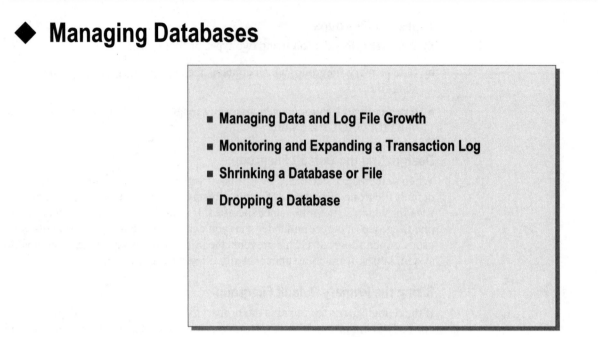

- Managing Data and Log File Growth
- Monitoring and Expanding a Transaction Log
- Shrinking a Database or File
- Dropping a Database

As your database grows or changes, you can expand or shrink the database size automatically or manually. When you no longer need a database, you can drop it, along with all associated files.

Managing Data and Log File Growth

- **Using Automatic File Growth**
- **Expanding Database Files**
- **Adding Secondary Database Files**

```
ALTER DATABASE Sample
    MODIFY FILE ( NAME = 'SampleLog',
    SIZE = 15MB)
GO

ALTER DATABASE Sample
ADD FILE
  (NAME = SampleData2,
   FILENAME='c:\Program Files\..\..\
      Data\Sample2.ndf',
   SIZE=15MB,
   MAXSIZE=20MB)
GO
```

When data files grow, or when data modification activity increases, you may need to expand the size of the data or log files. You can manage database growth by using SQL Server Enterprise Manager or the ALTER DATABASE statement. You must be in the **master** database to use the ALTER DATABASE statement.

You can control the size of the database by:

- Configuring the database and log files to grow automatically.

- Manually increasing or decreasing the current or maximum size of existing database and log files.

- Manually adding secondary database and log files.

Using Automatic File Growth

You can set the automatic file growth option by using the ALTER DATABASE statement or SQL Server Enterprise Manager to specify that database files automatically expand by a specified amount whenever necessary. Using automatic file growth reduces the administrative tasks involved with manually increasing the database size.

You can specify the initial size, maximum size, and growth increment of each file. Although it is possible to specify file growth in megabytes or kilobytes, you should specify file growth by percentage. If you do not specify a maximum size, a file can continue to grow until it uses all available space on the disk.

When you use automatic file growth with multiple files, SQL Server uses a proportional fill strategy across all the files in each filegroup. As data is written to the filegroup, SQL Server writes an amount proportional to the free space in the file to each file in the filegroup, instead of writing all the data to the first file until it is full and then writing to the next file.

For optimum performance:

- Allocate sufficient initial size to the database and the log to avoid frequently activating automatic growth.

- Set a maximum size for data files if you have multiple databases.

- Set the data and log file growth increments to sufficient sizes to avoid frequently activating automatic growth.

  For example, if the log grows by 40 MB daily, set the autogrow increment to 50 MB or 100 MB—rather than to 1 MB.

Expanding Database Files

If you do not configure an existing file to grow automatically, you still can increase its size. A value of zero for the growth increment indicates that it does not grow automatically.

Adding Secondary Database Files

You can create secondary database files to expand the size of a database. Use secondary database files to place data files on separate physical disks when you do not use the disk-striping capabilities of RAID systems.

Partial Syntax

ALTER DATABASE *database*
  { ADD FILE < filespec > [,...n] [TO FILEGROUP *filegroup_name*]
  | ADD LOG FILE < filespec > [,...*n*]
  | REMOVE FILE *logical_file_name* [WITH DELETE]
  | ADD FILEGROUP *filegroup_name*
  | REMOVE FILEGROUP *filegroup_name*
  | MODIFY FILE < filespec >
  | MODIFY NAME = *new_dbname*
  | MODIFY FILEGROUP *filegroup_name*
    {*filegroup_property* | NAME = *new_filegroup_name* }
  | SET < optionspec > [,...*n*] [WITH < termination >]
  | COLLATE < *collation_name* >
  }

Example

The following example increases the current log size and adds a secondary data file to the **Sample** database.

```
ALTER DATABASE Sample
   MODIFY FILE ( NAME = 'SampleLog',
   SIZE = 15MB)
GO

ALTER DATABASE Sample
ADD FILE
(NAME = 'SampleData2' ,
FILENAME='c:\Program Files\
   Microsoft SQL Server\MSSQL\Data\Sample2.ndf',
SIZE=15MB ,
MAXSIZE=20MB)
GO
```

Monitoring and Expanding a Transaction Log

- **Monitoring the Log**

- **Monitoring Situations That Produce Extensive Log Activity**

  - Mass loading of data into indexed table

  - Large transactions

  - Performing logged text or image operations

- **Expanding the Log When Necessary**

When a database grows, or when data modification activity increases, you may need to expand the transaction log.

Monitoring the Log

Plan carefully so that you do not have too little log space. Monitoring the log on a regular basis helps you determine the optimal time to expand it.

Warning   If your transaction log runs out of space, SQL Server cannot record transactions and does not allow changes to your database.

You can monitor the transaction log with SQL Server Enterprise Manager, the DBCC SQLPERF (LOGSPACE) statement, or Microsoft Windows® 2000 System Monitor.

You can monitor the transaction logs of individual databases by using SQL Server:Database object counters in System Monitor. These counters include ones listed in the following table.

Object counter	Displays
Log Bytes Flushed/sec	Number of bytes in the log buffer when buffer is flushed
Log Flushes/sec	Number of log flushes
Log Flush Waits/Sec	Number of commits that are waiting on log flush
Percent Log Used	Percent of space in the log that is in use
Log File(s) Size (KB)	Cumulative size of all of the log files in the database
Log Cache Hit Ratio	Percent of log cache reads that were successful from the log cache

Monitoring Situations That Produce Extensive Log Activity

Some situations that produce additional transaction log activity are:

- Loading information into a table that has indexes. SQL Server logs all inserts and index changes. When loading tables without indexes, SQL Server logs only extent allocations.

- Transactions that perform many modifications (INSERT, UPDATE, and DELETE statements) to a table in a single transaction. This typically occurs when the statement lacks a WHERE clause or when the WHERE clause is too general, causing a large number of records to be affected.

- Adding or modifying text or image data in a table.

Expanding the Log When Necessary

You can expand the transaction log by using SQL Server Enterprise Manager or the ALTER DATABASE statement.

Shrinking a Database or File

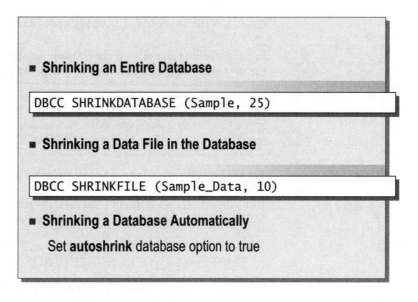

- **Shrinking an Entire Database**

  DBCC SHRINKDATABASE (Sample, 25)

- **Shrinking a Data File in the Database**

  DBCC SHRINKFILE (Sample_Data, 10)

- **Shrinking a Database Automatically**

  Set **autoshrink** database option to true

When too much space is allocated, or when space requirements decrease, you can shrink an entire database or specific data files in a database.

Shrinking an Entire Database

You can shrink an entire database by using SQL Server Enterprise Manager or by executing the Database Consistency Checker (DBCC) statement SHRINKDATABASE. This shrinks the size of all data files in the database.

SQL Server shrinks log files by using a deferred shrink operation, and does so as if all of the log files existed in one contiguous log pool. Log files are reset when the log is truncated; SQL Server attempts to shrink the truncated log files to as close to the targeted size as possible.

Syntax

DBCC SHRINKDATABASE (*database_name* [, *target_percent*] [, {NOTRUNCATE | TRUNCATEONLY}])

The following table describes the DBCC SHRINKDATABASE options.

Option	Description
target_percent	Specifies the wanted percentage of free space left in the database file after SQL Server has shrunk the database.
NOTRUNCATE	Causes SQL Server to retain the freed file space in the database files. The default is to release the freed file space to the operating system.
TRUNCATEONLY	Causes any unused space in the data files to be released to the operating system and shrinks the file to the last allocated extent, reducing the file size without moving any data. No attempt is made to relocate rows to unallocated pages. SQL Server ignores *target_percent* when you use this option.

Example

This example shrinks the size of the **SampleData** so that the file will have free space of 25 percent.

```
DBCC SHRINKDATABASE (SampleData, 25)
```

In the preceding example, if the **Sample** database file contains 6 MB of data, the new size of the database will be 8 MB (6 MB of data, 2 MB of free space).

Note   SQL Server does not shrink a file to a size smaller than the amount of space that the data occupies. Also, it does not shrink a file beyond the size specified in the SIZE parameter of the CREATE DATABASE statement.

Shrinking a Data File in the Database

You can shrink a data file in a database by using SQL Server Enterprise Manager or by executing the DBCC statement SHRINKFILE.

Syntax

DBCC SHRINKFILE ({*file_name* | *file_id*} [, *target_size*] [, { EMPTYFILE | NOTRUNCATE | TRUNCATEONLY}])

The following table describes the DBCC SHRINKFILE options.

Option	Description
target_size	Specifies the wanted size for the data file in megabytes, expressed as an integer. If not specified, DBCC SHRINKFILE reduces the size as much as possible.
EMPTYFILE	Migrates all data from the specified file to other files in the same filegroup. SQL Server no longer allows data to be placed on the file used with the EMPTY_FILE option. Use this option to drop the file by using the ALTER DATABASE statement.

Example

This example shrinks the size of the **sample** data file to 10 MB.

```
DBCC SHRINKFILE (Sample, 10)
```

Shrinking a Database Automatically

Autoshrink is not enabled by default. By setting the **autoshrink** database option to true, you can set a database option to recover unused space automatically. You can also change this option with SQL Server Enterprise Manager.

Consider the following facts and guidelines when you shrink a database or a data file:

- The resulting database must be larger than the size of the **model** database or the existing data in the database or data file.

- Before you shrink a database or a data file, you should back up the database, and the **master** database.

- DBCC SHRINKDATABASE and SHRINKFILE perform some actions on a deferred basis, so you may not see the database or file size reduced immediately.

- DBCC SHRINKFILE can reduce the size of a database to smaller than the size specified when the database was created or altered, but not to smaller than the size that the data occupies.

Dropping a Database

- **Methods of Dropping a Database**
  - SQL Server Enterprise Manager
  - DROP DATABASE statement

  ```
  DROP DATABASE Northwind, pubs
  ```

- **Restrictions on Dropping a Database**
  - While it is being restored
  - When a user is connected to it
  - When publishing as part of replication
  - If it is a system database

You can drop a database when you no longer need it. Dropping a database deletes the database and the disk files that the database uses.

Methods of Dropping a Database

You can drop databases by using SQL Server Enterprise Manager or by executing the DROP DATABASE statement.

Syntax

DROP DATABASE *database_name* [,...*n*]

Example

This example drops multiple databases by using one statement.

```
DROP DATABASE Northwind, pubs
```

When you drop a database, consider the following facts and guidelines:

- With SQL Server Enterprise Manager, you can drop only one database at a time.

- With Transact-SQL, you can drop several databases at once.

- After you drop a database, every login ID that used that particular database as its default database will not have a default database.

Note Back up the **master** database after you drop a database.

Restrictions on Dropping a Database

The following restrictions apply to dropping databases. You cannot drop:

- A database that is in the process of being restored.

- A database that is open for reading or writing by any user.

- A database that is publishing any of its tables as part of SQL Server replication.

- A system database.

◆ Introduction to Data Structures

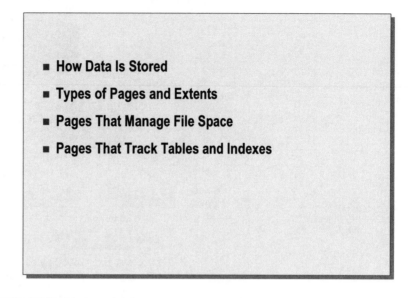

- How Data Is Stored
- Types of Pages and Extents
- Pages That Manage File Space
- Pages That Track Tables and Indexes

This section describes the data structures that SQL Server uses to store data.

How Data Is Stored

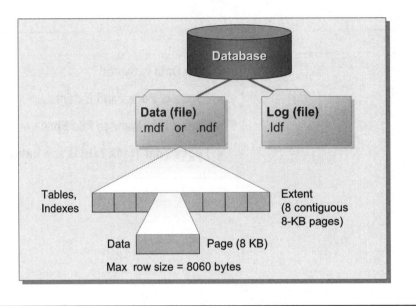

When creating a database, it is important to understand how SQL Server stores data so that you can calculate and specify the amount of disk space to allocate for the database. Consider the following facts and guidelines about data storage:

- All databases have a primary data file, identified by the .mdf file name extension, and one or more transaction log files, identified by the .ldf file name extension. A database also may have secondary data files, which are identified by the .ndf file name extension. These physical files have both operating system file names and logical file names that you can use in Transact-SQL statements.

- When you create a database, a copy of the **model** database, which includes the system tables, is copied to the database. The minimum size of a database must be equal to or greater than the size of the **model** database.

- SQL Server stores, reads, and writes data in 8-KB blocks of contiguous disk space called *pages*. This means that a database can store 128 pages per megabyte.

- Rows cannot span pages. Thus, the maximum amount of data in a single row, subtracting the space required for row overhead, is 8060 bytes.

- All pages are stored in *extents*. An extent is eight contiguous pages, or 64 KB. Therefore, a database has 16 extents per megabyte.

- Transaction log files hold all of the information necessary for recovery of the database in the event of a system failure. By default, the size of the transaction log is 25 percent of the size of the data files. Use this figure as a starting point and adjust it according to the needs of your application.

Types of Pages and Extents

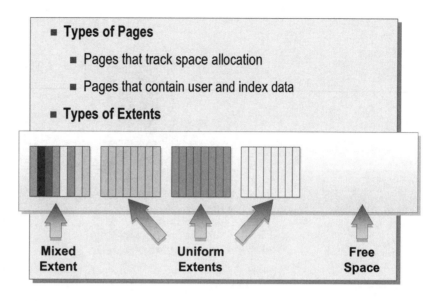

- **Types of Pages**
  - Pages that track space allocation
  - Pages that contain user and index data
- **Types of Extents**

Mixed Extent Uniform Extents Free Space

Pages and extents are the primary data structures in the SQL Server physical database.

Types of Pages

SQL Server uses several types of pages: some track space allocation, and some contain user and index data. The pages that track allocation contain densely packed information. This allows SQL Server to efficiently keep them in memory for easy tracking.

Types of Extents

SQL Server uses two types of extents:

- Extents that contain pages from two or more objects are called *mixed extents*. Every table starts as a mixed extent. You use mixed extents primarily for pages that track space and contain small objects.

- Extents that have all eight pages allocated to a single object are called *uniform extents*. They are used when tables or indexes need more than 64 KB of space.

Pages That Manage File Space

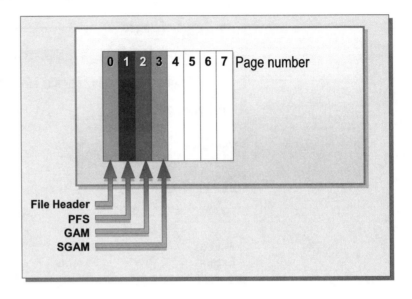

The first extent of each file is a mixed extent that contains a file header page followed by three allocation pages. SQL Server allocates this mixed extent when you create the primary data file and uses these pages internally.

File Header Page

The file header page contains the attributes of the file, such as the name of the database that owns the file, its file group, minimum size, and growth increment. It is the first page in every file (Page 0).

PFS Page

The Page Free Space (PFS) page is an allocation page that contains information about free space available on the pages in a file. Page 1 of each file is a PFS page. SQL Server adds other PFS pages as needed.

Each PFS page can track 8,000 contiguous pages, which is nearly 64 MB of data. For each page, the PFS page contains a byte that tracks:

- Whether the page has been allocated.
- Whether the page is on a mixed or uniform extent.
- An approximation of how much space is available on the page.

GAM and SGAM Pages

SQL Server uses Global Allocation Map (GAM) and Secondary Global Allocation Map (SGAM) pages to determine the location of free extents or mixed extents with free pages.

GAM Pages

The GAM page is an allocation page that contains information about allocated extents. Page 2 of each file is a GAM page. SQL Server adds additional GAM pages as needed.

Each GAM page covers 63,904 extents, or nearly 4 gigabytes (GB) of data. The GAM page contains one bit for each extent that it covers. The bit is set to 0 if the extent is allocated, and set to 1 if it is free.

SGAM Pages

The SGAM page is an allocation page that contains information about allocated mixed extents. Page 3 of each file is an SGAM page. SQL Server adds additional SGAM pages as needed.

SGAM pages track mixed extents that currently have at least one unused page. They also cover 63,904 extents. A bit set to 0 indicates that an extent is either a uniform extent or a mixed extent without any free pages. A bit set to 1 indicates a mixed extent with one or more free pages.

The following table summarizes the setting of the GAM and SGAM bits:

If the GAM bit is set to...	And the SGAM is set to...	Then ...
1	0	It is an available extent. This extent is not in use.
0	1	It is an available page. This mixed extent has an unassigned page or pages.
0	0	It is an extent with nothing available. The extent is assigned as a uniform extent or a full mixed extent.

Pages That Track Tables and Indexes

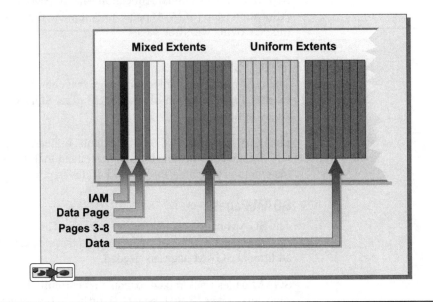

SQL Server initially assigns every table and index an allocation page and at least one data page in a mixed extent. As the object grows, SQL Server assigns up to seven more pages from mixed extents as needed. When the object exceeds eight pages, SQL Server assigns additional pages from uniform extents.

SQL Server uses four types of pages to manage tables and indexes. They may appear at any location in the file. They are the IAM, Data, Text/Image, and Index pages.

IAM Page

The IAM page is an allocation page that contains information about the extents that a table or index uses.

The IAM page contains the location of the eight initial pages and a bitmap of extents indicating which extents are in use for that object. A single IAM page can track up to 512,000 data pages. SQL Server adds more IAM pages for larger tables.

IAM pages are always allocated from mixed extents and can appear anywhere in a file or filegroup. SQL Server attempts to group IAM pages together for speedy retrieval.

Data Page

The Data page contains content other than **text**, **ntext**, and **image** data.

Text/Image Page

The Text/Image page contains **text**, **ntext**, and **image** content.

Index Page

The Index page contains index structures.

Recommended Practices

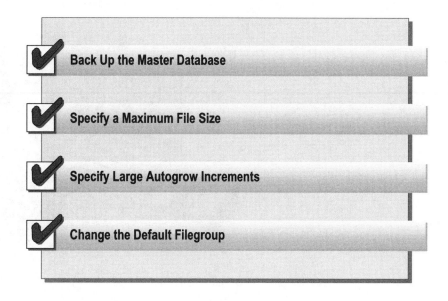

The following recommended practices will help you create and manage databases:

- Back up the **master** database immediately after you create or modify a database.

  This is important because the **master** database has the **system** catalog.

- Specify a maximum size when you use automatic file growth.

  This will prevent any single file from filling the entire hard disk.

- Specify large autogrow increments to avoid frequent file growth.

  This will reduce SQL Server administrative activity and help keep the file from becoming fragmented on the hard disk.

- Change the default filegroup.

  If your database has multiple filegroups, assign one of the user-defined filegroups as the default. This will prevent any unexpected table growth from adversely affecting the system tables in the primary filegroup.

Lab A: Creating and Managing Databases

Objectives

After completing this lab, you will be able to:

- Create a database.
- Manage the growth of a database.
- Change database options to control how often the transaction log is cleared.

Prerequisites

Before working on this lab, you must have:

- Script files for this lab, which are located in C:\Moc\2073A\Labfiles\L03.
- Answer files for this lab, which are located in
  C:\Moc\2073A\Labfiles\L03\Answers.

Lab Setup

To complete this lab, you must have completed the prior lab.

Note   This course is based on the **Northwind** database. The schema for the **Northwind** database is in Appendix A. The labs use a parallel version of the **Northwind** database that is called **ClassNorthwind**.

For More Information

If you require help when executing files, search SQL Query Analyzer Help for "Execute a query".

Other resources that you can use include:

- The **Northwind** database schema.
- Microsoft SQL Server Books Online.

Scenario

The organization of the classroom is meant to simulate that of a worldwide trading firm named Northwind Traders. Its fictitious domain name is nwtraders.msft. The primary DNS server for nwtraders.msft is the instructor computer, which has an Internet Protocol (IP) address of 192.168.x.200 (where x is the assigned classroom number). The name of the instructor computer is London.

The following table provides the user name, computer name, and IP address for each student computer in the fictitious **nwtraders.msft** domain. Find the user name for your computer, and make a note of it.

User name	Computer name	IP address
SQLAdmin1	Vancouver	192.168.x.1
SQLAdmin2	Denver	192.168.x.2
SQLAdmin3	Perth	192.168.x.3
SQLAdmin4	Brisbane	192.168.x.4
SQLAdmin5	Lisbon	192.168.x.5
SQLAdmin6	Bonn	192.168.x.6
SQLAdmin7	Lima	192.168.x.7
SQLAdmin8	Santiago	192.168.x.8
SQLAdmin9	Bangalore	192.168.x.9
SQLAdmin10	Singapore	192.168.x.10
SQLAdmin11	Casablanca	192.168.x.11
SQLAdmin12	Tunis	192.168.x.12
SQLAdmin13	Acapulco	192.168.x.13
SQLAdmin14	Miami	192.168.x.14
SQLAdmin15	Auckland	192.168.x.15
SQLAdmin16	Suva	192.168.x.16
SQLAdmin17	Stockholm	192.168.x.17
SQLAdmin18	Moscow	192.168.x.18
SQLAdmin19	Caracas	192.168.x.19
SQLAdmin20	Montevideo	192.168.x.20
SQLAdmin21	Manila	192.168.x.21
SQLAdmin22	Tokyo	192.168.x.22
SQLAdmin23	Khartoum	192.168.x.23
SQLAdmin24	Nairobi	192.168.x.24

Estimated time to complete this lab: 30 minutes

Exercise 1
Creating the ClassNorthwind Database

In this exercise, you will create the **ClassNorthwind** database and define the files used for data and the transaction log.

▶ To create the ClassNorthwind database

In this procedure, you will use SQL Server Enterprise Manager to create the **ClassNorthwind** database.

A complete Transact-SQL script for this procedure is located in C:\MOC\2073A\Labfiles\L03\Answers\Creabase.sql.

1. Log on to the **NWTraders** classroom domain by using the information in the following table.

Option	Value
User name	**SQLAdmin*x*** (where *x* corresponds to your computer name as designated in the **nwtraders.msft** classroom domain)
Password	**password**

2. Open SQL Server Enterprise Manager.

   You have permission to log in to and administer the installation of SQL Server on your computer because your **SQLAdmin*x*** account is a member of the Microsoft Windows® 2000 local group **Administrators**, which is automatically mapped to the SQL Server **sysadmin** role.

3. Expand Microsoft SQL Servers, expand SQL Server Group, and then expand your computer.

4. Right-click **Databases**, and then click **New Database**.

5. Use the values in the following table to create the **ClassNorthwind** database.

For this parameter	Use this value
Database name	**ClassNorthwind**
Database file name	**ClassNorthwind_Data**
Location	(Default)
Initial size	25 MB
Filegroup	Primary
File growth	10 percent
Maximum file size	100 MB
Transaction log file name	**ClassNorthwind_Log**
Location	(Default)
Initial size	15 MB
File growth	10 percent
Log file maximum size	40 MB

6. After you create the **ClassNorthwind** database, in the console tree, expand **Databases**, and then click **ClassNorthwind**.

   Review the information available in the details pane on the **General** tab.

7. Open SQL Query Analyzer and connect by using Windows 2000 Authentication.

8. Execute the **sp_helpdb** system stored procedure to view information on the **ClassNorthwind** database.

Exercise 2
Managing the Growth of the ClassNorthwind Transaction Log File

In this exercise, you will modify the maximum size of the **ClassNorthwind** transaction log file.

▶ To increase the size of the ClassNorthwind transaction log file

In this procedure, you will write and execute a statement to increase the maximum size of the **ClassNorthwind** transaction log file to 50 MB and the current log size to 20 MB.

A complete Transact-SQL script for this procedure is located in C:\MOC\2073A\Labfiles\L03\Answers\Altebase.sql.

1. Write and execute a statement that increases the maximum size of the **ClassNorthwind** transaction log file to 50 MB.

2. Write and execute a statement that increases the current size of the **ClassNorthwind** transaction log file to 25 MB.

3. Write and execute a statement that increases the growth increment of the **ClassNorthwind** transaction log file to 20 percent.

4. Execute the **sp_helpdb** system stored procedure to view information on the **ClassNorthwind** database and to verify the changes.

Exercise 3
Setting the Database Recovery Model

In this exercise, you will set the database recovery model to SIMPLE. This will allow SQL Server to reclaim log space after the log space is no longer needed for recovery. It also reduces space requirements.

▶ **To set the database recovery model**

In this procedure, you will write and execute a statement to set the **ClassNorthwind** database recovery model to SIMPLE. You will use the ALTER DATABASE statement.

A complete Transact-SQL script for this procedure is located in C:\MOC\2073A\Labfiles\L03\Answers\RecovModel.sql.

1. Execute the following statement to turn on the option that clears the transaction log automatically each time that SQL Server performs a checkpoint:

```
ALTER DATABASE ClassNorthwind SET RECOVERY SIMPLE
GO
```

2. Execute the **sp_helpdb** system stored procedure to view information on the **ClassNorthwind** database to verify that the recovery model has been changed.

Review

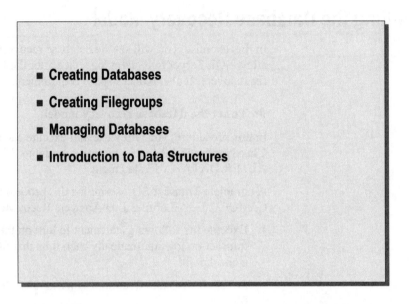

1. You are creating a database that is updated infrequently; it is used mainly for decision support and read-only queries. What percentage of the database would you allocate to the transaction log?

2. What are the advantages of using filegroups?

3. You are responsible for managing the mission-critical accounting records of your organization. Which database recovery model would be appropriate for this database?

4. The GAM, SGAM, and IAM pages all track data allocation. How is the IAM page different from the GAM and SGAM pages?

Microsoft®
Training &
Certification

Module 4: Creating Data Types and Tables

Contents

Microsoft®

Project Lead: Rich Rose
Instructional Designers: Rich Rose, Cheryl Hoople, Marilyn McGill
Instructional Software Design Engineers: Karl Dehmer, Carl Raebler, Rick Byham
Technical Lead: Karl Dehmer
Subject Matter Experts: Karl Dehmer, Carl Raebler, Rick Byham
Graphic Artist: Kirsten Larson (Independent Contractor)
Editing Manager: Lynette Skinner
Editor: Wendy Cleary
Copy Editor: Edward McKillop (S&T Consulting)
Production Manager: Miracle Davis
Production Coordinator: Jenny Boe
Production Support: Lori Walker (S&T Consulting)
Test Manager: Sid Benavente
Courseware Testing: TestingTesting123
Classroom Automation: Lorrin Smith-Bates
Creative Director, Media/Sim Services: David Mahlmann
Web Development Lead: Lisa Pease
CD Build Specialist: Julie Challenger
Online Support: David Myka (S&T Consulting)
Localization Manager: Rick Terek
Operations Coordinator: John Williams
Manufacturing Support: Laura King; Kathy Hershey
Lead Product Manager, Release Management: Bo Galford
Lead Product Manager, Data Base: Margo Crandall
Group Manager, Courseware Infrastructure: David Bramble
Group Product Manager, Content Development: Dean Murray
General Manager: Robert Stewart

Overview

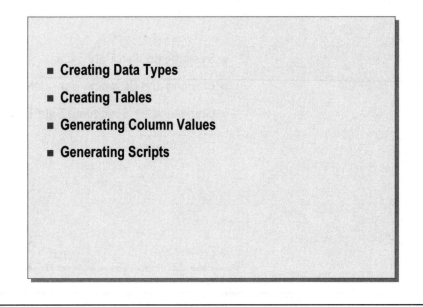

This module describes how to create data types and tables, and generate Transact-SQL scripts containing statements that create a database and its objects.

After completing this module, students will be able to:

- Create and drop user-defined data types.
- Create and drop user tables.
- Generate column values.
- Generate scripts.

◆ Creating Data Types

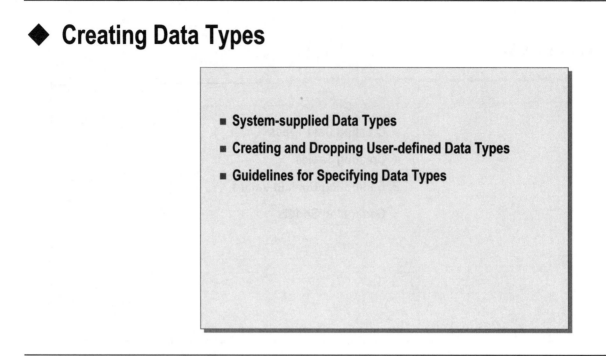

- System-supplied Data Types
- Creating and Dropping User-defined Data Types
- Guidelines for Specifying Data Types

Before you can create a table, you must define the data types for the table. Data types specify the type of information (characters, numbers, or dates) that a column can hold, as well as how the data is stored. Microsoft® SQL Server™ 2000 supplies various system data types. SQL Server also allows user-defined data types that are based on system data types.

System-supplied Data Types

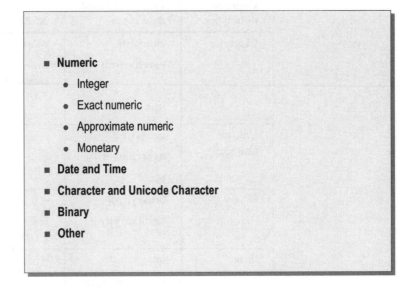

- **Numeric**
  - Integer
  - Exact numeric
  - Approximate numeric
  - Monetary
- **Date and Time**
- **Character and Unicode Character**
- **Binary**
- **Other**

Data types define the data value allowed for each column. SQL Server provides a number of different data types. Certain common data types have several associated SQL Server data types. You should choose appropriate data types to optimize performance and conserve disk space.

Categories of System-supplied Data Types

The following table maps common types of data to SQL Server system-supplied data types. The table includes data type synonyms for ANSI compatibility.

Common data types	SQL Server system-supplied data types	ANSI synonym	Number of bytes
Integer	**int**	*integer*	4
	bigint	–	8
	smallint, tinyint	–	2, 1
Exact numeric	**decimal[(p[, s])]**	*dec*	2–17
	numeric[(p[, s])]	–	
Approximate numeric	**float[(n)]**	*double precision, float[(n)] for n=8-15*	8
	real	*float[(n)] for n=1-7*	4
Monetary	**money, smallmoney**	–	8, 4
Date and time	**Datetime, smalldatetime**	–	8 4

(continued)

Common data types	SQL Server system-supplied data types	ANSI synonym	Number of bytes
Character	**char[(n)]**	*character*[(*n*)]	0–8000
	varchar[(n)]	*char VARYING*[(*n*)] *character VARYING*[(*n*)] –	
	text		0–2 GB
Unicode character	**nchar[(n)]**	–	0–8000
	nvarchar[(n)]		(4000 characters)
	ntext		0–2 GB
Binary	**binary[(n)]**	–	0–8000
	varbinary[(n)]	*binary VARYING*[(*n*)]	
Image	**image**	–	0–2 GB
Global identifier	**uniqueidentifier**	–	16
Special	**bit, cursor, uniqueidentifier**	–	1, 0–8
	timestamp	**rowversion**	8
	sysname	–	256
	table	–	
	sql_variant	–	0–8016

Exact and Approximate Numeric Data Types

How you plan to use a data type should determine whether you choose an exact numeric or an approximate numeric data type.

Exact Numeric Data Types

Exact numeric data types let you specify *exactly* the scale and precision to use. For example, you can specify three digits to the right of the decimal and four to the left. A query always returns exactly what you entered. SQL Server supports two exact numeric data types for ANSI compatibility: **decimal** and **numeric**.

In general, you would use exact numeric data types for financial applications in which you want to portray the data consistently (always two decimal places) and to query on that column (for example, to find all loans with an interest rate of 8.75 percent).

Approximate Numeric Data Types

Approximate numeric data types store data as accurately as possible. For example, the fraction 1/3 is represented in a decimal system as .33333 (repeating). The number cannot be stored accurately, so an approximation is stored. SQL Server supports two approximate data types: **float** and **real**.

If you are rounding numbers or performing quality checks between values, you should avoid using approximate numeric data types.

Note   It is best to avoid referencing columns with the **float** or **real** data type in WHERE clauses.

Creating and Dropping User-defined Data Types

```
Creating

EXEC sp_addtype    city, 'nvarchar(15)', NULL
EXEC sp_addtype    region, 'nvarchar(15)', NULL
EXEC sp_addtype    country, 'nvarchar(15)', NULL

Dropping

EXEC  sp_droptype city
```

User-defined data types are based on system-supplied data types. They allow you to refine data types further to ensure consistency when working with common data elements in different tables or databases. A user-defined data type is defined for a specific database.

Note User-defined data types that you create in the **model** database are automatically included in all databases that are subsequently created. Each user-defined data type is added as a row in the **systypes** table.

You can create and drop user-defined data types by using SQL Server Enterprise Manager or system stored procedures. Data type names must follow the rules for identifier names and must be unique to each database. Define each user-defined data type in terms of a system-supplied data type, preferably by specifying NULL or NOT NULL.

Creating a User-defined Data Type

The **sp_addtype** system stored procedure creates user-defined data types.

Syntax

sp_addtype {*type*}, [*system_data_type*] [, ['NULL' | 'NOT NULL']] [, '*owner_name*']

Example

The following example creates three user-defined data types.

```
EXEC  sp_addtype  city, 'nvarchar(15)', NULL
EXEC  sp_addtype  region, 'nvarchar(15)', NULL
EXEC  sp_addtype  country, 'nvarchar(15)', NULL
```

Dropping a User-Defined Data Type

The **sp_droptype** system stored procedure deletes user-defined data types from the **systypes** system table. A user-defined data type cannot be dropped if tables or other database objects reference it.

Syntax

sp_droptype {'*type*'}

Example

The following example drops a user-defined data type.

```
EXEC sp_droptype city
```

Note   Execute the **sp_help** system stored procedure to retrieve a list of currently defined data types.

Guidelines for Specifying Data Types

- **If Column Length Varies, Use a Variable Data Type**

- **Use tinyint Appropriately**

- **For Numeric Data Types, Commonly Use decimal**

- **If Storage Is Greater Than 8000 Bytes, Use text or image**

- **Use money for Currency**

- **Do Not Use float or real as Primary Keys**

Consider the following guidelines for selecting data types and balancing storage size with requirements:

- If column length varies, use one of the variable data types. For example, if you have a list of names, you can set it to **varchar** instead of **char** (fixed).

- If you own a growing bookselling business with many locations, and you have specified the **tinyint** data type for the store identifier in the database, you will have problems when you decide to open store number 256.

- For numeric data types, the size and required level of precision helps to determine your choice. In general, use **decimal**.

- If the storage is greater than 8000 bytes, use **text** or **image**. If it is less than 8000, use **binary** or **char**. When possible, it is best to use **varchar** because it has more functionality than **text** and **image**.

- Use the **money** data type for currency.

- Do not use the approximate data types **float** and **real** as primary keys. Because the values of these data types are not precise, it is not appropriate to use them in comparisons.

◆ Creating Tables

- How SQL Server Organizes Data in Rows
- How SQL Server Organizes text, ntext, and image Data
- Creating and Dropping a Table
- Adding and Dropping a Column

After you define all of the data types for your table, you can create tables, add and drop columns, and generate column values.

How SQL Server Organizes Data in Rows

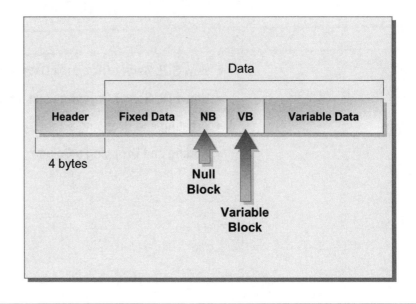

A data row consists of a row header and a data portion. It is important to understand the elements of the data portion of each row to accurately estimate the size of a table.

Row Header

The 4-byte row header contains information about the columns in the data row, such as a pointer to the location of the end of the fixed-data portion of the row, and whether variable-length columns exist in the row.

Data Portion

The data portion of a row may contain the following elements:

- *Fixed-length data.* Fixed-length data is entered into the page before variable-length data. An empty fixed-length data row takes up as much space as a populated fixed-length data row. A table with only fixed-length columns always stores the same number of rows on a page.

- *Null block.* A null block is a variable-length set of bytes. It consists of two bytes storing the number of columns followed by a null bitmap indicating whether each individual column is null. The size of a null bitmap is equal to one bit per column, rounded up to the nearest byte. One to eight columns require a 1-byte bitmap. Nine to sixteen columns require a 2-byte bitmap.

- *Variable block.* A variable block consists of two bytes that describe how many variable-length columns are present. An additional two bytes per column point to the end of each variable-length column. The variable block is omitted if there are no variable-length columns.

- *Variable-length data.* Variable-length data is entered into the page after the variable block. An empty variable-length data row takes up no space. A table with variable-length columns may have a few long rows or many short rows.

Tip   When possible, keep row length compact to allow more rows to fit on a page. This reduces input/output (I/O) and improves the buffer cache hit ratio.

How SQL Server Organizes text, ntext, and image Data

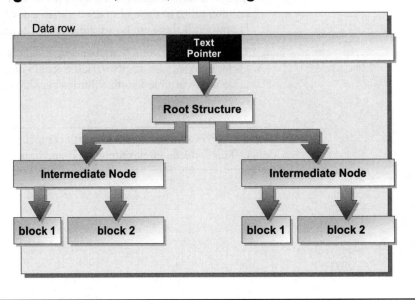

Variable-length data types can be stored as one collection of pages or in data rows. They are the:

- **text** data type, which can hold 2,147,483,647 characters. The non-Unicode **text** data type cannot be used for variables or parameters in stored procedures.

- **ntext** data type, which can hold a maximum of 2^{30} -1 (1,073,741,823) characters or 2^{31} -1 bytes, which is 2,147,483,647 bytes of variable-length Unicode data. The SQL-92 synonym for **ntext** is national text.

- **image** data type, which can hold from 0 through 2,147,483,647 bytes of binary data.

Because **text**, **ntext**, and **image** data types are usually large, SQL Server stores them outside of rows. A 16-byte pointer in the data row points to a root structure that holds the data. The text root structure forms the root node of the B-Tree, which points to the data blocks. If there are more than 32 kilobytes (KB) of data, intermediate nodes in the B-Tree are added between the root node and the blocks of data. This permits quick B-Tree navigation starting in the middle of a string.

With small- to medium-sized **text**, **ntext**, and **image** content, SQL Server provides the option to store values in the data row rather than in a separate B-Tree structure. You can specify this **text in row** option. You can also set the option limit; the range is 24 through 7,000 bytes.

You can enable the **text in row** option for a table by using the **sp_tableoption** system stored procedure.

Example

This example sets the **sp_tableoption** system stored procedure **text in row** option ON and specifies that up to 1000 **text**, **ntext**, or **image** characters will be stored in the data page.

```
EXEC sp_tableoption N'Employees', 'text in row', '1000'
```

Note If you specify ON, but do not specify a value, the default is 256 bytes. The default value ensures that small values and text pointers can be stored in the data rows.

Creating and Dropping a Table

- **Creating a Table**

Column name	Data type	NULL or NOT NULL
CREATE TABLE dbo.Categories (CategoryID	int IDENTITY (1,1)	NOT NULL,
CategoryName	nvarchar(15)	NOT NULL,
Description	ntext	NULL,
Picture	image	NULL)

- **Column Collation**

- **Specifying NULL or NOT NULL**

- **Computed Columns**

- **Dropping a Table**

When you create a table, you must specify the table name, column names, and column data types. Column names must be unique to a specific table, but you can use the same column name in different tables within the same database. You must specify a data type for each column.

Creating a Table

Consider the following facts when you create tables in SQL Server. You can have up to:

- Two billion tables per database.

- 1,024 columns per table.

- 8060 bytes per row (this approximate maximum length does not apply to **image**, **text**, and **ntext** data types).

Column Collation

SQL Server supports storing objects with different collations in the same database. Separate SQL Server collations can be specified at the column-level, so that each column in a table can be assigned a different collation.

Specifying NULL or NOT NULL

You can specify in the table definition whether to allow null values in each column. If you do not specify NULL or NOT NULL, SQL Server provides the NULL or NOT NULL characteristic, based on the session- or database-level default. However, these defaults can change, so do not rely on them. NOT NULL is the SQL Server default.

Partial Syntax

CREATE TABLE *table_name*
   column_name data type [COLLATE<*collation_name*>]
   [NULL | NOT NULL]
   | *column_name* AS *computed_column_expression*
   [,....*n*]

Example

The following example creates the **dbo.CategoriesNew** table, specifying the columns of the table, a data type for each column, and whether that column allows null values.

```
CREATE TABLE dbo.CategoriesNew
    (CategoryID      int IDENTITY
                     (1, 1)            NOT NULL,
     CategoryName    nvarchar(15)      NOT NULL,
     Description     ntext             NULL,
     Picture         image             NULL)
```

Note   To view table properties, right-click a table in SQL Server Enterprise Manager, or execute the **sp_help** system stored procedure and then scroll to the right.

Computed Columns

A *computed column* is a virtual column that is not physically stored in the table. SQL Server uses a formula that you create to calculate this column value by using other columns in the same table. Using a computed column name in a query can simplify the query syntax.

Dropping a Table

Dropping a table removes the table definition and all data, as well as the permission specifications for that table.

Before you can drop a table, you should remove any dependencies between the table and other objects. To view existing dependencies, execute the **sp_depends** system stored procedure.

Syntax

DROP TABLE *table_name* [,...*n*]

Adding and Dropping a Column

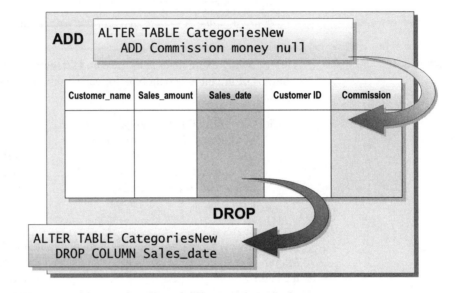

Adding and dropping columns are two ways to modify tables.

Partial Syntax

ALTER TABLE *table*
 {| [ALTER COLUMN *column_name*]
  |{ ADD
   { <column_definition> ::=
    column_name data_type
    { [NULL | NOT NULL]
  | DROP column *column_name*} [,...*n*]

Adding a Column

The type of information that you specify when you add a column is similar to that which you supply when you create a table.

Example

This example adds a column that allows null values.

```
ALTER TABLE CategoriesNew
 ADD Commission money null
```

Dropping a Column

Dropped columns are unrecoverable. Therefore, be certain that you want to remove a column before doing so.

Example

This example drops a column from a table.

```
ALTER TABLE CategoriesNew
 DROP COLUMN Sales_date
```

Note All indexes and constraints that are based on a column must be removed before you drop the column.

◆ Generating Column Values

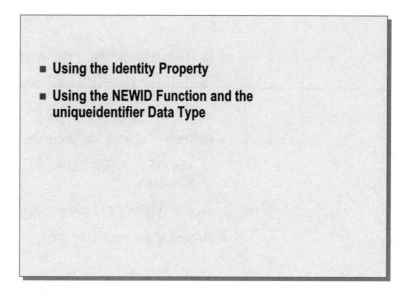

- Using the Identity Property

- Using the NEWID Function and the uniqueidentifier Data Type

Several features allow you to generate column values: the **Identity** property, the NEWID function, and the **uniqueidentifier** data type.

Using the Identity Property

- **Requirements for Using the Identity Property**
  - Only one identity column is allowed per table
  - Use with **integer, numeric,** and **decimal** data types
- **Retrieving Information About the Identity Property**
  - Use IDENT_SEED and IDENT_INCR for definition information
  - Use **@@identity** to determine most recent value
- **Managing the Identity Property**

You can use the **Identity** property to create columns (referred to as identity columns) that contain system-generated sequential values identifying each row inserted into a table. An identity column is often used for primary key values.

Having SQL Server automatically provide key values can reduce costs and improve performance. It simplifies programming, keeps primary key values short, and reduces user-transaction bottlenecks.

Partial Syntax

CREATE TABLE *table*
  (*column_name data_type*
  [IDENTITY [(*seed, increment*)]] NOT NULL)

Consider the following requirements for using the **Identity** property:

- Only one identity column is allowed per table.

- It must be used with **integer (int, bigint, smallint,** or **tinyint), numeric,** or **decimal** data types. The **numeric** and **decimal** data types must be specified with a scale of 0.

- It cannot be updated.

- You can use the IDENTITYCOL keyword in place of the column name in a query. This allows you to reference the column in the table having the **Identity** property without having to know the column name.

- It does not allow null values.

You can retrieve information about the **Identity** property in several ways:

- Two system functions return information about an identity column definition: IDENT_SEED (returns the seed, or starting, value) and IDENT_INCR (returns the increment value).

- You can retrieve data from identity columns using the **@@identity** global variable, which determines the value of the last row inserted into an identity column during a session.

- SCOPE_IDENTITY returns the last IDENTITY value inserted into an indentity column in the same scope. A scope is a stored procedure, trigger, function, or batch.

- IDENT_CURRENT returns the last identity value generated for a specified table in any session and any scope.

You can manage the **Identity** property in several ways:

- You can allow explicit values to be inserted into the identity column of a table by setting the IDENTITY_INSERT option ON. When IDENTITY_INSERT is ON, INSERT statements must supply a value.

- To check and possibly correct the current identity value for a table, you can use the DBCC CHECKIDENT statement. DBCC CHECKIDENT allows you to compare the current identity value with the maximum value in the identity column.

Note The **Identity** property does not enforce uniqueness. To enforce uniqueness, create a unique index.

Example

This example creates a table with two columns, **StudentId** and **Name**. The **Identity** property is used to increment the value automatically in each row added to the **StudentId** column. The seed is set to 100, and the increment value is 5. The values in the column would be 100, 105, 110, 115, and so on. Using 5 as an increment value allows you to insert records between the values at a later time.

```
CREATE TABLE Class
  (StudentID int  IDENTITY(100, 5) NOT NULL,
  Name varchar(16))
```

Using the NEWID Function and the uniqueidentifier Data Type

- **These Features Are Used Together**
- **Ensure Globally Unique Values**
- **Use with the DEFAULT Constraint**

```
CREATE TABLE Customer
(CustID uniqueidentifier NOT NULL DEFAULT NEWID(),
 CustName char(30) NOT NULL)
```

The **uniqueidentifier** data type and the NEWID function are two features that are used together. Use these features when data is collated from many tables into a larger table and when uniqueness among all records must be maintained:

- The **uniqueidentifier** data type stores a unique identification number as a 16-byte binary string. This data type is used for storing a globally unique identifier (GUID).

- The NEWID function creates a unique identifier number that can store a GUID by using the **uniqueidentifier** data type.

- The **uniqueidentifier** data type does not automatically generate new IDs for inserted rows the way the **Identity** property does. To get new **uniqueidentifier** values, you must define a table with a DEFAULT constraint that specifies the NEWID function. When you use an INSERT statement, you must also specify the NEWID function.

Example

In this example, the **Customer** table customer ID column is created with a **uniqueidentifier** data type, with a default value generated by the NEWID function. A unique value for the **CustID** column will be generated for each new and existing row.

```
CREATE TABLE Customer
(CustID uniqueidentifier NOT NULL DEFAULT NEWID(),
 CustName char(30) NOT NULL)
```

Generating Scripts

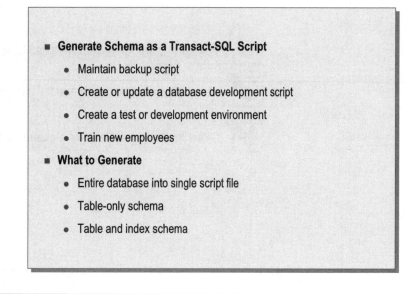

- **Generate Schema as a Transact-SQL Script**
  - Maintain backup script
  - Create or update a database development script
  - Create a test or development environment
  - Train new employees
- **What to Generate**
  - Entire database into single script file
  - Table-only schema
  - Table and index schema

When you create objects in a database, it is important to save all object definitions in a script file.

Generate Schema as a Transact-SQL Script

You can use SQL Server Enterprise Manager to document an existing database structure (schema) by generating it as one or more Transact-SQL scripts. These Transact-SQL scripts contain descriptions of the statements that were used to create a database and its objects.

Schema generated as Transact-SQL scripts can be used to:

- Maintain a backup script that allows a user to recreate all users, groups, logins, and permissions.
- Create or update a database development script.
- Create a test or development environment from an existing schema.
- Train newly hired employees.

What to Generate

You can generate:

- An entire database into a single script file.
- Table-only schema for one, some, or all tables in a database into one or more script files.
- Table and index schema into one script file, stored procedures into another script file, and defaults and rules into yet another script file.

Recommended Practices

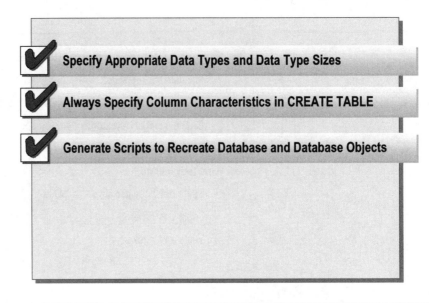

The following recommended practices will help you create data types and tables:

- Specify appropriate data types and data type sizes.

- When writing a CREATE TABLE statement, always specify column characteristics.

- After you create a database and database objects, generate a script that allows you to recreate the database and its objects.

Lab A: Creating Data Types and Tables

Objectives

After completing this lab, you will be able to:

- Create user-defined data types.
- Create tables.
- Add and drop columns.
- Generate Transact-SQL scripts from a database.

Prerequisites

Before working on this lab, you must have:

- Script files for this lab, which are located in C:\Moc\2073A\Labfiles\L04.
- Answer files for this lab, which are located in
  C:\Moc\2073A\Labfiles\L04\Answers.

Lab Setup

To complete this lab, you must have either:

- Completed the prior lab, or
- Executed the C:\Moc\2073A\Batches\Restore04.cmd batch file.

  This command file restores the **ClassNorthwind** database to a state required
  for this lab.

For More Information

If you require help in executing files, search SQL Query Analyzer Help for
"Execute a query".

Other resources that you can use include:

- The **Northwind** database schema.
- Microsoft SQL Server Books Online.

Scenario

The organization of the classroom is meant to simulate that of a worldwide trading firm named Northwind Traders. Its fictitious domain name is nwtraders.msft. The primary DNS server for nwtraders.msft is the instructor computer, which has an Internet Protocol (IP) address of 192.168.x.200 (where x is the assigned classroom number). The name of the instructor computer is London.

The following table provides the user name, computer name, and IP address for each student computer in the fictitious **nwtraders.msft** domain. Find the user name for your computer, and make a note of it.

User name	Computer name	IP address
SQLAdmin1	Vancouver	192.168.x.1
SQLAdmin2	Denver	192.168.x.2
SQLAdmin3	Perth	192.168.x.3
SQLAdmin4	Brisbane	192.168.x.4
SQLAdmin5	Lisbon	192.168.x.5
SQLAdmin6	Bonn	192.168.x.6
SQLAdmin7	Lima	192.168.x.7
SQLAdmin8	Santiago	192.168.x.8
SQLAdmin9	Bangalore	192.168.x.9
SQLAdmin10	Singapore	192.168.x.10
SQLAdmin11	Casablanca	192.168.x.11
SQLAdmin12	Tunis	192.168.x.12
SQLAdmin13	Acapulco	192.168.x.13
SQLAdmin14	Miami	192.168.x.14
SQLAdmin15	Auckland	192.168.x.15
SQLAdmin16	Suva	192.168.x.16
SQLAdmin17	Stockholm	192.168.x.17
SQLAdmin18	Moscow	192.168.x.18
SQLAdmin19	Caracas	192.168.x.19
SQLAdmin20	Montevideo	192.168.x.20
SQLAdmin21	Manila	192.168.x.21
SQLAdmin22	Tokyo	192.168.x.22
SQLAdmin23	Khartoum	192.168.x.23
SQLAdmin24	Nairobi	192.168.x.24

Estimated time to complete this lab: 30 minutes

Exercise 1
Creating User-defined Data Types

In this exercise, you will create user-defined data types for the **ClassNorthwind** database.

▶ **To execute a script that creates a user-defined data type**

In this procedure, you will execute a script to create a user-defined data type in the **ClassNorthwind** database.

1. Log on to the **NWTraders** classroom domain by using the information in the following table.

Option	Value
User name	**SQLAdminx** (where *x* corresponds to your computer name as designated in the **nwtraders.msft** classroom domain)
Password	**password**

2. Open SQL Query Analyzer and, if requested, log in to the (local) server with Microsoft Windows® Authentication.

    You have permission to log in to and administer SQL Server because you are logged as **SQLAdminx**, which is a member of the Microsoft Windows 2000 local group, Administrators. All members of this group are automatically mapped to the SQL Server **sysadmin** role.

3. In the **DB** list, click **ClassNorthwind**.

4. Open and review the Creatyp1.sql script file in C:\Moc\2073A\Labfiles\L04.

    This script creates a new data type named **postalcode** that contains up to 10 bytes of character data and that may be NULL.

5. Execute Creatyp1.sql.

6. Open, review and execute the Vertype.sql script file in C:\Moc\2073A\Labfiles\L04. Verify that the data type was created.

▶ **To create user-defined data types**

In this procedure, you will write and execute statements that create user-defined data types in the **ClassNorthwind** database.

A complete Transact-SQL script for this procedure is located in C:\MOC\2073A\Labfiles\L04\Answers\Creatyp2.sql.

1. Verify that you are using the **ClassNorthwind** database.

2. Write and execute statements to create the user-defined data types described in the following table.

Data type	Description of data
City	Up to 15 bytes of character data that may be NULL
Region	Up to 15 bytes of character data that may be NULL
Country	Up to 15 bytes of character data that may be NULL

3. Open and execute Vertype.sql to verify that the data types were created.

Exercise 2
Creating Tables in the ClassNorthwind Database

In this exercise, you will create all of the tables for the **ClassNorthwind** database.

▶ **To execute a script that creates a table**

In this procedure, you will execute a script that creates the **Employees** table in the **ClassNorthwind** database.

1. Open and review the Creatab1.sql script file in C:\Moc\2073A\Labfiles\L04.

   This script creates the **Employees** table in the **ClassNorthwind** database.

2. Execute Creatab1.sql.

▶ **To create a table by using statements**

In this procedure, you will write and execute a statement that creates the **Suppliers** table in the **ClassNorthwind** database.

A complete Transact-SQL script for this procedure is located in C:\Moc\2073A\Labfiles\L04\Answers\ Creatab2.sql.

1. Verify that you are using the **ClassNorthwind** database.

2. Write and execute a statement to create the **Suppliers** table, defining the following column names with their respective data types.

Ensure that the **SupplierID** and **CompanyName** columns do not allow null values, and that all other columns do allow null values.

Column name	Data type	Allows NULLs	Identity property
SupplierID	**int**	No	Seed = 1 Increment = 1
CompanyName	**nvarchar (40)**	No	No
ContactName	**nvarchar (30)**	Yes	No
ContactTitle	**nvarchar (30)**	Yes	No
Address	**nvarchar (60)**	Yes	No
City	**city**	Yes	No
Region	**region**	Yes	No
PostalCode	**postalcode**	Yes	No
Country	**country**	Yes	No
Phone	**nvarchar (24)**	Yes	No
Fax	**nvarchar (24)**	Yes	No
HomePage	**ntext**	Yes	No

Which data types are user-defined?

_____

_____

▶ **To create a table by using SQL Server Enterprise Manager**

In this procedure, you will use SQL Server Enterprise Manager to create the **Customers** table in the **ClassNorthwind** database.

1. Open SQL Server Enterprise Manager.

2. Expand Microsoft SQL Servers, expand SQL Server Group, expand your server, and then expand Databases.

3. Right-click **ClassNorthwind**, point to **New**, and then click **Table**.

4. Use the information in the following table to create the **Customers** table, defining the column names with their respective data types.

   Make sure that the **CustomerID** and **CompanyName** columns do not allow null values. Make sure that all other columns allow null values.

Column name	Data type	Allows NULLs?
CustomerID	nchar (5)	No
CompanyName	nvarchar (40)	No
ContactName	nvarchar (40)	Yes
ContactTitle	nvarchar (30)	Yes
Address	nvarchar (60)	Yes
City	city	Yes
Region	region	Yes
PostalCode	postalcode	Yes
Country	country	Yes
Phone	nvarchar (24)	Yes
Fax	nvarchar (24)	Yes

5. Save the new table as **Customers** and close the New Table window.

▶ **To execute a script that creates all tables in the ClassNorthwind database**

In this procedure, you will execute a script that creates all of the tables in the **ClassNorthwind** database.

1. Switch to SQL Query Analyzer.

2. Open, review and execute the Creatab3.sql script file in C:\Moc\2073A\Labfiles\L04.

   This script creates all of the tables in the **ClassNorthwind** database. It first drops all previously created tables.

Exercise 3
Adding and Dropping Columns

In this exercise, you will use the ALTER TABLE statement to add columns to a table and drop columns from a table in the **ClassNorthwind** database.

▶ **To add a column to a table**

In this procedure, you will write and execute a statement that adds a column to the **Employees** table in the **ClassNorthwind** database.

A complete Transact-SQL script for this procedure is located in C:\Moc\2073A\Labfiles\L04\Answers\Addcol.sql.

1. Verify that you are using the **ClassNorthwind** database.

2. Write and execute a statement to add a column to the **Employees** table. The column should be named **Age**, use the **tinyint** data type, and allow null values.

3. Execute the **sp_help** system stored procedure on the **Employees** table to verify that the **Age** column was defined as you specified. Notice that the **Age** column appears as the final column in the table.

▶ **To drop a column from a table**

After discussing client requirements with your users, you have determined that the **Age** column is not needed after all. In this procedure, you will write and execute a statement that drops the **Age** column from the **Employees** table in the **ClassNorthwind** database.

A complete Transact-SQL script for this procedure is located in C:\Moc\2073A\Labfiles\L04\Answers\Dropcol.sql.

1. Verify that you are using the **ClassNorthwind** database.

2. Write and execute a statement that drops the **Age** column from the **Employees** table.

3. Execute the **sp_help** system stored procedure on the **Employees** table to verify that the **Age** column was dropped.

Exercise 4
Generating Transact-SQL Scripts

In this exercise, you will use SQL Server Enterprise Manager to generate a Transact-SQL script of objects that you have created in the **ClassNorthwind** database.

▶ **To generate scripts to recreate objects**

In this procedure, you will use SQL Server Enterprise Manager to generate a Transact-SQL script that allows you to recreate all objects that you have created in the **ClassNorthwind** database.

1. Switch to SQL Server Enterprise Manager.

2. Expand Microsoft SQL Servers, expand SQL Server Group, expand your server, and then expand Databases.

3. Right-click **ClassNorthwind**, point to **All Tasks**, and then click **Generate SQL Script**.

4. On the **General** tab, click **Show All**.

5. Select the **All tables** and the **All user-defined data types** check boxes, and then click **OK**.

6. Save this script file as L04.sql.

7. Open and review the generated script.

Exercise 5
Loading the ClassNorthwind Database with Data

In this exercise, you will run a script to populate the **ClassNorthwind** database with data.

▶ **To load data into the ClassNorthwind database**

In this procedure, you will execute scripts that will generate and load sample data into the **ClassNorthwind** database.

1. Switch to SQL Query Analyzer.

2. Open and review the **Loaddata.sql** script file in
   C:\Moc\2073A\Labfiles\L04

3. Execute **Loaddata.sql**. This may take a minute or two to complete. Review the output in the results pane.

Review

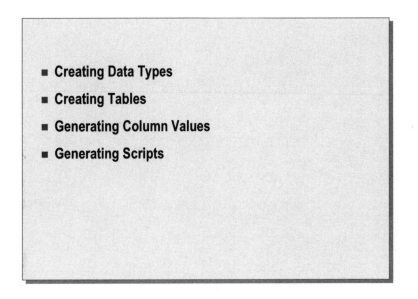

- Creating Data Types
- Creating Tables
- Generating Column Values
- Generating Scripts

1. Can a user-defined data type in one database be used in another database on the same SQL Server?

2. You are designing a database that stores information about millions of different products. You want to minimize the storage space that you use to store the product information. Each product has a description line in the **products** table. Occasionally, a product description will require up to 200 characters, but most product descriptions will only require 50 characters. What data type would you use?

3. You need to run a script that was created using SQL Server Enterprise Manager. How do you do this?

Microsoft®
Training &
Certification

Module 5: Implementing Data Integrity

Contents

***Microsoft*®**

Project Lead: Rich Rose
Instructional Designers: Rich Rose, Cheryl Hoople, Marilyn McGill
Instructional Software Design Engineers: Karl Dehmer, Carl Raebler, Rick Byham
Technical Lead: Karl Dehmer
Subject Matter Experts: Karl Dehmer, Carl Raebler, Rick Byham
Graphic Artist: Kirsten Larson (Independent Contractor)
Editing Manager: Lynette Skinner
Editor: Wendy Cleary
Copy Editor: Edward McKillop (S&T Consulting)
Production Manager: Miracle Davis
Production Coordinator: Jenny Boe
Production Support: Lori Walker (S&T Consulting)
Test Manager: Sid Benavente
Courseware Testing: TestingTesting123
Classroom Automation: Lorrin Smith-Bates
Creative Director, Media/Sim Services: David Mahlmann
Web Development Lead: Lisa Pease
CD Build Specialist: Julie Challenger
Online Support: David Myka (S&T Consulting)
Localization Manager: Rick Terek
Operations Coordinator: John Williams
Manufacturing Support: Laura King; Kathy Hershey
Lead Product Manager, Release Management: Bo Galford
Lead Product Manager, Data Base: Margo Crandall
Group Manager, Courseware Infrastructure: David Bramble
Group Product Manager, Content Development: Dean Murray
General Manager: Robert Stewart

Overview

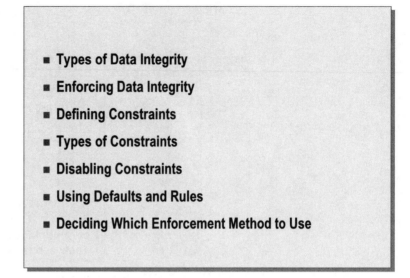

- **Types of Data Integrity**
- **Enforcing Data Integrity**
- **Defining Constraints**
- **Types of Constraints**
- **Disabling Constraints**
- **Using Defaults and Rules**
- **Deciding Which Enforcement Method to Use**

This module begins with an introduction to data integrity concepts, including the methods available for enforcing data integrity. The module then introduces constraints, which are the key method for ensuring data integrity, and the various types of constraints. The module discusses the creation and implementation of constraints in detail, as well as the means to disable constraints when necessary.

The module discusses defaults and rules as an alternate way to enforce data integrity, although the emphasis remains on constraints. The module concludes with a comparison of the different data integrity methods.

After completing this module, you will be able to:

- Describe the types of data integrity.
- Describe the methods to enforce data integrity.
- Determine which constraint to use and create constraints.
- Define and use DEFAULT, CHECK, PRIMARY KEY, UNIQUE, and FOREIGN KEY constraints.
- Disable constraint checking.
- Describe and use defaults and rules.
- Determine which data integrity enforcement methods to use.

Types of Data Integrity

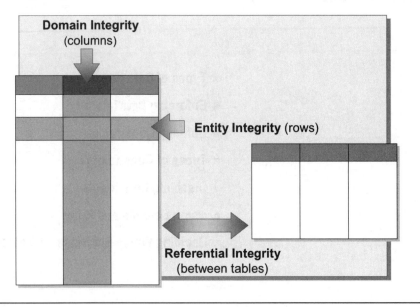

An important step in database planning is deciding the best way to enforce the integrity of the data. Data integrity refers to the consistency and accuracy of data that is stored in a database. The different types of data integrity are as follows.

Domain Integrity

Domain (or column) integrity specifies a set of data values that are valid for a column and determines whether null values are allowed. Domain integrity is often enforced through the use of validity checking and can also be enforced by restricting the data type, format, or range of possible values allowed in a column.

Entity Integrity

Entity (or table) integrity requires that all rows in a table have a unique identifier, known as the *primary key value*. Whether the primary key value can be changed, or whether the whole row can be deleted, depends on the level of integrity required between the primary key and any other tables.

Referential Integrity

Referential integrity ensures that the relationships among the primary keys (in the referenced table) and *foreign keys* (in the referencing tables) are always maintained. A row in a referenced table cannot be deleted, nor the primary key changed, if a foreign key refers to the row, unless the cascade action is permitted. You can define referential integrity relationships within the same table or between separate tables.

Enforcing Data Integrity

- **Declarative Data Integrity**
  - Criteria defined in object definitions
  - SQL Server enforces automatically
  - Implement by using constraints, defaults, and rules
- **Procedural Data Integrity**
  - Criteria defined in script
  - Script enforces
  - Implement by using triggers and stored procedures

You can enforce data integrity through two methods: declarative data integrity or procedural data integrity.

Declarative Data Integrity

With *declarative* integrity, you define the criteria that the data must meet as part of an object definition, and then Microsoft® SQL Server™ 2000 automatically ensures that the data conforms to the criteria. The preferred method of implementing basic data integrity is to use declarative integrity. Consider the following facts about the declarative method:

- Declarative integrity is declared as part of the database definition, by using declarative constraints that you define directly on tables and columns.

- Implement declarative integrity by using constraints, defaults, and rules.

Procedural Data Integrity

With *procedural* integrity, you write scripts that define both the criteria that data must meet and enforce the criteria. You should limit your use of procedural integrity to more complicated business logic and exceptions. For example, use procedural integrity when you want to have a cascading delete. The following facts apply to procedural integrity:

- Procedural integrity can be implemented on the client or the server by using other programming languages and tools.

- Implement procedural integrity by using triggers and stored procedures.

◆ Defining Constraints

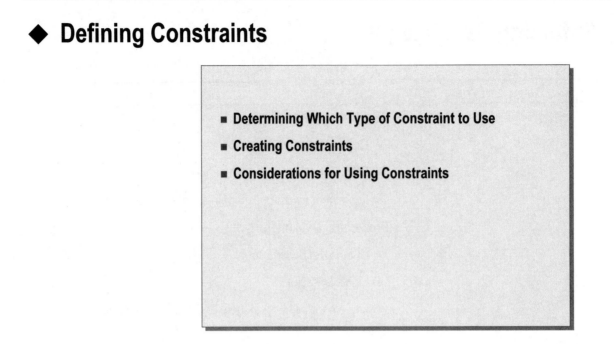

- Determining Which Type of Constraint to Use
- Creating Constraints
- Considerations for Using Constraints

Constraints are the preferred method of enforcing data integrity. This section discusses how to determine the type of constraint to use, what type of data integrity that each type of constraint enforces, and how to define constraints.

Determining Which Type of Constraint to Use

Type of integrity	Constraint type
Domain	DEFAULT
	CHECK
	REFERENTIAL
Entity	PRIMARY KEY
	UNIQUE
Referential	FOREIGN KEY
	CHECK

Constraints are an ANSI-standard method of enforcing data integrity. Each type of data integrity — domain, entity, and referential — is enforced with separate types of constraints. Constraints ensure that valid data values are entered in columns and that relationships are maintained between tables. The following table describes the different types of constraints.

Type of integrity	Constraint type	Description
Domain	DEFAULT	Specifies the value that will be provided for the column when a value has not been explicitly supplied in an INSERT statement.
	CHECK	Specifies data values that are acceptable in a column.
	REFERENTIAL	Specifies the data values that are acceptable to update, based on values in a column in another table.
Entity	PRIMARY KEY	Uniquely identifies each row—ensures that users do not enter duplicate values and that an index is created to enhance performance. Null values are not allowed.
	UNIQUE	Prevents duplication of alternate (non-primary) keys, and ensures that an index is created to enhance performance. Null values are allowed.
Referential	FOREIGN KEY	Defines a column or combination of columns with values that match the primary key of the same or another table.
	CHECK	Specifies the data values that are acceptable in a column based on values in other columns in the same table.

Creating Constraints

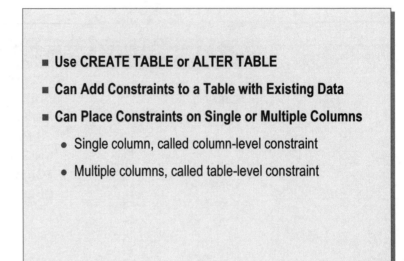

- **Use CREATE TABLE or ALTER TABLE**
- **Can Add Constraints to a Table with Existing Data**
- **Can Place Constraints on Single or Multiple Columns**
  - Single column, called column-level constraint
  - Multiple columns, called table-level constraint

You create constraints by using the CREATE TABLE or ALTER TABLE statement.

You can add constraints to a table with existing data, and you can place constraints on single or multiple columns:

- If the constraint applies to a single column, it is called a *column-level* constraint.

- If a constraint references multiple columns, it is called a *table-level* constraint, even if it does not reference all columns in the table.

Partial Syntax

CREATE TABLE *table_name*
   ({ < column_definition >
   | < table_constraint > } [,...*n*])

< column_definition > ::= { *column_name data_type* }
   [[DEFAULT *constant_expression*]
   [< column_constraint >] [,..*n*]

< column_constraint > ::=
   [CONSTRAINT *constraint_name*]
      | [{ PRIMARY KEY | UNIQUE }
         [CLUSTERED | NONCLUSTERED]]

    | [[FOREIGN KEY]
        REFERENCES *ref_table* [(*ref_column*)]
        [ON DELETE { CASCADE | NO ACTION }]
        [ON UPDATE { CASCADE | NO ACTION }]]
      | CHECK (*logical_expression*) }

```
< table_constraint > ::=
    [ CONSTRAINT constraint_name ]
    { [ { PRIMARY KEY | UNIQUE }
        [ CLUSTERED | NONCLUSTERED ]
        { ( column [ ASC | DESC ] [ ,...n ] ) } ]
    | FOREIGN KEY
        [ ( column [ ,...n ] ) ]
        REFERENCES ref_table [ ( ref_column [ ,...n ] ) ]
        [ ON DELETE { CASCADE | NO ACTION } ]
        [ ON UPDATE { CASCADE | NO ACTION } ]
    | CHECK ( search_conditions ) }
```

Example

This example creates the **Products** table, defines columns, and defines constraints at both the column and table level.

```
USE Northwind
CREATE TABLE dbo.Products
(
    ProductID       int IDENTITY (1,1) NOT NULL,
    ProductName     nvarchar (40) NOT NULL,
    SupplierID      int       NULL,
    CategoryID      int       NULL,
    QuantityPerUnit nvarchar (20) NULL,
    UnitPrice       money    NULL       CONSTRAINT DF_Products_UnitPrice   DEFAULT(0),
    UnitsInStock    smallint NULL       CONSTRAINT DF_Products_UnitsInStock DEFAULT(0),
    UnitsOnOrder    smallint NULL       CONSTRAINT DF_Products_UnitsOnOrder DEFAULT(0),
    ReorderLevel    smallint NULL       CONSTRAINT DF_Products_ReorderLevel DEFAULT(0),
    Discontinued    bit      NOT NULL CONSTRAINT DF_Products_Discontinued DEFAULT(0),

    CONSTRAINT PK_Products PRIMARY KEY CLUSTERED (ProductID),

    CONSTRAINT FK_Products_Categories FOREIGN KEY (CategoryID)
        REFERENCES dbo.Categories (CategoryID) ON UPDATE CASCADE,
    CONSTRAINT FK_Products_Suppliers  FOREIGN KEY (SupplierID)
        REFERENCES dbo.Suppliers  (SupplierID) ON DELETE CASCADE,

    CONSTRAINT CK_Products_UnitPrice CHECK (UnitPrice >= 0),
    CONSTRAINT CK_ReorderLevel        CHECK (ReorderLevel >= 0),
    CONSTRAINT CK_UnitsInStock        CHECK (UnitsInStock >= 0),
    CONSTRAINT CK_UnitsOnOrder        CHECK (UnitsOnOrder >= 0)
)
GO
```

Considerations for Using Constraints

- **Can Be Changed Without Recreating a Table**
- **Require Error-Checking in Applications and Transactions**
- **Verify Existing Data**

Consider the following facts when you implement or modify constraints:

- You can create, change, and drop constraints without having to drop and recreate a table.

- You must build error-checking logic into your applications and transactions to test whether a constraint has been violated.

- SQL Server verifies existing data when you add a constraint to a table.

You should specify names for constraints when you create them, because SQL Server provides complicated, system-generated names. Names must be unique to the database object owner and follow the rules for SQL Server identifiers.

For help with constraints, execute the **sp_helpconstraint** or **sp_help** system stored procedure, or query information schema views, such as **check_constraints**, **referential_constraints**, and **table_constraints**.

The following system tables store constraint definitions: **syscomments**, **sysreferences**, and **sysconstraints**.

◆ Types of Constraints

- DEFAULT Constraints
- CHECK Constraints
- PRIMARY KEY Constraints
- UNIQUE Constraints
- FOREIGN KEY Constraints
- Cascading Referential Integrity

This section describes the types of constraints. Syntax, examples, and considerations for use define each constraint.

DEFAULT Constraints

- **Apply Only to INSERT Statements**

- **Only One DEFAULT Constraint Per Column**

- **Cannot Be Used with IDENTITY Property or rowversion Data Type**

- **Allow Some System-supplied Values**

```
USE Northwind
ALTER TABLE dbo.Customers
ADD
CONSTRAINT DF_contactname DEFAULT 'UNKNOWN'
FOR ContactName
```

A DEFAULT constraint enters a value in a column when one is not specified in an INSERT statement. DEFAULT constraints enforce domain integrity.

Partial Syntax

```
[CONSTRAINT constraint_name]
    DEFAULT constant_expression
```

Example

This example adds a DEFAULT constraint that inserts the UNKNOWN value in the **dbo.Customers** table if a contact name is not provided.

```
USE Northwind
ALTER TABLE dbo.Customers
ADD
CONSTRAINT DF_contactname DEFAULT 'UNKNOWN' FOR ContactName
```

Consider the following facts when you apply a DEFAULT constraint:

- It verifies existing data in the table.

- It applies only to INSERT statements.

- Only one DEFAULT constraint can be defined per column.

- It cannot be placed on columns with the **Identity** property or on columns with the **rowversion** data type.

- It allows some system-supplied values—USER, CURRENT_USER, SESSION_USER, SYSTEM_USER, or CURRENT_TIMESTAMP—to be specified rather than user-defined values. These system-supplied values can be useful in providing a record of the users who have been inserting data.

CHECK Constraints

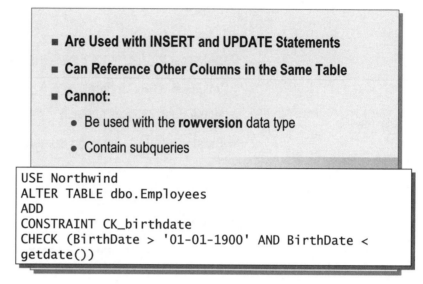

- **Are Used with INSERT and UPDATE Statements**

- **Can Reference Other Columns in the Same Table**

- **Cannot:**

  - Be used with the **rowversion** data type

  - Contain subqueries

```
USE Northwind
ALTER TABLE dbo.Employees
ADD
CONSTRAINT CK_birthdate
CHECK (BirthDate > '01-01-1900' AND BirthDate <
getdate())
```

A CHECK constraint restricts the data that users can enter into a particular column to specific values. CHECK constraints are similar to WHERE clauses in that you can specify the conditions under which data will be accepted.

Partial Syntax

[CONSTRAINT *constraint_name*]
   CHECK (*logical_expression*)

Example

This example adds a CHECK constraint to ensure that a birth date conforms to an acceptable range of dates.

```
USE Northwind
ALTER TABLE dbo.Employees
ADD
CONSTRAINT CK_birthdate
CHECK (BirthDate > '01-01-1900' AND BirthDate < getdate())
```

Consider the following facts when you apply a CHECK constraint:

- It verifies data every time that you execute an INSERT or UPDATE statement.

- It can reference other columns in the same table.

  For example, a **salary** column could reference a value in a **job_grade** column.

- It cannot be placed on columns with the **rowversion** data type.

- It cannot contain subqueries.

- If any data violates the CHECK constraint, you can execute the DBCC CHECKCONSTRAINTS statement to return the violating rows.

PRIMARY KEY Constraints

- **Only One PRIMARY KEY Constraint Per Table**

- **Values Must Be Unique**

- **Null Values Are Not Allowed**

- **Creates a Unique Index on Specified Columns**

```
USE Northwind
ALTER TABLE dbo.Customers
ADD
CONSTRAINT PK_Customers
  PRIMARY KEY NONCLUSTERED (CustomerID)
```

A PRIMARY KEY constraint defines a primary key on a table that uniquely identifies a row. It enforces entity integrity.

Partial Syntax

[CONSTRAINT *constraint_name*]
    PRIMARY KEY [CLUSTERED | NONCLUSTERED]
        { (*column*[,...*n*]) }

Example

This example adds a constraint that specifies that the primary key value of the **dbo.Customers** table is the customer identification and indicates that a nonclustered index will be created to enforce the constraint.

```
USE Northwind
ALTER TABLE dbo.Customers
ADD
CONSTRAINT PK_Customers
  PRIMARY KEY NONCLUSTERED (CustomerID)
```

Consider the following facts when you apply a PRIMARY KEY constraint:

- Only one PRIMARY KEY constraint can be defined per table.

- The values entered must be unique.

- Null values are not allowed.

- It creates a unique index on the specified columns. You can specify a clustered or nonclustered index (clustered is the default if it does not already exist).

Note   The index created for a PRIMARY KEY constraint cannot be dropped directly. It is dropped when you drop the constraint.

UNIQUE Constraints

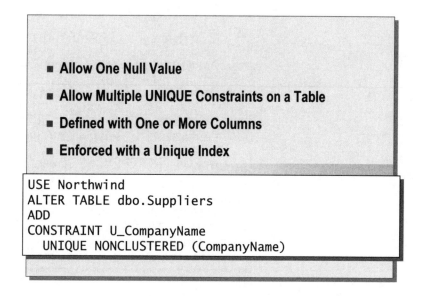

A UNIQUE constraint specifies that two rows in a column cannot have the same value. This constraint enforces entity integrity with a unique index.

A UNIQUE constraint is helpful when you already have a primary key, such as an employee number, but you want to guarantee that other identifiers, such as an employee's driver's license number, are also unique.

Partial Syntax

[CONSTRAINT *constraint_name*]
    UNIQUE [CLUSTERED | NONCLUSTERED]
        { (*column*[,...*n*]) }

Example

This example creates a UNIQUE constraint on the company name in the **dbo.Suppliers** table.

```
USE Northwind
ALTER TABLE dbo.Suppliers
ADD
CONSTRAINT U_CompanyName
    UNIQUE NONCLUSTERED (CompanyName)
```

Consider the following facts when you apply a UNIQUE constraint:

- It can allow one null value.
- You can place multiple UNIQUE constraints on a table.
- You can apply the UNIQUE constraint to one or more columns that must have unique values, but are not the primary key of a table.
- The UNIQUE constraint is enforced through the creation of a unique index on the specified column or columns.

FOREIGN KEY Constraints

- **Must Reference a PRIMARY KEY or UNIQUE Constraint**

- **Provide Single or Multicolumn Referential Integrity**

- **Do Not Automatically Create Indexes**

- **Users Must Have SELECT or REFERENCES Permissions on Referenced Tables**

- **Use Only REFERENCES Clause Within Same Table**

```
USE Northwind
ALTER TABLE dbo.Orders
ADD CONSTRAINT FK_Orders_Customers
  FOREIGN KEY (CustomerID)
  REFERENCES dbo.Customers(CustomerID)
```

A FOREIGN KEY constraint enforces referential integrity. The FOREIGN KEY constraint defines a reference to a column with a PRIMARY KEY or UNIQUE constraint in the same, or another table.

Partial Syntax

[CONSTRAINT *constraint_name*]
   [FOREIGN KEY] [(*column*[,...*n*])]
      REFERENCES *ref_table* [(*ref_column* [,...*n*])].

Example

This example uses a FOREIGN KEY constraint to ensure that customer identification in the **dbo.Orders** table is associated with a valid identification in the **dbo.Customers** table.

```
USE Northwind
ALTER TABLE dbo.Orders
ADD CONSTRAINT FK_Orders_Customers
  FOREIGN KEY (CustomerID)
  REFERENCES dbo.Customers(CustomerID)
```

Consider the following facts and guidelines when you apply a FOREIGN KEY constraint:

- It provides single or multicolumn referential integrity. The number of columns and data types that are specified in the FOREIGN KEY statement must match the number of columns and data types in the REFERENCES clause.

- Unlike PRIMARY KEY or UNIQUE constraints, FOREIGN KEY constraints do not create indexes automatically. However, if you will be using many joins in your database, you should create an index for the FOREIGN KEY to improve join performance.

- To modify data, users must have SELECT or REFERENCES permissions on other tables that are referenced with a FOREIGN KEY constraint.

- You can use only the REFERENCES clause without the FOREIGN KEY clause when you reference a column in the same table.

Cascading Referential Integrity

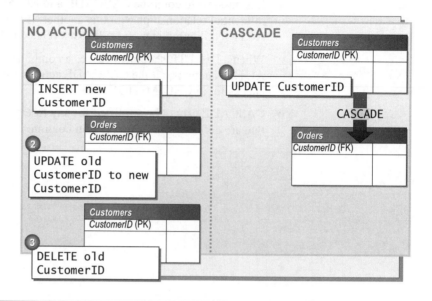

The FOREIGN KEY constraint includes a CASCADE option that allows any change to a column value that defines a UNIQUE or PRIMARY KEY constraint to automatically propagate the change to the foreign key value. This action is referred to as *cascading referential integrity*.

The REFERENCES clauses of the CREATE TABLE and ALTER TABLE statements support ON DELETE and ON UPDATE clauses. These clauses allow you to specify the CASCADE or NO ACTION option.

Partial Syntax

[CONSTRAINT *constraint_name*]
    [FOREIGN KEY] [(*column*[,...*n*])]
        REFERENCES *ref_table* [(*ref_column* [,...*n*])].
        [ON DELETE { CASCADE | NO ACTION }]
        [ON UPDATE { CASCADE | NO ACTION }]

NO ACTION specifies that any attempt to delete or update a key referenced by foreign keys in other tables raises an error and the change is rolled back. NO ACTION is the default.

If CASCADE is defined and a row is changed in the parent table, the corresponding row is then changed in the referencing table.

For example, in the **Northwind** database, the **Orders** table has a referential relationship with the **Customers** table; specifically, the **Orders.CustomerID** foreign key references the **Customers.CustomerID** primary key.

If an UPDATE statement is executed on **CustomerID** in the **Customers** table, and an ON UPDATE CASCADE action is specified for **Orders.CustomerID**, SQL Server checks for one or more dependent rows in the **Orders** table. If any exist, it updates the dependent rows in the **Orders** table, as well as the row referenced in the **Customers** table.

Consider these factors when applying the CASCADE option:

- It is possible to combine CASCADE and NO ACTION on tables that have referential relationships with one another. If SQL Server encounters NO ACTION, it terminates and rolls back related CASCADE actions.

  When a DELETE statement causes a combination of CASCADE and NO ACTION actions, all the CASCADE actions are applied before SQL Server checks for any NO ACTION.

- CASCADE cannot be specified for any foreign key or primary key columns that are defined with a **rowversion** column.

◆ Disabling Constraints

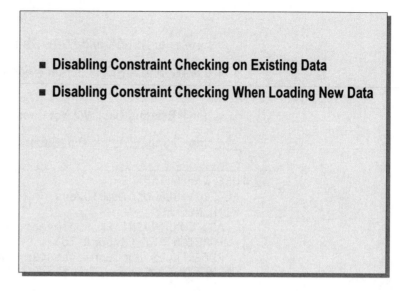

- ■ **Disabling Constraint Checking on Existing Data**
- ■ **Disabling Constraint Checking When Loading New Data**

For reasons of performance, it is sometimes advisable to disable constraints. For example, it is more efficient to allow large batch operations to process before enabling constraints. This section describes how to disable constraint checking, whether you are creating a new constraint or disabling an existing one.

Disabling Constraint Checking on Existing Data

- ■ **Applies to CHECK and FOREIGN KEY Constraints**

- ■ **Use WITH NOCHECK Option When Adding a New Constraint**

- ■ **Use if Existing Data Will Not Change**

- ■ **Can Change Existing Data Before Adding Constraints**

```
USE Northwind
ALTER TABLE dbo.Employees
WITH NOCHECK
  ADD CONSTRAINT FK_Employees_Employees
  FOREIGN KEY (ReportsTo)
  REFERENCES dbo.Employees(EmployeeID)
```

When you define a constraint on a table that already contains data, SQL Server checks the data automatically to verify that it meets the constraint requirements. However, you can disable constraint checking on existing data when you add a constraint to the table.

Consider the following guidelines for disabling constraint checking on existing data:

- ■ You can disable only CHECK and FOREIGN KEY constraints. Other constraints must be dropped and then added again.

- ■ To disable constraint checking when you add a CHECK or FOREIGN KEY constraint to a table with existing data, include the WITH NOCHECK option in the ALTER TABLE statement.

- ■ Use the WITH NOCHECK option if existing data will not change. Data must conform to CHECK constraints if the data is updated.

- ■ Be certain that it is appropriate to disable constraint checking. You can execute a query to change existing data before you decide to add a constraint.

Partial Syntax

ALTER TABLE *table*
  [WITH CHECK │ WITH NOCHECK]
  ADD CONSTRAINT *constraint*

    [FOREIGN KEY] [(*column*[,...*n*])]
      REFERENCES *ref_table* [(*ref_col* [,...*n*])]
    [CHECK (*search_conditions*)]

Example

In this example, you add a FOREIGN KEY constraint that verifies that all employees are associated with a valid manager. The constraint is not enforced on existing data at the time that the constraint is added.

```
USE Northwind
ALTER TABLE dbo.Employees
WITH NOCHECK
    ADD CONSTRAINT FK_Employees_Employees
    FOREIGN KEY (ReportsTo)
    REFERENCES dbo.Employees(EmployeeID)
```

Disabling Constraint Checking When Loading New Data

- **Applies to CHECK and FOREIGN KEY Constraints**
- **Use When:**
  - Data conforms to constraints
  - You load new data that does not conform to constraints

```
USE Northwind
ALTER TABLE dbo.Employees
NOCHECK
   CONSTRAINT FK_Employees_Employees
```

You can disable constraint checking on existing CHECK and FOREIGN KEY constraints so that any data that you modify or add to the table is not checked against the constraint.

To avoid the costs of constraint checking, you might want to disable constraints when:

- You already have ensured that the data conforms to the constraints.
- You want to load data that does not conform to the constraints. Later, you can execute queries to change the data and then re-enable the constraints.

Important Disabling constraints on one table does not affect constraints on other tables that reference the original table. Updates to a table still can generate constraint violation errors.

Enabling a constraint that has been disabled requires executing another ALTER TABLE statement that contains either a CHECK or CHECK ALL clause.

Partial Syntax

ALTER TABLE *table*
  {CHECK | NOCHECK} CONSTRAINT
  {ALL | *constraint*[,...*n*]}

Example

This example disables the **FK_Employees_Employees** constraint. It can be re-enabled by executing another ALTER TABLE statement with the CHECK clause.

```
USE Northwind
ALTER TABLE dbo.Employees
NOCHECK
    CONSTRAINT FK_Employees_Employees
```

To determine whether a constraint is enabled or disabled on a table, execute the **sp_help** system stored procedure, or use the **CnstIsDisabled** property in the OBJECTPROPERTY function.

Using Defaults and Rules

- **As Independent Objects They:**
  - Are defined once
  - Can be bound to one or more columns or user-defined data types

```
CREATE DEFAULT phone_no_default
  AS '(000)000-0000'
GO
EXEC sp_bindefault phone_no_default,
  'Customers.Phone'
```

```
CREATE RULE regioncode_rule
  AS @regioncode IN ('IA', 'IL', 'KS', 'MO')
GO
EXEC sp_bindrule regioncode_rule,
  'Customers.Region'
```

Defaults and rules are objects that can be bound to one or more columns or user-defined data types, making it possible to define them once and use them repeatedly. A disadvantage to using defaults and rules is that they are not ANSI-compliant.

Creating a Default

If a value is not specified when you insert data, a default specifies one for the column to which the object is bound. Consider these facts before you create defaults:

- Any rules that are bound to the column and the data types validate the value of a default.

- Any CHECK constraints on the column must validate the value of a default.

- You cannot create a DEFAULT constraint on a column that is defined with a user-defined data type if a default is already bound to the data type or column.

Syntax

CREATE DEFAULT *default*
  AS *constant_expression*

Binding a Default

After you create a default, you must bind it to a column or user-defined data type by executing the **sp_bindefault** system stored procedure. To detach a default, execute the **sp_unbindefault** system stored procedure.

Example

This example inserts a placeholder phone number in the correct format until the actual phone number can be supplied.

```
USE Northwind
GO
CREATE DEFAULT phone_no_default
 AS '(000)000-0000'
GO
EXEC sp_bindefault phone_no_default, 'Customers.Phone'
```

Creating a Rule

Rules specify the acceptable values that you can insert into a column. They ensure that data falls within a specified range of values, matches a particular pattern, or matches entries in a specified list. Consider these facts about rules:

- A rule definition can contain any expression that is valid in a WHERE clause.

- A column or user-defined data type can have only one rule that is bound to it.

Syntax

CREATE RULE *rule*
  AS *condition_expression*

Binding a Rule

After you create a rule, you must bind it to a column or user-defined data type by executing the **sp_bindrule** system stored procedure. To detach a rule, execute the **sp_unbindrule** system stored procedure.

Example

In this example, the rule ensures that only specified states are allowed.

```
USE Northwind
GO
CREATE RULE regioncode_rule
 AS @regioncode IN ('IA', 'IL', 'KS', 'MO')
GO
EXEC sp_bindrule regioncode_rule, 'Customers.Region'
```

Dropping a Default or Rule

The DROP statement removes a default or rule from the database.

Syntax

DROP DEFAULT *default* [,...*n*]

Syntax

DROP RULE *rule* [, ...*n*]

Deciding Which Enforcement Method to Use

Data integrity components	Functionality	Performance costs	Before or after modification
Constraints	Medium	Low	Before
Defaults and rules	Low	Low	Before
Triggers	High	Medium-High	After
Data types, Null/Not Null	Low	Low	Before

You should consider functionality and performance costs when you determine which methods to use to enforce data integrity:

- It is best to use declarative integrity for fundamental integrity logic, such as when enforcing valid values and maintaining the relationships between tables.

- If you want to maintain complex redundant data that is not part of a primary or foreign key relationship, you must use triggers or stored procedures.

  However, because triggers do not fire until a modification occurs, error checking happens after the statement is completed. When a trigger detects a violation, it must undo the changes.

Data integrity component	Impact	Functionality	Performance costs	Before or after modification
Constraints	Define with a table and validate the data before a transaction begins, resulting in better performance.	Medium	Low	Before
Defaults and rules	Implement data integrity as separate objects that can be associated with one or more tables.	Low	Low	Before
Triggers	Provide additional functionality, such as cascading and complex application logic. Any modifications must be rolled back.	High	Medium-High	After (except for INSTEAD OF triggers)
Data types, Null/Not Null	Provides the lowest level of data integrity. Implemented for each column when the table is created. Data is validated before a transaction begins.	Low	Low	Before

Recommended Practices

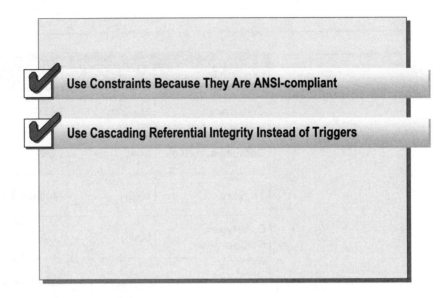

The following recommended practices should help you implement data integrity:

- Use constraints because they are ANSI-compliant and are supported by third-party development tools.
- Use cascading referential integrity instead of triggers.

Additional information on the following topics is available in SQL Server Books Online.

Topic	Search on
Developing databases	"data integrity"
Clustered and nonclustered indexes	"creating an index"
Cascading referential integrity	"cascading referential integrity restraints"
Triggers	"triggers"

Lab A: Implementing Data Integrity

Objectives

After completing this lab, you will be able to:

- Define and use DEFAULT and CHECK constraints to enforce domain integrity.
- Define and use PRIMARY KEY and FOREIGN KEY constraints to enforce entity and referential integrity.
- Create and use Microsoft SQL Server 2000 rules and defaults.

Prerequisites

Before working on this lab, you must have:

- Script files for this lab, which are located in C:\Moc\2073A\Labfiles\L05.
- Answer files for this lab, which are located in C:\Moc\2073A\Labfiles\L05\Answers.

Lab Setup

To complete this lab, you must have either:

- Completed the prior lab, or
- Executed the C:\Moc\2073A\Batches\Restore05.cmd batch file.

  This command file restores the **ClassNorthwind** database to a state required for this lab.

For More Information

If you require help with executing files, search SQL Query Analyzer Help for "Execute a query".

Other resources that you can use include:

- The **Northwind** database schema.
- SQL Server Books Online.

Scenario

The organization of the classroom is meant to simulate that of a worldwide trading firm named Northwind Traders. Its fictitious domain name is nwtraders.msft. The primary DNS server for nwtraders.msft is the instructor computer, which has an Internet Protocol (IP) address of 192.168.x.200 (where x is the assigned classroom number). The name of the instructor computer is London.

The following table provides the user name, computer name, and IP address for each student computer in the fictitious **nwtraders.msft** domain. Find the user name for your computer, and make a note of it.

User name	Computer name	IP address
SQLAdmin1	Vancouver	192.168.x.1
SQLAdmin2	Denver	192.168.x.2
SQLAdmin3	Perth	192.168.x.3
SQLAdmin4	Brisbane	192.168.x.4
SQLAdmin5	Lisbon	192.168.x.5
SQLAdmin6	Bonn	192.168.x.6
SQLAdmin7	Lima	192.168.x.7
SQLAdmin8	Santiago	192.168.x.8
SQLAdmin9	Bangalore	192.168.x.9
SQLAdmin10	Singapore	192.168.x.10
SQLAdmin11	Casablanca	192.168.x.11
SQLAdmin12	Tunis	192.168.x.12
SQLAdmin13	Acapulco	192.168.x.13
SQLAdmin14	Miami	192.168.x.14
SQLAdmin15	Auckland	192.168.x.15
SQLAdmin16	Suva	192.168.x.16
SQLAdmin17	Stockholm	192.168.x.17
SQLAdmin18	Moscow	192.168.x.18
SQLAdmin19	Caracas	192.168.x.19
SQLAdmin20	Montevideo	192.168.x.20
SQLAdmin21	Manila	192.168.x.21
SQLAdmin22	Tokyo	192.168.x.22
SQLAdmin23	Khartoum	192.168.x.23
SQLAdmin24	Nairobi	192.168.x.24

Estimated time to complete this lab: 30 minutes

Exercise 1
Defining DEFAULT Constraints

In this exercise, you will add DEFAULT constraints to the **Employees** table in the **ClassNorthwind** database.

▶ To define a DEFAULT constraint

In this procedure, you will execute a script that creates a default for the **Region** column in the **Employees** table, and then you will modify the same script to change the default region.

1. Log on to the **NWTraders** classroom domain by using the information in the following table.

Option	Value
User name	**SQLAdminx** (where *x* corresponds to your computer name as designated in the **nwtraders.msft** classroom domain)
Password	**password**

2. Open SQL Query Analyzer and, if requested, log in to the (local) server with Microsoft Windows® authentication.

   You have permission to log in to and administer SQL Server because you are logged as **SQLAdminx**, which is a member of the Microsoft Windows 2000 local group, Administrators. All members of this group are automatically mapped to the SQL Server **sysadmin** role.

3. In the **DB** list, click **ClassNorthwind**.

4. Open Labfiles\L05\DefConst.sql, and then review and execute it.

   This script will create a DEFAULT constraint that adds NY (New York) as the default for the **Region** column in the **Employees** table.

5. Execute **sp_helpconstraint** *tablename* and **sp_help** *constraintname* to view information on the DEFAULT constraint that you just created.

6. Modify Labfiles\L05\DefConst.sql to replace the DEFAULT constraint created in step 4 with a constraint that makes WA (Washington) the default for the **Region** column in the **Employees** table. L05\Answers\DefCons2.sql is a completed script for this step.

Exercise 2
Defining CHECK Constraints

In this exercise, you will add two CHECK constraints to the tables in the **ClassNorthwind** database.

▶ **To define a CHECK constraint**

In this procedure, you will execute a script to add a *title of courtesy* constraint to the **Employees** table, and then you will write and execute a statement to add a birth date constraint to the **Employee** table. Finally, you will write and execute a statement to test the new constraints.

1. Open Labfiles\L05\ChkConst.sql, and then review and execute it.

    This script will add a title of courtesy CHECK constraint to the **Employees** table of the **ClassNorthwind** database.

2. Write and execute a statement that adds a constraint to the **BirthDate** column in the **Employees** table called **CK_BirthDate**. The value in the **BirthDate** column must be earlier than today's date. L05\Answers\BirthDate.sql is a completed script for this step.

3. Execute statements that violate each constraint.

Use the following examples as a template.

```
USE ClassNorthwind
GO
UPDATE Employees SET TitleOfCourtesy = 'None'
WHERE EmployeeID = 1
GO
UPDATE Employees SET BirthDate = (GETDATE()+1)
WHERE EmployeeID = 1
GO
```

What happens?

_____

_____

4. Execute **sp_helpconstraint** *tablename* and **sp_help** *constraintname* to view information on the CHECK constraints that you created.

Exercise 3
Defining PRIMARY KEY Constraints

In this exercise, you will add PRIMARY KEY constraints to all of the tables in the **ClassNorthwind** database.

▶ **To define a PRIMARY KEY constraint**

In this procedure, you first will execute a script that creates a primary key on the **Employees** table, and then you will write a statement to create a PRIMARY KEY constraint on the **Customers** table. Finally, you will execute a script that adds PRIMARY KEY constraints to the other tables in the **ClassNorthwind** database.

1. Open Labfiles\L05\Prikey1.sql, and then review and execute it to create a PRIMARY KEY constraint on the **Employees** table in the **ClassNorthwind** database.

2. Write and execute a statement that adds a PRIMARY KEY constraint called **PK_Customers** on the **CustomerID** column in the **Customers** table. L05\Answers\PriTitle.sql is a completed script for this step.

   What is the impact on nonclustered indexes associated with the table when you create a PRIMARY KEY constraint?

   _____

   _____

3. Open Labfiles\L05\PriKey2.sql, and then review and execute it to create PRIMARY KEY constraints on the remaining tables in the **ClassNorthwind** database.

4. Execute the **sp_helpconstraint** system stored procedure to view information on the PRIMARY KEY constraint that you created for the **orders** table. Also execute the **sp_help** system stored procedure on the constraint on **PK_Employees** in the **ClassNorthwind** database.

Exercise 4
Defining FOREIGN KEY Constraints

In this exercise, you will add FOREIGN KEY constraints to tables in the **ClassNorthwind** database.

▶ **To define a FOREIGN KEY constraint**

In this procedure, you will first execute a script that creates a foreign key on the **Orders** table, and then you will write a statement to create a FOREIGN KEY constraint on the **Orders** table. Finally, you will execute a script that adds FOREIGN KEY constraints to the other tables in the **ClassNorthwind** database.

1. Open Labfiles\L05\ForKey1.sql, and then review and execute it to create a FOREIGN KEY constraint on the **Orders** table.

    Why was it not necessary to execute any DROP INDEX statements?

    _____

    _____

    Does the FOREIGN KEY constraint prevent the referenced table from being dropped or truncated?

    _____

    _____

2. Write and execute a statement that adds a FOREIGN KEY constraint, called **FK_Products_Categories**, to the **CategoryID** column in the **Products** table referencing the **CategoryID** column in the **Categories** table. Specify an option that does not verify that the existing data conforms to the new constraint. L05\Answers\ForeignKeyProd.sql is a completed script for this step.

3. Open Labfiles\L05\ForKey2.sql, and then review and execute it to create the remaining FOREIGN KEY constraints in the **ClassNorthwind** database.

4. Execute **sp_helpconstraint** *tablename* to view information on some of the FOREIGN KEY constraints that you created. You can use the following tables with FOREIGN KEY constraints for this step: **Products**, **Orders**, **Order Details**, **Suppliers**, and **Employees**.

If Time Permits
Creating Defaults and Rules

In this exercise, you will add defaults and rules to the **ClassNorthwind** database.

▶ **To create a default**

In this procedure, you will execute a script to create and bind a default, and then you will verify that the default is functioning correctly.

1. Open Labfiles\L05\CreaDefa.sql, and then review and execute it.

   This script creates and binds a default to the **Suppliers.Country** column. The default is Singapore.

2. Execute a statement that inserts a new record to verify that the default is working properly. The example below shows how to do this for the **Suppliers** table. You can change the example to include your favorite book title and author.

   ```
   USE ClassNorthwind
   INSERT Suppliers (CompanyName) VALUES ('Karl''s Bakery')
   GO
   ```

3. Write and execute a statement to query the **Suppliers** table to view the results. The example below assumes that you used the data supplied in the previous step.

   ```
   USE ClassNorthwind
   SELECT * FROM Suppliers
       WHERE Country = 'Singapore'
   GO
   ```

▶ **To create a rule**

In this procedure, you will execute a script to create and bind a rule, and then you will verify that the rule is functioning correctly.

1. Open Labfiles\L05\CreaRule.sql, and then review and execute it.

   This script creates a path rule that ensures that employee-photo paths follow the format described in the script.

2. Execute the following UPDATE statement to test the rule by attempting to update the **PhotoPath** column with an invalid path. The statement should fail because it violates the path rule.

   ```
   USE ClassNorthwind
   UPDATE Employees
       SET PhotoPath = 'http://accweb/xemmployees/new.bmp'
       WHERE LastName = 'Fuller'
   GO
   ```

Review

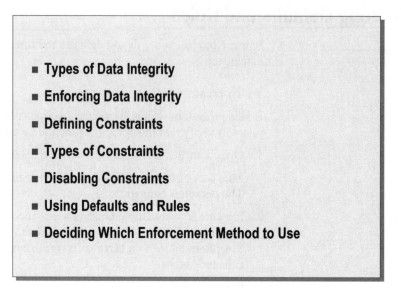

- Types of Data Integrity
- Enforcing Data Integrity
- Defining Constraints
- Types of Constraints
- Disabling Constraints
- Using Defaults and Rules
- Deciding Which Enforcement Method to Use

1. What type of constraint would you add to the Country field in your database to ensure that your Indonesian subsidiary does business only with other Indonesian companies?

2. After implementation of the constraint, or rule, in question 1, your data entry operators are complaining that they have to enter the word Indonesia over and over again. How can you fix this?

3. Your business has changed and you no longer do work in Indonesia. Your subsidiary has moved to Malaysia and is now doing business with several other East Asian countries. Currently, there are 4.5 million sales records that include Indonesia in the country field. How can you add the new countries and still preserve the rows that contain Indonesia?

4. Your order entry system has two main tables: **Orders** and **Customers**. What data integrity components should you consider if you want to ensure that each order and customer can be uniquely identified? How would you manage the relationship between the two tables?

Microsoft®
Training &
Certification

Module 6:
Planning Indexes

Contents

Microsoft®

Project Lead: Rich Rose
Instructional Designers: Rich Rose, Cheryl Hoople, Marilyn McGill
Instructional Software Design Engineers: Karl Dehmer, Carl Raebler, Rick Byham
Technical Lead: Karl Dehmer
Subject Matter Experts: Karl Dehmer, Carl Raebler, Rick Byham
Graphic Artist: Kirsten Larson (Independent Contractor)
Editing Manager: Lynette Skinner
Editor: Wendy Cleary
Copy Editor: Edward McKillop (S&T Consulting)
Production Manager: Miracle Davis
Production Coordinator: Jenny Boe
Production Support: Lori Walker (S&T Consulting)
Test Manager: Sid Benavente
Courseware Testing: TestingTesting123
Classroom Automation: Lorrin Smith-Bates
Creative Director, Media/Sim Services: David Mahlmann
Web Development Lead: Lisa Pease
CD Build Specialist: Julie Challenger
Online Support: David Myka (S&T Consulting)
Localization Manager: Rick Terek
Operations Coordinator: John Williams
Manufacturing Support: Laura King; Kathy Hershey
Lead Product Manager, Release Management: Bo Galford
Lead Product Manager, Data Base: Margo Crandall
Group Manager, Courseware Infrastructure: David Bramble
Group Product Manager, Content Development: Dean Murray
General Manager: Robert Stewart

Overview

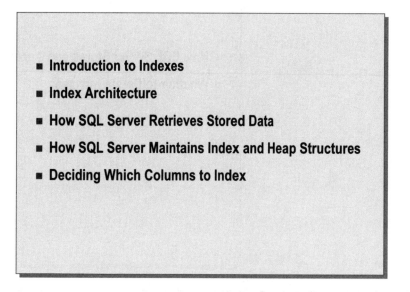

- **Introduction to Indexes**
- **Index Architecture**
- **How SQL Server Retrieves Stored Data**
- **How SQL Server Maintains Index and Heap Structures**
- **Deciding Which Columns to Index**

This module provides an overview of planning indexes. It explains how indexes can improve database performance. It discusses how Microsoft® SQL Server™ 2000 stores clustered and nonclustered indexes and how SQL Server retrieves rows by using indexes. It also explores how SQL Server maintains indexes. The module concludes with guidelines for deciding which columns to index.

After completing this module, you will be able to:

- Describe why and when to use an index.
- Describe how SQL Server uses clustered and nonclustered indexes.
- Describe how SQL Server index architecture facilitates the retrieval of data.
- Describe how SQL Server maintains indexes and heaps.
- Describe the importance of selectivity, density, and distribution of data when deciding which columns to index.

◆ Introduction to Indexes

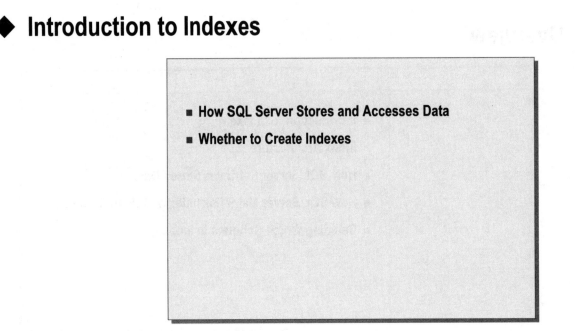

- How SQL Server Stores and Accesses Data
- Whether to Create Indexes

Using indexes can greatly improve database performance. This section introduces basic index concepts and discusses when and why indexes are used.

How SQL Server Stores and Accesses Data

- **How Data Is Stored**
  - Rows are stored in data pages
  - Heaps are a collection of data pages for a table
- **How Data Is Accessed**
  - Scanning all data pages in a table
  - Using an index that points to data on a page

Data Pages

Page 4		Page 5		Page 6		Page 7		Page 8		Page 9	
Con	...	Rudd	...	Akhtar	...	Smith	...	Martin	...	Ganio	...
Funk	...	White	...	Funk	...	Ota	...	Phua	...	Jones	...
White	...	Barr	...	Smith	...	Jones	...	Jones	...	Hall	...
...	...	...	...	Martin	...	...	...	Smith	...	...	...
...	...	...	...	...	...	...	...	...	...	...	...

Understanding how data is stored is the basis for understanding how SQL Server accesses data.

Note In the illustration, only the last names are shown in the data pages, although the data pages store complete rows.

How Data Is Stored

A heap is a collection of data pages containing rows for a table:

- Each data page contains 8 kilobytes (KB) of information. A group of eight adjacent pages is called an *extent*.
- The data rows are not stored in any particular order, and there is no particular order to the sequence of the data pages.
- The data pages are not linked in a linked list.
- When rows are inserted into a page and a page is full, the data pages split.

How Data Is Accessed

SQL Server accesses data in one of two ways:

■ Scanning all of the data pages of tables—called a *table scan*. When SQL Server performs a table scan, it:

- Starts at the beginning of the table.

- Scans from page-to-page through all of the rows in the table.

- Extracts the rows that meet the criteria of the query.

■ Using indexes. When SQL Server uses an index, it:

- Traverses the index tree structure to find rows that the query requests.

- Extracts only the needed rows that meet the criteria of the query.

SQL Server first determines whether an index exists. Then, the query optimizer, the component responsible for generating the optimum execution plan for a query, determines whether scanning a table or using the index is more efficient for accessing data.

Whether to Create Indexes

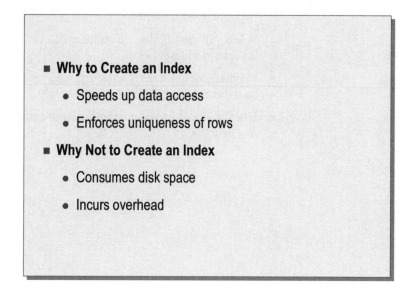

■ **Why to Create an Index**

    ● Speeds up data access

    ● Enforces uniqueness of rows

■ **Why Not to Create an Index**

    ● Consumes disk space

    ● Incurs overhead

When you are considering whether to create an index, evaluate two factors to ensure that the index will be more efficient than a table scan: the nature of the data and the nature of the queries based on the table.

Why to Create an Index

Indexes accelerate data retrieval. For example, without an index, you would have to go through an entire textbook one page at a time to find information about a topic.

SQL Server uses indexes to point to the location of a row on a data page instead of having to look through all of the data pages of a table. Consider the following facts and guidelines about indexes:

■ Indexes generally accelerate queries that join tables and perform sorting or grouping operations.

■ Indexes enforce the uniqueness of rows if uniqueness is defined when you create the index.

■ Indexes are created and maintained in ascending or descending sorted order.

■ Indexes are best created on columns with a high degree of selectivity—that is, columns or combinations of columns in which the majority of the data is unique.

Why Not to Create an Index

Indexes are useful, but they consume disk space and incur overhead and maintenance costs. Consider the following facts and guidelines about indexes:

- When you modify data on an indexed column, SQL Server updates the associated indexes.

- Maintaining indexes requires time and resources. Therefore, do not create an index that you will not use frequently.

- Indexes on columns containing a large amount of duplicate data may have few benefits.

◆ Index Architecture

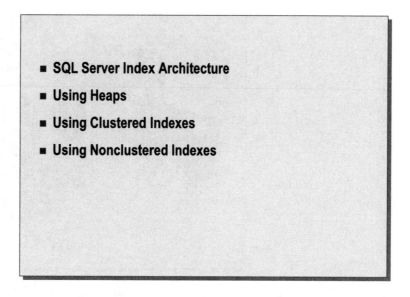

The index architecture for clustered and nonclustered indexes is different. Understanding the differences in architecture will help you create the most effective type of index.

Multimedia Presentation: SQL Server Index Architecture

The multimedia presentation presents the following concepts.

Clustered Indexes

In a clustered index, the leaf level is the actual data page. Data is physically stored on a data page in ascending order. The order of the values in the index pages is also ascending.

Nonclustered Indexes Built on Top of a Heap

When a nonclustered index is built on top of a heap, SQL Server uses row identifiers in the index pages that point to rows in the data pages. The row identifiers store data location information.

Nonclustered Indexes Built on Top of a Clustered Index

When a nonclustered index is built on top of a table with a clustered index, SQL Server uses a clustering key in the index pages that point to the clustered index. The clustering key stores data location information.

Using Heaps

SQL Server:

- **Uses Index Allocation Map Pages That:**
  - Contain information on where the extents of a heap are stored
  - Navigate through the heap and find available space for new rows being inserted
  - Connect data pages
- **Reclaims Space for New Rows in the Heap When a Row Is Deleted**

SQL Server maintains data pages in a heap unless a clustered index is defined on the table. SQL Server:

- Uses Index Allocation Map (IAM) pages to maintain heaps. IAM pages:
  - Contain information on where the extents of a heap are stored.

    The **sysindexes** system table stores a pointer to the first IAM page associated with a heap.

  - Are used to navigate through the heap and find available space for new rows being inserted.

  - Connect the data pages.

    The data pages and the rows within them are not in any specific order and are not linked together. The only logical connection between data pages is that which is recorded in the IAM pages.

- Reclaims space for new rows in the heap when a row is deleted.

Using Clustered Indexes

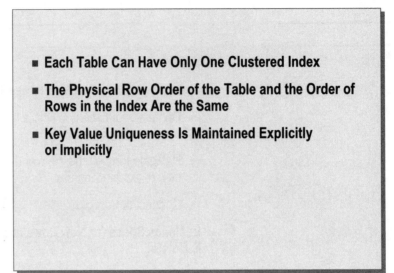

- **Each Table Can Have Only One Clustered Index**
- **The Physical Row Order of the Table and the Order of Rows in the Index Are the Same**
- **Key Value Uniqueness Is Maintained Explicitly or Implicitly**

Clustered indexes are useful for columns that are searched frequently for ranges of key values, or are accessed in sorted order. When you create a clustered index, consider the following facts and guidelines:

- Each table can have only one clustered index.

- The physical row order of the table and the order of rows in the index are the same. You should create clustered indexes before you create any nonclustered indexes because a clustered index changes the physical row order of the table. Rows are sorted into a sequenced order and maintained in that order.

- Key value uniqueness is maintained explicitly, with the UNIQUE keyword, or implicitly, with an internal unique identifier. These unique identifiers are internal to SQL Server and are not accessible to the user.

- The average size of a clustered index is about five percent of the table size. However, clustered index size varies depending on the size of the indexed column.

- When a row is deleted, space is reclaimed and is available for a new row.

- During index creation, SQL Server temporarily uses disk space from the current database. A clustered index requires about 1.2 times the table size for working space when the index is created. The disk space that is used during index creation is reclaimed automatically after the index is created.

Note Be sure that you have sufficient disk space in the database when you create clustered indexes.

Using Nonclustered Indexes

- **Nonclustered Indexes Are the SQL Server Default**
- **Existing Nonclustered Indexes Are Automatically Rebuilt When:**
  - An existing clustered index is dropped
  - A clustered index is created
  - The DROP_EXISTING option is used to change which columns define the clustered index

Nonclustered indexes are useful when users require multiple ways to search data. For example, a reader may frequently search through a gardening book, looking for both the common and scientific names of plants. You could create a nonclustered index for retrieving the scientific names and a clustered index for retrieving common names. When you create a nonclustered index, consider the following facts and guidelines:

- If an index type is not specified, the type will default to nonclustered index.
- SQL Server automatically rebuilds existing nonclustered indexes when any of the following occurs.
  - An existing clustered index is dropped.
  - A clustered index is created.
  - The DROP_EXISTING option is used to change which columns define the clustered index.
- The order of the leaf level pages of a nonclustered index differs from the physical order of the table. The leaf level is sorted in ascending order.
- Uniqueness is maintained at the leaf level with either clustering keys or row identifiers.
- You can have up to 249 nonclustered indexes per table.
- Nonclustered indexes are best created on columns in which the data selectivity ranges from highly selective to unique.
- Create clustered indexes before nonclustered indexes.
- The row identifiers specify the logical ordering of rows and consist of the file ID, page number, and row ID.

◆ How SQL Server Retrieves Stored Data

- ■ **How SQL Server Uses the sysindexes Table**
- ■ **Finding Rows Without Indexes**
- ■ **Finding Rows in a Heap with a Nonclustered Index**
- ■ **Finding Rows in a Clustered Index**
- ■ **Finding Rows in a Clustered Index with a Nonclustered Index**

To design efficient databases, it is important to understand how SQL Server retrieves stored data. This section describes how SQL Server index architecture facilitates the retrieval of data.

How SQL Server Uses the sysindexes Table

- **Describes the Indexes**

indid	Object Type
0	Heap
1	Clustered Index
2 to 250	Nonclustered Index
255	text, ntext, or image

- **Location of IAM, First, and Root of Indexes**
- **Number of Pages and Rows**
- **Distribution of Data**

The **sysindexes** system table is a central location for vital information about tables and indexes. It contains statistical information, such as the number of rows and data pages in each table. It describes how to find information stored in a data table.

Page pointers in the **sysindexes** table anchor all of the page collections for tables and indexes. Every table has one collection of data pages, plus additional collections of pages to implement each index defined for the table.

A row in **sysindexes** for each table and index is uniquely identified by the combination of the object identifier column (**id**) and the index identifier column (**indid**).

The indid Column

This is how the columns of the **sysindexes** table assist in locating data pages for different types of objects:

- A heap has a row in **sysindexes** with the **indid** column set to zero. The **FirstIAM** column in **sysindexes** points to the chain of IAM pages for the collection of data pages in the table. SQL Server must use the IAM pages to find the pages in the data page collection because these pages are not linked together.

- A clustered index created for a table has a row in **sysindexes** with the **indid** column set to 1. The **root** column in **sysindexes** points to the top of the clustered index *balanced tree* (B-Tree).

- Each nonclustered index created for a table has a row in **sysindexes** with a value in the **indid** column. The value for the **indid** column for a nonclustered index ranges from 2 to 250. The **root** column in **sysindexes** points to the top of the nonclustered index B-Tree.

- Each table that has at least one **text, ntext**, or **image** column also has a row in **sysindexes** with the **indid** column set to 255. The **FirstIAM** column in **sysindexes** points to the chain of IAM pages that manage the **text, ntext**, and **image** pages.

Finding Rows Without Indexes

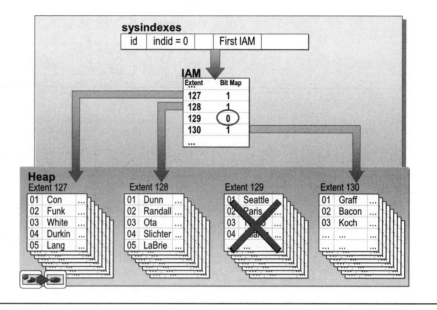

When an index does not exist on a table, SQL Server must use a table scan to retrieve rows. SQL Server uses the **sysindexes** table to find the IAM page. Because the IAM page contains a list of all pages related to that table, as a bitmap of eight-page extents, SQL Server can then read all data pages.

Initiating a data search on a heap by using an IAM page is efficient for a table scan, but it is not a good means to find a small number of rows in a large table.

The rows are returned unsorted. They may initially be returned in insertion order, but this order will not be maintained. After deletions have occurred, new inserts will fill in the gaps, making the order unpredictable.

Finding Rows in a Heap with a Nonclustered Index

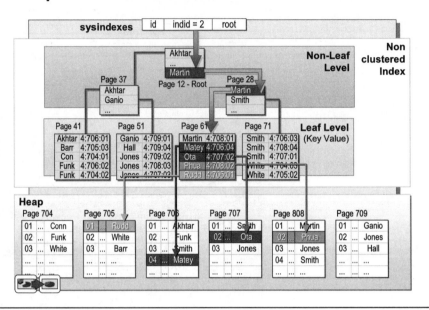

A nonclustered index is like the index of a textbook. The data is stored in one place and the index is stored in another. Pointers indicate the storage location of the indexed items in the underlying table.

SQL Server indexes are organized as B-Trees. Each page in an index holds a page header followed by index rows. Each index row contains a key value and a pointer to either another page or a data row.

Each page in an index is called an index node. The top node of the B-Tree is called the root node or root level. The bottom node is called the leaf node or leaf level. Any index levels between the root and the leaf nodes are intermediate levels. Each page in the intermediate or bottom layers has a pointer to the preceding and subsequent pages in a doubly linked list.

In a table that only contains a nonclustered index, the leaf nodes contain row locators with pointers to the data rows holding the key values. Each pointer (Row ID or RID) is built from the file ID, page number, and the number of the row on the page.

Example

```
SELECT lastname, firstname
FROM member
WHERE lastname
BETWEEN 'Masters' AND 'Rudd'
```

Finding Rows in a Clustered Index

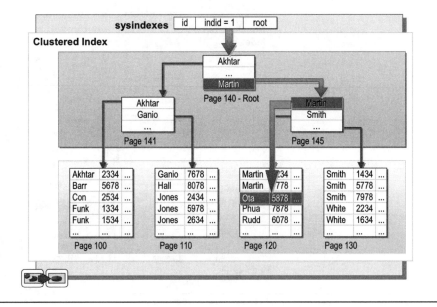

Clustered and nonclustered indexes share a similar B-Tree structure. The differences are that:

- The data pages of a clustered index are the leaf nodes of the B-Tree structure.

- The data rows of a clustered index are sorted and stored in a sequential order based on their clustered key.

A clustered index is like a telephone directory in which all of the rows for customers with the same last name are clustered together in the same part of the book. Just as the organization of a telephone directory makes it easy for a person to search, SQL Server quickly searches a table with a clustered index. Because a clustered index determines the sequence in which rows are stored in a table, there can only be one clustered index for a table at a time.

Keeping your clustered key value small increases the number of index rows that can be placed on an index page and decreases the number of levels that must be traversed. This minimizes I/O.

Note If there are duplicate values in a clustered index, SQL Server must distinguish between rows that contain identical values in the key column or columns. It does this by using a 4-byte integer (*uniquifier* value) in an additional system-only uniquifier column.

Example

```
SELECT lastname, firstname
FROM member
WHERE lastname = 'Ota'
```

Finding Rows in a Clustered Index with a Nonclustered Index

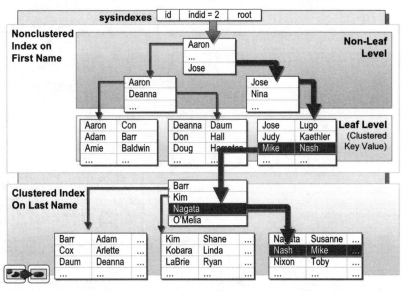

When a nonclustered index is added to a table that already has a clustered index, the row locator of each nonclustered index contains the clustered key index value for the row.

When using clustered and nonclustered indexes on the same table, the B-Tree structures of both indexes must be traversed to reach data. This generates additional I/O.

Because the key value of a clustered index is usually larger than the 8-byte RID used for heaps, nonclustered indexes can be substantially larger on clustered indexed tables than when built on heaps. Keeping the key values of the clustered index small helps you to build smaller, faster indexes.

Example

```
SELECT lastname, firstname, phone
FROM member
WHERE firstname = 'Mike'
```

◆ How SQL Server Maintains Index and Heap Structures

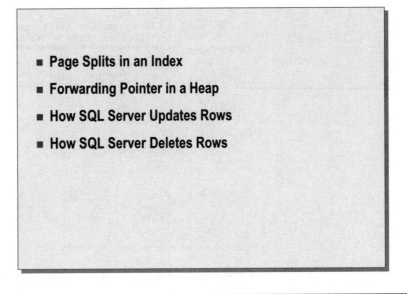

- Page Splits in an Index
- Forwarding Pointer in a Heap
- How SQL Server Updates Rows
- How SQL Server Deletes Rows

This section discusses how SQL Server maintains indexes and heaps when inserting, updating, and deleting rows.

Page Splits in an Index

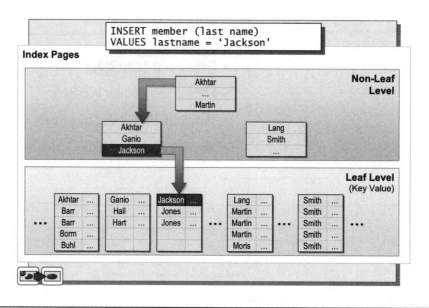

A clustered index directs an inserted or updated row to a specific page, which is determined by the clustered key value. If either the data page or index page does not have enough room to accommodate the data, a new page is added in a process known as a *page split*. Approximately half of the data remains on the old page, and the other half is moved to the new page.

Logically, the new page follows the original page; physically, the new page may be assigned to any available page. If an index experiences a large number of page splits, rebuilding the index will improve performance.

Note If a page splits in a clustered index, SQL Server does not need to maintain the nonclustered indexes for all of the rows that have moved to a new page. The row locator continues to identify the correct location in the clustering key.

Forwarding Pointer in a Heap

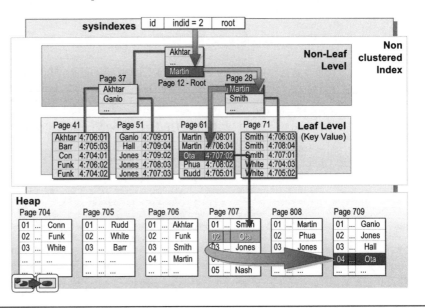

Page splits do not occur in a heap. SQL Server has a different means of handling updates and inserts when data pages are full.

Inserts to a Heap

The insert of a new row into a heap cannot cause a page split, because a new row can be inserted wherever room is available.

Forwarding Pointers

If an update to a row in a heap needs more room than is currently available on that page, the row will be moved to a new data page. The row leaves a *forwarding pointer* in its original location. If the row with the forwarding pointer must move again, the original pointer is redirected to the new location.

The forwarding pointer ensures that nonclustered indexes need not be changed. If an update causes the forwarded row to shrink enough to fit in its original place, the pointer is eliminated, and the record is restored to its original location by the update.

Page Splits in Nonclustered Indexes on a Heap

Although an insert or update cannot cause a page split in a heap, if a nonclustered index exists on the heap, an insert or update can still cause a page split in the nonclustered index.

How SQL Server Updates Rows

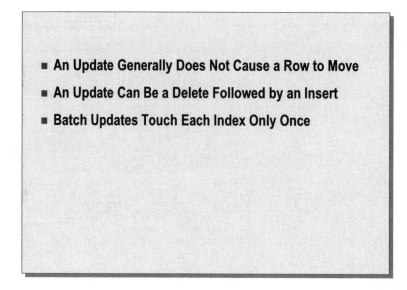

- An Update Generally Does Not Cause a Row to Move
- An Update Can Be a Delete Followed by an Insert
- Batch Updates Touch Each Index Only Once

Updates can often take place without impacting the structure of data rows.

An Update Generally Does Not Cause a Row to Move

Updates generally do not require rows to move. No move occurs if the update does not enlarge the record or if any enlargement still fits on the same page. Updates typically generate only a single log record.

An Update Can Be a Delete Followed by an Insert

An update causing a row to be moved is logged as a delete followed by an insert, if:

- The update does not fit on a page of a heap.
- The table has an update trigger.
- The table is marked for replication.
- The value of the clustered index key requires the row to be placed in a different location. For example, a last name changed from Abercrombie to Yukish would move that name in a telephone directory.

Batch Updates Touch Each Index Only Once

If a significant number of rows are inserted, updated or deleted in a table in a single SQL statement, SQL Server presorts the changes for each index so that the changes are performed in the order of the index. This batch update results in a significantly greater performance improvement than when using a series of Transact-SQL statements.

How SQL Server Deletes Rows

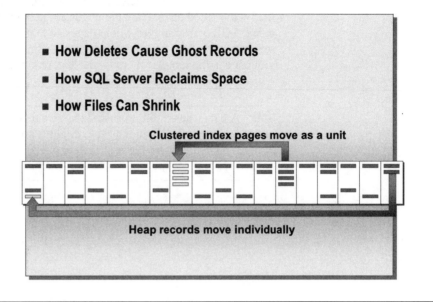

The deletion of rows impacts both the index and data pages.

How Deletes Cause Ghost Records

Rows deleted from the leaf level of an index are not removed immediately. They are marked as invalid and called *ghost records*. This process can prevent the need to lock adjacent records. It can also prevent lock contention over ranges of data. SQL Server periodically initializes a special housekeeping thread that checks indexes for the existence of ghost records and removes them.

How SQL Server Reclaims Space

When the last row is deleted from a data page, the entire page is deallocated, unless it is the only page remaining in the table.

Deleting Rows in an Index

Space in an index is available for use by adjacent rows immediately after a row is deleted, but some gaps usually remain until the index is rebuilt.

Deleting Rows in a Heap

Deleted rows in heaps are not compacted until the space is required for an insertion.

How Files Can Shrink

After records have been deleted, a file is able to shrink. SQL Server shrinks a file by moving data to available pages at the beginning of the file. Within an index, SQL Server moves whole pages so that the rows stay in their proper, sorted relationship. Page pointers adjust to link the moved page into the correct sequence in the table. If there is no clustered index, individual rows can move wherever there is room in the file.

Note A database option, **autoshrink**, tries to shrink the database without manual intervention. It does so five minutes after startup and every thirty minutes thereafter. The file is shrunk to a size where 25 percent of the file is unused space, or to the size of the file when it was created, whichever is greater.

◆ Deciding Which Columns to Index

- ■ **Understanding the Data**
- ■ **Indexing Guidelines**
- ■ **Choosing the Appropriate Clustered Index**
- ■ **Indexing to Support Queries**
- ■ **Determining Selectivity**
- ■ **Determining Density**
- ■ **Determining Distribution of Data**

Planning useful indexes is one of the most important aspects of improving query performance. It requires both an understanding of index structure and how the data is used.

Understanding the Data

- **Logical and Physical Design**
- **Data Characteristics**
- **How Data Is Used**
  - The types of queries performed
  - The frequency of queries that are typically performed

Before you create an index, you should have a thorough understanding of the data, including:

- Logical and physical design.
- Data characteristics.
- How data is used.

  To design useful and effective indexes, you must rely on the analysis of queries that users send. A poor analysis of how users access data becomes apparent in the form of slow query response or even unnecessary table locks. You should be aware of how users access data by observing:

  - The types of queries performed.
  - The frequency of queries that are typically performed.

Having a thorough understanding of the user's data requirements helps to determine which columns to index and what types of indexes to create. You might have to sacrifice some speed on one query to gain better performance on another.

Indexing Guidelines

- **Columns to Index**
  - Primary and foreign keys
  - Those frequently searched in ranges
  - Those frequently accessed in sorted order
  - Those frequently grouped together during aggregation
- **Columns Not to Index**
  - Those seldom referenced in queries
  - Those that contain few unique values
  - Those defined with **text**, **ntext**, or **image** data types

Your business environment, data characteristics, and use of the data determine the columns that you specify to build an index. The usefulness of an index is directly related to the percentage of rows returned from a query. Low percentages or high selectivity are more efficient.

Note When you create an index on a column, the column is referred to as the index column. A value within an index column is called a key value.

Columns to Index

Create indexes on frequently searched columns, such as:

- Primary keys.
- Foreign keys or columns that are used frequently in joining tables.
- Columns that are searched for ranges of key values.
- Columns that are accessed in sorted order.
- Columns that are grouped together during aggregation.

Columns Not to Index

Do not index columns that:

- You seldom reference in a query.
- Contain few unique values. For example, an index on a column with two values, male and female, returns a high percentage of rows.
- Are defined with **text**, **ntext**, and **image** data types. Columns with these data types cannot be indexed.

Choosing the Appropriate Clustered Index

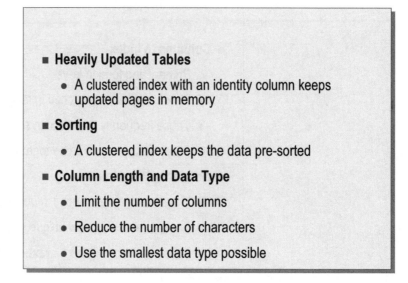

Consider how the table is used when you choose the clustered index for each table.

Heavily Updated Tables

When you optimize performance for data insertion to a heavily used table, consider creating a clustered index on a primary key identity column. By forcing inserts to a small group of pages at the end of the table, speed increases. The frequent access keeps these pages in memory.

Sorting

Tables that are frequently sorted for reports, grouped for aggregation, or searched for ranges of data can benefit from a clustered index on the sorting column. Using a clustered index is particularly helpful when many columns of the table are returned and a nonclustered index is impractical. For example, a mailing list table would benefit from a clustered index on the postal code, because the mailing labels must be printed and applied in a specified order.

Column Length and Data Type

SQL Server uses the clustered index value as the row identifier within each nonclustered index. The clustered index value can be repeated many times in your table structure.

To prevent large clustered indexes from making their associated nonclustered indexes larger and slower:

- Limit the number of columns in your clustered index.

- Reduce the average number of characters by using a **varchar** data type instead of a **char** data type.

- Use the smallest data type possible, such as **tinyint** instead of **int**.

Indexing to Support Queries

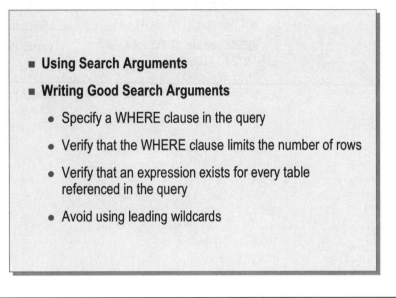

- **Using Search Arguments**
- **Writing Good Search Arguments**
  - Specify a WHERE clause in the query
  - Verify that the WHERE clause limits the number of rows
  - Verify that an expression exists for every table referenced in the query
  - Avoid using leading wildcards

Query performance is dependent on how well you have designed your indexes. It is also important to write your queries with a search argument that can take advantage of an indexed column.

Using Search Arguments

A search argument limits a search to an exact match, a range of values, or a combination of two or more items joined by an AND operator. A search argument contains a constant expression that acts on a column by using an operator. When you write queries that contain search arguments, you increase the opportunity for the query optimizer to use an index.

Writing Good Search Arguments

If an expression does not limit a search, it is considered a non-search argument. In many cases, you should rewrite queries to convert non-search arguments into search arguments.

To limit the search, you should:

- Specify a WHERE clause in the query.
- Verify that the WHERE clause limits the number of rows.
- Verify that an expression exists for every table referenced in the query.
- Avoid using leading wildcard characters.

The following table shows good search arguments:

Good search argument	Query
WHERE cust_id = 47635	Limits the search because **cust_id** is unique
WHERE date BETWEEN '07/23/2000' AND '07/30/2000'	Limits the search to only a small range of data
WHERE lastname LIKE 'Gre%'	Limits the search to only last names that begin with the letters Gre

Determining Selectivity

member_no	last_name	first_name
1	Randall	Joshua
2	Flood	Kathie
.		SELECT *
.		FROM member
.		WHERE member_no > 8999
10000	Anderson	Bill

High selectivity

$$\frac{\text{Number of rows meeting criteria}}{\text{Total number of rows in table}} = \frac{1000}{10000} = 10\%$$

member_no	last_name	first_name
1	Randall	Joshua
2	Flood	Kathie
.		SELECT *
.		FROM member
.		WHERE member_no < 9001
10000	Anderson	Bill

Low selectivity

$$\frac{\text{Number of rows meeting criteria}}{\text{Total number of rows in table}} = \frac{9000}{10000} = 90\%$$

A concept and term that is frequently used when discussing indexes is *selectivity*. When determining which columns to index and choosing the type of index to create, you should consider how selective the data values are.

Defining Selectivity

Selectivity is derived from the percentage of rows in a table that are accessed or returned by a query. The query optimizer determines selectivity for SELECT, UPDATE, or DELETE statements. When creating indexes, you should create them on:

- Columns that are often referenced in join operations or in the WHERE clause.

- Data that is highly selective.

High Selectivity and Low Selectivity

In *high selectivity*, the search criteria limit the number of rows returned to a low percentage of the total possible. One row returned is the highest selectivity that can be achieved.

In *low selectivity*, the search criteria return a high percentage of the rows in the table.

Estimating Selectivity

You can determine how selective a query is by estimating the number of rows returned, relative to the total number of rows in a table for a specific query.

Example 1

In this example, assuming that there are 10,000 rows in the **member** table and that the member numbers are in the range of 1 to 10,000—all unique values—the query returns one row.

```
SELECT *
FROM member
WHERE member_no = 8999
```

Example 2

In this example, assuming that there are 10,000 rows in the **member** table and that the member numbers are in the range of 1 to 10,000—all unique values—the query returns 999 rows.

```
SELECT *
FROM member
WHERE member_no > 9001
```

Example 3

In this example, assuming that there are 10,000 rows in the **member** table and that the member numbers are in the range of 1 to 10,000—all unique values—the query returns 9,000 rows.

```
SELECT *
FROM member
WHERE member_no < 9001
```

Determining Density

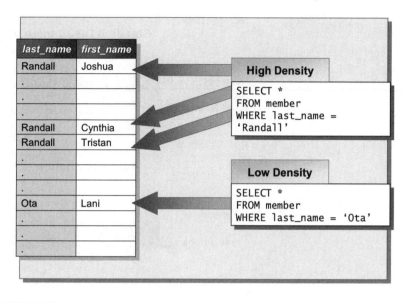

A related concept to selectivity is the concept of *density*. When determining which columns to index, you should examine the density of your data.

Defining Density

Density is the average percentage of duplicate rows in an index. If your data or query is not very selective (low selectivity), you have a high amount of density.

- An index with a large number of duplicates has high density.

  For example, an index on the **lastname** column can be very dense.

- A unique index has low density.

  An example of this would be an index on social security number, ID, driver's license number, or last name and first name (composite).

Relating Density to the Data

When determining the density of your data, remember that density relates to the specific data elements. Density can vary. Consider an index on the **lastname** column. Data elements of this index are very dense for popular last names such as Randall, whereas the last name Ota is not likely to be very dense.

How Density Affects the Query Plan

Because data is not distributed evenly, the query optimizer might or might not use an index. In the illustration, the query optimizer might:

- Perform a table scan to retrieve the last name Randall.
- Use an index to access the last name Ota.

Determining Distribution of Data

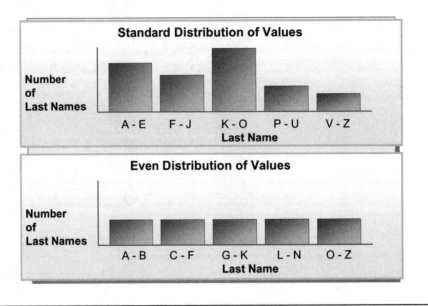

The distribution of data is related to the concept of density. When determining the density of the data, you should also examine how the data is distributed.

Defining Distribution of Data

The *distribution of data* indicates the amount of data that exists for a range of values in a given table and how many rows fall in that range. If an indexed column has very few unique values, data retrieval may be slow because of the distribution of data. For example, a telephone directory sorted alphabetically on last name may show that there is a high occurrence of people with the last name Randall or Jones.

Standard or Even Distribution

In a standard distribution, the key value ranges remain constant while the number per range changes. An even distribution allows the query optimizer to easily determine the selectivity of a query by estimating the number of qualifying rows as a percentage of the total rows in the table.

Relating Density to Distribution of Data

Similar to density, data elements of the index can vary in how the data is distributed. Typically, data is not evenly distributed. For example, if the **member** table contains 10,000 rows and has an index on the **lastname** column, the last names are typically not evenly distributed.

Estimating the Percentage of Rows Returned

In many cases, you can approximate the percentage of data to be returned in a result set. For example, if the criterion is male/female, the result set for females can be estimated at 50 percent. When estimating the percentage of rows returned on values such as last name, city, or other demographic data, it is critical that you know your data, because data distribution varies widely in different environments.

Example

This query is used to show the distribution (amount of duplicates) of column values on an existing database. In this example, the query returns each value only once with a number (count) that indicates how many times it occurs in the table.

```
SELECT column, count(*) AS 'Data Count'
FROM table
GROUP BY column
ORDER BY 'Data count' DESC
```

Recommended Practices

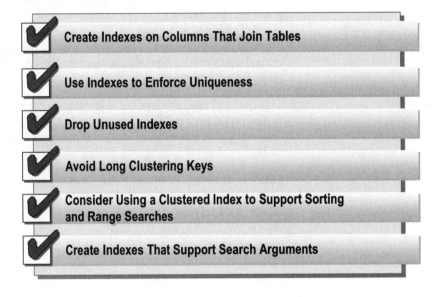

- Create Indexes on Columns That Join Tables
- Use Indexes to Enforce Uniqueness
- Drop Unused Indexes
- Avoid Long Clustering Keys
- Consider Using a Clustered Index to Support Sorting and Range Searches
- Create Indexes That Support Search Arguments

The following recommended practices should help you plan indexes effectively:

- Create indexes on columns that join tables, including primary keys or foreign keys.

- Create unique indexes to enforce uniqueness in a column or group of columns.

- Review your indexes and drop those that are not being used. Indexes require disk space and time to maintain them. Databases with high data insert activity should have fewer indexes. Databases with high read activity should have more indexes.

- Avoid including unnecessary columns in the clustered index. When possible, use small data types, such as **varchar** instead of **char**.

- Consider using a clustered index to support sorting and range searches. When you optimize a table for data retrieval, the clustered index should support the retrieval of groups of records. Select the column or columns for the clustering key that sorts data in a frequently needed order or that groups records that must be accessed together.

- Create indexes that support the search arguments of common queries. Highly selective columns are good candidates for indexes. Columns with high density are poor candidates for indexes.

Lab A: Determining the Indexes of a Table

Objectives

After completing this lab, you will be able to:

- Use the **sp_help** system stored procedure to determine the index structure of a table.

- Query the **sysindexes** table to identify the index structure of a table.

Prerequisites

Before working on this lab, you must have script files for this lab, which are located in C:\Moc\2073A\Labfiles\L06.

Lab Setup

To complete this lab, you must have either:

- Completed the prior lab, or

- Executed the C:\Moc\2073A\Batches\Restore06.cmd batch file.

  This command file restores the **credit** database to a state required for this lab.

For More Information

If you require help in executing files, search SQL Query Analyzer Help for "Execute a query".

Other resources that you can use include:

- The **credit** database schema.

- Microsoft SQL Server Books Online.

Scenario

The organization of the classroom is meant to simulate that of a worldwide trading firm named Northwind Traders. Its fictitious domain name is nwtraders.msft. The primary DNS server for nwtraders.msft is the instructor computer, which has an Internet Protocol (IP) address of 192.168.*x*.200 (where *x* is the assigned classroom number). The name of the instructor computer is London.

The following table provides the user name, computer name, and IP address for each student computer in the fictitious nwtraders.msft domain. Find the user name for your computer, and make a note of it.

User name	Computer name	IP address
SQLAdmin1	Vancouver	192.168.*x*.1
SQLAdmin2	Denver	192.168.*x*.2
SQLAdmin3	Perth	192.168.*x*.3
SQLAdmin4	Brisbane	192.168.*x*.4
SQLAdmin5	Lisbon	192.168.*x*.5
SQLAdmin6	Bonn	192.168.*x*.6
SQLAdmin7	Lima	192.168.*x*.7
SQLAdmin8	Santiago	192.168.*x*.8
SQLAdmin9	Bangalore	192.168.*x*.9
SQLAdmin10	Singapore	192.168.*x*.10
SQLAdmin11	Casablanca	192.168.*x*.11
SQLAdmin12	Tunis	192.168.*x*.12
SQLAdmin13	Acapulco	192.168.*x*.13
SQLAdmin14	Miami	192.168.*x*.14
SQLAdmin15	Auckland	192.168.*x*.15
SQLAdmin16	Suva	192.168.*x*.16
SQLAdmin17	Stockholm	192.168.*x*.17
SQLAdmin18	Moscow	192.168.*x*.18
SQLAdmin19	Caracas	192.168.*x*.19
SQLAdmin20	Montevideo	192.168.*x*.20
SQLAdmin21	Manila	192.168.*x*.21
SQLAdmin22	Tokyo	192.168.*x*.22
SQLAdmin23	Khartoum	192.168.*x*.23
SQLAdmin24	Nairobi	192.168.*x*.24

Estimated time to complete this lab: 15 minutes

Exercise 1
Identifying Indexes Using sp_help

In this exercise, you will use the **sp_help** system stored procedure to determine the index structure of a table.

► To use sp_help

In this procedure, you will use the **sp_help** system stored procedure to determine the name, type, and key columns of the indexes on a table.

1. Log on to the **NWTraders** classroom domain by using the information in the following table.

Option	Value
User name	**SQLAdmin***x* (where *x* corresponds to your computer name as designated in the nwtraders.msft classroom domain)
Password	**password**

2. Open SQL Query Analyzer and, if requested, log in to the (local) server with Microsoft Windows® Authentication.

   You have permission to log in to and administer SQL Server because you are logged as **SQLAdmin***x*, which is a member of the Microsoft Windows 2000 local group, Administrators. All members of this group are automatically mapped to the SQL Server **sysadmin** role.

3. In the **DB** list, click **credit**.

4. Open C:\Moc\2073A\Labfiles\L06\Inspect_corporation.sql, and then review and execute it.

   This script will use **sp_help** to return information about the **corporation** table. This stored procedure returns nine grids of data.

5. Navigate to the sixth grid, called **index_name**.

   What are the names of the indexes on the **corporation** table?

   _____

   _____

   Is the primary key of the **corporation** table a clustered or a nonclustered index?

   _____

   _____

Exercise 2
Viewing Entries in the sysindexes Table

In this exercise, you will query the **sysindexes** system table and identify indexes.

▶ **To view the sysindexes system table**

In this procedure, you will execute a script that queries the **sysindexes** system table.

1. Open C:\Moc\2073A\Labfiles\L06\Inspect_sysindexes.sql, and then review and execute it.

    This script will query the **sysobjects** and **sysindexes** tables for user-created tables, sorted by the table name.

    Which tables do not have a clustered index? How can you tell?

    _____

    _____

    What type of indexes does the **corporation** table have?

    _____

    _____

2. Review the column names in the **sysindexes** table.

    How many rows are in the **member** table? How many pages are used?

    _____

    _____

    How does SQL Server locate the root of an index or the first IAM page in a heap?

    _____

    _____

Review

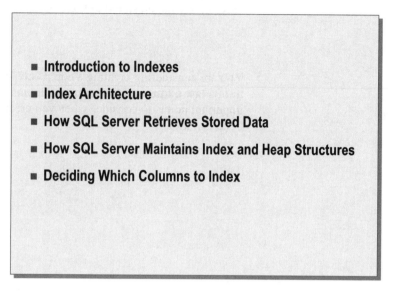

- Introduction to Indexes
- Index Architecture
- How SQL Server Retrieves Stored Data
- How SQL Server Maintains Index and Heap Structures
- Deciding Which Columns to Index

1. If a customer table has no indexes, how does SQL Server find the row for a customer named Eva Corets?

2. How many clustered indexes can be created for a table?

3. How does a nonclustered index identify the parent rows when a table has a clustered index? How does a nonclustered index identify the data rows when a table does *not* have a clustered index?

4. The expansion of a field that is not included in an index causes a page split. This page split has moved the row to a new page. What is the impact of this move on the nonclustered indexes in the table?

5. You are considering creating a composite, clustered index on the **company name**, **last name**, and **first name** columns of a table. What are some important points to consider when you create the index, and why? Is there a better solution?

Microsoft®
Training &
Certification

Module 7: Creating and Maintaining Indexes

Contents

Microsoft®

Project Lead: Rich Rose
Instructional Designers: Rich Rose, Cheryl Hoople, Marilyn McGill
Instructional Software Design Engineers: Karl Dehmer, Carl Raebler, Rick Byham
Technical Lead: Karl Dehmer
Subject Matter Experts: Karl Dehmer, Carl Raebler, Rick Byham
Graphic Artist: Kirsten Larson (Independent Contractor)
Editing Manager: Lynette Skinner
Editor: Wendy Cleary
Copy Editor: Edward McKillop (S&T Consulting)
Production Manager: Miracle Davis
Production Coordinator: Jenny Boe
Production Support: Lori Walker (S&T Consulting)
Test Manager: Sid Benavente
Courseware Testing: TestingTesting123
Classroom Automation: Lorrin Smith-Bates
Creative Director, Media/Sim Services: David Mahlmann
Web Development Lead: Lisa Pease
CD Build Specialist: Julie Challenger
Online Support: David Myka (S&T Consulting)
Localization Manager: Rick Terek
Operations Coordinator: John Williams
Manufacturing Support: Laura King; Kathy Hershey
Lead Product Manager, Release Management: Bo Galford
Lead Product Manager, Data Base: Margo Crandall
Group Manager, Courseware Infrastructure: David Bramble
Group Product Manager, Content Development: Dean Murray
General Manager: Robert Stewart

Overview

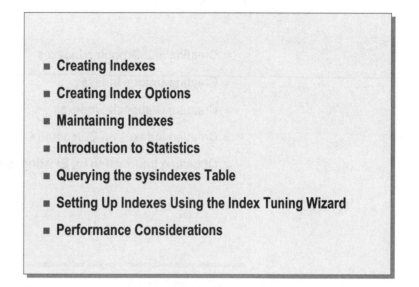

- **Creating Indexes**
- **Creating Index Options**
- **Maintaining Indexes**
- **Introduction to Statistics**
- **Querying the sysindexes Table**
- **Setting Up Indexes Using the Index Tuning Wizard**
- **Performance Considerations**

When you program a database, you want to create useful indexes that enable you to quickly gain access to data. By using Microsoft® Windows® 2000, you can create and maintain indexes and statistics. When you use the Index Tuning Wizard, Microsoft SQL Server™ 2000 creates indexes, analyzes your queries, and determines the indexes that you should create.

After completing this module, you will be able to:

- Create indexes and indexed views with unique or composite characteristics.
- Use the CREATE INDEX options.
- Describe how to maintain indexes over time.
- Describe how the query optimizer creates, stores, maintains, and uses statistics to optimize queries.
- Query the **sysindexes** table.
- Describe how the Index Tuning Wizard works and when to use it.
- Describe performance considerations that affect creating and maintaining indexes.

◆ Creating Indexes

- **Creating and Dropping Indexes**
- **Creating Unique Indexes**
- **Creating Composite Indexes**
- **Creating Indexes on Computed Columns**
- **Obtaining Information on Existing Indexes**

Now that you are familiar with the different index architectures, we will discuss creating and dropping indexes and obtaining information on existing indexes.

Creating and Dropping Indexes

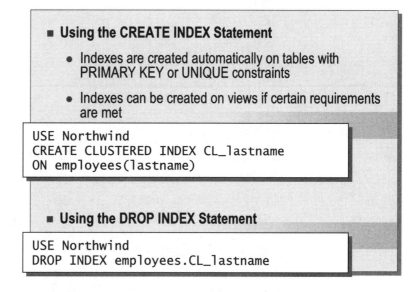

- **Using the CREATE INDEX Statement**
  - Indexes are created automatically on tables with PRIMARY KEY or UNIQUE constraints
  - Indexes can be created on views if certain requirements are met

```
USE Northwind
CREATE CLUSTERED INDEX CL_lastname
ON employees(lastname)
```

- **Using the DROP INDEX Statement**

```
USE Northwind
DROP INDEX employees.CL_lastname
```

You create indexes by using the CREATE INDEX statement and can remove them by using the DROP INDEX statement.

Note   You must be the table owner to execute either statement in a database.

Using the CREATE INDEX Statement

Use the CREATE INDEX statement to create indexes. You also can use the Create Index Wizard in SQL Server Enterprise Manager. When you create an index on one or more columns in a table, consider the following facts and guidelines:

- SQL Server automatically creates indexes when a PRIMARY KEY or UNIQUE constraint is created on a table. Defining a PRIMARY KEY or UNIQUE constraint is preferred over creating standard indexes.

- You must be the table owner to execute the CREATE INDEX statement.

- Indexes can be created on views.

- SQL Server stores index information in the **sysindexes** system table.

- Before you create an index on a column, determine whether indexes already exist on that column.

- Keep your indexes small by defining them on columns that are small in size. Typically, smaller indexes are more efficient than indexes with larger key values.

- Select columns on the basis of uniqueness so that each key value identifies a small number of rows.

- When you create a clustered index, all existing nonclustered indexes are rebuilt.

Syntax

```
CREATE [ UNIQUE ] [ CLUSTERED | NONCLUSTERED ]
INDEX index_name ON { table | view } ( column [ ASC | DESC ] [ ,...n ] )
[WITH
[PAD_INDEX ]
[[,] FILLFACTOR = fillfactor ]
[[,] IGNORE_DUP_KEY ]
[[,] DROP_EXISTING ]
[[,] STATISTICS_NORECOMPUTE ]
[[,] SORT_IN_TEMPDB ]
]
[ON filegroup ]
```

Example 1

This example creates a clustered index on the **LastName** column in the **Employees** table.

```
CREATE CLUSTERED INDEX CL_lastname
  ON employees(lastname)
```

Using the DROP INDEX Statement

Use the DROP INDEX statement to remove an index on a table. When you drop an index, consider the following facts:

- SQL Server reclaims disk space that is occupied by the index when you execute the DROP INDEX statement.

- You cannot use the DROP INDEX statement on indexes that are created by PRIMARY KEY or UNIQUE constraints. You must drop the constraint in order to drop these indexes.

- When you drop a table, all indexes for that table are also dropped.

- When you drop a clustered index, all nonclustered indexes on the table are rebuilt automatically.

- You must be in the database in which an index resides in order to drop that index.

- The DROP INDEX statement cannot be used on system tables.

Syntax

DROP INDEX 'table.index | view.index' [, ...n]

Example 2

This example drops the **cl_lastname** index from the **Member** table.

```
USE Northwind
DROP INDEX employees.CL_lastname
```

Creating Unique Indexes

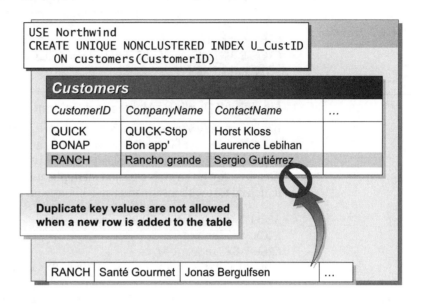

```
USE Northwind
CREATE UNIQUE NONCLUSTERED INDEX U_CustID
    ON customers(CustomerID)
```

Customers

CustomerID	CompanyName	ContactName	...
QUICK	QUICK-Stop	Horst Kloss	
BONAP	Bon app'	Laurence Lebihan	
RANCH	Rancho grande	Sergio Gutiérrez	

Duplicate key values are not allowed when a new row is added to the table

| RANCH | Santé Gourmet | Jonas Bergulfsen | ... |

A *unique* index ensures that all data in an indexed column is unique and does not contain duplicate values.

Unique indexes ensure that data in indexed columns is unique. If the table has a PRIMARY KEY or UNIQUE constraint, SQL Server automatically creates a unique index when you execute the CREATE TABLE or ALTER TABLE statement.

Ensuring That Data in Indexed Columns Is Unique

Create a unique index for clustered or nonclustered indexes when the data itself is inherently unique.

However, if uniqueness must be enforced, create PRIMARY KEY or UNIQUE constraints on the column rather than creating a unique index. When you create a unique index, consider the following facts and guidelines:

- SQL Server automatically creates unique indexes on columns in a table defined with PRIMARY KEY or UNIQUE constraints.

- If a table contains data, SQL Server checks for duplicate values when you create the index.

- SQL Server checks for duplicate values each time that you use the INSERT or UPDATE statement. If duplicate key values exist, SQL Server cancels your statement and returns an error message with the first duplicate.

- Ensure that each row has a unique value—no two rows can have the same identification number if a unique index is created on that column. This regulation ensures that each entity is identified uniquely.

- Create unique indexes only on columns in which entity integrity can be enforced. For example, you would not create a unique index on the **LastName** column of the **Employees** table because some employees may have the same last names.

Example 1

This example creates a unique, nonclustered index named **U_CustID** on the **Customers** table. The index is built on the **CustomerID** column. The value in the **CustomerID** column must be a unique value for each row of the table.

```
USE Northwind
CREATE UNIQUE NONCLUSTERED INDEX U_CustID
  ON customers(CustomerID)
```

Finding All Duplicate Values in a Column

If duplicate key values exist when you create a unique index, the CREATE INDEX statement fails. SQL Server returns an error message with the first duplicate, but other duplicate values may exist, as well. Use the following sample script on any table to find all duplicate values in a column. Replace the italicized text with information specific to your query.

```
SELECT index_col, COUNT (index_col)
FROM tablename
GROUP BY index_col
HAVING COUNT(index_col)>1 ORDER BY index_col
```

Example 2

This example determines whether duplicate customer identification exists in the **CustomerID** column in the **Customers** table. If so, SQL Server returns the customer identification and number of duplicate entries in the result set.

```
SELECT CustomerID, COUNT(CustomerID) AS '# of Duplicates'
FROM Northwind.dbo.Customers
GROUP BY CustomerID
HAVING COUNT(CustomerID)>1
ORDER BY CustomerID
```

Result

CustomerID	# of Duplicates

```
(0 row(s) affected)
```

Creating Composite Indexes

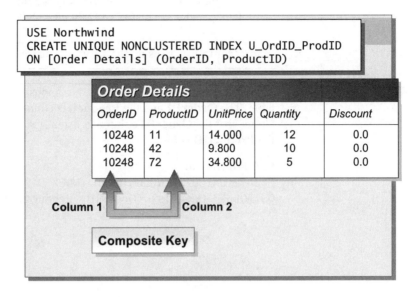

```
USE Northwind
CREATE UNIQUE NONCLUSTERED INDEX U_OrdID_ProdID
ON [Order Details] (OrderID, ProductID)
```

Order Details

OrderID	ProductID	UnitPrice	Quantity	Discount
10248	11	14.000	12	0.0
10248	42	9.800	10	0.0
10248	72	34.800	5	0.0

Column 1   Column 2

Composite Key

Composite indexes specify more than one column as the key value. You create composite indexes:

- When two or more columns are best searched as a key.

- If queries reference only the columns in the index.

For example, a telephone directory is a good example of where a composite index would be useful. The directory is organized by last names. Within the last names, it is organized by first names, because entries with the same last name often exist.

When you create a composite index, consider the following facts and guidelines:

- You can combine as many as 16 columns into a single composite index. The sum of the lengths of the columns that make up the composite index cannot exceed 900 bytes.

- All columns in a composite index must be from the same table, except when an index is created on a view.

- Define the most unique column first. The first column defined in the CREATE INDEX statement is referred to as the *highest order*.

- The WHERE clause of a query must reference the first column of the composite index for the query optimizer to use the composite index.

- An index on (**column1**, **column2**) is not the same as an index on (**column2**, **column1**)—each has a distinct column order. The column that contains more selective data or that would return the lowest percentage of rows often determines the column order.

- Composite indexes are useful for tables with multiple column keys.

- Use composite indexes to increase query performance and reduce the number of indexes that you create on a table.

Note   Multiple indexes on the same columns are typically not useful.

Example

This example creates a nonclustered, composite index on the **Order Details** table. The **OrderID** and the **ProductID** columns are the composite key values. Notice that the **OrderID** column is listed first because it is more selective than the **ProductID** column.

```
USE Northwind
CREATE UNIQUE NONCLUSTERED INDEX U_OrdID_ProdID
ON [Order Details] (OrderID, ProductID)
```

Creating Indexes on Computed Columns

■ **You Can Create Indexes on Computed Columns When:**

- Computed_column_expression is deterministic and precise
- ANSI_NULL connection-level option is ON
- Computed column cannot evaluate to the **text, ntext**, or **image** data types
- Required SET options are set ON when you create the index and when INSERT, UPDATE, or DELETE statements change the index value
- NUMERIC_ROUNDABORT option is set OFF

■ **Query Optimizer May Ignore an Index on a Computed Column**

You can create indexes on computed columns when:

■ The computed_column_expression is *deterministic*. Deterministic expressions always return the same result.

■ The ANSI_NULL connection-level option is ON when the CREATE TABLE statement is executed. The OBJECTPROPERTY function reports whether the option is on through the **IsAnsiNullsOn** property.

■ The computed_column_expression that is defined for the computed column cannot evaluate the **text, ntext**, or **image** data types.

■ The connection on which the index is created, and all connections attempting INSERT, UPDATE, or DELETE statements that will change values in the index, have six SET options set ON and one option set OFF. These options must be set on:

- ANSI_NULLS
- ANSI_PADDING
- ANSI_WARNINGS
- ARITHABORT
- CONCAT_NULL_YIELDS_NULL
- QUOTED_IDENTIFIER

■ In addition to these ON settings, the NUMERIC_ROUNDABORT option must be set OFF.

Note The query optimizer ignores an index on a computed column for any SELECT statement that is executed by a connection that does not have these same option settings.

Obtaining Information on Existing Indexes

- **Using the sp_helpindex System Stored Procedure**

```
USE Northwind
EXEC sp_helpindex Customers
```

- **Using the sp_help *tablename* System Stored Procedure**

You may require information about existing indexes before you create, modify, or remove an index.

Using the sp_helpindex System Stored Procedure

You can use SQL Server Enterprise Manager or execute the **sp_helpindex** system stored procedure to obtain index information, such as index name, type, and options for a specific table.

Example

This example lists the indexes on the **Customers** table.

```
USE Northwind
EXEC sp_helpindex Customers
```

Result

index_name	index_description	index_keys
PK_Customers	clustered, unique, Primary Key located on PRIMARY	CustomerID
PostalCode	nonclustered located on PRIMARY	PostalCode
City	nonclustered located on PRIMARY	City

```
(1 row(s) affected)
```

Using the sp_help *tablename* System Stored Procedure

You can also execute the **sp_help** *tablename* system stored procedure to obtain information on indexes, as well as other table information.

◆ Creating Index Options

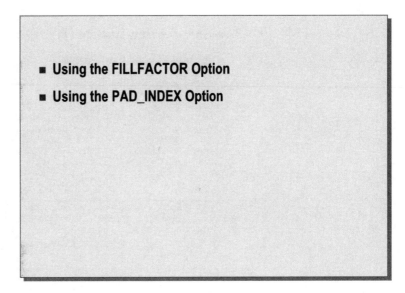

- ■ Using the FILLFACTOR Option
- ■ Using the PAD_INDEX Option

SQL Server offers creating index options that can speed up index creation and also enhance index performance over time.

Using the FILLFACTOR Option

- **Specifies How Much to Fill the Page**
- **Impacts Leaf-Level Pages**

Data Pages Full

Con ... 470401	Akhtar ... 470601	Martin ... 470801
Funk ... 470402	Funk ... 470602	Phua ... 470802
White ... 470403	Smith ... 470603	Jones ... 470803
Rudd ... 470501	Martin ... 470604	Smith ... 470804
White ... 470502	Smith ... 470701	Ganio ... 470901
Barr ... 470503	Ota ... 470702	Jones ... 470902

Fillfactor 50 = Leaf Pages 50% Full

Con ... 470401	Rudd ... 470501	Akhtar ... 470601	Martin ... 470604	Martin ... 470801	Smith ... 470804
Funk ... 470402	White ... 470502	Funk ... 470402	Smith ... 470701	Phua ... 470802	Ganio ... 470901
White ... 470403	Barr ... 470503	Smith ... 470603	Ota ... 470702	Jones ... 470803	White ... 470902

You can use the FILLFACTOR option to optimize the performance of INSERT and UPDATE statements on tables that contain clustered or nonclustered indexes.

When an index page becomes full, SQL Server must take time to split the page to make room for new rows. Use the FILLFACTOR option to allocate a percentage of free space on the leaf-level index pages to reduce page splitting.

Note The FILLFACTOR option is applied only when the index is created or rebuilt. SQL Server does not dynamically maintain the specified percentage of allocated space on the index pages.

The fillfactor value that you specify on a table depends on how often data is modified (INSERT and UPDATE statements) and your organization's environment. Generally, you should:

- Use a low fillfactor value for online transaction processing (OLTP) environments.
- Use a high fillfactor value for SQL Server Analysis Services environments.

The following table shows the FILLFACTOR option settings and the typical environments in which these fillfactor values are used.

FILLFACTOR percentage	Leaf-level pages	Non-leaf-level pages	Activity on key values	Typical business environment
0 (default)	Fill completely	Leave room for one index entry	None to light modification	Analysis Services
1–99	Fill to specified percentage	Leave room for one index entry	Moderate to heavy modification	Mixed or OLTP
100	Fill completely	Leave room for one index entry	None to light modification	Analysis Services

When you use the FILLFACTOR option, consider the following facts and guidelines:

- Fillfactor values range from 1 to 100 percent.

- The default fillfactor value is 0. This value fills the leaf-level index pages to 100 percent and leaves room for the maximum size of one index entry in the non-leaf-level index pages. You cannot explicitly specify fillfactor = 0.

- You can change the default fillfactor value at the server level by using the **sp_configure** system stored procedure.

- The **sysindexes** system table stores the fillfactor value that was last applied, along with other index information.

- The fillfactor value is specified in percentages. The percentage determines how much the leaf-level pages should be filled. For example, a fillfactor of 65 percent fills the leaf-level pages 65 percent, leaving 35 percent of the page space free for new rows. The size of the row has an impact on how many rows can fit into or fill the page for the specified fillfactor percentage.

- Use the FILLFACTOR option on tables into which many rows are inserted, or when clustered index key values are frequently modified.

Using the PAD_INDEX Option

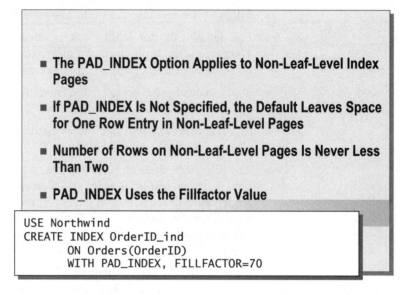

■ The PAD_INDEX Option Applies to Non-Leaf-Level Index Pages

■ If PAD_INDEX Is Not Specified, the Default Leaves Space for One Row Entry in Non-Leaf-Level Pages

■ Number of Rows on Non-Leaf-Level Pages Is Never Less Than Two

■ PAD_INDEX Uses the Fillfactor Value

```
USE Northwind
CREATE INDEX OrderID_ind
    ON Orders(OrderID)
        WITH PAD_INDEX, FILLFACTOR=70
```

The PAD_INDEX option specifies the percentage to which to fill the non-leaf-level index pages. You can use the PAD_INDEX option only when FILLFACTOR is specified, because the PAD_INDEX percentage value is determined by the percentage value specified for FILLFACTOR.

The following table shows the impact of FILLFACTOR option settings when you use the PAD_INDEX option, and the typical environment in which PAD_INDEX values are used.

FILLFACTOR percentage	Leaf-level pages	Non-leaf-level pages	Activity on key values	Typical business environment
1–99	Fill to specified percentage	Fill to specified percentage	Moderate to heavy modification	OLTP

When you use the PAD_INDEX option, consider the following facts:

■ SQL Server applies the percentage that the FILLFACTOR option specifies to the leaf-level and non-leaf-level pages.

■ By default, SQL Server always leaves enough room to accommodate at least one row of the maximum index size for each non-leaf-level page, regardless of how high the fillfactor value is.

■ The number of items on the non-leaf-level index page is never fewer than two, regardless of how low the fillfactor value is.

■ PAD_INDEX uses the fillfactor value.

Example

This example creates the **OrderID_ind** index on the **OrdersID** column in the **Orders** table. By specifying the PAD_INDEX option with the FILLFACTOR option, SQL Server creates leaf-level and non-leaf-level pages that are 70 percent full. However, if you do not use the PAD_INDEX option, the leaf-level pages are 70 percent full, and the non-leaf-level pages are almost completely filled.

```
USE Northwind
CREATE INDEX OrderID_ind
  ON Orders(OrderID)
  WITH PAD_INDEX, FILLFACTOR=70
```

◆ Maintaining Indexes

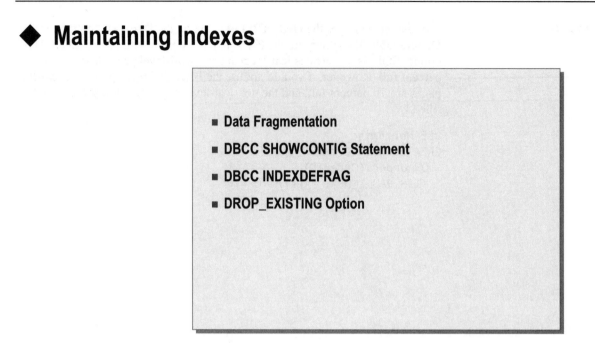

- Data Fragmentation
- DBCC SHOWCONTIG Statement
- DBCC INDEXDEFRAG
- DROP_EXISTING Option

You must maintain indexes after you create them to ensure optimal performance. Over time, data becomes fragmented. You manage data fragmentation according to your organization's environment.

SQL Server provides an Index Tuning Wizard that tracks the usage of your indexes automatically and assists with maintaining and creating indexes that perform optimally.

You also can use various options and tools to help you rebuild indexes and verify index optimization.

Data Fragmentation

- **How Fragmentation Occurs**
  - SQL Server reorganizes index pages when data is modified
  - Reorganization causes index pages to split
- **Methods of Managing Fragmentation**
  - Drop and recreate an index and specify a fillfactor value
  - Rebuild an index and specify a fillfactor value
- **Business Environment**
  - Data fragmentation can be good for OLTP environment
  - Data fragmentation can be bad for Analysis Services environment

---

Depending on your business environment, fragmentation can be either good or bad for performance.

How Fragmentation Occurs

Fragmentation occurs when data is modified. For example, when rows of data are added to or deleted from a table, or when values in the indexed columns are changed, SQL Server adjusts the index pages to accommodate the changes and to maintain the storage of the indexed data. The adjustment of the index pages is known as a *page split*. The splitting process increases the size of a table and the time that is needed to process queries.

Methods of Managing Fragmentation

There are two methods of managing fragmentation in SQL Server. The first method is to drop and recreate a clustered index and to specify a fillfactor value by using the FILLFACTOR option. The second method is to rebuild an index and specify a fillfactor value.

Business Environment

The degree of fragmentation that is acceptable in your database depends on your environment:

- In an OLTP environment, fragmentation can be beneficial, because an OLTP environment is write-intensive. A typical OLTP system has large numbers of concurrent users who are actively adding and modifying data.

- Fragmentation can be detrimental in an Analysis Services environment because that environment is read-intensive.

DBCC SHOWCONTIG Statement

- **What DBCC SHOWCONTIG Determines**
  - Whether a table or index is heavily fragmented
  - Whether data and index pages are full
- **When to Execute**
  - If tables have been heavily modified
  - If tables contain imported data
  - If tables seem to cause poor query performance

The DBCC SHOWCONTIG statement displays fragmentation information on the data and indexes of a specified table.

What DBCC SHOWCONTIG Statement Determines

When you execute the DBCC SHOWCONTIG statement, SQL Server goes across the index pages at the leaf level to determine whether a table or specified index is heavily fragmented. The DBCC SHOWCONTIG statement also determines whether the data and index pages are full.

When to Execute

Execute the DBCC SHOWCONTIG statement on heavily modified tables, tables that contain imported data, or tables that seem to cause poor query performance. When you execute the DBCC SHOWCONTIG statement, consider the following facts and guidelines:

- SQL Server requires you to reference either a table or index ID when you execute the DBCC SHOWCONTIG statement. Query the **sysindexes** table to obtain the table or index ID.

- Determine how often you should execute the DBCC SHOWCONTIG statement. Measure the activity level on a table on a daily, weekly, or monthly basis.

The following table describes the statistics that the DBCC SHOWCONTIG statement returns.

Statistic	Description
Pages scanned	Number of pages in the table or index.
Extents scanned	Number of extents in the table or index.
Extent switches	Number of times that the DBCC statement left an extent while it was traversing the pages of the extent.
Average pages per extent	Number of pages per extent in the page chain.
Scan density [Best Count: Actual Count]	The number in scan density is 100 (a percentage) if everything is contiguous; if it is below 100, some fragmentation exists. Best Count is the ideal number of extent changes that would be present if everything were contiguously linked. Actual Count is the actual number of extent changes.
Logical scan fragmentation	Percentage of out-of-order pages returned from scanning the leaf pages of an index. This number is not relevant to heaps and text indexes. An out-of-order page is one for which the next page indicated in an Index Allocation Map (IAM) is a different page than the page pointed to by the next-page pointer in the leaf page.
Extent scan fragmentation	Percentage of out-of-order extents in scanning the leaf pages of an index. This number is not relevant to heaps. An out-of-order extent is one for which the extent containing the current page for an index is not the next physical extent—after the extent containing the previous page for an index.
Average bytes free per page	Average number of free bytes on the scanned pages. The higher the number, the less full the pages are—lower numbers are better. Be aware, however, that this number is also affected by row size. A large row size may result in a higher number.
Average page density (full)	Value that shows the fullness of a page. This value considers row size, so it is a more accurate indication of the fullness of a page. Higher percentages are better than lower percentages.

Syntax

```
DBCC SHOWCONTIG
[({table_name | table_id | view_name | view_id }
[, index_name | index_id ] )]
[ WITH
{ ALL_INDEXES | FAST
[, ALL_INDEXES ] | TABLERESULTS
[, { ALL_INDEXES } ]
[, { FAST | ALL_LEVELS } ]
      }
]
```

Example

This example executes a statement that accesses the **Customers** table.

```
USE Northwind
DBCC SHOWCONTIG (Customers, PK_Customers)
```

Result

```
DBCC SHOWCONTIG scanning 'Customers' table...
Table: 'Customers' (2073058421); index ID: 1, database ID: 6
TABLE level scan performed.
Pages Scanned:                              3
Extents Scanned:                            2
Extent Switches:                            1
Avg. Pages per Extent:                      1.5
Scan Density [Best Count:Actual Count]:     50.00% [1:2]
Logical Scan Fragmentation                  0.00%
Extent Scan Fragmentation:                  50.00%
Avg. Bytes Free per Page:                   246.7
Avg. Page Density (full):                   96.95%
DBCC execution completed. If DBCC printed error messages,
contact your system administrator.
```

DBCC INDEXDEFRAG Statement

- **DBCC INDEXDEFRAG**
  - Defragments the leaf level of an index
  - Arranges leaf-level pages so that the physical order of the pages matches the left-to-right logical order
  - Improves index-scanning performance
- **Index Defragmenting vs. Index Rebuilding**

As data in a table changes, the indexes on the table sometimes become *fragmented*. The DBCC INDEXDEFRAG statement can *defragment* the leaf level of clustered and nonclustered indexes on tables and views. Defragmenting arranges the pages so that the physical order of the pages matches the left-to-right logical order of the leaf nodes. This rearrangement improves index-scanning performance.

Using the DBCC INDEXDEFRAG Statement

When you use DBCC INDEXDEFRAG, it:

- Compacts the pages of an index, taking into account the FILLFACTOR specified when the index was created. Any empty pages created as a result of this compaction will be removed.
- Defragments one file at a time when an index spans more than one file. Pages do not migrate between files.
- Reports to the user an estimated percentage completed. Reporting is done every five minutes. The DBCC INDEXDEFRAG statement can be terminated at any point in the process, and any completed work is retained.
- Is an online operation. It does not hold locks for an extended time, and does not block running queries or updates. Defragmentation is always fully logged, regardless of the database recovery model setting.

Index Defragmenting vs. Index Rebuilding

The time required to defragment is related to the amount of fragmentation. A very fragmented index might require more time to defragment than to rebuild. A relatively unfragmented index defragments faster than rebuilding a new index.

Note Using the DBCC INDEXDEFRAG statement does not improve performance when indexes are physically defragmented on disk. To physically defragment an index, rebuild the index.

Syntax

```
DBCC INDEXDEFRAG
    ( { database_name | database_id | 0 }
        , { table_name | table_id | 'view_name' | view_id }
        , { index_name | index_id }
    )  [ WITH NO_INFOMSGS ]
```

Example

This example executes the DBCC INDEXDEFRAG statement on the **mem_no_CL** index of the **Member** table in the **credit** database.

```
DBCC INDEXDEFRAG(credit, member, mem_no_CL)
```

Result

Pages scanned	Pages moved	Pages removed
150	28	9

```
(1 row(s) affected)
```

DROP_EXISTING Option

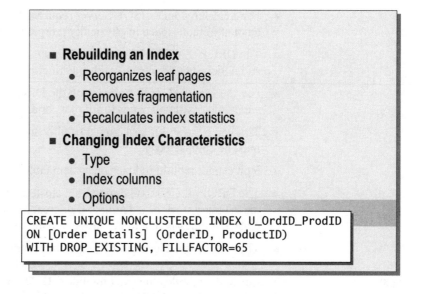

Use the DROP_EXISTING option to change the characteristics of an index or to rebuild indexes without having to drop the index and recreate it. The benefit of using the DROP_EXISTING option is that you can modify indexes created with PRIMARY KEY or UNIQUE constraints.

Rebuilding an Index

Execute the CREATE INDEX statement with the DROP_EXISTING option to rebuild a named clustered or nonclustered index:

- Reorganize the leaf-level pages by compressing or expanding rows

- Remove fragmentation

- Recalculate the index statistics

Changing Index Characteristics

When you use the DROP_EXISTING option, you can change the following index characteristics:

- Type
  - You can change a nonclustered index into a clustered index.
  - You cannot change a clustered index into a nonclustered index.
- Index columns
  - You can change the index definition to specify different columns.
  - You can specify additional columns or remove specified columns from a composite index.
  - You can change the index columns to be unique or not unique.
- Options
  - You can change the FILLFACTOR or PAD INDEX percentage value.

When you use the DROP_EXISTING option, consider the following facts and guidelines:

- For a clustered index, SQL Server requires that you have 1.2 times the amount of table space to physically reorganize the data.

- The DROP_EXISTING option accelerates the process of building clustered and nonclustered indexes by eliminating the sorting process.

- Use the FILLFACTOR option with the DROP_EXISTING option if you want your leaf-level pages to fill to a certain percentage.

  This can be useful if space must be allocated for new data or if the index must be compacted.

- You cannot rebuild indexes on system tables.

- The DROP_EXISTING option on a clustered index helps you avoid the unnecessary work of deleting and re-creating nonclustered indexes if the clustered index is rebuilt on the same column.

- The nonclustered indexes are rebuilt once, and only if the keys are different.

Example

This example rebuilds the existing index, **U_OrdID_ProdID** , for the **Order Details** table. The index is redefined as a clustered, composite index with a specified option of filling each data page to 65 percent. This statement will fail if a clustered index already exists on the **Order Details** table.

```
CREATE UNIQUE NONCLUSTERED INDEX U_OrdID_ProdID
ON [Order Details] (OrderID, ProductID)
WITH DROP_EXISTING, FILLFACTOR=65
```

Lab A: Creating and Maintaining Indexes

Objectives

After completing this lab, you will be able to:

- Create indexes.

- Determine the size and density of indexes.

Prerequisites

Before working on this lab, you must have:

- Script files for this lab, which are located in C:\Moc\2073A\Labfiles\L07.

- Answer files for this lab, which are located in
  C:\Moc\2073A\Labfiles\L07\Answers.

Lab Setup

To complete this lab, you must have either:

- Completed the prior lab, or

- Executed the C:\Moc\2073A\Batches\Restore07A.cmd batch file.

  This command file restores the **ClassNorthwind** database to a state required
  for this lab.

For More Information

If you require help with executing files, search SQL Query Analyzer Help for
"Execute a query".

Other resources that you can use include:

- The **Northwind** database schema.

- The **credit** database schema.

- Microsoft SQL Server Books Online.

Scenario

The organization of the classroom is meant to simulate that of a worldwide trading firm named Northwind Traders. Its fictitious domain name is nwtraders.msft. The primary DNS server for nwtraders.msft is the instructor computer, which has an Internet Protocol (IP) address of 192.168.x.200 (where x is the assigned classroom number). The name of the instructor computer is London.

The following table provides the user name, computer name, and IP address for each student computer in the fictitious **nwtraders.msft** domain. Find the user name for your computer, and make a note of it.

User name	Computer name	IP address
SQLAdmin1	Vancouver	192.168.x.1
SQLAdmin2	Denver	192.168.x.2
SQLAdmin3	Perth	192.168.x.3
SQLAdmin4	Brisbane	192.168.x.4
SQLAdmin5	Lisbon	192.168.x.5
SQLAdmin6	Bonn	192.168.x.6
SQLAdmin7	Lima	192.168.x.7
SQLAdmin8	Santiago	192.168.x.8
SQLAdmin9	Bangalore	192.168.x.9
SQLAdmin10	Singapore	192.168.x.10
SQLAdmin11	Casablanca	192.168.x.11
SQLAdmin12	Tunis	192.168.x.12
SQLAdmin13	Acapulco	192.168.x.13
SQLAdmin14	Miami	192.168.x.14
SQLAdmin15	Auckland	192.168.x.15
SQLAdmin16	Suva	192.168.x.16
SQLAdmin17	Stockholm	192.168.x.17
SQLAdmin18	Moscow	192.168.x.18
SQLAdmin19	Caracas	192.168.x.19
SQLAdmin20	Montevideo	192.168.x.20
SQLAdmin21	Manila	192.168.x.21
SQLAdmin22	Tokyo	192.168.x.22
SQLAdmin23	Khartoum	192.168.x.23
SQLAdmin24	Nairobi	192.168.x.24

Estimated time to complete this lab: 30 minutes

Exercise 1
Creating Indexes

In this exercise, you will create several indexes to complement FOREIGN KEY constraints on tables in the **ClassNorthwind** database.

▶ To create an index on the Orders table

In this procedure, you will open a script file that creates an index, review the contents of the script, execute it, and then verify that the index was created.

1. Log on to the **NWTraders** classroom domain by using the information in the following table.

Option	Value
User name	**SQLAdmin**x (where *x* corresponds to your computer name as designated in the **nwtraders.msft** classroom domain)
Password	**password**

2. Open SQL Query Analyzer and, if requested, log in to the (local) server with Microsoft Windows Authentication.

   You have permission to log in to and administer SQL Server because you are logged as **SQLAdmin**x, which is a member of the Windows 2000 local group, Administrators. All members of this group are automatically mapped to the SQL Server **sysadmin** role.

3. In the **DB** list, click **ClassNorthwind**.

4. Open the C:\Moc\2073A\Labfiles\L07\CreaIndx1.sql script file.

5. Review the CREATE INDEX statement.

   This script creates a nonclustered index named **Orders_Customers_link** on the **CustomerID** column in the **Orders** table with a fillfactor value of 75.

6. Execute the script file.

7. Verify that the **Orders_Customers_link** index was created by executing the following statement:

   ```
   EXEC sp_help Orders
   ```

   The results of the **sp_help** system stored procedure show that the **Orders_Customers_link** nonclustered index exists on the **CustomerID** column in the **Orders** table.

▶ **To create indexes on foreign keys that reference the Products table**

In this procedure, you will create clustered and nonclustered indexes for all foreign key references in the **Products** table by using the following information. You can use the Create Index wizard in SQL Server Enterprise Manager or write a Transact-SQL statement in SQL Query Analyzer. C:\Moc\2073A\Labfiles\L07\Answers\CreaIndx2.sql is a completed script for this procedure.

1. Verify that you are using the **ClassNorthwind** database.

2. Write and execute a script that creates the following indexes.

Index type	Name	Table	Column	Fillfactor value
Clustered	**Products_CategoryID_link**	**Products**	**CategoryID**	0
Nonclustered	**Products_SupplierID_link**	**Products**	**SupplierID**	0

3. Query the **sysindexes** system table to verify that the indexes were created.

▶ **To verify the existence of the indexes that you created**

In this procedure, you will execute statements to verify that the indexes that you created exist and are correct.

1. Execute the **sp_helpindex** system stored procedure on the **Orders** table.

   What are the results?

   _____

   _____

2. Execute the **sp_helpindex** system stored procedure on the **Products** table. Why are there indexes on the foreign key columns?

   _____

   _____

   Why are all of the indexes not unique?

   _____

   _____

Exercise 2
Examining Index Structures

In this exercise, you will use SQL Query Analyzer to examine the table structure before creating indexes. You will create various types of indexes with different fillfactors and observe the effects on the table structure.

You can open, review, and execute sections of the ExamIndex.sql script file in the C:\Moc\SQL2073A\Labfiles\L07 folder, or type and execute the provided Transact-SQL statements.

▶ **To observe the initial table structure**

In this procedure, you will execute a Transact-SQL statement to obtain information about the **Member** table.

1. Type and execute these statements individually to obtain information about the **Member** table:

```
USE credit
GO
EXEC sp_spaceused member

SELECT * FROM sysindexes WHERE id = OBJECT_ID('member')

DBCC SHOWCONTIG ('member')
```

2. Record the statistical information in the following table.

Information	Source	Result
Number of rows	**sp_spaceused**: rows	
Number of indexes	**SELECT * FROM sysindexes WHERE id = OBJECT_ID('member')**	
Number of pages	SHOWCONTIG: Pages Scanned	
Number of rows per page	Calculate and round up the results. (# of rows/ # of pages) = # of rows per page	
Number of extents	SHOWCONTIG: Extent Switches	
Average extent fill	SHOWCONTIG: Avg. Pages per Extent	
Average page fill	SHOWCONTIG: Avg. Page Density (full)	

▶ **To create a clustered index**

In this procedure, you will create a unique clustered index and observe changes to the table structure. You also will obtain information about the index structure.

1. Type and execute this statement to create a unique clustered index on the **member_no** column of the **Member** table, without specifying a fillfactor:

```
USE credit
CREATE UNIQUE CLUSTERED INDEX mem_no_CL
    ON member (member_no)
```

2. Type and execute the following statement to obtain information about the **Member** table:

```
USE credit
SELECT * FROM sysindexes WHERE id = OBJECT_ID('member')

DBCC SHOWCONTIG ('member')
```

3. Record the statistical information in the following table.

Information	Source	Result
Number of clustered index pages	**sysindexes** row: **used**	
Number of data pages in the clustered index	**sysindexes** row: **dpages**	
Number of non-data pages in the clustered index	**(used – dpages)**	
Number of indexes	**SELECT * FROM sysindexes**	
Number of pages	SHOWCONTIG: Pages Scanned	
Number of rows per page	Calculate and round up the results. (# of rows/ # of pages) = # of rows per page	
Number of extents	SHOWCONTIG: Extent Switches	
Average extent fill	SHOWCONTIG: Avg. Pages per Extent	
Average page fill	SHOWCONTIG: Avg. Page Density (full)	

Are the pages still full?

_____

_____

Is the table still contiguous?

_____

_____

Will creating a clustered index always make the data pages more compact?
Why or why not?

_____

_____

_____

▶ **To create a nonclustered index**

In this procedure, you will create a nonclustered index and obtain information
about the index structure.

1. Type and execute this statement to drop the previously created index:

    ```
    USE credit
    EXEC index_cleanup member
    ```

2. Type and execute this statement to create a nonclustered index on the
    firstname column of the **Member** table, without specifying a fillfactor:

    ```
    USE credit
    CREATE NONCLUSTERED INDEX indx_fname
       ON member(firstname)
    ```

3. Type and execute this SELECT statement that returns the **sysindexes** rows for the **Member** table:

```
USE credit
SELECT * FROM sysindexes WHERE id = OBJECT_ID('member')
```

4. Record the statistical information in the following table.

Information	Source	Result
Number of pages in the nonclustered index on the **firstname** column	**sysindexes** row: used	
Number of pages in the leaf level	**sysindexes** row: **dpages**	
Approximate number of rows per leaf page	(# rows in table/# leaf-level pages)	

▶ **To create a nonclustered index with a fillfactor**

In this procedure, you will create a nonclustered index and observe changes to the table structure.

1. Type and execute this statement to drop the nonclustered index from the **Member** table:

```
USE credit
EXEC index_cleanup member
```

2. Type and execute this statement to create the same index, with a fillfactor of 25 percent:

```
USE credit
CREATE NONCLUSTERED INDEX indx_fname
    ON member(firstname)
    WITH FILLFACTOR=25
```

3. Type and execute this SELECT statement that returns the **sysindexes** rows for the **Member** table:

```
USE credit
SELECT * FROM sysindexes WHERE id = OBJECT_ID('member')
```

4. Record the statistical information in the following table.

Information	Source	Result
Number of pages in this index	**sysindexes** row: used	
Number of pages in the leaf level	**sysindexes** row: **dpages**	
Approximate number of rows per leaf page	(# rows in table/# leaf-level pages)	

Is the increase in the leaf-level size in proportion to the fillfactor?

_____

How can you determine whether the increase in the leaf-level size is proportional to the fillfactor of 25 percent?

_____

_____

◆ Introduction to Statistics

- **How Statistics Are Gathered**

- **How Statistics Are Stored**

- **Creating Statistics**

- **Updating Statistics**

- **Viewing Statistics**

Statistics are created on indexes and can be created on columns. Because the query optimizer uses statistics to optimize queries, you should know how they are gathered, stored, created, updated, and viewed.

How Statistics Are Gathered

- **Reads Column Values or a Sampling of Column Values**
  - Produces an evenly distributed sorted list of values
- **Performs a Full Scan or Sampling of Rows**
  - Dynamically determines the percentage of rows to be sampled based on the number of rows in the table
- **Selects Samplings**
  - From the table or from the smallest nonclustered index on the columns
  - All of the rows on the data page are used to update the statistical information

Statistics are a sampling of column values.

Reads Column Values or a Sampling of Column Values

SQL Server gathers statistics by reading all of the column values or a sampling of column values to produce an evenly distributed and sorted list of values known as *distribution steps*. SQL Server generates distribution steps by performing a full scan or sample scan and then by selecting samplings.

Performs a Full Scan or Sampling of Rows

SQL Server dynamically determines the percentage of rows to be sampled based on the number of rows in the table. The query optimizer performs either a full scan or a sampling of rows when gathering statistics.

- The SAMPLE option is the default for updating and creating statistics.
- The FULLSCAN option is used when:
  - Indexes are created.
  - The FULLSCAN option is specified in the CREATE STATISTICS statement.
  - The UPDATE STATISTICS statement is executed.

Selects Samplings

The sampling is randomly selected across data pages from the table or from the smallest nonclustered index on the columns needed by the statistics. After a data page has been read from disk, all of the rows on the data page are used to update the statistical information.

When the query optimizer gathers samplings:

- The table size determines which method is chosen.

- A minimum number of values are sampled to derive useful statistics.

- If the number of rows specified is too few to be useful, the query optimizer automatically corrects the sampling, based on the number of existing rows in the table.

- Statistics are kept only on the first column defined in a composite index.

How Statistics Are Stored

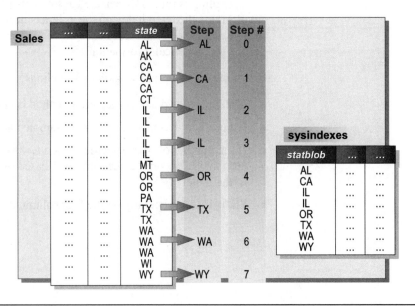

Statistics are stored in the **statblob** column of the **sysindexes** system table.

Distribution Steps

Each value stored in the **statblob** column is called a distribution step. Distribution steps refer to space between data samplings, or how many rows are stepped across before the next sampling is taken and stored. The first and last key values in the index are always included in the statistics. There can be as many as 300 values, of which the end point is the 300th value.

Contents in the statblob Column

In addition to storing distribution steps, the **statblob** column also stores:

- Date and time when statistics were last updated.
- Number of rows in the table.
- Number of rows sampled to create the histogram and determine density.
- Number of distribution steps.
- Average key length.
- Density for individual columns and all of the columns combined.
- Number of rows that fall within a histogram step.
- Number of rows that are equal in value to the upper bound of the histogram step.
- Number of distinct values within a histogram step.

Note The **statblob** column is defined as an **image** data type.

Creating Statistics

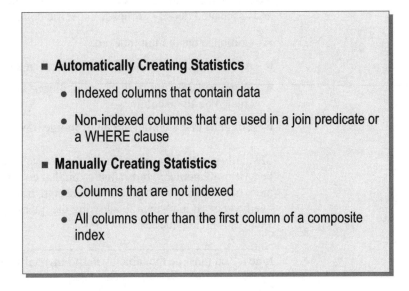

- **Automatically Creating Statistics**
  - Indexed columns that contain data
  - Non-indexed columns that are used in a join predicate or a WHERE clause
- **Manually Creating Statistics**
  - Columns that are not indexed
  - All columns other than the first column of a composite index

You can create statistics automatically or manually. However, you should allow SQL Server to create statistics automatically for you.

Automatically Creating Statistics

When the **auto create statistics** database option default is set to ON, SQL Server automatically creates statistics for:

- Indexed columns that contain data.
- Non-indexed columns that are used in a join predicate or a WHERE clause.

The query optimizer activates the automatic creation of statistics when optimizing a query. This can be a disadvantage if the query optimizer determines that statistics are missing. The execution plan will include the statistics creation action, which requires additional time when processing the query.

Note When you execute a query and view the execution plan, the query optimizer may suggest remedial action, such as creating or updating statistics, or creating an index. At that point, you can immediately create or update statistics and indexes.

Manually Creating Statistics

You can execute the CREATE STATISTICS statement to create a histogram and associated density groups for specific columns. You can create statistics on:

- Columns that are not indexed.

- All columns other than the first column of a composite index.

- Computed columns only if the conditions are such that an index can be created on these columns.

- Columns that are not defined of **image**, **text**, and **ntext** data types.

Manually creating statistics is useful when you have a column that may not benefit from an index, but statistics on that column may be useful for creating more optimal execution plans. Having statistics on those columns eliminates the overhead of an index, while allowing the query optimizer to use the column when optimizing queries.

Note   You must be the table owner to manually create statistics on a table.

Partial Syntax   CREATE STATISTICS *statistics_name* ON {*table*| *view*} (*column* [,...*n*])

Updating Statistics

- **Frequency of Updating Statistics**

- **Automatically Updating Statistics**

- **Manually Updating Statistics**

  - If you create an index before any data is put into the table

  - If a table is truncated

  - If you add many rows to a table that contains minimal or no data, and you plan to immediately query against that table

Over time, statistics can become outdated, which can affect the performance of the query optimizer.

Frequency of Updating Statistics

SQL Server updates statistical information when the information becomes outdated. The volume of data in the column relative to the amount of changing data determines the frequency of the update. For example:

- The statistics for a table containing 10,000 rows may require updating when 1,000 index values have changed, because 1,000 index values represent a significant percentage of the table.

- The statistics for a table containing 10 million index entries may not require updating when 1,000 index values have changed, because 1,000 index values represents a small percentage of the table.

SQL Server always samples a minimum number of rows. Tables that are smaller than 8 megabytes (MB) are always fully scanned to gather statistics.

Note SQL Server issues a warning when statistics are out-of-date or unavailable. This warning appears when the execution plan is viewed by using the execution plan. You can use SQL Profiler to monitor the **Missing Column Statistics** event class. This event class indicates when statistics are missing.

Automatically Updating Statistics

You should allow SQL Server to automatically update statistics for you. When the **auto update statistics** database option is set to ON (default), SQL Server automatically updates existing statistics when they become outdated.

For example, if a table is substantially updated since the last time that the statistics were created or updated, SQL Server automatically updates the statistics to optimize a query that uses the table.

The query optimizer activates the automatic updating of statistics when optimizing a query. This can be a disadvantage if the query optimizer determines that statistics are out-of-date. The execution plan will include the statistics update action, which requires additional time in processing the query.

Manually Updating Statistics

You can execute the UPDATE STATISTICS statement to update information about the distribution of key values for one or more statistics in a specified table. You may want to manually update statistics for a table or column in the following situations:

- If you create an index before any data is put into a table.
- If a table is truncated.
- If you add many rows to a table that contains minimal or no data, and you plan to immediately query against that table.

Partial Syntax

UPDATE STATISTICS *table| view* [*index* | (*statistics_name*[,...*n*])]

Note   To see a list of index names and descriptions, execute the **sp_helpindex** system stored procedure with the table name.

Viewing Statistics

- **The DBCC SHOW_STATISTICS Statement Returns Statistical Information in the Distribution Page for an Index or Column**
- **Statistical Information Includes:**
  - The time when the statistics were last updated
  - The number of rows sampled to produce the histogram
  - Density information
  - Average key length
  - Histogram step information

You can view statistical information in the distribution page for an index or a column by executing the DBCC SHOW_STATISTICS statement.

The following table describes the information that the DBCC SHOW_STATISTICS statement returns.

Column name	Description
Updated	Date and time the statistics were last updated
Rows	Number of rows in the table
Rows sampled	Number of rows sampled for statistics information
Steps	Number of distribution steps
Density	Selectivity of the first index column prefix (non-frequent)
Average key length	Average length of the first index column prefix
All density	Selectivity of a set of index column prefixes (frequent)
Average length	Average length of a set of index column prefixes
Columns	Names of index column prefixes for which **All density** and **Average length** are displayed
RANGE_HI_KEY	Upper bound value of a histogram step
RANGE_ROWS	Number of rows from the sample that fall in a histogram step, excluding the upper bound

(continued)

Column name	Description
EQ_ROWS	Number of rows from the sample that are equal in value to the upper bound of the histogram step
DISTINCT_RANGE_ROWS	Number of distinct values within a histogram step, excluding the upper bound
AVG_RANGE_ROWS	Average number of duplicate values within a histogram step, excluding the upper bound (RANGE_ROWS / DISTINCT_RANGE_ROWS for DISTINCT_RANGE_ROWS > 0)

Syntax

DBCC SHOW_STATISTICS (*table*, *target*)

Viewing statistics is typically useful when you do high-end performance tuning for specific queries. In most applications, it is not necessary to view statistics.

Querying the sysindexes Table

- **Stores Table and Index Information**
  - Type of index (**indid**)
  - Space used (**dpages**, **reserved**, and **used**)
  - Fillfactor (**OrigFillFactor**)
- **Stores Statistics for Each Index**

You can query the **sysindexes** table to get index and table information, in addition to statistics for each index. The following table is a partial list of the information that you can view that comes from the data stored in the **sysindexes** table.

Column	Description	Values
indid (type of index)	ID of the index (type of index)	Possible values are: • 0 for nonclustered table • 1 for clustered index • >1 for nonclustered index • 255 for tables that have text or image data
dpages (space used)	Count of leaf-level index pages	For **indid** = 0 or **indid** = 1, **dpages** is the count of data pages used. For **indid**=255, **dpages** is set to 0. Otherwise, **dpages** is the count of nonclustered index pages used.
reserved (space used)	Count of reserved pages for an index	For **indid** = 0 or **indid** = 1, **reserved** is the count of pages allocated for all indexes and table data. For **indid** = 255, **reserved** is a count of the pages allocated for text or image data. Otherwise, **reserved** is the count of pages allocated for the index.
used (space used)	Count of space used by an index	For **indid** = 0 or **indid** = 1, **used** is the count of the total pages used for all index and table data. For **indid** = 255, **used** is a count of the pages used for text or image data. Otherwise, **used** is the count of pages used for the index.

(continued)

Column	Description	Values
OrigFillFactor (fillfactor)	Original fillfactor value used when the index was created	This value is not maintained; however, it can be helpful if you need to recreate an index and do not remember which fillfactor value was used.
minlen	Minimum size of a row	Integer value.
xmaxlen	Maximum size of a row	Integer value.
maxirow	Maximum size of a non-leaf index row	Integer value.
keys	Description of key columns	Applies only if entry is an index.
statversion	Number of times the statistics have been updated	Integer value.
statblob	Statistics binary large object (BLOB)	Stores statistical information.

Example

This example executes a statement that accesses the index ID and other information from the **sysindexes** system table. Specify the clustered index name (*index_name*) in the WHERE clause to obtain the index ID of a clustered index.

```
SELECT id, indid, reserved, used, origfillfactor, name
FROM Northwind.dbo.sysindexes
WHERE name = 'PK_customers'
```

Result

id	indid	reserved	used	origfillfactor	name
2073058421	1	15	15	0	PK_Customers

```
(1 row(s) affected)
```

Setting Up Indexes Using the Index Tuning Wizard

- **Use the Index Tuning Wizard to:**
  - Recommend or verify optimal index configuration
  - Provide cost analysis reports
  - Recommend ways to tune the database
  - Specify criteria when a workload is evaluated
- **Do Not Use the Index Tuning Wizard on:**
  - Tables referenced by cross-database queries that do not exist
  - System tables, PRIMARY KEY constraints, unique indexes

Whether you are a novice or an advanced SQL Server user, the Index Tuning Wizard can help you create appropriate indexes on a new database or verify existing indexing on your current database. The Index Tuning Wizard looks at the query load to determine which indexes are useful, whereas the execution plan feature displays which indexes are used in queries.

Determining When to Use the Index Tuning Wizard

Novice users can use the wizard to quickly create an optimal index configuration. Advanced users can use the wizard for establishing a baseline index configuration. Advanced users can then custom-tune or verify their existing index configurations.

The Index Tuning Wizard can:

- Recommend or verify the optimal index configuration for a database, given an applied workload or trace file, by using the query optimizer costing analysis.

- Provide cost-analysis reports on the effects of the proposed changes, including:

  - Index usage on current and recommended indexes.

  - Query performance improvement for the 100 most expensive queries and table participation in a workload.

- Recommend ways to tune the database for a small set of problem queries.

- Specify criteria to consider when the Index Tuning Wizard evaluates a workload, such as maximum queries to tune, maximum space for recommended indexes, and maximum columns per index.

Determining How To Use the Wizard

When you want to use the Index Tuning Wizard, consider the following facts and guidelines:

- The user invoking the Index Tuning Wizard must be a member of the **sysadmin** fixed server role because the queries in the workload are analyzed in the security context of the user.

- It is not recommended that you use the Index Tuning Wizard on:

  - Tables referenced by cross-database queries that do not exist in the currently selected database.

  - System tables.

  - PRIMARY KEY constraints and unique indexes.

    The wizard may drop or replace a clustered index that is not unique, or currently created on a PRIMARY KEY constraint.

- It is not recommended that you drop any indexes when the **Keep all existing indexes** option is selected.

  The wizard recommends only new indexes, if appropriate. Clearing this option can result in a greater overall improvement in the performance of the workload.

- It is recommended that you leave the **Add indexed views** option selected.

- Hints can prevent the Index Tuning Wizard from choosing a better execution plan. Consider removing any index hints from queries before analyzing the workload.

- When you want to reduce the execution time of the Index Tuning Wizard, you should:

  - Ensure that **Perform thorough analysis** is not selected in the **Select Server and Database** dialog box. Performing a thorough analysis causes the Index Tuning Wizard to perform an exhaustive analysis of the queries, resulting in a longer execution time. Selecting this option can result in a greater overall improvement in the performance of the tuned workload.

  - Tune only a subset of the tables in the database.

  - Reduce the size of the workload file.

Note When you use the Index Tuning Wizard to analyze a Transact-SQL script that does not have a file name extension of .sql, such as My_script.txt, and you open the file with **File Format** set to **Auto**, the wizard generates the error message **Not a valid File Format**. Set **File Format** to **ANSI SQL** or **UNICODE SQL** instead.

Performance Considerations

- Create Indexes on Foreign Keys

- Create the Clustered Index Before Nonclustered Indexes

- Consider Creating Composite Indexes

- Create Multiple Indexes for a Table That Is Read Frequently

- Use the Index Tuning Wizard

Take the following actions to reduce the impact on performance when you create or use indexes:

- Create indexes on foreign keys, because foreign keys are typically referenced in queries.

- Create the clustered index before nonclustered indexes, because a clustered index changes the physical row order of the table.

- Create composite indexes. Query performance is enhanced with composite indexes, especially when users regularly search for information in more than one way.

- Create multiple indexes for a table, especially if the table is read frequently. Query performance is enhanced when a table has a clustered index and nonclustered indexes.

- Use the Index Tuning Wizard to track the usage of your indexes automatically and to assist you with maintaining and creating indexes that perform optimally.

Recommended Practices

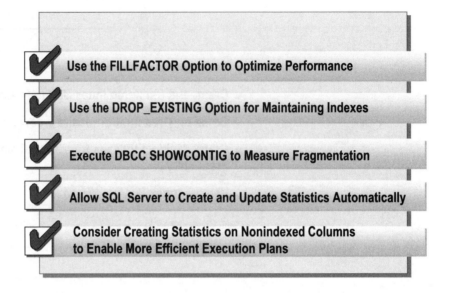

- Use the FILLFACTOR Option to Optimize Performance
- Use the DROP_EXISTING Option for Maintaining Indexes
- Execute DBCC SHOWCONTIG to Measure Fragmentation
- Allow SQL Server to Create and Update Statistics Automatically
- Consider Creating Statistics on Nonindexed Columns to Enable More Efficient Execution Plans

To get the most out of your indexes, consider the following practices:

- Use the FILLFACTOR option to optimize the performance of INSERT and UPDATE statements. This option allows you to specify a percentage of free space on the leaf-level pages.

- Use the DROP_EXISTING option to rebuild indexes quickly.

- Execute the DBCC SHOWCONTIG statement to determine the fragmentation of a table. The DBCC SHOWCONTIG statement shows the percentage of fragmentation and the average page density in a table.

- Allow SQL Server to create and update statistics for you automatically. Over time, statistics sometimes become outdated, which can affect the performance of the query optimizer. You should set **auto update statistics** and **auto create statistics** to ON.

- Consider creating statistics on nonindexed columns and secondary columns of a composite index. You can enhance query performance without incurring the overhead of maintaining additional indexes. Creating statistics allows the query optimizer to create more efficient execution plans.

Additional information on the following topics is available in SQL Server Books Online.

Topic	Search on
Index statistics	sp_autostats
	DBCC SHOW_STATISTICS
	"update statistics"
Creating indexes	"index tuning recommendations"
Computed columns	"SET options that affect results"
Functions	"deterministic and nondeterministic functions"

Lab B: Viewing Index Statistics

Objectives

After completing this lab, you will be able to:

- Estimate density and determine selectivity of indexes.
- View index statistics to determine whether the index is selective.

Prerequisites

Before working on this lab, you must have:

- Script files for this lab, which are located in C:\Moc\2073A\Labfiles\L07.
- Answer files for this lab, which are located in
  C:\Moc\2073A\Labfiles\L07\Answers.

Lab Setup

To complete this lab, you must have either:

- Completed the prior lab, or
- Executed the C:\Moc\2073A\Batches\Restore07B.cmd batch file.

  This command file restores the **ClassNorthwind** database to a state required
  for this lab.

For More Information

If you require help in executing files, search SQL Query Analyzer Help for
"Execute a query".

Other resources that you can use include:

- The **credit** database schema.
- Microsoft SQL Server Books Online.

Scenario

The organization of the classroom is meant to simulate that of a worldwide trading firm named Northwind Traders. Its fictitious domain name is nwtraders.msft. The primary DNS server for nwtraders.msft is the instructor computer, which has an Internet Protocol (IP) address of 192.168.x.200 (where x is the assigned classroom number). The name of the instructor computer is London.

The following table provides the user name, computer name, and IP address for each student computer in the fictitious **nwtraders.msft** domain. Find the user name for your computer, and make a note of it.

User name	Computer name	IP address
SQLAdmin1	Vancouver	192.168.x.1
SQLAdmin2	Denver	192.168.x.2
SQLAdmin3	Perth	192.168.x.3
SQLAdmin4	Brisbane	192.168.x.4
SQLAdmin5	Lisbon	192.168.x.5
SQLAdmin6	Bonn	192.168.x.6
SQLAdmin7	Lima	192.168.x.7
SQLAdmin8	Santiago	192.168.x.8
SQLAdmin9	Bangalore	192.168.x.9
SQLAdmin10	Singapore	192.168.x.10
SQLAdmin11	Casablanca	192.168.x.11
SQLAdmin12	Tunis	192.168.x.12
SQLAdmin13	Acapulco	192.168.x.13
SQLAdmin14	Miami	192.168.x.14
SQLAdmin15	Auckland	192.168.x.15
SQLAdmin16	Suva	192.168.x.16
SQLAdmin17	Stockholm	192.168.x.17
SQLAdmin18	Moscow	192.168.x.18
SQLAdmin19	Caracas	192.168.x.19
SQLAdmin20	Montevideo	192.168.x.20
SQLAdmin21	Manila	192.168.x.21
SQLAdmin22	Tokyo	192.168.x.22
SQLAdmin23	Khartoum	192.168.x.23
SQLAdmin24	Nairobi	192.168.x.24

Estimated time to complete this lab: 30 minutes

Exercise 1
Examining the Use of Indexes

In this exercise, you will create indexes, execute a series of SELECT statements to examine the density of four columns in the **Charge** table, and determine selectivity.

You can open, review, and execute sections of the ExamUse.sql script file in the C:\Moc\SQL2073A\Labfiles\L07 folder, or type and execute the provided Transact-SQL statements.

▶ To create indexes

In this procedure, you will drop existing indexes on the **Charge** table and create nonclustered indexes.

1. Log on to the **NWTraders** classroom domain by using the information in the following table.

Option	Value
User name	**SQLAdminx** (where *x* corresponds to your computer name as designated in the **nwtraders.msft** classroom domain)
Password	**password**

2. Open SQL Query Analyzer and, if requested, log in to the (local) server with Microsoft Windows® Authentication.

   You have permission to log in to and administer SQL Server because you are logged as **SQLAdminx**, which is a member of the Windows 2000 local group, Administrators. All members of this group are automatically mapped to the SQL Server **sysadmin** role.

3. Type and execute this statement to create unique, nonclustered indexes on the **charge_no**, **member_no**, **provider_no**, and **category_no** columns of the **charge** table:

```
USE credit
CREATE UNIQUE NONCLUSTERED INDEX charge_no_CL
        ON charge (charge_no)
CREATE NONCLUSTERED INDEX indx_member_no
        ON charge (member_no)
CREATE NONCLUSTERED INDEX indx_provider_no
        ON charge (provider_no)
CREATE NONCLUSTERED INDEX indx_category_no
        ON charge (category_no)
GO
```

▶ **To review the charge table structure**

In this procedure, you will creates indexes on the **Charge** table and determine the minimum and maximum values for the indexed columns.

1. Type or select these statements, and execute them to obtain the minimum and maximum values for the **charge_no**, **member_no**, **provider_no**, and **category_no** columns:

```
SELECT 'Charge_No ', MIN(Charge_No) AS 'Minimum Value',
       MAX(Charge_No) AS 'Maximum Value' FROM charge
UNION
SELECT 'Member_No ', MIN(Member_No) AS 'Minimum Value',
       MAX(Member_No) AS 'Maximum Value' FROM charge
UNION
SELECT 'Provider_No ', MIN(Provider_No) AS 'Minimum Value',
       MAX(Provider_No) AS 'Maximum Value' FROM charge
UNION
SELECT 'Category_No ', MIN(Category_No) AS 'Minimum Value',
       MAX(Category_No) AS 'Maximum Value' FROM charge
GO
```

2. Record the information in the following table.

Value	charge_no	member_no	provider_no	category_no
Min				
Max				

▶ **To determine selectivity**

In this procedure, you will execute a series of SELECT statements that select all rows from the **Charge** table. A table scan is performed for each SELECT statement. For each SELECT statement, you will first select the query and then view the estimated execution plan. You will modify the WHERE clause so that the query optimizer uses an index to retrieve the rows, and then you execute that query. After executing the query, you will record and evaluate the maximum number of rows that can be returned by using an index.

```
USE credit
SELECT * FROM charge
WHERE charge_no BETWEEN 1 AND 100000

USE credit
SELECT * FROM charge
WHERE member_no BETWEEN 1 AND 10000

USE credit
SELECT * FROM charge
WHERE provider_no BETWEEN 1 AND 500

USE credit
SELECT * FROM charge
WHERE category_no between 1 AND 10
```

1. Select the first statement, but do not execute it.

2. In the query window, on the **Query** menu, click **Display Estimated Execution Plan**.

   Notice the query plan for the statement.

3. Modify the range in the SELECT statements so that the query optimizer uses an index to retrieve the rows, rather than the optimizer using a table scan or full index scan.

   When choosing a range, remember that:

   - Each page has approximately 172 charges.

   - Older members and providers are less active than newer ones.

   - All categories are equally popular.

4. Execute the statements.

5. In the following table, record the maximum number of rows that can be returned by using an index.

WHERE clause	Approximate number of rows
WHERE **charge_no** BETWEEN 1 AND n	
WHERE **member_no** BETWEEN 1 AND n	
WHERE **provider_no** BETWEEN 1 AND n	
WHERE **category_no** BETWEEN 1 AND n	

6. Repeat steps 1 through 5 for the remaining SELECT statements.

Note You will notice that it is not easy to predict the selectivity of a query, even when you know the values of all of the arguments. It is best to let the query optimizer decide how to execute the query.

Is the number of rows accessed by the query optimizer the same for all indexes? Why or why not?

_____

_____

_____

_____

_____

_____

_____

_____

Exercise 2
Viewing Index Statistics and Evaluating Index Selectivity

In this exercise, you will create various indexes on the **Member** table, obtain index statistics, and evaluate whether an index is useful to the query optimizer based on its selectivity.

You can open, review, and execute sections of the IndexStats.sql script file in C:\Moc\SQL2073A\Labfiles\L07, or type and execute the provided Transact-SQL statements.

► To create indexes

In this procedure, you will execute a script that checks for any existing indexes and statistics, drops them, and then creates appropriate indexes. You will view the statistics based on the indexes created.

1. Using SQL Query Analyzer, type and execute this statement to drop existing indexes on the **Member** table:

```
USE credit
EXEC index_cleanup member
```

2. Type and execute these statements to create three indexes on the **Member** table:

```
USE credit
CREATE UNIQUE INDEX indx_member_no ON member (member_no)
CREATE INDEX indx_corp_lname ON member(corp_no,lastname)
CREATE INDEX indx_lastname ON member (lastname)
GO
```

▶ **To view index statistics and evaluate selectivity of indexes**

In this procedure, you will obtain index statistics for the new indexes, record the statistical information, and evaluate the selectivity of the indexes.

1. Type and execute this statement to display index statistical information on the **member_no** column of the **Member** table:

```
USE credit
DBCC SHOW_STATISTICS (member,indx_member_no)
```

2. Record the statistical information in the following table.

Information	Result
Rows	
Steps	
Density	
All density	

How selective is the index on the **member_no** column?

_____

_____

3. Type and execute this statement to display index statistical information on a composite index on the **corp_no** and **lastname** columns of the **Member** table:

```
USE credit
DBCC SHOW_STATISTICS (member,indx_corp_lname)
```

4. Record the statistical information in the following table.

Information	Result
Rows	
Steps	
Density	
All density (**corp_no**)	
(**corp_no, lastname**)	

How selective is this index?

_____

_____

5. Type and execute this statement to display index statistical information on the **lastname** column of the **Member** table:

```
USE credit
DBCC SHOW_STATISTICS (member,indx_lastname)
```

6. Record the statistical information in the following table.

Information	Result
Rows	
Steps	
Density	
All density	

How selective is this index?

_____

_____

Review

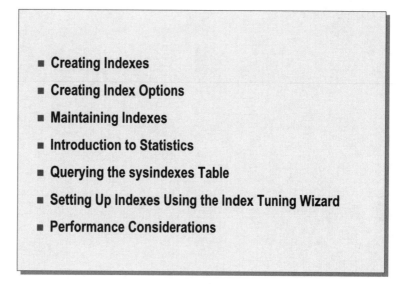

- Creating Indexes
- Creating Index Options
- Maintaining Indexes
- Introduction to Statistics
- Querying the sysindexes Table
- Setting Up Indexes Using the Index Tuning Wizard
- Performance Considerations

1. You are the database administrator responsible for a large customer database. Lately, the order processing department has been encountering slower system response times when submitting customer orders. Your experience says that the indexing on the **Orders** and **Order Details** tables is correct. What other factors may be causing the slow performance?

2. What are the advantages of having the SQL Server automatically create and update statistics?

3. You now have the responsibility of maintaining a database that the Sales department uses for taking customer orders. The **Sales** database has performed poorly. Your manager asks you to improve performance in two days. What is the appropriate tool to use to solve this problem?

Microsoft®
Training &
Certification

Module 8:
Implementing Views

Contents

Microsoft®

Project Lead: Rich Rose
Instructional Designers: Rich Rose, Cheryl Hoople, Marilyn McGill
Instructional Software Design Engineers: Karl Dehmer, Carl Raebler, Rick Byham
Technical Lead: Karl Dehmer
Subject Matter Experts: Karl Dehmer, Carl Raebler, Rick Byham
Graphic Artist: Kirsten Larson (Independent Contractor)
Editing Manager: Lynette Skinner
Editor: Wendy Cleary
Copy Editor: Edward McKillop (S&T Consulting)
Production Manager: Miracle Davis
Production Coordinator: Jenny Boe
Production Support: Lori Walker (S&T Consulting)
Test Manager: Sid Benavente
Courseware Testing: TestingTesting123
Classroom Automation: Lorrin Smith-Bates
Creative Director, Media/Sim Services: David Mahlmann
Web Development Lead: Lisa Pease
CD Build Specialist: Julie Challenger
Online Support: David Myka (S&T Consulting)
Localization Manager: Rick Terek
Operations Coordinator: John Williams
Manufacturing Support: Laura King; Kathy Hershey
Lead Product Manager, Release Management: Bo Galford
Lead Product Manager, Data Base: Margo Crandall
Group Manager, Courseware Infrastructure: David Bramble
Group Product Manager, Content Development: Dean Murray
General Manager: Robert Stewart

Overview

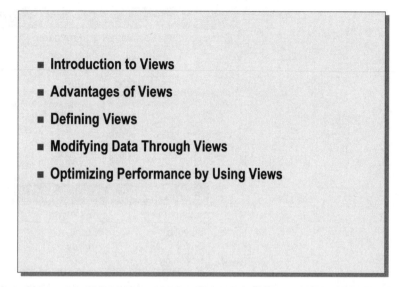

- **Introduction to Views**
- **Advantages of Views**
- **Defining Views**
- **Modifying Data Through Views**
- **Optimizing Performance by Using Views**

This module defines views and their advantages. The module then describes creating views and provides examples of projections and joins. These examples illustrate how to include computed columns and built-in functions in view definitions. The module then covers restrictions on modifying data through views. The last section discusses how views can improve performance.

After completing this module, you will be able to:

- Describe the concept of a view.
- List the advantages of views.
- Define a view by using the CREATE VIEW statement.
- Modify data through views.
- Optimize performance by using views.

Introduction to Views

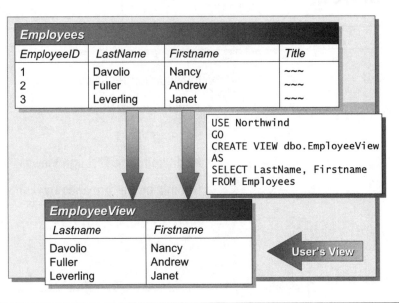

A view provides the ability to store a predefined query as an object in the database for later use. The tables queried in a view are called *base tables*. With a few exceptions, you can name and store any SELECT statement as a view. Common examples of views are:

- A subset of rows or columns of a base table.

- A union of two or more base tables.

- A join of two or more base tables.

- A statistical summary of a base table.

- A subset of another view, or some combination of views and base tables.

Example

This example creates the **dbo.EmployeeView** view in the **Northwind** database. The view displays two columns in the **Employees** table.

```
USE Northwind
GO
CREATE VIEW dbo.EmployeeView
AS
SELECT LastName, Firstname
FROM Employees
```

Query

```
SELECT * from EmployeeView
```

Result

LastName	FirstName
Davolio	Nancy
Fuller	Andrew
Leverling	Janet
.	
.	
.	

```
(9 row(s) affected)
```

Advantages of Views

- **Focus the Data for Users**
  - Focus on important or appropriate data only
  - Limit access to sensitive data
- **Mask Database Complexity**
  - Hide complex database design
  - Simplify complex queries, including distributed queries to heterogeneous data
- **Simplify Management of User Permissions**
- **Improve Performance**
- **Organize Data for Export to Other Applications**

Views offer several advantages, including focusing data for users, masking data complexity, simplifying permission management, and organizing data for export to other applications.

Focus the Data for Users

Views create a controlled environment that allows access to specific data while other data is concealed. Data that is unnecessary, sensitive, or inappropriate can be left out of a view. Users can manipulate the display of data in a view, as is possible in a table. In addition, with the proper permissions and a few restrictions, users can modify the data that a view produces.

Mask Database Complexity

Views shield the complexity of the database design from the user. This provides developers with the ability to change the design without affecting user interaction with the database. In addition, users can see a friendlier version of the data by using names that are easier to understand than the cryptic names that are often used in databases.

Complex queries, including distributed queries to heterogeneous data, can also be masked through views. The user queries the view instead of writing the query or executing a script.

Simplify Management of User Permissions

Instead of granting permission for users to query specific columns in base tables, database owners can grant permission for users to query data through views only. This also protects changes in the design of the underlying base tables. Users can continue to query the view without interruption.

Improve Performance

Views allow you to store results of complex queries. Other queries can use these summarized results. Views also allow you to partition data. You can place individual partitions on separate computers.

Organize Data for Export to Other Applications

You can create a view based on a complex query that joins two or more tables and then export the data to another application for further analysis.

◆ Defining Views

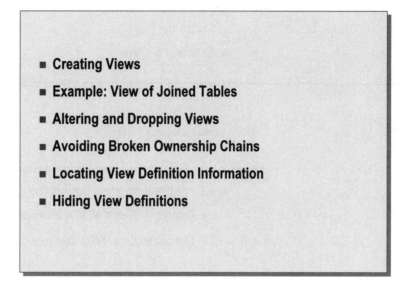

- ■ Creating Views
- ■ Example: View of Joined Tables
- ■ Altering and Dropping Views
- ■ Avoiding Broken Ownership Chains
- ■ Locating View Definition Information
- ■ Hiding View Definitions

This section describes creating, altering and dropping views. It also covers how to avoid broken ownership chains, to hide view definitions, and to obtain information on views within your database.

Creating Views

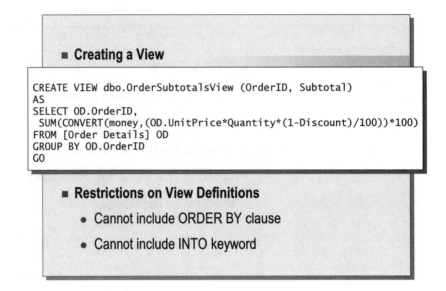

```
■ Creating a View

CREATE VIEW dbo.OrderSubtotalsView (OrderID, Subtotal)
AS
SELECT OD.OrderID,
 SUM(CONVERT(money,(OD.UnitPrice*Quantity*(1-Discount)/100))*100)
FROM [Order Details] OD
GROUP BY OD.OrderID
GO
```

■ **Restrictions on View Definitions**

- Cannot include ORDER BY clause

- Cannot include INTO keyword

You can create views by using the Create View Wizard, SQL Server Enterprise Manager, or Transact-SQL. You can create views only in the current database.

Creating a View

When you create a view, Microsoft® SQL Server™ 2000 verifies the existence of objects that are referenced in the view definition. Your view name must follow the rules for identifiers. Specifying a view owner name is optional. You should develop a consistent naming convention to distinguish views from tables. For example, you could add the word view as a suffix to each view object that you create. This allows similar objects (tables and views) to be easily distinguished when you query the **INFORMATION_SCHEMA.TABLES** view.

Syntax

CREATE VIEW *owner.view_name* [(*column* [,*n*])]
    [WITH {ENCRYPTION | SCHEMABINDING | VIEW_METADATA} [,n]]
    AS
    select_statement

[WITH CHECK OPTION]

To execute the CREATE VIEW statement, you must be a member of the system administrators (**sysadmin**) role, database owner (**db_owner**) role, or the data definition language administrator (**db_ddladmin**) role, or you must have been granted the CREATE VIEW permission. You must also have SELECT permission on all tables or views that are referenced within the view.

To avoid situations in which the owner of a view and the owner of the underlying tables differ, it is recommended that the **dbo** user own all objects in a database. Always specify the **dbo** user as the owner name when you create the object; otherwise, the object will be created with your user name as the object owner.

You specify the contents of a view by using a SELECT statement. With a few limitations, views can be as complex as you like. You must specify column names if:

- Any of the columns of the view are derived from an arithmetical expression, built-in function, or constant.

- Any columns in tables that will be joined share the same name.

Important   When you create views, it is important to test the SELECT statement that defines the view to ensure that SQL Server returns the expected result set. After you have written and tested the SELECT statement and verified the results, create the view.

Restrictions on View Definitions

When you create views, consider the following restrictions:

- The CREATE VIEW statement cannot include the COMPUTE, or COMPUTE BY clauses. The CREATE VIEW statement cannot include the INTO keyword.

- The CREATE VIEW statement can include the ORDER BY clause, only if the TOP keyword is used.

- Views cannot reference temporary tables.

- Views cannot reference more than 1,024 columns.

- The CREATE VIEW statement cannot be combined with other Transact-SQL statements in a single batch.

Example 1

Here is an example of a view that creates a column (**Subtotal**) that calculates the subtotals of an order from the **UnitPrice**, **Quantity**, and **Discount** columns.

```
CREATE VIEW dbo.OrderSubtotalsView (OrderID, Subtotal)
AS
SELECT OD.OrderID,
    SUM(CONVERT
      (money,(OD.UnitPrice*Quantity*(1- Discount)/100))*100)
FROM [Order Details] OD
GROUP BY OD.OrderID
GO
```

Example 2

This example queries the view to see the results.

```
SELECT * FROM OrderSubtotalsView
```

Result

OrderID	Subtotal
10271	48.0000
10977	2233.0000
10440	4924.1400
.	
.	
.	

```
(830 row(s) affected)
```

Example: View of Joined Tables

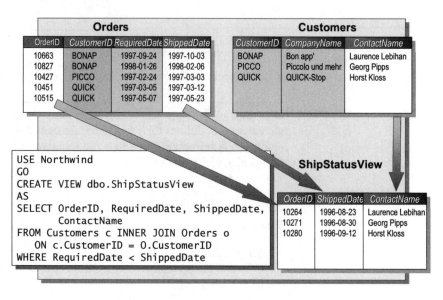

You often create views to provide a convenient way of looking at information from two or more joined tables in one central location.

Example 1

In this example, **ShipStatusView** joins the **Customers** and **Orders** tables.

```
USE Northwind
GO
CREATE VIEW dbo.ShipStatusView
AS
SELECT OrderID, ShippedDate, ContactName
FROM Customers c INNER JOIN Orders o
   ON c.CustomerID = O.CustomerID
WHERE RequiredDate < ShippedDate

SELECT * FROM ShipStatusView
```

Result

OrderID	ShippedDate	ContactName
10264	1996-08-23	Maria Larsson
10271	1996-08-30	Art Braunschweiger
10280	1996-09-12	Christina Berglund
.		
.		
.		

(37 row(s) affected)

Altering and Dropping Views

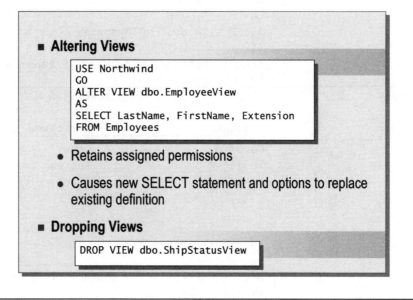

- **Altering Views**

```
USE Northwind
GO
ALTER VIEW dbo.EmployeeView
AS
SELECT LastName, FirstName, Extension
FROM Employees
```

  - Retains assigned permissions

  - Causes new SELECT statement and options to replace existing definition

- **Dropping Views**

```
DROP VIEW dbo.ShipStatusView
```

You often alter views in response to requests from users for additional information or to changes in the underlying table definition. You can alter a view by dropping and recreating it or by executing the ALTER VIEW statement.

Altering Views

The ALTER VIEW statement changes the definition of a view, including indexed views, without affecting dependent stored procedures or triggers. This allows you to retain permissions for the view. This statement is subject to the same restrictions as the CREATE VIEW statement. If you drop a view and then recreate it, you must reassign permissions to it.

Syntax

ALTER VIEW *owner.view_name*
  [(*column* [,...*n*])]
  [WITH {ENCRYPTION | SCHEMABINDING | VIEW_METADATA} [,...n]]
  AS
  select_statement
  [WITH CHECK OPTION]

Note If you use the WITH CHECK OPTION, WITH ENCRYPTION, WITH SCHEMABINDING, or WITH VIEW_METADATA option when you create the view, you must include it in the ALTER VIEW statement if you want to retain the functionality that the option provides.

Example

The following example alters **EmployeeView** to add the **Extension** column.

```
USE Northwind
GO
ALTER VIEW dbo.EmployeeView
AS
SELECT LastName, FirstName, Extension
FROM Employees
```

Query

```
SELECT * from  dbo.EmployeeView
```

Result

LastName	FirstName	Extension
Davolio	Nancy	5467
Fuller	Andrew	3457
Leverling	Janet	3355
.		
.		
.		

```
(9 row(s) affected)
```

Note If you define a view with a SELECT * statement, and then alter the structure of the underlying tables by adding columns, the new columns do not appear in the view. When all columns are selected in a CREATE VIEW statement, the column list is interpreted only when you first create the view. To see the new columns in the view, you must alter the view.

Dropping Views

If you no longer need a view, you can remove its definition from the database by executing the DROP VIEW statement. Dropping a view removes its definition and all permissions assigned to it. Furthermore, if users query any views that reference the dropped view, they receive an error message. However, dropping a table that references a view does not drop the view automatically. You must drop it explicitly.

Note The permission to drop a view goes to the view owner and is nontransferable. This is the default. However, the system administrator or database owner can drop any object by specifying the owner name in the DROP VIEW statement.

Avoiding Broken Ownership Chains

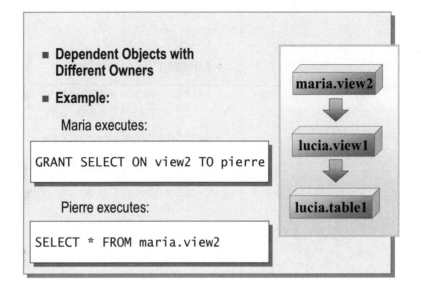

SQL Server allows the owner of the original object to retain control over users who are authorized to access the object.

Dependent Objects with Different Owners

View definitions depend on underlying objects (views or tables). These dependencies can be thought of as the ownership chain. If the owner of a view also owns the underlying objects, the owner only has to grant permission for the view. When the object is used, permissions are checked only on the view.

To avoid broken ownership chains, the **dbo** user should own all views. When the object is used, permissions are checked on each dependent object with a different owner.

Example

Maria creates **view2**. With the following statement, she grants permission to Pierre to query it.

Syntax

```
GRANT select ON view2 TO pierre
```

However, **maria.view2** depends on an object (**view1**) owned by another user (Lucia). Permissions are checked on each dependent object with a different owner.

Pierre queries the view by using the following statement:

Syntax

```
SELECT * FROM maria.view2
```

Because **maria.view2** depends on **lucia.view1**, SQL Server checks the permissions on **maria.view2** and **lucia.view1**. If Lucia has previously granted permission to Pierre on **view1**, Pierre is allowed access. If Lucia has not previously granted permission to Pierre, access is denied, allowing Lucia to retain control over individuals who are authorized to access the objects that she creates.

Locating View Definition Information

- **Locating View Definitions**
  - Not available if view was created using WITH ENCRYPTION option
- **Locating View Dependencies**
  - Lists objects upon which view depends
  - Lists objects that depend on a view

You may want to see the definition of a view in order to alter the view definition or to understand how its data is derived from the base tables.

Locating View Definitions

You can locate view definition information with SQL Server Enterprise Manager or by querying the following views and system tables.

Information schema view or system table	Displays information on
INFORMATION_SCHEMA.TABLES or **sysobjects**	View names.
INFORMATION_SCHEMA.VIEW_TABLE_USAGE or **sysdepends**	Base object names.
INFORMATION_SCHEMA.VIEWS or **syscomments**	View definition.
INFORMATION_SCHEMA.VIEW_COLUMN_USAGE or **syscolumns**	Columns that are defined in a view.

Note INFORMATION_SCHEMA.VIEW_TABLE_USAGE and INFORMATION_SCHEMA.VIEW_COLUMN_USAGE display information for your user name only.

To display the text that was used to create a view, use SQL Server Enterprise Manager, query **INFORMATION_SCHEMA.VIEWS,** or execute the **sp_helptext** system stored procedure with the view name as the parameter.

Syntax

sp_helptext *objname*

Locating View Dependencies

To retrieve a report of the tables or views on which a view depends and of objects that depend on a particular view, use SQL Server Enterprise Manager or execute the **sp_depends** system stored procedure.

You should view dependencies before you drop any object. Before you alter or drop a table, use the **sp_depends** system stored procedure to determine whether any objects reference the table.

Syntax

sp_depends *objname*

Hiding View Definitions

- **Use the WITH ENCRYPTION Option**

- **Do Not Delete Entries in the syscomments Table**

```
USE Northwind
GO
CREATE VIEW dbo.[Order Subtotals]
    WITH ENCRYPTION
AS
SELECT OrderID,
  Sum(CONVERT(money,(UnitPrice*Quantity*(1-Discount)/100))*100)
    AS Subtotal
FROM [Order Details]
GROUP BY OrderID
GO
```

Because users may display the definition of a view by using SQL Server Enterprise Manager, by querying **INFORMATION_SCHEMA.VIEWS**, or by querying the **syscomments** system table, you might want to hide certain view definitions.

Use the WITH ENCRYPTION Option

You can encrypt the **syscomments** table entries that contain the text of the CREATE VIEW statement by specifying the WITH ENCRYPTION option in the view definition.

Before you encrypt a view, ensure that the view definition (script) is saved to a file. To decrypt the text of a view, you must drop the view and recreate it, or alter the view and use the original syntax.

Example

In this example, **dbo.[Order Subtotals]** is created by using the WITH ENCRYPTION option so that the view definition is hidden.

```
USE Northwind
GO
CREATE VIEW dbo.[Order Subtotals]
    WITH ENCRYPTION
AS
SELECT OrderID,
  Sum(CONVERT(money,(UnitPrice*Quantity*(1-Discount)/100))*100)
    AS Subtotal
FROM [Order Details]
GROUP BY OrderID
```

Do Not Delete Entries in the syscomments Table

When security considerations require that the view definition be unavailable to users, use encryption. Never delete entries from the **syscomments** table. This prevents you from using the view, and it prevents SQL Server from recreating the view when you upgrade a database to a newer version of SQL Server.

Modifying Data Through Views

- **Cannot Affect More Than One Underlying Table**

- **Cannot Be Made to Certain Columns**

- **Can Cause Errors If They Affect Columns That Are Not Referenced in the View**

- **Are Verified If the WITH CHECK OPTION Has Been Specified**

Views do not maintain a separate copy of data. Instead, they show the result set of a query on one or more base tables. Therefore, whenever you modify data in a view, you are actually modifying the base table.

With some restrictions, you can insert, update, or delete table data freely through a view. In general, the view must be defined on a single table and must not include aggregate functions or GROUP BY clauses in the SELECT statement.

Specifically, modifications that are made by using views:

- Cannot affect more than one underlying table.

  You can modify views that are derived from two or more tables, but each update or modification can affect only one table.

- Cannot be made on certain columns.

  SQL Server does not allow you to change a column that is the result of a calculation, such as columns that contain computed values, built-in functions, or row aggregate functions.

- Can cause errors if modifications affect columns that are not referenced in the view.

  For example, you will receive an error message if you insert a row into a view that is defined on a table that contains columns that are not referenced in the view and that do not allow NULLs or contain default values.

- Are verified if the WITH CHECK OPTION has been specified in the view definition.

  The WITH CHECK OPTION forces all data modification statements that are executed against the view to adhere to certain criteria. These criteria are specified within the SELECT statement that defines the view. If the changed values are out of the range of the view definition, SQL Server rejects the modifications.

◆ Optimizing Performance by Using Views

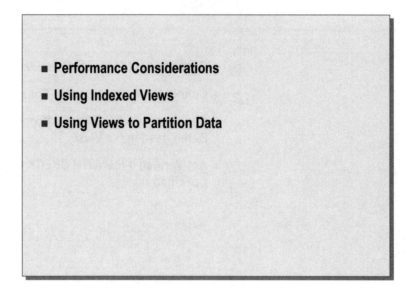

- Performance Considerations
- Using Indexed Views
- Using Views to Partition Data

This section describes performance considerations for using views, and how views allow you optimize performance by storing results of complex queries and partitioning data.

Performance Considerations

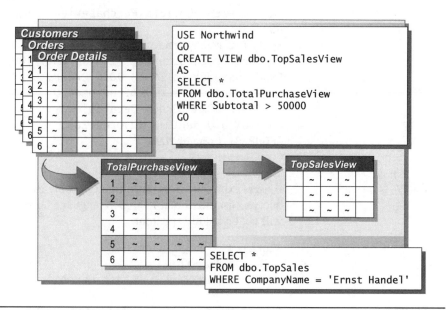

When views that join several tables and evaluate complex expressions are nested within another view, the immediate source of any performance problems may be difficult to determine. Therefore, you may want to consider creating separate view definitions rather than nesting views.

Example

In the following example, **TopSalesView** queries a subset of rows from **TotalPurchaseView**.

```
USE Northwind
GO
CREATE VIEW dbo.TopSalesView
AS
SELECT *
FROM dbo.TotalPurchaseView
WHERE Subtotal > 50000
GO
```

The view definition of **dbo.TopSalesView** hides the complexity of the underlying query that is used to create TotalPurchaseView, which joins three base tables.

```
USE Northwind
GO
CREATE VIEW dbo.TotalPurchaseView
AS
SELECT CompanyName, Sum(CONVERT(money,
    (UnitPrice*Quantity*(1-Discount)/100))*100) AS Subtotal
FROM Customers c INNER JOIN Orders o
    ON c.CustomerID=o.CustomerID
    INNER JOIN [Order Details] od
      ON o.OrderID = od.OrderID
GROUP BY CompanyName
GO
```

Query

If users experience any performance problems when they execute the following query to list the available French language books, the source of the problem will not be readily apparent.

```
SELECT *
FROM dbo.TopSales
WHERE CompanyName = 'Ernst Handel'
```

Result

CompanyName	Subtotal
Ernst Handel	104874.98

(1 row(s) affected)

Using Indexed Views

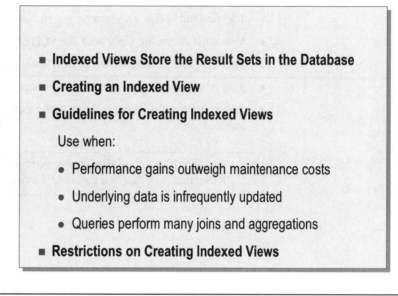

- **Indexed Views Store the Result Sets in the Database**
- **Creating an Indexed View**
- **Guidelines for Creating Indexed Views**

  Use when:

  - Performance gains outweigh maintenance costs
  - Underlying data is infrequently updated
  - Queries perform many joins and aggregations
- **Restrictions on Creating Indexed Views**

You can create indexes on views. An *indexed view* stores the result set of a view in the database. Because of the fast retrieval time, you can use indexed views to improve query performance.

Creating an Indexed View

Create an indexed view by implementing a UNIQUE CLUSTERED index on a view. The results of the view are stored in the leaf-level pages of the clustered index. After you create the UNIQUE CLUSTERED index, you can create other indexes on that view.

An indexed view automatically reflects modifications made to data in the base tables. As data changes, the UNIQUE CLUSTERED index is updated.

Guidelines for Creating Indexed Views

The query optimizer automatically determines whether a given query will benefit from using an indexed view. It can determine this even if the query does not reference the indexed view. As a general practice, allow the query optimizer to determine when to use indexed views.

By using the Index Tuning Wizard, you can greatly enhance your ability to determine the best mix of indexes and indexed views to optimize query performance.

Create indexed views when:

- The performance gain of improved speed in retrieving results outweighs the increased maintenance cost.
- The underlying data is infrequently updated.
- Queries perform a significant amount of joins and aggregations that either process many rows or are performed frequently by many users.

Restrictions on Creating Indexed Views

Consider the following guidelines when you create indexed views:

- The first index that you create on a view must be a unique clustered index.

- You must create the view with the SCHEMABINDING option.

- The view can reference base tables, but it cannot reference other views.

- You must use two-part names to reference tables and user-defined functions.

- Subsequent connections must have the same option settings to use the indexed view.

Note   You should use the **IsIndexable** property of the OBJECTPROPERTY function to make sure that you can index a view.

Using Views to Partition Data

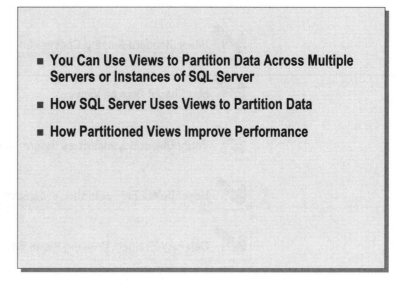

- **You Can Use Views to Partition Data Across Multiple Servers or Instances of SQL Server**
- **How SQL Server Uses Views to Partition Data**
- **How Partitioned Views Improve Performance**

You can use views to partition data across multiple databases or instances of SQL Server to improve performance.

How SQL Server Uses Views to Partition Data

You can use the UNION set operator within a view to combine the results of two or more queries from separate tables into a single result set. This appears to the user as a single table called a *partitioned view*. You can update partitioned views even though they reference multiple tables.

Partitioned views can be based on data from multiple heterogeneous sources, such as remote servers, not just tables in the same database. This allows you to distribute database processing across a group of servers. The group of servers can support the processing needs for large e-commerce applications or corporate data centers.

How Partitioned Views Improve Performance

If the tables in a partitioned view are on different servers, or on a computer with multiple processors, each table involved in the query can be scanned in parallel, thereby improving query performance. In addition, maintenance tasks, such as rebuilding indexes or backing up a table, can execute faster.

Note You cannot create an index on a partitioned view. The view definition required to build the indexed view only allows two-part names; a partitioned view requires the use of three- or four-part names, such as, *Servername.databasename.ownername.objectname.*

Recommended Practices

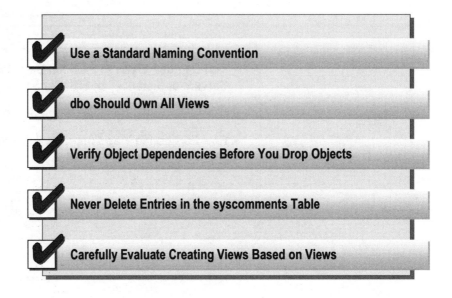

- Use a Standard Naming Convention
- dbo Should Own All Views
- Verify Object Dependencies Before You Drop Objects
- Never Delete Entries in the syscomments Table
- Carefully Evaluate Creating Views Based on Views

The following recommended practices should help you use and manage views in your databases:

- You should develop a consistent naming convention to distinguish views from tables.

- Specify **dbo** as the owner when you create views. The **dbo** should own all objects referenced in the view definition. This prevents the need to specify the owner name when you query the view, because the database owner is the default owner. The database owner also has permission on all underlying objects in the database, thereby preventing potential broken ownership chains.

- Verify object dependencies before you drop objects from the database. Execute the **sp_depends** system stored procedure, or display the dependencies in SQL Server Enterprise Manager to ensure that dependencies do not exist on an object that you plan to drop.

- Never delete entries in the **syscomments** system table. If your application requires that the definition is invisible to others, include the WITH ENCRYPTION option with either the CREATE VIEW or ALTER VIEW statement. Be sure to save your script definition before you encrypt the script.

- Carefully evaluate whether to create views based on views. They can hide complexities and could be the source of performance problems.

Additional information on the following topics is available in SQL Server Books Online.

Topic	Search on
CREATE VIEW	"create view"
ALTER VIEW	"alter view"
DROP VIEW	"drop view"
Broken ownership chains	"ownership chain"
Generating SQL scripts	"documenting and scripting databases"

Lab A: Implementing Views

Objectives

After completing this lab, you will be able to:

- Create a view using a wizard.
- Alter a view to encrypt its definition.
- Alter a view by using WITH CHECK OPTION.
- Use information schema to obtain information about views.

Prerequisites

Before working on this lab, you must have:

- Script files for this lab, which are located in C:\Moc\2073A\Labfiles\L08.
- Answer files for this lab, which are located in
  C:\Moc\2073A\Labfiles\L08\Answers.

Lab Setup

To complete this lab, you must have either:

- Completed the prior lab, or
- Executed the C:\Moc\2073A\Batches\Restore08.cmd batch file.

  This command file restores the **ClassNorthwind** database to a state required
  for this lab.

For More Information

If you require help with executing files, search SQL Query Analyzer Help for
"Execute a query".

Other resources that you can use include:

- The **Northwind** database schema.
- Microsoft SQL Server Books Online.

Scenario

The organization of the classroom is meant to simulate that of a worldwide trading firm named Northwind Traders. Its fictitious domain name is nwtraders.msft. The primary DNS server for nwtraders.msft is the instructor computer, which has an Internet Protocol (IP) address of 192.168.x.200 (where x is the assigned classroom number). The name of the instructor computer is London.

The following table provides the user name, computer name, and IP address for each student computer in the fictitious **nwtraders.msft** domain. Find the user name for your computer, and make a note of it.

User name	Computer name	IP address
SQLAdmin1	Vancouver	192.168.x.1
SQLAdmin2	Denver	192.168.x.2
SQLAdmin3	Perth	192.168.x.3
SQLAdmin4	Brisbane	192.168.x.4
SQLAdmin5	Lisbon	192.168.x.5
SQLAdmin6	Bonn	192.168.x.6
SQLAdmin7	Lima	192.168.x.7
SQLAdmin8	Santiago	192.168.x.8
SQLAdmin9	Bangalore	192.168.x.9
SQLAdmin10	Singapore	192.168.x.10
SQLAdmin11	Casablanca	192.168.x.11
SQLAdmin12	Tunis	192.168.x.12
SQLAdmin13	Acapulco	192.168.x.13
SQLAdmin14	Miami	192.168.x.14
SQLAdmin15	Auckland	192.168.x.15
SQLAdmin16	Suva	192.168.x.16
SQLAdmin17	Stockholm	192.168.x.17
SQLAdmin18	Moscow	192.168.x.18
SQLAdmin19	Caracas	192.168.x.19
SQLAdmin20	Montevideo	192.168.x.20
SQLAdmin21	Manila	192.168.x.21
SQLAdmin22	Tokyo	192.168.x.22
SQLAdmin23	Khartoum	192.168.x.23
SQLAdmin24	Nairobi	192.168.x.24

Estimated time to complete this lab: 30 minutes

Exercise 1
Creating and Testing Views

In this exercise, you will create views to manage daily requests on the **ClassNorthwind** database. You will use the Create View Wizard and execute a script that creates several views. Finally, you will query the views to verify that you received the expected results.

▶ **To use the Create View Wizard**

In this procedure, you will use the Create View Wizard to quickly create a view.

1. Log on to the **NWTraders** classroom domain by using the information in the following table.

Option	Value
User name	**SQLAdmin***x* (where *x* corresponds to your computer name as designated in the **nwtraders.msft** classroom domain)
Password	**password**

2. Open SQL Server Enterprise Manager.

3. In the console tree, click your server.

4. On the **Tools** menu, click **Wizards**.

5. Expand Database, and then double-click **Create View Wizard**.

6. Use the information in the following table to create a view that lists the products from a particular supplier.

Option	Value
Select a database	**ClassNorthwind**
Select tables	**Products**
Select columns	**ProductID, ProductName, SupplierID, CategoryID, QuantityPerUnit, UnitPrice, Discontinued**
Define restriction	`WHERE SupplierID = 14`
Name the view	**FormaggiProductsView**

7. Query the view to ensure that you received the expected result set.

▶ **To create views from a script**

In this procedure, you will execute a script to create views.

1. Open SQL Query Analyzer and, if requested, log in to the (local) server with Microsoft Windows® Authentication.

   You have permission to log in to and administer SQL Server because you are logged as **SQLAdmin*x***, which is a member of the Microsoft Windows 2000 local group, Administrators. All members of this group are automatically mapped to the SQL Server **sysadmin** role.

2. Open, review, and execute Labfiles\L08\CreaView.sql to create the following views.

View name	View description
FormaggiProductsView	All products from supplier ID of 14
Customer and Suppliers by City	All customers and all suppliers listed (UNION)
Current Product List	All products that are not discontinued
Orders Qry	All customers orders and order information
Products Above Average Price	All products that are priced above the average product unit price
Products by Category	All products listed by category
Invoices	All invoice information
Order Details Extended	All order details extended price information
Sales by Category	All sales for 1997 listed by category

3. Open a new query window and execute the **sp_depends** system stored procedure. List the tables on which the **Order Details Extended** view depends, as well as objects that depend on **Order Details Extended**.

   _____

   _____

4. Switch to SQL Server Enterprise Manager to determine the dependencies on the **Orders** table.

5. In the console tree, expand the **ClassNorthwind** database, and then click **Tables**.

6. In the details pane, right-click the **Orders** table; on the shortcut menu, click **All Tasks**, and then click **Display Dependencies**.

   What objects are dependent on the **Orders** table?

   _____

   _____

Exercise 2
Encrypting a View Definition

In this exercise, you will alter a view to encrypt its definition so that it will be invisible.

▶ **To alter and encrypt the Sales by Category view**

In this procedure, you will use SQL Server Enterprise Manager to display the script that created the **Sales by Category** view. Then, you will alter the view to encrypt the script. L08\Answers\EncryptView.sql is a completed script for this procedure.

1. Open SQL Server Books Online to the topic "How to generate a script (Enterprise Manager)."

2. Use the procedure in SQL Server Books Online to generate a script for the **Sales by Category** view.

3. Save your script as SaleByCatView.sql

Note If you display the properties of the view or select preview when you generate the script, you can copy and paste the view definition into a query window for modification.

---

4. In a query window, revise the script to alter **Sales by Category** so that it is created by using the WITH ENCRYPTION option.

5. Execute the modified script to alter **Sales by Category**.

6. Save your revised script as SaleByCatView.sql

▶ **To test that the statements have been encrypted**

In this procedure, you will use the **sp_helptext** system stored procedure and SQL Server Enterprise Manager to observe the effect of using the encryption option.

1. Execute the **sp_helptext** system stored procedure that displays the script that created **Sales by Category**.

   The Results window will display the following statement: "The object's comments have been encrypted."

2. In SQL Server Enterprise Manager, in the details pane, right-click **Sales by Category**, and then click **Properties**.

   Can you see the CREATE VIEW syntax that was used to create **Sales by Category**?

   _____

3. How would you decrypt the **Sales by Category** view?

   _____

Exercise 3
Modifying Data Through Views

In this exercise, you will alter **FormaggiProductsView** to include WITH CHECK OPTION so that data modifications can only be made that adhere to the view definition.

▶ To alter FormaggiProductsView to enable WITH CHECK OPTION

In this procedure, you will alter **FormaggiProductsView** to enable WITH CHECK OPTION. L08\Answers\Supplier14.sql is a completed script for this procedure.

1. Generate a script for the **FormaggiProductsView** view.

2. Modify your script to enable WITH CHECK OPTION.

3. Execute the script and save the file with your modifications.

▶ To update the title table through FormaggiProductsView

In this procedure, you will update the **Products** table with data that is out of the range of **FormaggiProductsView**. You then will observe the results.

1. Write an UPDATE statement to change the products listed in **FormaggiProductsView** from supplier 14 to supplier 12, where product ID equals 31.

2. Execute the UPDATE statement.

    What was the result?

    _____

    _____

Exercise 4
Locating View Definitions

In this exercise, you will query the information schema views to obtain information about the views that you have created in the **ClassNorthwind** database. L08\Answers\Schema.sql is a completed script for this exercise.

▶ **To display information about views**

In this procedure, you will query the information schema views to display details about views in the **ClassNorthwind** database.

1. Verify that you are using the **ClassNorthwind** database.

2. Query **INFORMATION_SCHEMA.VIEWS** to display all views and their definitions.

    What information was displayed about **FormaggiProductsView** and **Products Above Average Price**?

    _____

    _____

3. Which information schema view displays a list of table and view names?

    _____

    _____

4. Query **INFORMATION_SCHEMA.VIEW_COLUMN_USAGE** to display a list of columns that are referenced in the **Invoices** view.

5. Query **INFORMATION_SCHEMA.VIEW_TABLE_USAGE** to display
    a list of tables that are referenced in the **Sales by Category** view.

    What tables were listed?

    _____

    _____

    Why were you able to see the tables that are referenced in **Sales by
    Category** when this view is encrypted?

    _____

    _____

    Which system tables, system functions, or system stored procedures could
    also have been used to display information about views?

    _____

    _____

Review

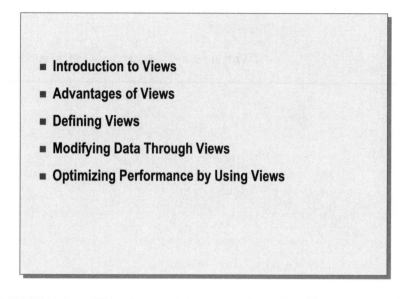

- Introduction to Views
- Advantages of Views
- Defining Views
- Modifying Data Through Views
- Optimizing Performance by Using Views

1. What are the benefits of views?

2. You have developed a query that joins the **Customer**, **Orders**, and **Order Details** tables to list the details of each customer order, such as the quantity of an item and the date that delivery is required. When customers change an existing order, employees need to be able to update the **Orders** and **Order Details** tables. How would you accomplish this task without granting permission on the underlying tables?

3. What is the benefit of using the WITH CHECK OPTION in your view definition?

4. What are some considerations to remember when you use views?

Microsoft®
Training &
Certification

Module 9: Implementing Stored Procedures

Contents

Microsoft®

Project Lead: Rich Rose
Instructional Designers: Rich Rose, Cheryl Hoople, Marilyn McGill
Instructional Software Design Engineers: Karl Dehmer, Carl Raebler, Rick Byham
Technical Lead: Karl Dehmer
Subject Matter Experts: Karl Dehmer, Carl Raebler, Rick Byham
Graphic Artist: Kirsten Larson (Independent Contractor)
Editing Manager: Lynette Skinner
Editor: Wendy Cleary
Copy Editor: Edward McKillop (S&T Consulting)
Production Manager: Miracle Davis
Production Coordinator: Jenny Boe
Production Support: Lori Walker (S&T Consulting)
Test Manager: Sid Benavente
Courseware Testing: TestingTesting123
Classroom Automation: Lorrin Smith-Bates
Creative Director, Media/Sim Services: David Mahlmann
Web Development Lead: Lisa Pease
CD Build Specialist: Julie Challenger
Online Support: David Myka (S&T Consulting)
Localization Manager: Rick Terek
Operations Coordinator: John Williams
Manufacturing Support: Laura King; Kathy Hershey
Lead Product Manager, Release Management: Bo Galford
Lead Product Manager, Data Base: Margo Crandall
Group Manager, Courseware Infrastructure: David Bramble
Group Product Manager, Content Development: Dean Murray
General Manager: Robert Stewart

Overview

- ■ **Introduction to Stored Procedures**
- ■ **Creating, Executing, Modifying, and Dropping Stored Procedures**
- ■ **Using Parameters in Stored Procedures**
- ■ **Executing Extended Stored Procedures**
- ■ **Handling Error Messages**

Objectives

After completing this module, you will be able to:

- ■ Describe how a stored procedure is processed.
- ■ Create, execute, modify, and drop a stored procedure.
- ■ Create stored procedures that accept parameters.
- ■ Execute extended stored procedures.
- ■ Create custom error messages.

◆ Introduction to Stored Procedures

- Defining Stored Procedures
- Initial Processing of Stored Procedures
- Subsequent Processing of Stored Procedures
- Advantages of Stored Procedures

This section introduces the different types of Microsoft® SQL Server™ 2000 stored procedures, describes how stored procedures are processed—both initially and on subsequent execution—and lists some of the advantages of using stored procedures.

Defining Stored Procedures

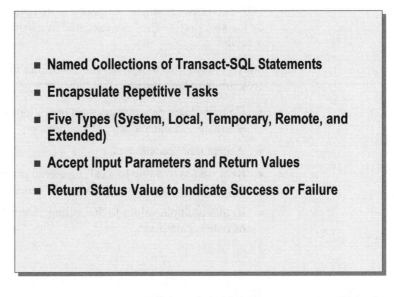

- **Named Collections of Transact-SQL Statements**
- **Encapsulate Repetitive Tasks**
- **Five Types (System, Local, Temporary, Remote, and Extended)**
- **Accept Input Parameters and Return Values**
- **Return Status Value to Indicate Success or Failure**

A stored procedure is a named collection of Transact-SQL statements that is stored on the server. Stored procedures are a method of encapsulating repetitive tasks. Stored procedures support user-declared variables, conditional execution, and other powerful programming features.

SQL Server supports five types of stored procedures:

System Stored Procedures (sp_)   Stored in the **master** database, system stored procedures (identified by the sp_ prefix) provide an effective method to retrieve information from system tables. They allow system administrators to perform database administration tasks that update system tables even though the administrators do not have permission to update the underlying tables directly. System stored procedures can be executed in any database.

Local Stored Procedures   Local stored procedures are created in individual user databases.

Temporary Stored Procedures   Temporary stored procedures can be local, with names that start with a single number sign (#), or global, with names that start with a double number sign (##). Local temporary stored procedures are available within a single user session; global temporary stored procedures are available for all user sessions.

Remote Stored Procedures   Remote stored procedures are an earlier feature of SQL Server. Distributed queries now support this functionality.

Extended Stored Procedures (xp_)   Extended stored procedures are implemented as dynamic-link libraries (DLLs) executed outside of the SQL Server environment. Extended stored procedures are typically identified by the xp_ prefix. They are executed in a manner similar to that of stored procedures.

Stored procedures in SQL Server are similar to procedures in other programming languages, in that they can:

- Contain statements that perform operations in the database, including the ability to call other stored procedures.

- Accept input parameters.

- Return a status value to a calling stored procedure or batch to indicate success or failure (and the reason for failure).

- Return multiple values to the calling stored procedure or batch in the form of output parameters.

Initial Processing of Stored Procedures

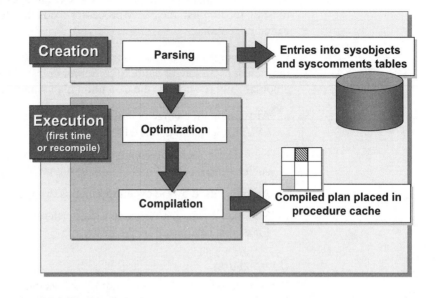

Processing a stored procedure includes creating it and then executing it the first time, which places its execution plan in the procedure cache. The procedure cache is a pool of memory containing the execution plans for all currently executing Transact-SQL statements. The size of the procedure cache fluctuates dynamically according to activity levels. The procedure cache is located in the memory pool, which is the main unit of memory for SQL Server. It contains most of the data structures that use memory in SQL Server.

Creation

When a stored procedure is created, the statements in it are parsed for syntactical accuracy. SQL Server then stores the name of the stored procedure in the **sysobjects** system table and the text of the stored procedure in the **syscomments** system table in the current database. An error is returned if a syntax error is encountered, and the stored procedure is not created.

Delayed Name Resolution

A process called delayed name resolution allows stored procedures to refer to objects that do not exist when the stored procedure is created. This process permits flexibility, because stored procedures and the objects that they reference do not have to be created in a particular order. The objects must exist by the time the stored procedure is executed. Delayed name resolution is performed at the time the stored procedure is executed.

Execution (First Time or Recompile)

The first time that a stored procedure is executed, or if the stored procedure must be recompiled, the query processor reads the stored procedure in a process called resolution.

Certain changes in a database can cause an execution plan to be either inefficient or no longer valid. SQL Server detects these changes and automatically recompiles the execution plan when any of the following apply:

- Any structural change is made to a table or view referenced by the query (ALTER TABLE and ALTER VIEW).

- New distribution statistics are generated, either explicitly from a statement, such as UPDATE STATISTICS, or automatically.

- An index used by the execution plan is dropped.

- Significant changes are made to keys (the INSERT or DELETE statement) for a table referenced by the query.

Optimization

When a stored procedure successfully passes the resolution stage, the SQL Server query optimizer analyzes the Transact-SQL statements in the stored procedure and creates a plan that contains the fastest method to access the data. To do so, the query optimizer takes into account:

- The amount of data in the tables.

- The presence and nature of table indexes and the distribution of data in the indexed columns.

- The comparison operators and comparison values that are used in WHERE clause conditions.

- The presence of joins and the UNION, GROUP BY, or ORDER BY clause.

Compilation

Compilation refers to the process of analyzing the stored procedure and creating an execution plan that is in the procedure cache. The procedure cache contains the most valuable stored procedure execution plans. Factors that increase the value of a plan include the following:

- Time required to recompile (high compile cost)
- Frequent usage

Subsequent Processing of Stored Procedures

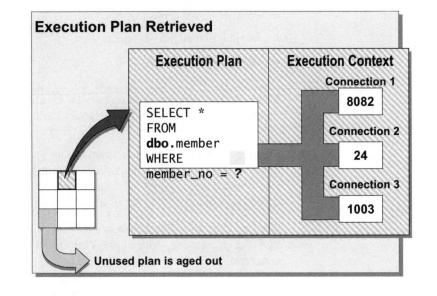

Subsequent processing of stored procedures is faster than initial processing, because SQL Server uses the optimized execution plan in the procedure cache.

If the following conditions apply, SQL Server uses the in-memory plan to execute the query subsequently:

- The current environment is the same as the environment in which the plan was compiled.

  Server, database, and connection settings determine the environment.

- Objects to which the stored procedure refers do not require name resolution.

  Objects require name resolution when objects that are owned by different users have the same names. For example, if the **sales** role owns a **Product** table, and the **development** role owns a **Product** table, SQL Server must determine the table on which to operate each time that a **Product** table is referenced.

SQL Server execution plans have two main components:

- Execution Plan—most of the execution plan is in this reentrant, read-only data structure that any number of users can use.

- Execution Context—each user currently executing the query has this reusable data structure that holds the data specific to his or her execution, such as parameter values. If a user executes a query, and one of the structures is not in use, it is reinitialized with the context for the new user.

At most, there will always be one compiled plan in the cache for each unique combination of stored procedure plus environment. There can be many plans in cache for the same stored procedure if each is for a different environment.

The following factors result in different environments that affect compilation choices:

- Parallel versus serial compiled plans
- Implicit ownership of objects
- Different SET options

Note For more information on parallel execution plans, see the "Degree of Parallelism" topic in SQL Server Books Online.

Developers should choose an environment for their applications and use it. Objects whose implicit ownership resolution is ambiguous should use explicit resolution by specifying the object owner. SET options should be consistent; they should be set at the start of a connection and not changed.

After an execution plan is generated, it stays in the procedure cache. SQL Server ages old, unused plans out of the cache only when space is needed.

Advantages of Stored Procedures

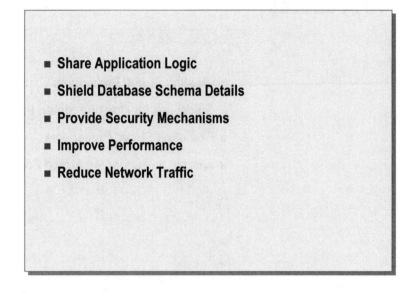

- Share Application Logic
- Shield Database Schema Details
- Provide Security Mechanisms
- Improve Performance
- Reduce Network Traffic

Stored procedures offer numerous advantages. They can:

- Share application logic with other applications, thereby ensuring consistent data access and modification.

  Stored procedures can encapsulate business functionality. Business rules or policies encapsulated in stored procedures can be changed in a single location. All clients can use the same stored procedures to ensure consistent data access and modification.

- Shield users from exposure to the details of the tables in the database. If a set of stored procedures supports all of the business functions that users need to perform, users never need to access the tables directly.

- Provide security mechanisms. Users can be granted permission to execute a stored procedure even if they do not have permission to access the tables or views to which the stored procedure refers.

- Improve performance. Stored procedures implement many tasks as a series of Transact-SQL statements. Conditional logic can be applied to the results of the first Transact-SQL statements to determine which subsequent Transact-SQL statements are executed. All of these Transact-SQL statements and conditional logic become part of a single execution plan on the server.

- Reduce network traffic. Rather than sending hundreds of Transact-SQL statements over the network, users can perform a complex operation by sending a single statement, which reduces the number of requests that pass between client and server.

◆ Creating, Executing, Modifying, and Dropping Stored Procedures

- ■ Creating Stored Procedures
- ■ Guidelines for Creating Stored Procedures
- ■ Executing Stored Procedures
- ■ Altering and Dropping Stored Procedures

This section describes how to create, execute, modify, and drop stored procedures.

Creating Stored Procedures

- **Create in Current Database Using the CREATE PROCEDURE Statement**

```
USE Northwind
GO
CREATE PROC dbo.OverdueOrders
AS
  SELECT *
  FROM dbo.Orders
  WHERE RequiredDate < GETDATE() AND ShippedDate IS Null
GO
```

- **Can Nest to 32 Levels**
- **Use sp_help to Display Information**

You can create a stored procedure in the current database only—except for temporary stored procedures, which are always created in the **tempdb** database. Creating a stored procedure is similar to creating a view. First, write and test the Transact-SQL statements that you want to include in the stored procedure. Then, if you receive the results that you expect, create the stored procedure.

Using CREATE PROCEDURE

You create stored procedures by using the CREATE PROCEDURE statement. Consider the following facts when you create stored procedures:

- Stored procedures can reference tables, views, user-defined functions, and other stored procedures, as well as temporary tables.

- If a stored procedure creates a local temporary table, the temporary table only exists for the purpose of the stored procedure and disappears when stored procedure execution completes.

- A CREATE PROCEDURE statement cannot be combined with other Transact-SQL statements in a single batch.

- The CREATE PROCEDURE definition can include any number and type of Transact-SQL statements, with the exception of the following object creation statements: CREATE DEFAULT, CREATE PROCEDURE, CREATE RULE, CREATE TRIGGER, and CREATE VIEW. Other database objects can be created within a stored procedure and should be qualified with the name of the object owner.

- To execute the CREATE PROCEDURE statement, you must be a member of the system administrators (**sysadmin**) role, database owner (**db_owner**) role, or the Data Definition Language (DDL) administrator (**db_ddladmin**) role, or you must have been granted CREATE PROCEDURE permission.

- The maximum size of a stored procedure is 128 megabytes (MB), depending on available memory.

Partial Syntax

CREATE PROC [EDURE] *procedure_name* [; *number*]
   [{ @*parameter data_type* }
      [VARYING] [= *default*] [OUTPUT]
   ] [,...n]
   [WITH
      { RECOMPILE | ENCRYPTION | RECOMPILE , ENCRYPTION }]
   [FOR REPLICATION]
   AS *sql_statement* [...n]

Example

The following statements create a stored procedure that lists all overdue orders in the **Northwind** database.

```
USE Northwind
GO
CREATE PROC dbo.OverdueOrders
AS
  SELECT *
  FROM dbo.Orders
  WHERE RequiredDate < GETDATE() AND ShippedDate IS Null
GO
```

Nesting Stored Procedures

Stored procedures can be nested (one stored procedure calls another). Characteristics of nesting include the following:

- Stored procedures can be nested to 32 levels. Attempting to exceed 32 levels of nesting causes the entire calling stored procedure chain to fail.

- The current nesting level is stored in the **@@nestlevel** system function.

- If one stored procedure calls a second stored procedure, the second stored procedure can access all of the objects that the first stored procedure created, including temporary tables.

- Nested stored procedures can be recursive. For example, Stored Procedure X can call Stored Procedure Y. While Stored Procedure Y is executing, it can call Stored Procedure X.

Viewing Information About Stored Procedures

As with other database objects, the following system stored procedures can be used to find additional information about all types of stored procedures: **sp_help**, **sp_helptext**, and **sp_depends**. To print a list of stored procedures and owner names in the database, use the **sp_stored_procedures** system stored procedure. You can also query the **sysobjects**, **syscomments**, and **sysdepends** system tables to obtain information.

Guidelines for Creating Stored Procedures

- **dbo User Should Own All Stored Procedures**
- **One Stored Procedure for One Task**
- **Create, Test, and Troubleshoot**
- **Avoid sp_ Prefix in Stored Procedure Names**
- **Use Same Connection Settings for All Stored Procedures**
- **Minimize Use of Temporary Stored Procedures**
- **Never Delete Entries Directly From Syscomments**

Consider the following guidelines when you create stored procedures:

- To avoid situations in which the owner of a stored procedure and the owner of the underlying tables differ, it is recommended that the **dbo** user own all objects in a database. Because a user can be a member of multiple roles, always specify the **dbo** user as the owner name when you create the object. Otherwise, the object will be created with your user name as the owner:

  - You must also have appropriate permissions on all of the tables or views that are referenced within the stored procedure.

  - Avoid situations in which the owner of a stored procedure and the owner of the underlying tables differ.

  Note If you are creating a user-defined system stored procedure, you must be logged in as a member of the system administrators (**sysadmin**) role and use the **master** database.

- Design each stored procedure to accomplish a single task.

- Create, test, and troubleshoot your stored procedure on the server; then test it from the client.

- To easily distinguish system stored procedures, avoid using the **sp_** prefix when you name local stored procedures.

- All stored procedures should use the same connection settings.

  SQL Server saves the settings of both SET QUOTED_IDENTIFIER and SET ANSI_NULLS when a stored procedure is created or altered. These original settings are used when the stored procedure is executed. Therefore, any client session settings for these SET options are ignored during stored procedure execution.

  Other SET options, such as SET ARITHABORT, SET ANSI_WARNINGS, and SET ANSI_PADDINGS, are not saved when a stored procedure is created or altered.

  To determine whether the ANSI SET options were enabled when a stored procedure was created, query the OBJECTPROPERTY system function. SET options should not be changed during the execution of stored procedures.

- Minimize use of temporary stored procedures to avoid contention on the system tables in **tempdb**, a situation that can adversely affect performance.

- Use **sp_executesql** instead of using the EXECUTE statement to dynamically execute a string in a stored procedure. **sp_executesql** is more efficient because it generates execution plans that SQL Server is more likely to reuse. SQL Server compiles the Transact-SQL statement or statements in the string into an execution plan that is separate from the execution plan of the stored procedure. You can use **sp_executesql** when executing a Transact-SQL statement multiple times, if the only variation is in the parameter values supplied to the Transact-SQL statement.

- Never delete entries directly from the **syscomments** system table. If you do not want users to be able to view the text of your stored procedures, you must create them by using the WITH ENCRYPTION option. If you do not use WITH ENCRYPTION, users can use SQL Server Enterprise Manager or execute the **sp_helptext** system stored procedure to view the text of stored procedures located in the **syscomments** system table.

Executing Stored Procedures

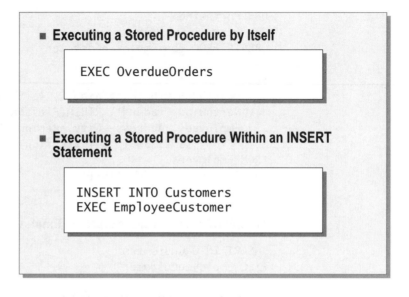

You can execute a stored procedure by itself or as part of an INSERT statement. You must have been granted EXECUTE permission on the stored procedure.

Executing a Stored Procedure by Itself

You can execute a stored procedure by issuing the EXECUTE statement along with the name of the stored procedure and any parameters.

Syntax

```
[ [ EXEC [ UTE ] ]
    {
        [ @return_status = ]
            { procedure_name [ ;number ] | @procedure_name_var
    }
    [ [ @parameter = ] { value | @variable [ OUTPUT ] | [ DEFAULT ] ]
        [ ,...n ]
    [ WITH RECOMPILE ]
```

Example 1

The following statement executes a stored procedure that lists all overdue orders in the **Northwind** database.

```
EXEC OverdueOrders
```

Executing a Stored Procedure Within an INSERT Statement

The INSERT statement can populate a local table with a result set that is returned from a local or remote stored procedure. SQL Server loads the table with data that is returned from SELECT statements in the stored procedure. The table must already exist, and data types must match.

Example 2

The following statement creates the **EmployeeCustomer** stored procedure, which inserts employees into the **Customers** table of the **Northwind** database.

```
USE Northwind
GO
CREATE PROC dbo.EmployeeCustomer
AS
SELECT
    UPPER(SUBSTRING(LastName, 1, 4)+SUBSTRING(FirstName, 1,1)),
    'Northwind Traders', RTRIM(FirstName)+' '+LastName,
    'Employee', Address, City, Region, PostalCode, Country,
    ('(206) 555-1234'+' x'+Extension), NULL
FROM Employees
WHERE HireDate < GETDATE ()
GO
```

The following statements execute the **EmployeeCustomer** stored procedure.

```
INSERT INTO Customers
EXEC EmployeeCustomer
```

The number of employees hired earlier than today's date is added to the **Customers** table.

Result

```
(9 row(s) affected)
```

Altering and Dropping Stored Procedures

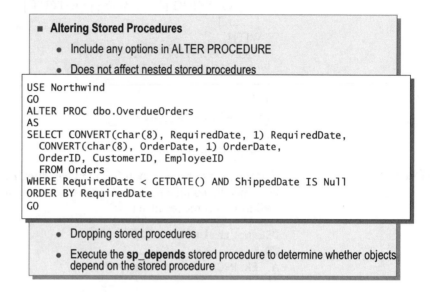

- **Altering Stored Procedures**
  - Include any options in ALTER PROCEDURE
  - Does not affect nested stored procedures

```
USE Northwind
GO
ALTER PROC dbo.OverdueOrders
AS
SELECT CONVERT(char(8), RequiredDate, 1) RequiredDate,
  CONVERT(char(8), OrderDate, 1) OrderDate,
  OrderID, CustomerID, EmployeeID
  FROM Orders
WHERE RequiredDate < GETDATE() AND ShippedDate IS Null
ORDER BY RequiredDate
GO
```

  - Dropping stored procedures
  - Execute the **sp_depends** stored procedure to determine whether objects depend on the stored procedure

Stored procedures are often modified in response to requests from users or to changes in the underlying table definitions.

Altering Stored Procedures

To modify an existing stored procedure and retain permission assignments, use the ALTER PROCEDURE statement. SQL Server replaces the previous definition of the stored procedure when it is altered with ALTER PROCEDURE.

Caution It is strongly recommended that you do not modify system stored procedures directly. Instead, create a user-defined system stored procedure by copying the statements from an existing system stored procedure, and then modify it to meet your needs.

Consider the following facts when you use the ALTER PROCEDURE statement:

- If you want to modify a stored procedure that was created with any options, such as the WITH ENCRYPTION option, you must include the option in the ALTER PROCEDURE statement to retain the functionality that the option provides.

- ALTER PROCEDURE alters only a single procedure. If your procedure calls other stored procedures, the nested stored procedures are not affected.

- Permission to execute this statement defaults to the creators of the initial stored procedure, members of the **sysadmin** server role, and members of the **db_owner** and **db_ddladmin** fixed database roles. You cannot grant permission to execute ALTER PROCEDURE.

Syntax

```
ALTER PROC [ EDURE ] procedure_name [ ; number ]
   [ { @parameter data_type }
      [ VARYING ] [ = default ] [ OUTPUT ]
   ] [ ,...n ]
   [ WITH
      { RECOMPILE | ENCRYPTION
         | RECOMPILE , ENCRYPTION
      }
   ]
   [ FOR REPLICATION ]
   AS
      sql_statement [ ...n ]
```

Example

The following example modifies the **OverdueOrders** stored procedure to select only specific column names rather than all columns from the **Orders** table, as well as to sort the result set.

```
USE Northwind
GO
ALTER PROC dbo.OverdueOrders
AS
SELECT CONVERT(char(8), RequiredDate, 1) RequiredDate,
   CONVERT(char(8), OrderDate, 1) OrderDate,
   OrderID, CustomerID, EmployeeID
   FROM Orders
WHERE RequiredDate < GETDATE() AND ShippedDate IS Null
ORDER BY RequiredDate
GO
```

The following statement executes the **OverdueOrders** stored procedure.

```
EXEC OverdueOrders
```

Result

If the **OverdueOrders** stored procedure is executed based on today's date, the result set will look similar to the following.

RequiredDate	OrderDate	OrderID	CustomerID	EmployeeID
05/06/98	04/08/98	11008	ERNSH	7
05/11/98	04/13/98	11019	RANCH	6
05/19/98	04/21/98	11039	LINOD	1
05/21/98	04/22/98	11040	GREAL	4
05/25/98	04/23/98	11045	BOTTM	6

.

.

.

```
(21 row(s) affected)
```

Dropping Stored Procedures

Use the DROP PROCEDURE statement to remove user-defined stored procedures from the current database.

Before you drop a stored procedure, execute the **sp_depends** stored procedure to determine whether objects depend on the stored procedure.

Syntax

DROP PROCEDURE { *procedure* } [,...n]

Example

This example drops the **OverdueOrders** stored procedure.

```
USE Northwind
GO
DROP PROC dbo.OverdueOrders
GO
```

Lab A: Creating Stored Procedures

Objectives

After completing this lab, you will be able to:

- Create a stored procedure by using SQL Query Analyzer.
- Display information about stored procedures that you create.

Prerequisites

Before working on this lab, you must have:

- Script files for this lab, which are located in C:\Moc\2073A\Labfiles\L09.
- Answer files for this lab, which are located in
  C:\Moc\2073A\Labfiles\L09\Answers.

Lab Setup

To complete this lab, you must have either:

- Completed the prior lab, or
- Executed the C:\Moc\2073A\Batches\Restore09A.cmd batch file.

  This command file restores the **ClassNorthwind** database to a state required
  for this lab.

For More Information

If you require help in executing files, search SQL Query Analyzer Help for
"Execute a query".

Other resources that you can use include:

- The **Northwind** database schema.
- Microsoft SQL Server Books Online.

Scenario

The organization of the classroom is meant to simulate that of a worldwide trading firm named Northwind Traders. Its fictitious domain name is nwtraders.msft. The primary DNS server for nwtraders.msft is the instructor computer, which has an Internet Protocol (IP) address of 192.168.x.200 (where x is the assigned classroom number). The name of the instructor computer is London.

The following table provides the user name, computer name, and IP address for each student computer in the fictitious nwtraders.msft domain. Find the user name for your computer, and make a note of it.

User name	Computer name	IP address
SQLAdmin1	Vancouver	192.168.x.1
SQLAdmin2	Denver	192.168.x.2
SQLAdmin3	Perth	192.168.x.3
SQLAdmin4	Brisbane	192.168.x.4
SQLAdmin5	Lisbon	192.168.x.5
SQLAdmin6	Bonn	192.168.x.6
SQLAdmin7	Lima	192.168.x.7
SQLAdmin8	Santiago	192.168.x.8
SQLAdmin9	Bangalore	192.168.x.9
SQLAdmin10	Singapore	192.168.x.10
SQLAdmin11	Casablanca	192.168.x.11
SQLAdmin12	Tunis	192.168.x.12
SQLAdmin13	Acapulco	192.168.x.13
SQLAdmin14	Miami	192.168.x.14
SQLAdmin15	Auckland	192.168.x.15
SQLAdmin16	Suva	192.168.x.16
SQLAdmin17	Stockholm	192.168.x.17
SQLAdmin18	Moscow	192.168.x.18
SQLAdmin19	Caracas	192.168.x.19
SQLAdmin20	Montevideo	192.168.x.20
SQLAdmin21	Manila	192.168.x.21
SQLAdmin22	Tokyo	192.168.x.22
SQLAdmin23	Khartoum	192.168.x.23
SQLAdmin24	Nairobi	192.168.x.24

Estimated time to complete this lab: 15 minutes

Exercise 1
Writing and Executing a Stored Procedure

In this exercise, you will create a stored procedure that lists the five most expensive products ordered by price.

▶ To create a stored procedure by using SQL Query Analyzer

In this procedure, you will create a stored procedure that lists the five most expensive products.
C:\Moc\2073A\Labfiles\L09\Answers\FiveMostExpensiveProducts.sql is a completed script for this procedure.

1. Log on to the **NWTraders** classroom domain by using the information in the following table.

Option	Value
User name	**SQLAdmin***x* (where *x* corresponds to your computer name as designated in the nwtraders.msft classroom domain)
Password	**password**

2. Open SQL Query Analyzer and, if requested, log in to the (local) server with Microsoft Windows® Authentication.

   You have permission to log in to and administer SQL Server because you are logged as **SQLAdmin***x*, which is a member of the Microsoft Windows 2000 local group, Administrators. All members of this group are automatically mapped to the SQL Server **sysadmin** role.

3. Verify that you are using the **ClassNorthwind** database.

4. Write a query against the **Products** table that lists only the product name and unit price. Limit the rows returned to the five most expensive products, and order the result set by unit price.

5. Test your query to ensure that it returns the expected result set.

6. Modify your query to create a stored procedure named **FiveMostExpensiveProducts**.

7. Save your script as C:\MOC\2073A\Labfiles\L09\FiveMostExpensiveProducts.sql.

8. Execute your stored procedure to verify that it works as expected.

   What are the five most expensive products?

   _____

   _____

Exercise 2
Locating Stored Procedure Information

In this exercise, you will execute system stored procedures and use SQL Server Enterprise Manager and SQL Query Analyzer to display information about the stored procedures that you have created.

▶ To display stored procedure definitions

In this procedure, you will use SQL Server Enterprise Manager and SQL Query Analyzer to display stored procedure definitions.

1. Open SQL Server Enterprise Manager.

2. Expand your server, expand **Databases**, expand **ClassNorthwind**, and then expand **Stored Procedures**.

3. In the details pane, right-click **FiveMostExpensiveProducts**, and then click **Properties**.

4. Review the stored procedure definition.

5. Open SQL Query Analyzer.

6. Verify that you are using the **ClassNorthwind** database.

7. In the query window, execute the following system stored procedure.

```
sp_helptext FiveMostExpensiveProducts
```

8. Review the stored procedure definition.

▶ To display metadata information about stored procedures

In this procedure, you will use the OBJECT_ID and OBJECTPROPERTY functions to display metadata about stored procedures.

1. Using SQL QueryAnalyzer, determine the object ID of the **FiveMostExpensiveProducts** stored procedure by executing the following statement:

```
SELECT OBJECT_ID('FiveMostExpensiveProducts')
```

Write the object ID below.

---

2. Execute the following statement to determine whether the ANSI NULLs connection settings were turned on when you created the **FiveMostExpensiveProducts** stored procedure. Substitute the object ID of your stored procedure for x.

```
SELECT OBJECTPROPERTY(x, 'ExecIsAnsiNullsOn')
```

What was the result?

---

3. Execute the following statement to determine whether the ANSI quoted identifer connection setting was turned on when you created the **FiveMostExpensiveProducts** stored procedure. Substitute the object ID of your stored procedure for *x*.

```
SELECT OBJECTPROPERTY(x, 'ExecIsQuotedIdentOn')
```

What was the result?

_____

_____

◆ Using Parameters in Stored Procedures

- **Using Input Parameters**
- **Executing Stored Procedures Using Input Parameters**
- **Returning Values Using Output Parameters**
- **Explicitly Recompiling Stored Procedures**

Parameters extend the functionality of stored procedures. You can pass information into and out of stored procedures by using parameters. They enable you to use the same stored procedure to search a database many times.

For example, you can add a parameter to a stored procedure that searches the **Employee** table for employees whose hire dates match a date that you specify. You then can execute the stored procedure each time that you want to specify a different hire date.

SQL Server supports two types of parameters: input parameters and output parameters.

Using Input Parameters

- **Validate All Incoming Parameter Values First**

- **Provide Appropriate Default Values and Include Null Checks**

```
CREATE PROCEDURE dbo.[Year to Year Sales]
   @BeginningDate DateTime, @EndingDate DateTime
AS
IF @BeginningDate IS NULL OR @EndingDate IS NULL
BEGIN
    RAISERROR('NULL values are not allowed', 14, 1)
    RETURN
END
SELECT O.ShippedDate,
       O.OrderID,
       OS.Subtotal,
       DATENAME(yy,ShippedDate) AS Year
FROM ORDERS O INNER JOIN [Order Subtotals] OS
   ON O.OrderID = OS.OrderID
WHERE O.ShippedDate BETWEEN @BeginningDate AND @EndingDate
GO
```

Input parameters allow information to be passed into a stored procedure. To define a stored procedure that accepts input parameters, you declare one or more variables as parameters in the CREATE PROCEDURE statement.

Partial Syntax

@parameter data_type [*= default*]

Consider the following facts and guidelines when you specify parameters:

- All incoming parameter values should be checked at the beginning of a stored procedure to trap missing and invalid values early.

- You should provide appropriate default values for a parameter.

  If a default is defined, a user can execute the stored procedure without specifying a value for that parameter.

Note   Parameter defaults must be constants or NULL. When you specify NULL as a default value for a parameter, you must use =Null; IS NULL will not work because the syntax does not support the ANSI NULL designation.

- The maximum number of parameters in a stored procedure is 1,024.

- The maximum number of local variables in a stored procedure is limited only by available memory.

- Parameters are local to a stored procedure. The same parameter names can be used in other stored procedures.

Parameter information is stored in the **syscolumns** system table.

Example

The following example creates the **Year to Year Sales** stored procedure, which returns all sales between specific dates.

```
CREATE PROCEDURE dbo.[Year to Year Sales]
   @BeginningDate DateTime, @EndingDate DateTime
AS
IF @BeginningDate IS NULL OR @EndingDate IS NULL
BEGIN
    RAISERROR('NULL values are not allowed', 14, 1)
    RETURN
END
SELECT O.ShippedDate,
       O.OrderID,
       OS.Subtotal,
       DATENAME(yy,ShippedDate) AS Year
FROM ORDERS O INNER JOIN [Order Subtotals] OS
   ON O.OrderID = OS.OrderID
WHERE O.ShippedDate BETWEEN @BeginningDate AND @EndingDate
GO
```

Executing Stored Procedures Using Input Parameters

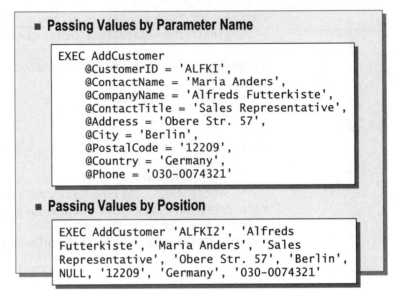

- **Passing Values by Parameter Name**

```
EXEC AddCustomer
    @CustomerID = 'ALFKI',
    @ContactName = 'Maria Anders',
    @CompanyName = 'Alfreds Futterkiste',
    @ContactTitle = 'Sales Representative',
    @Address = 'Obere Str. 57',
    @City = 'Berlin',
    @PostalCode = '12209',
    @Country = 'Germany',
    @Phone = '030-0074321'
```

- **Passing Values by Position**

```
EXEC AddCustomer 'ALFKI2', 'Alfreds
Futterkiste', 'Maria Anders', 'Sales
Representative', 'Obere Str. 57', 'Berlin',
NULL, '12209', 'Germany', '030-0074321'
```

You can set the value of a parameter by either passing the value to the stored procedure, by parameter name, or by position. You should not mix the different formats when you supply values.

Passing Values by Parameter Name

Specifying a parameter in an EXECUTE statement in the format *@parameter = value* is referred to as *passing by parameter name*. When you pass values by parameter name, the parameter values can be specified in any order, and you can omit parameters that allow null values or that have a default.

The default value of a parameter, if defined for the parameter in the stored procedure, is used when:

- No value for the parameter is specified when the stored procedure is executed.

- The DEFAULT keyword is specified as the value for the parameter.

Syntax

```
[ [ EXEC [ UTE ] ]
    {
        [ @return_status = ]
            { procedure_name [ ;number ] | @procedure_name_var
    }
    [ [ @parameter = ] { value | @variable [ OUTPUT ] | [ DEFAULT ] ]
        [ ,...n ]
[ WITH RECOMPILE ]
```

Partial Example 1

The following partial example creates the **AddCustomer** stored procedure, which adds a new customer to the **Northwind** database. Notice that all variables except for **CustomerID** and **CompanyName** are specified to allow a null value.

```
USE Northwind
GO
CREATE PROCEDURE dbo.AddCustomer
    @CustomerID      nchar (5),
    @CompanyName     nvarchar (40),
    @ContactName     nvarchar (30) = NULL,
    @ContactTitle    nvarchar (30) = NULL,
    @Address         nvarchar (60) = NULL,
    @City            nvarchar (15) = NULL,
    @Region          nvarchar (15) = NULL,
    @PostalCode      nvarchar (10) = NULL,
    @Country         nvarchar (15) = NULL,
    @Phone           nvarchar (24) = NULL,
    @Fax             nvarchar (24) = NULL
    AS
    .
    .
    .
```

Partial Example 2

The following example passes values by parameter name to the **AddCustomer** stored procedure. Notice that the order of the values is different from the CREATE PROCEDURE statement.

Also notice that values for the **@Region** and **@Fax** parameters are not specified. If the Region and Fax columns in the table allow null values, the **AddCustomer** stored procedure will execute successfully. However, if the Region and Fax columns do not allow null values, you must pass a value to a parameter, regardless of whether you have defined the parameter to allow a null value.

```
EXEC AddCustomer
    @CustomerID = 'ALFKI',
    @ContactName = 'Maria Anders',
    @CompanyName = 'Alfreds Futterkiste',
    @ContactTitle = 'Sales Representative',
    @Address = 'Obere Str. 57',
    @City = 'Berlin',
    @PostalCode = '12209',
    @Country = 'Germany',
    @Phone = '030-0074321'
    .
    .
    .
```

Passing Values by Position

Passing only values (without reference to the parameters to which they are being passed) is referred to as *passing values by position*. When you specify only a value, the parameter values must be listed in the order in which they are defined in the CREATE PROCEDURE statement.

When you pass values by position, you can omit parameters where defaults exist, but you cannot interrupt the sequence. For example, if a stored procedure has five parameters, you can omit both the fourth and fifth parameters, but you cannot omit the fourth parameter and specify the fifth.

Partial Example 3

The following example passes values by position to the **AddCustomer** stored procedure. Notice that the **@Region** and **@Fax** parameter have no values. However, only the **@Region** parameter is supplied with NULL. The **@Fax** parameter is omitted because it is the last parameter.

```
EXEC AddCustomer 'ALFKI2', 'Alfreds Futterkiste', 'Maria
Anders', 'Sales Representative', 'Obere Str. 57', 'Berlin',
NULL, '12209', 'Germany', '030-0074321'
```

Returning Values Using Output Parameters

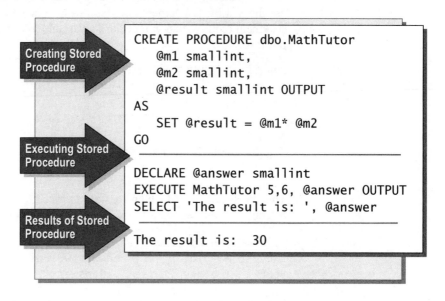

```
                          CREATE PROCEDURE dbo.MathTutor
Creating Stored              @m1 smallint,
Procedure                    @m2 smallint,
                             @result smallint OUTPUT
                          AS
                             SET @result = @m1* @m2
                          GO
Executing Stored
Procedure
                          DECLARE @answer smallint
                          EXECUTE MathTutor 5,6, @answer OUTPUT
                          SELECT 'The result is: ', @answer
Results of Stored
Procedure
                          The result is:   30
```

Stored procedures can return information to the calling stored procedure or client with output parameters (variables designated with the OUTPUT keyword). By using output parameters, any changes to the parameter that result from the execution of the stored procedure can be retained, even after the stored procedure completes execution.

To use an output parameter, you must specify the OUTPUT keyword in both the CREATE PROCEDURE and EXECUTE statements. If the keyword OUTPUT is omitted when the stored procedure is executed, the stored procedure still executes but does not return a value. Output parameters have the following characteristics:

- The calling statement must contain a variable name to receive the return value. It is not possible to pass constants.

- You can use the variable subsequently in additional Transact-SQL statements in the batch or the calling stored procedure.

- The parameter can be of any data type, except **text** or **image**.

- They can be cursor placeholders.

Example 1

This example creates a **MathTutor** stored procedure that calculates the product of two numbers. This example uses the SET statement. However, you can also use the SELECT statement to dynamically concatenate a string. A SET statement requires that you declare a variable in order to print the string "The result is:"

```
CREATE PROCEDURE dbo.MathTutor
    @m1 smallint,
    @m2 smallint,
    @result smallint OUTPUT
AS
    SET @result = @m1* @m2
GO
```

This batch calls the **MathTutor** stored procedure and passes the values of 5 and 6. These values become variables, which are entered into the SET statement.

```
DECLARE @answer smallint
EXECUTE MathTutor 5,6, @answer OUTPUT
SELECT 'The result is: ', @answer
```

Result

The **@result** parameter is designated with the OUTPUT keyword. SQL Server prints the content of the **@result** variable when you execute the **MathTutor** stored procedure. The result variable is defined as the product of the two values, 5 and 6.

```
The result is: 30
```

Explicitly Recompiling Stored Procedures

- **Recompile When**
  - Stored procedure returns widely varying result sets
  - A new index is added to an underlying table
  - The parameter value is atypical
- **Recompile by Using**
  - CREATE PROCEDURE [WITH RECOMPILE]
  - EXECUTE [WITH RECOMPILE]
  - **sp_recompile**

Stored procedures can be recompiled explicitly, but you should do so infrequently, and only when:

- Parameter values are passed to a stored procedure that returns widely varying result sets.
- A new index is added to an underlying table from which a stored procedure might benefit.
- The parameter value that you are supplying is atypical.

SQL Server provides three methods for recompiling a stored procedure explicitly.

CREATE PROCEDURE...[WITH RECOMPILE]

The CREATE PROCEDURE...[WITH RECOMPILE] statement indicates that SQL Server does not cache a plan for this stored procedure. Instead, the option recompiles the stored procedure each time that it is executed.

Example 1

The following example creates a stored procedure called **OrderCount** that is recompiled each time that it is executed.

```
USE Northwind
GO
CREATE PROC dbo.OrderCount
@CustomerID nchar (10)
WITH RECOMPILE
AS
    SELECT count(*) FROM [Orders Qry]
    WHERE CustomerID = @CustomerID
GO
```

EXECUTE...[WITH RECOMPILE]

The EXECUTE...[WITH RECOMPILE] statement creates a new execution plan each time that the procedure is executed, if you specify WITH RECOMPILE. The new execution plan is not stored in the cache. Use this option if the parameter that you are passing varies greatly from those that are usually passed to the stored procedure. Because this optimized plan is the exception rather than the rule, when execution is completed, you should re-execute the stored procedure by using a parameter that is typically passed. This option is also useful if the data has changed significantly since the stored procedure was last compiled.

Example 2

This example recompiles the **CustomerInfo** stored procedure at the time that it is executed.

```
EXEC  CustomerInfo WITH RECOMPILE
```

sp_recompile

The **sp_recompile** system stored procedure recompiles the specified stored procedure or trigger the next time that it is executed. If the **@objname** parameter specifies a table or view, all stored procedures that use the named object will be recompiled the next time that they are executed.

Use the **sp_recompile** system stored procedure with the *tablename* option if you have added a new index to an underlying table that the stored procedure references, and if you believe that the performance of the stored procedure will benefit from the new index.

Example 3

This example recompiles all stored procedures or triggers that reference the **Customers** table in the **Northwind** database.

```
EXEC sp_recompile Customers
```

Note   You can use DBCC FREEPROCCACHE to clear all stored procedure plans from the cache.

Executing Extended Stored Procedures

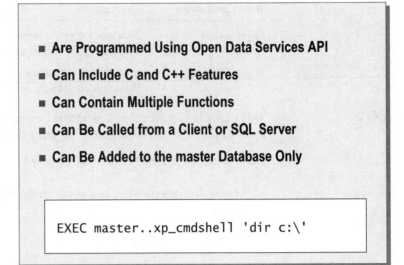

- **Are Programmed Using Open Data Services API**
- **Can Include C and C++ Features**
- **Can Contain Multiple Functions**
- **Can Be Called from a Client or SQL Server**
- **Can Be Added to the master Database Only**

```
EXEC master..xp_cmdshell 'dir c:\'
```

Extended stored procedures are functions inside a DLL that increase SQL Server functionality. They are executed in the same way as stored procedures, and they support input parameters, return status codes, and output parameters.

Example 1

This example executes the **xp_cmdshell** extended stored procedure that displays a list of files and subdirectories by executing the **dir** operating system command.

```
EXEC master..xp_cmdshell 'dir c:\ '
```

Extended stored procedures:

- Are programmed by using the Open Data Services (ODS) application programming interface (API).

- Allow you to create your own external routines in programming languages such as Microsoft Visual C++® and Visual C.

- Can contain multiple functions.

- Can be called from a client or SQL Server.

- Can be added to the **master** database only.

Note You can execute an extended stored procedure from the **master** database only, or by explicitly specifying the location **master**. You can also create a user-defined system stored procedure that calls the extended stored procedure. This allows you to execute the extended stored procedure from within any database.

The following table includes some commonly used extended stored procedures.

Extended stored procedure	Description
xp_cmdshell	Executes a given command string as an operating system command shell and returns output as rows of text
xp_logevent	Logs a user-defined message in a SQL Server log file or in the Windows 2000 Event Viewer.

Example 2

This example executes the **sp_helptext** system stored procedure to display the name of the DLL that contains the **xp_cmdshell** extended stored procedure.

```
EXEC master..sp_helptext xp_cmdshell
```

Result

This result displays the DLL that contains the **xp_cmdshell** extended stored procedure.

```
xplog70.dll
```

You can also create your own extended stored procedures. Generally, you call extended stored procedures to communicate with other applications or the operating system. For example, Sqlmap70.dll allows you to send e-mail messages from within SQL Server by using the **xp_sendmail** extended stored procedure.

When you select **Development Tools** during SQL Server Setup, SQL Server installs sample extended stored procedures in the C:\Program Files\Microsoft SQL Server\80\Tools\Devtools\Samples\ODS folder as a compressed self-extracting executable.

Handling Error Messages

- **RETURN Statement Exits Query or Procedure Unconditionally**

- **sp_addmessage Creates Custom Error Messages**

- **@@error Contains Error Number for Last Executed Statement**

- **RAISERROR Statement**

  - Returns user-defined or system error message

  - Sets system flag to record error

To enhance the effectiveness of stored procedures, you should include error messages that communicate transaction status (success or failure) to the user. You should perform the task logic, business logic, and error checking *before* you begin transactions, and you should keep your transactions short.

You can use coding strategies, such as existence checks, to recognize errors. When an error occurs, provide as much information as possible to the client. You can check the following in your error handling logic: return codes, SQL Server errors, and custom error messages.

RETURN Statement

The RETURN statement exits from a query or stored procedure unconditionally. It also can return an integer status value (return code).

A return value of 0 indicates success. Return values 0 through -14 are currently in use, and return values from -15 through -99 are reserved for future use. If a user-defined return value is not provided, the SQL Server value is used. User-defined return values always take precedence over those that SQL Server supplies.

Example 1

This example creates the **GetOrders** stored procedure that retrieves information from the **Orders** and **Customers** tables by querying the **Orders Qry** view. The RETURN statement in the **GetOrders** stored procedure returns the total number of rows from the SELECT statement to another stored procedure. You could also nest the **GetOrders** stored procedure within another stored procedure.

```
USE Northwind
GO
CREATE PROCEDURE dbo.GetOrders
    @CustomerID nchar (10)
AS
    SELECT OrderID, CustomerID, EmployeeID
    FROM [Orders Qry]
    WHERE CustomerID = @CustomerID
    RETURN (@@ROWCOUNT)
GO
```

sp_addmessage

This stored procedure allows developers to create custom error messages. SQL Server treats both system and custom error messages the same way. All messages are stored in the **sysmessages** table in the **master** database. These error messages also can be written automatically to the Windows 2000 application log.

Example 2

This example creates a user-defined error message that requires the message to be written to the Windows 2000 application log when it occurs.

```
EXEC sp_addmessage
@msgnum = 50010,
@severity = 10,
@msgtext = 'Customer cannot be deleted.',
@with_log = 'true'
```

@@error

This system function contains the error number for the most recently executed Transact-SQL statement. It is cleared and reset with each statement that is executed. A value of 0 is returned if the statement executes successfully. You can use the **@@error** system function to detect a specific error number or to exit a stored procedure conditionally.

Example 3

This example creates the **AddSupplierProduct** stored procedure in the **Northwind** database. This stored procedure uses the **@@error** system function to determine whether an error occurs when each INSERT statement is executed. If the error does occur, the transaction is rolled back.

```
USE Northwind
GO
CREATE PROCEDURE dbo.AddSupplierProduct
        @CompanyName nvarchar (40) = NULL,
        @ContactName nvarchar (40) = NULL,
        @ContactTitle nvarchar (40)= NULL,
        @Address nvarchar (60) = NULL,
        @City nvarchar (15) = NULL,
        @Region nvarchar (40) = NULL,
        @PostalCode nvarchar (10) = NULL,
        @Country nvarchar (15) = NULL,
        @Phone nvarchar (24) = NULL,
        @Fax nvarchar (24) = NULL,
        @HomePage ntext = NULL,
        @ProductName nvarchar (40) = NULL,
        @CategoryID int = NULL,
        @QuantityPerUnit nvarchar (20) = NULL,
        @UnitPrice money = NULL,
        @UnitsInStock smallint = NULL,
        @UnitsOnOrder smallint = NULL,
        @ReorderLevel smallint = NULL,
        @Discontinued bit  = NULL
AS
BEGIN TRANSACTION
    INSERT Suppliers (
        CompanyName,
        ContactName,
        Address,
        City,
        Region,
        PostalCode,
        Country,
        Phone)
    VALUES (
        @CompanyName,
        @ContactName,
        @Address,
        @City,
        @Region,
        @PostalCode,
        @Country,
        @Phone)
    IF @@error <> 0
        BEGIN
          ROLLBACK TRAN
              RETURN
        END
    DECLARE @InsertSupplierID int
    SELECT @InsertSupplierID=@@identity
    INSERT Products (
        ProductName,
        SupplierID,
        CategoryID,
        QuantityPerUnit,
        Discontinued)
    VALUES (
```

```
                    @ProductName,
                    @InsertSupplierID,
                    @CategoryID,
                    @QuantityPerUnit,
                    @Discontinued)
        IF @@error <> 0
            BEGIN
                ROLLBACK TRAN
                    RETURN
            END
    COMMIT TRANSACTION
```

RAISERROR Statement

The RAISERROR statement returns a user-defined error message and sets a system flag to record that an error has occurred. You must specify an error severity level and message state when using the RAISERROR statement.

The RAISERROR statement allows the application to retrieve an entry from the **master..sysmessages** system table or build a message dynamically with user-specified severity and state information. The RAISERROR statement can write error messages to the SQL Server Error Log and to the Windows 2000 application log.

Example 4

This example raises a user-defined error message and writes the message to the Windows 2000 application log.

```
RAISERROR(50010, 16, 1) WITH LOG
```

Notes The PRINT statement returns a user-defined message to the message handler of the client; however, unlike the RAISERROR statement, the PRINT statement does not store the error number in the **@@error** system function.

Demonstration: Handling Error Messages

Follow this script as the instructor points out the error handling techniques that are included in it.

```
/* UpdateCustomerPhone
Updates a customer phone number
Error checking ensures that a valid customer
identification number is supplied
*/
/*
The following user-defined message supports the
UpdateCustomerPhone stored procedure*/
EXEC sp_addmessage 50010, 16, 'CustomerID not found.',
@replace='replace'
USE Northwind
GO
CREATE PROCEDURE UpdateCustomerPhone
  @CustomerID nchar (5) = NULL,
  @Phone nvarchar (24) = NULL
AS
IF @CustomerID IS NULL
   BEGIN
      PRINT 'You must supply a valid CustomerID.'
      RETURN
END
/* Ensure a valid CustomerID is supplied' */
IF NOT EXISTS
   (SELECT * FROM Customers WHERE CustomerID = @CustomerID)
      BEGIN
         RAISERROR (50010, 16, 1) --Customer not found.
         RETURN
      END
```

```
BEGIN TRANSACTION
UPDATE Customers
   SET Phone = @Phone
   WHERE CustomerID = @CustomerID

/* Display message that the phone number for CompanyName has
been updated */
SELECT 'The phone number for ' + @CustomerID + ' has been
updated to ' +
@Phone
COMMIT TRANSACTION
GO
```

Performance Considerations

- **Windows 2000 System Monitor**
  - Object: SQL Server: Cache Manager
  - Object: SQL Statistics
- **SQL Profiler**
  - Can monitor events
  - Can test each statement in a stored procedure

You can use the following tools to help you find the source of performance problems that may be related to stored procedure execution.

Windows 2000 System Monitor

Windows 2000 System Monitor monitors the use of the procedure cache, in addition to many other related activities.

The following objects and counters provide general information about the compiled plans in the procedure cache and the number of recompilations. You can also monitor a specific instance, such as **procedure plan**.

Object	Counters
SQL Server: Cache Manager	Cache Hit-Ratio
	Cache Object Counts
	Cache Pages
	Cache Use Count/sec
SQL Statistics	SQL Re-compilations/sec

SQL Profiler

SQL Profiler is a graphical tool that allows you to monitor events, such as when the stored procedure has started or completed, or when individual Transact-SQL statements within a stored procedure have started or completed. In addition, you can monitor whether a stored procedure is found in the procedure cache.

In the development phase of a project, you can also test stored procedure statements one line at a time to confirm that the statements work as expected.

Note Use caution when you create nested stored procedures. Nesting stored procedures adds a level of complexity that can make troubleshooting performance problems difficult.

Recommended Practices

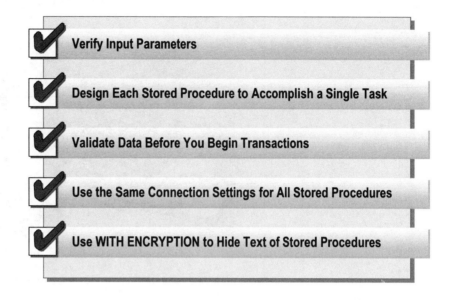

- ✔ Verify Input Parameters
- ✔ Design Each Stored Procedure to Accomplish a Single Task
- ✔ Validate Data Before You Begin Transactions
- ✔ Use the Same Connection Settings for All Stored Procedures
- ✔ Use WITH ENCRYPTION to Hide Text of Stored Procedures

To write more effective and efficient stored procedures, follow these recommended practices:

- Verify all input parameters at the beginning of each stored procedure to trap missing and invalid values early.
- Design each stored procedure to accomplish a single task.
- Perform task and business logic error checking and data validation *before* you begin transactions. Keep your transactions short.
- Use the same connection settings for all stored procedures.
- To conceal the text of stored procedures, use the WITH ENCRYPTION option. Never delete entries from the **syscomments** system table.

Additional information on the following topic is available in SQL Server Books Online.

Topic	Search on
Procedure cache	"SQL Server memory pool"
	"execution plan caching and reuse"

Lab B: Creating Stored Procedures Using Parameters

Objectives

After completing this lab, you will be able to:

- Create a stored procedure by using the Create Stored Procedure Wizard.
- Test a stored procedure that includes error-handling techniques.
- Create custom error messages.
- Create stored procedures that return codes.

Prerequisites

Before working on this lab, you must have:

- Script files for this lab, which are located in C:\Moc\2073A\Labfiles\L09.
- Answer files for this lab, which are located in
  C:\Moc\2073A\Labfiles\L09\Answers.

Lab Setup

To complete this lab, you must have either:

- Completed the prior lab, or
- Executed the C:\Moc\2073A\Batches\Restore09B.cmd batch file.

  This command file restores the **ClassNorthwind** database to a state required
  for this lab.

For More Information

If you require help in executing files, search SQL Query Analyzer Help for
"Execute a query".

Other resources that you can use include:

- The **Northwind** database schema.

- Microsoft SQL Server Books Online.

Scenario

The organization of the classroom is meant to simulate that of a worldwide trading firm named Northwind Traders. Its fictitious domain name is nwtraders.msft. The primary DNS server for nwtraders.msft is the instructor computer, which has an Internet Protocol (IP) address of 192.168.*x*.200 (where *x* is the assigned classroom number). The name of the instructor computer is London.

The following table provides the user name, computer name, and IP address for each student computer in the fictitious nwtraders.msft domain. Find the user name for your computer, and make a note of it.

User name	Computer name	IP address
SQLAdmin1	Vancouver	192.168.*x*.1
SQLAdmin2	Denver	192.168.*x*.2
SQLAdmin3	Perth	192.168.*x*.3
SQLAdmin4	Brisbane	192.168.*x*.4
SQLAdmin5	Lisbon	192.168.*x*.5
SQLAdmin6	Bonn	192.168.*x*.6
SQLAdmin7	Lima	192.168.*x*.7
SQLAdmin8	Santiago	192.168.*x*.8
SQLAdmin9	Bangalore	192.168.*x*.9
SQLAdmin10	Singapore	192.168.*x*.10
SQLAdmin11	Casablanca	192.168.*x*.11
SQLAdmin12	Tunis	192.168.*x*.12
SQLAdmin13	Acapulco	192.168.*x*.13
SQLAdmin14	Miami	192.168.*x*.14
SQLAdmin15	Auckland	192.168.*x*.15
SQLAdmin16	Suva	192.168.*x*.16
SQLAdmin17	Stockholm	192.168.*x*.17
SQLAdmin18	Moscow	192.168.*x*.18
SQLAdmin19	Caracas	192.168.*x*.19
SQLAdmin20	Montevideo	192.168.*x*.20
SQLAdmin21	Manila	192.168.*x*.21
SQLAdmin22	Tokyo	192.168.*x*.22
SQLAdmin23	Khartoum	192.168.*x*.23
SQLAdmin24	Nairobi	192.168.*x*.24

Estimated time to complete this lab: 45 minutes

Exercise 1
Using the Create Stored Procedure Wizard

In this exercise, you will use the Create Stored Procedure Wizard to create a stored procedure in the **ClassNorthwind** database that updates the phone number of an employee.

▶ **To use the Create Stored Procedure Wizard**

In this procedure, you will use the Create Stored Procedure Wizard to create a stored procedure that updates an employee's phone number.

1. Log on to the **NWTraders** classroom domain by using the information in the following table.

Option	Value
User name	**SQLAdmin**x (where x corresponds to your computer name as designated in the nwtraders.msft classroom domain)
Password	**password**

2. Open SQL Server Enterprise Manager.

3. In the console tree, click your server.

4. On the **Tools** menu, click **Wizards**.

5. Expand **Database**, and then double-click Create Stored Procedure Wizard.

6. Select the **ClassNorthwind** database.

7. Create a stored procedure that updates an employee's phone number. The phone number is maintained in the **Employees** table. Select the **Update** action for the **Employees** table.

8. Click the **Edit** button to edit the stored procedure properties.

9. Name your stored procedure **UpdateEmployeePhone**.

10. Include only the **HomePhone** column in the SET clause and only **EmployeeID** in the WHERE clause.

11. In the console tree, expand the **ClassNorthwind** database, and then expand **Stored Procedures**.

12. Verify that the **UpdateEmployeePhone** stored procedure is listed in the details pane.

13. Review the properties of the **UpdateEmployeePhone** stored procedure.

    What parameters were defined in the stored procedure?

    _____

    _____

14. Open SQL Query Analyzer and, if requested, log in to the (local) server with Windows Authentication.

    You have permission to log in to and administer SQL Server because you are logged as **SQLAdminx**, which is a member of the Windows 2000 local group, Administrators. All members of this group are automatically mapped to the SQL Server **sysadmin** role.

15. Execute the **UpdateEmployeePhone** stored procedure to verify that it works as expected. Update the phone number to (503) 555-1212 for employee Nancy Davolio, whose EmployeeID is 1.

▶ **To generate a script**

In this procedure, you will generate and save a script for the stored procedure that you created with the Create Stored Procedure Wizard.

1. Switch to SQL Server Enterprise Manager.

2. In the console tree, expand **Databases**, expand **ClassNorthwind**, and then click **Stored Procedures**.

3. In the details pane, right-click **UpdateEmployeePhone**, point to **All Tasks**, and then click **Generate SQL Script**.

4. Click **OK** to generate the script.

5. Save the script as **UpdateEmployeePhone.sql**.

6. Open and review the saved script.

Exercise 2
Using Error Handling in Stored Procedures

In this exercise, you will execute a script that creates a stored procedure to add a supplier and a product to the **ClassNorthwind** database. You will then test the error handling contained in this script.

▶ **To create and test a stored procedure**

In this procedure, you will open and review a script that creates a stored procedure to add a new supplier and a new product. Then you will test to ensure that the stored procedure executes as expected by using it to insert a new supplier and a new product. Finally, you will test the error handling of the stored procedure.

1. Switch to SQL Query Analyzer.

2. Open C:\Moc\2073A\Labfiles\L09\SupplierProduct.sql, and review its contents.

   What is the benefit of using the **@@error** system function while inserting values into the **Suppliers** and **Products** tables?

   _____

   _____

3. Execute the script to create the **SupplierProductInsert** stored procedure.

4. Open C:\Moc\2073A\Labfiles\L09\SupplierProductInsert.sql. Modify the script by entering the appropriate values to add a new supplier and a new product. (You may use any values that you want.)

5. Execute the modified script.

6. Test the error handling in the **SupplierProductInsert** stored procedure by modifying the values and placing an in-line comment in front of the **@contactname** parameter. Execute your modified script to ensure that the value will be ignored.

   What error message did you receive?

   _____

   _____

Exercise 3
Customizing Error Messages

In this exercise, you will create a custom error message that will be logged into the Windows 2000 Event Viewer application log that lists the supplier ID that was inserted, along with the SQL Server user who performed the insertion.

▶ To create a custom error message

In this procedure, you will modify the **SupplierProduct** stored procedure to call custom error messages.
C:\Moc\2073A\Labfiles\L09\Answers\CustomErrorAnswer.sql is a complete script for this procedure.

1. Open C:\Moc\2073A\Labfiles\L09\CustomError.sql, review its contents, and then execute it.

2. Search for the comment /* #1 Substitute student code here */, and then add a variable to the **CustomError** stored procedure that will store the value of the user name that inserts the supplier.

Tip   Use the SUSER_SNAME system function.

---

3. Search for the next comment /* #2 Substitute student code here */. Add a RAISERROR statement that indicates that a new supplier has been added.

   The RAISERROR statement should call error #50018 and pass the parameters for the supplier number and the user who is executing the stored procedure.

   See SQL Server Books Online for additional information about the RAISERROR statement.

4. Search for the next comment /* #3 Substitute student code here */ to create the error message number 50018 by using the **sp_addmessage** system stored procedure. Include the Supplier and UserName values in your error message.

5. Execute the script to create the **CustomError** stored procedure.

6. Open C:\Moc\2073A\Labfiles\L09\SupplierProductInsert.sql. Modify the script by entering the appropriate values to add a new supplier and a new product. (You may use any values that you want.)

7. Execute the modified script.

8. Review the results, and then open Event Viewer and view the application log to verify that your information message was recorded.

Exercise 4
Using Return Codes

In this exercise, you will create a stored procedure with the OUTPUT keyword by using the C:\Moc\2073A\Labfiles\L09\Return1.sql script. Then you will execute that stored procedure and test it for different return codes by using the Return2.sql and Return3.sql scripts.

▶ To create the OrderCount stored procedure

In this procedure, you will create a stored procedure named **OrderCount** that counts the number of unfilled orders for a customer. If the customer has at least one unfilled order, it returns a status of 1. If the customer does not have unfilled orders, it returns a status of 0. This is an example of a nested stored procedure.

1. Using SQL Query Analyzer, open C:\Moc\2073A\Labfiles\L09\Return1.sql, review its contents, and then execute it.

2. Type and execute the following procedure:

    ```
    EXEC OrderCount 1,1
    ```

    What is the result?

    _____

    _____

▶ To execute the OrderCount stored procedure with the OUTPUT option

In this procedure, you will observe the effects of using the OUTPUT option in the **OrderCount** stored procedure.

1. Using SQL Query Analyzer, open C:\Moc\2073A\Labfiles\L09\Return2.sql, review its contents, and then execute it.

    This script executes the **OrderCount** stored procedure and passes a value of a CustomerID that has unfilled orders.

    What is the result?

    _____

    _____

2. Open C:\Moc\2073A\Labfiles\L09\Return3.sql, review its contents, and then execute it.

    This script executes the **OrderCount** stored procedure and passes a value of a CustomerID that has unfilled orders.

    What is the result?

    _____

    _____

If Time Permits
Executing Extended Stored Procedures

In this exercise, you will execute an extended stored procedure and view the DLL file name in which the function is defined.

▶ To execute an extended stored procedure

In this procedure, you will execute the **xp_cmdshell** extended stored procedure to list all of the files and folders in the root of drive C.

1. Using SQL Query Analyzer, verify that you are using the **master** database.

2. Execute the **xp_cmdshell** extended stored procedure to view the list of all files in the C:\ folder.

   ```
   EXEC master..xp_cmdshell 'dir c:\'
   ```

   What was the result?

   _____

   _____

3. Execute the **sp_helptext** system stored procedure to view the definition for **xp_cmdshell**.

   ```
   EXEC master..sp_helptext xp_cmdshell
   ```

   What was the result?

   _____

   _____

If Time Permits
Tracing Stored Procedures Using SQL Profiler

In this exercise, you will use the SQL Profiler graphical tool to trace individual stored procedures.

► To trace stored procedure events by using SQL Profiler

In this procedure, you will start a SQL Profiler trace by using a custom trace template to monitor stored procedures.

1. Open SQL Profiler.

2. On the toolbar, click **New Trace**.

3. Connect to the (local) server with Windows Authentication.

4. On the **Events** tab, add all stored procedures and Transact-SQL event classes.

5. Click **Run**.

6. Switch to SQL Query Analyzer, open C:\Moc\2073A\Labfiles\L09\SupplierProductInsert.sql, review its contents, and then execute it.

7. Switch to SQL Profiler.

8. Stop and then review the trace.

Review

- **Introduction to Stored Procedures**
- **Creating, Executing, Modifying, and Dropping Stored Procedures**
- **Using Parameters in Stored Procedures**
- **Executing Extended Stored Procedures**
- **Handling Error Messages**

1. You have created a stored procedure to remove a customer from your database. You would like to have a custom error message written to the Windows 2000 application log when the delete transaction completes. How would you perform this task?

2. You want users in the payroll department to be able to insert, update, and delete data in the **payroll** database. However, you do not want them to have access to the underlying tables. How would you accomplish this goal, besides creating a view?

3. You must modify a stored procedure in your database. Several users have been granted permission to execute this stored procedure. What statement would you execute to perform the modification without affecting the existing permissions?

Module 10: Implementing User-defined Functions

Contents

Microsoft®

Project Lead: Rich Rose
Instructional Designers: Rich Rose, Cheryl Hoople, Marilyn McGill
Instructional Software Design Engineers: Karl Dehmer, Carl Raebler, Rick Byham
Technical Lead: Karl Dehmer
Subject Matter Experts: Karl Dehmer, Carl Raebler, Rick Byham
Graphic Artist: Kirsten Larson (Independent Contractor)
Editing Manager: Lynette Skinner
Editor: Wendy Cleary
Copy Editor: Edward McKillop (S&T Consulting)
Production Manager: Miracle Davis
Production Coordinator: Jenny Boe
Production Support: Lori Walker (S&T Consulting)
Test Manager: Sid Benavente
Courseware Testing: TestingTesting123
Classroom Automation: Lorrin Smith-Bates
Creative Director, Media/Sim Services: David Mahlmann
Web Development Lead: Lisa Pease
CD Build Specialist: Julie Challenger
Online Support: David Myka (S&T Consulting)
Localization Manager: Rick Terek
Operations Coordinator: John Williams
Manufacturing Support: Laura King; Kathy Hershey
Lead Product Manager, Release Management: Bo Galford
Lead Product Manager, Data Base: Margo Crandall
Group Manager, Courseware Infrastructure: David Bramble
Group Product Manager, Content Development: Dean Murray
General Manager: Robert Stewart

Overview

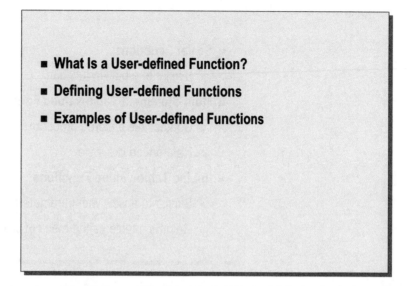

- ■ **What Is a User-defined Function?**
- ■ **Defining User-defined Functions**
- ■ **Examples of User-defined Functions**

This module provides an overview of user-defined functions. It explains why and how you use them, as well as the syntax for creating them.

After completing this module, you will be able to:

- ■ Describe the three types of user-defined functions.
- ■ Create and alter user-defined functions.
- ■ Create each of the three types of user-defined functions.

What Is a User-defined Function?

- **Scalar Functions**
  - Similar to a built-in function
- **Multi-Statement Table-valued Functions**
  - Content like a stored procedure
  - Referenced like a view
- **In-Line Table-valued Functions**
  - Similar to a view with parameters
  - Returns a table as the result of single SELECT statement

With Microsoft® SQL Server™ 2000, you can design your own functions to supplement and extend the system-supplied (built-in) functions.

A user-defined function takes zero, or more, input parameters and returns either a *scalar* value or a table. Input parameters can be any data type except **timestamp**, **cursor**, or **table**. User-defined functions do not support output parameters.

SQL Server 2000 supports three types of user-defined functions:

Scalar Functions

A scalar function is similar to a built-in function.

Multi-Statement Table-valued Functions

A multi-statement table-valued function returns a table built by one or more Transact-SQL statements and is similar to a stored procedure. Unlike a stored procedure, a multi-statement table-valued function can be referenced in the FROM clause of a SELECT statement as if it were a view.

In-Line Table-valued Functions

An in-line table-valued function returns a table that is the result of a single SELECT statement. It is similar to a view but offers more flexibility than views in the use of parameters, and extends the features of indexed views.

◆ Defining User-defined Functions

- Creating a User-defined Function
- Creating a Function with Schema Binding
- Setting Permissions for User-defined Functions
- Altering and Dropping User-defined Functions

This section covers creating, altering, and dropping a user-defined function. It also covers permissions.

Creating a User-defined Function

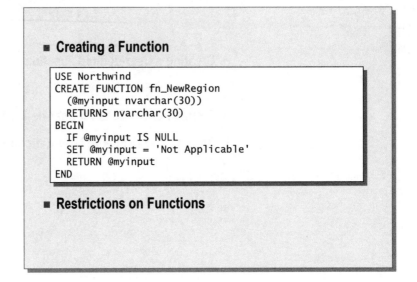

- **Creating a Function**

```
USE Northwind
CREATE FUNCTION fn_NewRegion
  (@myinput nvarchar(30))
  RETURNS nvarchar(30)
BEGIN
  IF @myinput IS NULL
  SET @myinput = 'Not Applicable'
  RETURN @myinput
END
```

- **Restrictions on Functions**

You create a user-defined function in nearly the same way that you create a view or stored procedure.

Creating a Function

You create user-defined functions by using the CREATE FUNCTION statement. Each fully qualified user-defined function name (database_name.owner_name.function_name) must be unique. The statement specifies the input parameters with their data types, the processing instructions, and the value returned with each data type.

Syntax

CREATE FUNCTION [owner_name.] function_name
  ([{ @parameter_name scalar_parameter_data_type [= default] } [,...n]])
  RETURNS scalar_return_data_type
  [WITH < function_option> [,...n]]
  [AS]
  BEGIN
  function_body
  RETURN scalar_expression
  END

Example

This example creates a user-defined function to replace a null value with the words Not Applicable.

```
USE Northwind
GO

CREATE FUNCTION fn_NewRegion
(@myinput nvarchar(30))
RETURNS nvarchar(30)
BEGIN
  IF @myinput IS NULL
  SET @myinput = 'Not Applicable'
  RETURN @myinput
END
```

When referencing a scalar user-defined function, specify the function owner and the function name in two-part syntax.

```
SELECT LastName, City, dbo.fn_NewRegion(Region) AS Region,
    Country
FROM dbo.Employees
```

Result

LastName	City	Region	Country
Davolio	Seattle	WA	USA
Fuller	Tacoma	WA	USA
Leverling	Kirkland	WA	USA
Peacock	Redmond	WA	USA
Buchanan	London	Not Applicable	UK
Suyama	London	Not Applicable	UK
King	London	Not Applicable	UK
Callahan	Seattle	WA	USA
Dodsworth	London	Not Applicable	UK

Restrictions on Functions

Nondeterministic functions are functions, such as GETDATE(), that could return different result values each time that they are called with the same set of input values. Built-in nondeterministic functions are not allowed in the body of user-defined functions. The following built-in functions are nondeterministic.

@@ERROR	FORMATMESSAGE	IDENTITY	USER_NAME
@@IDENTITY	GETANSINULL	NEWID	@@ERROR
@@ROWCOUNT	GETDATE	PERMISSIONS	@@IDENTITY
@@TRANCOUNT	GetUTCDate	SESSION_USER	@@ROWCOUNT
APP_NAME	HOST_ID	STATS_DATE	@@TRANCOUNT
CURRENT_TIMESTAMP	HOST_NAME	SYSTEM_USER	
CURRENT_USER	IDENT_INCR	TEXTPTR	
DATENAME	IDENT_SEED	TEXTVALID	

Creating a Function with Schema Binding

- **Referenced User-defined Functions and Views Are Also Schema Bound**
- **Objects Are Not Referenced with a Two-Part Name**
- **Function and Objects Are All in the Same Database**
- **Have Reference Permission on Required Objects**

You can use schema binding to bind the function to the database objects that it references. If a function is created with the SCHEMABINDING option, then the database objects that the function references cannot be altered (by using the ALTER statement) or dropped (by using a DROP statement).

A function can be schema-bound only if the following conditions are true:

- Any user-defined functions and views referenced by the function are also schema-bound.

- The objects that the function references are not referenced with a two-part name in the **owner.objectname** format.

- The function and the objects that it references belong to the same database.

- The user who executed the CREATE FUNCTION statement has REFERENCE permission on all of the database objects that the function references.

Setting Permissions for User-defined Functions

- **Need CREATE FUNCTION Permission**

- **Need EXECUTE Permission**

- **Need REFERENCE Permission on Cited Tables, Views, or Functions**

- **Must Own the Function to Use in CREATE or ALTER TABLE Statement**

The permission requirements for user-defined functions are similar to that of other database objects.

- You must have CREATE FUNCTION permission to create, alter, or drop user-defined functions.

- Users other than the owner must be granted EXECUTE permission on a function before they can use it in a Transact-SQL statement.

- If the function is being schema-bound, you must have REFERENCE permission on tables, views, and functions referenced by the function. REFERENCE permissions can be granted through the GRANT statement to views and user-defined functions, as well as tables.

- If a CREATE TABLE or ALTER TABLE statement references a user-defined function in a CHECK constraint, DEFAULT clause, or computed column, the table owner must also own the function.

Altering and Dropping User-defined Functions

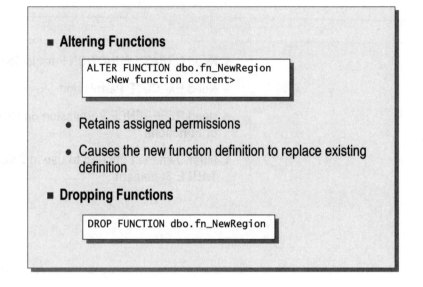

- **Altering Functions**

  ```
  ALTER FUNCTION dbo.fn_NewRegion
      <New function content>
  ```

  - Retains assigned permissions
  - Causes the new function definition to replace existing definition

- **Dropping Functions**

  ```
  DROP FUNCTION dbo.fn_NewRegion
  ```

You can alter and drop user-defined functions by using the ALTER FUNCTION statement.

The benefit of altering a function instead of dropping and recreating it is the same as it is for views and procedures. The permissions on the function remain and immediately apply to the revised function.

Altering Functions

You modify a user-defined function by using the ALTER FUNCTION statement.

Example

This example shows how to alter a function.

```
ALTER FUNCTION dbo.fn_NewRegion
    <New function content>
```

Dropping Functions

You drop a user-defined function by using the DROP FUNCTION statement.

Example

This example shows how to drop a function.

```
DROP FUNCTION dbo.fn_NewRegion
```

◆ Examples of User-defined Functions

- Using a Scalar User-defined Function

- Example of a Scalar User-defined Function

- Using a Multi-Statement Table-valued Function

- Example of a Multi-Statement Table-valued Function

- Using an In-Line Table-valued Function

- Example of an In-Line Table-valued Function

This section describes the three types of user-defined functions. It describes their purpose and provides examples of the syntax that you can use to create and call them.

Using a Scalar User-defined Function

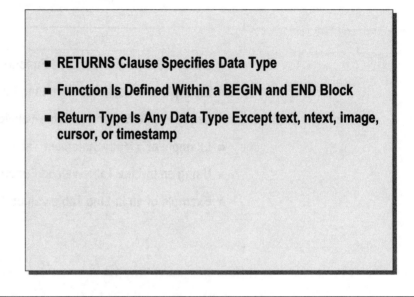

- RETURNS Clause Specifies Data Type

- Function Is Defined Within a BEGIN and END Block

- Return Type Is Any Data Type Except text, ntext, image, cursor, or timestamp

A scalar function returns a single data value of the type defined in a RETURNS clause. The body of the function, defined in a BEGIN...END block, contains the series of Transact-SQL statements that return the value. The return type can be any data type except **text**, **ntext**, **image**, **cursor**, or **timestamp**.

Example of a Scalar User-defined Function

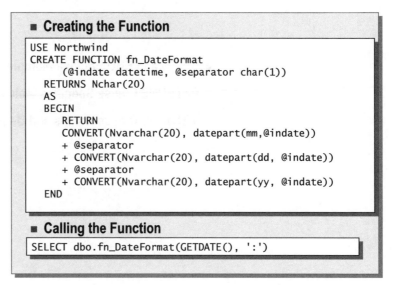

■ **Creating the Function**

```
USE Northwind
CREATE FUNCTION fn_DateFormat
    (@indate datetime, @separator char(1))
RETURNS Nchar(20)
AS
BEGIN
    RETURN
    CONVERT(Nvarchar(20), datepart(mm,@indate))
    + @separator
    + CONVERT(Nvarchar(20), datepart(dd, @indate))
    + @separator
    + CONVERT(Nvarchar(20), datepart(yy, @indate))
END
```

■ **Calling the Function**

```
SELECT dbo.fn_DateFormat(GETDATE(), ':')
```

A scalar user-defined function is similar to a built-in function. After you create it, you can reuse it.

Example

This example creates a user-defined function that receives date and column separators as variables and reformats the date as a character string.

```
USE Northwind
GO
CREATE FUNCTION fn_DateFormat
    (@indate datetime, @separator char(1))
RETURNS Nchar(20)
AS
BEGIN
    RETURN
    CONVERT(Nvarchar(20), datepart(mm,@indate))
    + @separator
    + CONVERT(Nvarchar(20), datepart(dd, @indate))
    + @separator
    + CONVERT(Nvarchar(20), datepart(yy, @indate))
END
```

You can call a scalar user-defined function in the same way that you do a built-in function.

```
SELECT dbo.fn_DateFormat(GETDATE(), ':')
```

Using a Multi-Statement Table-valued Function

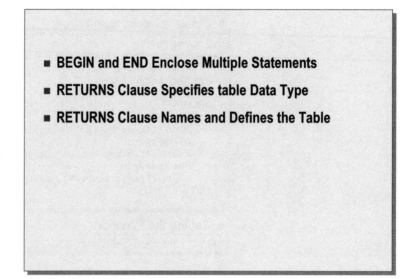

- **BEGIN and END Enclose Multiple Statements**
- **RETURNS Clause Specifies table Data Type**
- **RETURNS Clause Names and Defines the Table**

A multi-statement table-valued function is a combination of a view and a stored procedure. You can use user-defined functions that return a table to replace stored procedures or views.

A table-valued function (like a stored procedure) can use complex logic and multiple Transact-SQL statements to build a table. In the same way that you use a view, you can use a table-valued function in the FROM clause of a Transact-SQL statement.

When using a multi-statement table-valued function, consider the following facts:

- The BEGIN and END delimit the body of the function.
- The RETURNS clause specifies **table** as the data type returned.
- The RETURNS clause defines a name for the table and defines the format of the table. The scope of the return variable name is local to the function.

Example of a Multi-Statement Table-valued Function

■ **Creating the Function**

```
USE Northwind
GO
CREATE FUNCTION fn_Employees (@length nvarchar(9))
RETURNS @fn_Employees table
    (EmployeeID int PRIMARY KEY NOT NULL,
    [Employee Name] nvarchar(61) NOT NULL)
AS
BEGIN
    IF @length = 'ShortName'
        INSERT @fn_Employees SELECT EmployeeID, LastName
        FROM Employees
    ELSE IF @length = 'LongName'
        INSERT @fn_Employees SELECT EmployeeID,
        (FirstName + ' ' + LastName) FROM Employees
RETURN
END
```

■ **Calling the Function**

```
SELECT * FROM dbo.fn_Employees('LongName')
Or
SELECT * FROM dbo.fn_Employees('ShortName')
```

You can create functions by using many statements that perform complex operations.

Example

This example creates a multi-statement table-valued function that returns the last name or both the first and last names of an employee, depending on the parameter provided.

```
USE Northwind
GO

CREATE FUNCTION fn_Employees
    (@length nvarchar(9))
RETURNS @fn_Employees TABLE
    (EmployeeID int PRIMARY KEY NOT NULL,
    [Employee Name] Nvarchar(61) NOT NULL)
AS
BEGIN
    IF @length = 'ShortName'
        INSERT @fn_Employees SELECT EmployeeID, LastName
        FROM Employees
    ELSE IF @length = 'LongName'
        INSERT @fn_Employees SELECT EmployeeID,
        (FirstName + ' ' + LastName) FROM Employees
RETURN
END
```

You can call the function instead of a table or view.

```
SELECT * FROM dbo.fn_Employees('LongName')
```

or

```
SELECT * FROM dbo.fn_Employees('ShortName')
```

Using an In-Line Table-valued Function

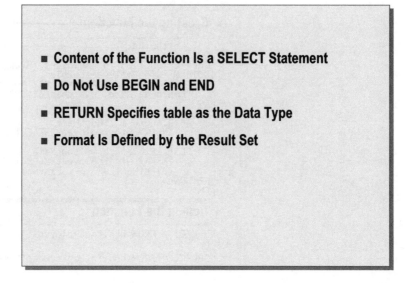

- Content of the Function Is a SELECT Statement
- Do Not Use BEGIN and END
- RETURN Specifies table as the Data Type
- Format Is Defined by the Result Set

In-line user-defined functions return a table and are referenced in the FROM clause, just like a view. When using in-line user-defined functions, consider the following facts and guidelines:

- The RETURN clause contains a single SELECT statement in parentheses. The result set of the SELECT statement forms the table that the function returns. The SELECT statement used in an in-line function is subject to the same restrictions as SELECT statements used in views.

- BEGIN and END do not delimit the body of the function.

- RETURN specifies **table** as the data type returned.

- You do not have to define the format of a return variable, because it is set by the format of the result set of the SELECT statement in the RETURN clause.

Example of an In–Line Table-valued Function

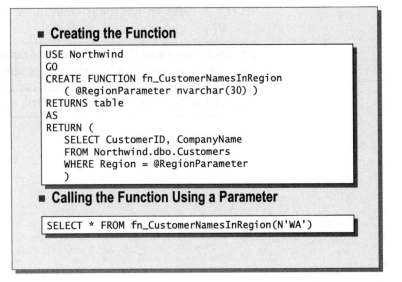

- **Creating the Function**

```
USE Northwind
GO
CREATE FUNCTION fn_CustomerNamesInRegion
    ( @RegionParameter nvarchar(30) )
RETURNS table
AS
RETURN (
    SELECT CustomerID, CompanyName
    FROM Northwind.dbo.Customers
    WHERE Region = @RegionParameter
    )
```

- **Calling the Function Using a Parameter**

```
SELECT * FROM fn_CustomerNamesInRegion(N'WA')
```

You can use in-line functions to achieve the functionality of parameterized views.

You are not allowed to include a user-provided parameter within the view when you create it. You can usually resolve this by providing a WHERE clause when calling the view. However, this may require building a string for dynamic execution, which can increase the complexity of the application. You can achieve the functionality of a parameterized view by using an in-line table-valued function.

Example

This example creates an in-line table-valued function that takes a region value as a parameter.

```
USE Northwind
GO

CREATE FUNCTION fn_CustomerNamesInRegion
    ( @RegionParameter nvarchar(30) )
RETURNS table
AS
RETURN (
    SELECT CustomerID, CompanyName
    FROM Northwind.dbo.Customers
    WHERE Region = @RegionParameter
    )
```

To call the function, provide the function name as the FROM clause and provide a region value as a parameter.

```
SELECT * FROM fn_CustomerNamesInRegion(N'WA')
```

Tip In-line functions can greatly increase performance when used with indexed views. SQL Server performs complex aggregation and join operations when the index is created. Subsequent queries can use an in-line function with a parameter to filter rows from the simplified, stored result set.

Recommended Practices

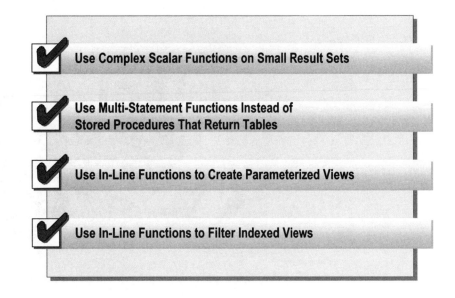

- Use Complex Scalar Functions on Small Result Sets
- Use Multi-Statement Functions Instead of Stored Procedures That Return Tables
- Use In-Line Functions to Create Parameterized Views
- Use In-Line Functions to Filter Indexed Views

The following recommended practices should help you implement user-defined functions:

- Use complex scalar functions on small result sets. User-defined functions provide a way for you to encapsulate complex reasoning into a simple query, but if all users of the function do not appreciate the complexity of the underlying calculation, the function could result in time-consuming calculations that the user does not see. Do not apply a complex aggregation on each member of a large result set.

- Use multi-statement functions instead of stored procedures that return tables. Writing stored procedures that return tables as multi-statement user-defined functions can improve efficiency.

- Use in-line functions to create views by using parameters. Using parameters with in-line functions can simplify references to tables and views.

- Use in-line functions to filter views. Using in-line functions with indexed views can greatly increase performance.

Additional information on the following topics is available in SQL Server Books Online.

Topic	Search on
Creating user-defined functions	"CREATE FUNCTION"
Describing the purpose and types of user-defined functions	"user-defined functions"
Definition and list of deterministic and nondeterministic functions.	"nondeterministic functions"

Lab A: Creating User-defined Functions

Objectives

After completing this lab, you will be able to:

- Create scalar user-defined functions.
- Create multi-statement table-valued user-defined functions.
- Create in-line table-valued user-defined functions.

Prerequisites

Before working on this lab, you must have:

- Script files for this lab, which are located in C:\Moc\2073A\Labfiles\L10.
- Answer files for this lab, which are located in
  C:\Moc\2073A\Labfiles\L10\Answers.

Lab Setup

To complete this lab, you must have either:

- Completed the prior lab, or
- Executed the C:\Moc\2073A\Batches\Restore10.cmd batch file.

  This command file restores the **ClassNorthwind** database to a state required
  for this lab.

For More Information

If you require help with executing files, search SQL Query Analyzer Help for
"Execute a query".

Other resources that you can use include:

- The **Northwind** database schema.
- Microsoft SQL Server Books Online.

Scenario

The organization of the classroom is meant to simulate that of a worldwide trading firm named Northwind Traders. Its fictitious domain name is nwtraders.msft. The primary DNS server for nwtraders.msft is the instructor computer, which has an Internet Protocol (IP) address of 192.168.x.200 (where x is the assigned classroom number). The name of the instructor computer is London.

The following table provides the user name, computer name, and IP address for each student computer in the fictitious **nwtraders.msft** domain. Find the user name for your computer, and make a note of it.

User name	Computer name	IP address
SQLAdmin1	Vancouver	192.168.x.1
SQLAdmin2	Denver	192.168.x.2
SQLAdmin3	Perth	192.168.x.3
SQLAdmin4	Brisbane	192.168.x.4
SQLAdmin5	Lisbon	192.168.x.5
SQLAdmin6	Bonn	192.168.x.6
SQLAdmin7	Lima	192.168.x.7
SQLAdmin8	Santiago	192.168.x.8
SQLAdmin9	Bangalore	192.168.x.9
SQLAdmin10	Singapore	192.168.x.10
SQLAdmin11	Casablanca	192.168.x.11
SQLAdmin12	Tunis	192.168.x.12
SQLAdmin13	Acapulco	192.168.x.13
SQLAdmin14	Miami	192.168.x.14
SQLAdmin15	Auckland	192.168.x.15
SQLAdmin16	Suva	192.168.x.16
SQLAdmin17	Stockholm	192.168.x.17
SQLAdmin18	Moscow	192.168.x.18
SQLAdmin19	Caracas	192.168.x.19
SQLAdmin20	Montevideo	192.168.x.20
SQLAdmin21	Manila	192.168.x.21
SQLAdmin22	Tokyo	192.168.x.22
SQLAdmin23	Khartoum	192.168.x.23
SQLAdmin24	Nairobi	192.168.x.24

Estimated time to complete this lab: 30 minutes

Exercise 1
Creating a Scalar User-defined Function

The products that your company sells are subject to varying tax rates that are based on the product categories. Some products such as beverages are heavily taxed, and some products such as condiments have no tax. You decide to create a user-defined function to encapsulate the tax logic. This user-defined function gives you a central point for administering the tax rates and reducing the number of locations in which you must repeat and maintain the logic.

In this exercise, you will create and execute a script that creates a scalar user-defined function. After you create the function, you will test it to verify that it works.

▶ **To create a scalar user-defined function**

In this procedure, you will create a trigger by executing a script file.

1. Log on to the **NWTraders** classroom domain by using the information in the following table.

Option	Value
User name	**SQLAdmin**x (where x corresponds to your computer name as designated in the nw**traders.msft** classroom domain)
Password	**password**

2. Open SQL Query Analyzer and, if requested, log in to the (local) server with Microsoft Windows® authentication.

   You have permission to log in to and administer SQL Server because you are logged as **SQLAdmin**x, which is a member of the Microsoft Windows 2000 local group, Administrators. All members of this group are automatically mapped to the SQL Server **sysadmin** role.

3. In the **DB** list, click **ClassNorthwind**.

4. Open, examine, and execute TaxRate.sql in the C:\Moc\2073A\Labfiles\L10 folder.

   This script demonstrates a CASE statement that calculates a tax rate for each product, based on its product category.

5. Create a scalar user-defined function called **fn_TaxRate** to encapsulate the CASE statement. Accept a parameter as **@ProdID int** and a return a **numeric(5,4)** data type.

   C:\Moc\2073A\Labfiles\L10\Answers\fn_TaxRate.sql is a completed script containing this function.

▶ **To test the function**

In this procedure, you will test the function that you just created by selecting columns from the **Products** table.

- Execute the following SELECT statement to select **ProductName**, **UnitPrice**, **CategoryID**, **TaxRate**, and a calculated **PriceWithTax** value from the **Products** table:

```
SELECT ProductName, UnitPrice, CategoryID,
    ClassNorthwind.dbo.fn_TaxRate(ProductID) AS TaxRate,
    UnitPrice * ClassNorthwind.dbo. fn_TaxRate(ProductID)
        AS PriceWithTax
FROM Products
```

The **TaxRate** column should contain values of 1.00, 1.05, or 1.10 for each product.

The **PriceWithTax** column should contain the **UnitPrice** multiplied by the **TaxRate**.

Exercise 2
Creating a Multi-Statement Table-valued User-defined Function

In this exercise, you will create a multi-statement table-valued user-defined function that queries the **Employees** table in the **ClassNorthwind** database and that shows all direct and non-direct reports.

▶ **To create a multi-statement table-valued user-defined function**

The **Employees** table in the **ClassNorthwind** database contains a column called **ReportsTo** that contains the employee ID number of the manager to whom each employee reports.

In this exercise, you will create a user-defined function that takes the **EmployeeID** number of a manager as a parameter and iterates through the **Employee** table, gathering employees that report to that designated manager at any level.

- Open, review, and execute fn_FindReports.sql in the C:\Moc\2073A\Labfiles\L10 folder.

  This script creates a function called **fn_FindReports** that returns a table of reporting employees.

▶ **To test the function**

In this procedure, you will test the function that you just created by selecting columns from the **fn_FindReports** function.

1. Execute the following SELECT statement to select **EmployeeID**, **Name**, **Title**, and **MgrEmployeeID** columns from the **fn_FindReports** function.

   ```
   SELECT EmployeeID, [Name], Title, MgrEmployeeID
   FROM dbo.fn_FindReports(5)
   ```

   This SELECT statement returns the employees who report to Steven Buchanan (**EmployeeID** 5).

2. Execute the following SELECT statement to select the **EmployeeID**, **Name**, **Title**, and **MgrEmployeeID** from the **fn_FindReports** function.

   ```
   SELECT EmployeeID, Name, Title, MgrEmployeeID
   FROM dbo.fn_FindReports(2)
   ```

   This statement returns a table containing the names of employees who report to Andrew Fuller (**EmployeeID** 2).

   C:\Moc\2073A\Labfiles\L10\Answers\Call_fn_FindReports.sql is a completed script containing this statement.

Exercise 3
Creating an In-Line Table-valued User-defined Function

In this exercise, you will create an in-line table-valued user-defined function as an alternative to a view. This function, called **fn_LargeFreight**, will accept a dollar amount as a parameter and return freight orders with amounts that exceed the dollar amount.

▶ **To create an in-line table-valued user-defined function**

The **Orders** table in the **ClassNorthwind** database contains a column called **Freight** that contains the dollar amount charged for freight for each order. You want to join that table with the **Shippers** table to return both order and shipping information. You also want to filter the result set to show only those orders that have expensive freight charges.

In this procedure, you will create an in-line table-valued user-defined function that serves as a parameterized view.

* Create an in-line table-valued user-defined function called **fn_LargeFreight** that accepts a parameter called **@FreightAmt** of data type **money** and returns the output from the following SELECT statement:

```
SELECT S.ShipperID, S.CompanyName,
    O.OrderID, O.ShippedDate, O.Freight
FROM Shippers AS S JOIN Orders AS O
    ON S.ShipperID = O.ShipVia
WHERE O.Freight > @FreightAmt
```

C:\Moc\2073A\Labfiles\L10\Answers\fn_LargeFreight.sql is a completed script containing this function.

▶ **To test the function**

In this procedure, you will test the function that you just created by selecting columns from the **fn_LargeFreight** function.

* Execute the following SELECT statement to select rows from the **fn_LargeFreight** function that have dollar sales greater than $600.

```
SELECT * FROM fn_LargeFreight(600)
```

C:\Moc\2073A\Labfiles\L10\Answers\Call_fn_LargeFreight.sql is a completed script containing this statement.

Review

- **What Is a User-defined Function?**
- **Defining User-defined Functions**
- **Examples of User-defined Functions**

1. Describe the three types of user-defined functions.

2. What built-in functions are not permitted in the body of a user-defined function?

3. What types of user-defined functions require you to specify the names and data types of the output columns?

Microsoft®
Training &
Certification

Module 11:
Implementing Triggers

Contents

Project Lead: Rich Rose
Instructional Designers: Rich Rose, Cheryl Hoople, Marilyn McGill
Instructional Software Design Engineers: Karl Dehmer, Carl Raebler, Rick Byham
Technical Lead: Karl Dehmer
Subject Matter Experts: Karl Dehmer, Carl Raebler, Rick Byham
Graphic Artist: Kirsten Larson (Independent Contractor)
Editing Manager: Lynette Skinner
Editor: Wendy Cleary
Copy Editor: Edward McKillop (S&T Consulting)
Production Manager: Miracle Davis
Production Coordinator: Jenny Boe
Production Support: Lori Walker (S&T Consulting)
Test Manager: Sid Benavente
Courseware Testing: TestingTesting123
Classroom Automation: Lorrin Smith-Bates
Creative Director, Media/Sim Services: David Mahlmann
Web Development Lead: Lisa Pease
CD Build Specialist: Julie Challenger
Online Support: David Myka (S&T Consulting)
Localization Manager: Rick Terek
Operations Coordinator: John Williams
Manufacturing Support: Laura King; Kathy Hershey
Lead Product Manager, Release Management: Bo Galford
Lead Product Manager, Data Base: Margo Crandall
Group Manager, Courseware Infrastructure: David Bramble
Group Product Manager, Content Development: Dean Murray
General Manager: Robert Stewart

Overview

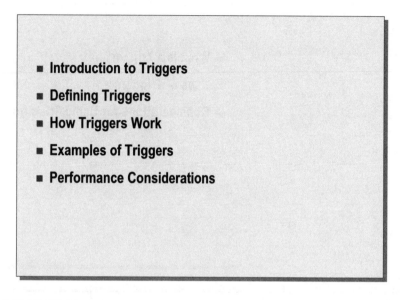

- ■ **Introduction to Triggers**
- ■ **Defining Triggers**
- ■ **How Triggers Work**
- ■ **Examples of Triggers**
- ■ **Performance Considerations**

A *trigger* is a stored procedure that executes when data in a specified table is modified. You often create triggers to enforce referential integrity or consistency among logically related data in different tables. Because users cannot circumvent triggers, you can use triggers to enforce complex business rules that maintain data integrity.

After completing this module, you will be able to:

- ■ Create a trigger.
- ■ Drop a trigger.
- ■ Alter a trigger.
- ■ Describe how various triggers work.
- ■ Evaluate the performance considerations that affect using triggers.

◆ Introduction to Triggers

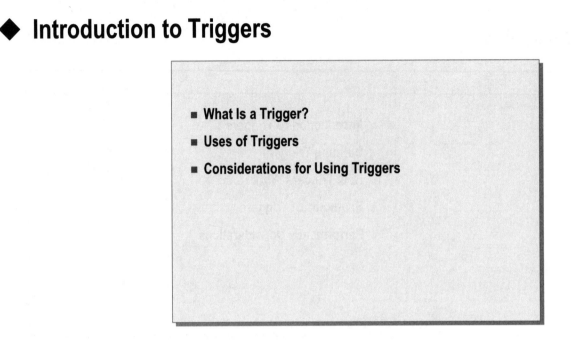

- What Is a Trigger?
- Uses of Triggers
- Considerations for Using Triggers

This section introduces triggers and describes when and how to use them.

What Is a Trigger?

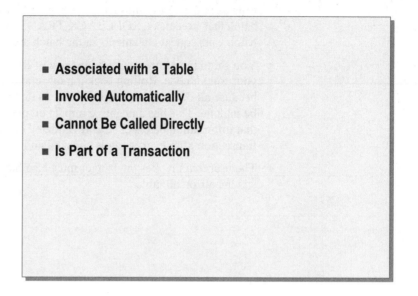

- **Associated with a Table**
- **Invoked Automatically**
- **Cannot Be Called Directly**
- **Is Part of a Transaction**

A trigger is a special kind of stored procedure that executes whenever an attempt is made to modify data in a table that the trigger protects. Triggers are tied to specific tables.

Associated with a Table

Triggers are defined on a specific table, which is referred to as the trigger table.

Invoked Automatically

When an attempt is made to insert, update, or delete data in a table, and a trigger for that particular action has been defined on the table, the trigger executes automatically. It cannot be circumvented.

Cannot Be Called Directly

Unlike standard system-stored procedures, triggers cannot be called directly and do not pass or accept parameters.

Is Part of a Transaction

The trigger and the statement that fires it are treated as a single transaction that can be rolled back from anywhere within the trigger. When using triggers, consider these facts and guidelines:

- Trigger definitions can include a ROLLBACK TRANSACTION statement even if an explicit BEGIN TRANSACTION statement does not exist.

- If a ROLLBACK TRANSACTION statement is encountered, the entire transaction rolls back. If a statement in the trigger script follows the ROLLBACK TRANSACTION statement, the statement is executed. It may be necessary to use a RETURN clause in an IF statement to prevent the processing of other statements.

- If a trigger that includes a ROLLBACK TRANSACTION statement is fired from within a user-defined transaction, the ROLLBACK TRANSACTION rolls back the entire transaction. A trigger that is executed from within a batch that executes a ROLLBACK TRANSACTION statement cancels the batch; subsequent statements in the batch are not executed.

- You should minimize or avoid the use of ROLLBACK TRANSACTION in your trigger code. Rolling back a transaction creates additional work because all of the work that was done to that point in the transaction has to be undone. This has a negative impact on performance. It is recommended that information be checked and validated outside the transaction. Start the transaction after everything is checked and verified.

- The user that invokes the trigger must also have permission to perform all statements on all tables.

Uses of Triggers

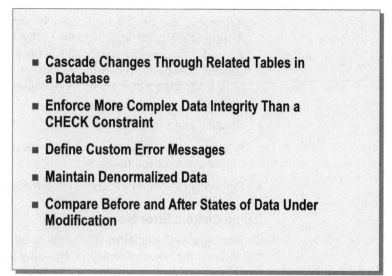

- Cascade Changes Through Related Tables in a Database

- Enforce More Complex Data Integrity Than a CHECK Constraint

- Define Custom Error Messages

- Maintain Denormalized Data

- Compare Before and After States of Data Under Modification

Triggers are best used to maintain low-level data integrity, *not* to return query results. The primary benefit of triggers is that they can contain complex processing logic. Triggers can cascade changes through related tables in a database, enforce more complex data integrity than a CHECK constraint, define custom error messages, maintain *denormalized* data, and compare before and after states of data under modification.

Cascade Changes Through Related Tables in a Database

You can use a trigger to cascade updates and deletes through related tables in a database. For example, a delete trigger on the **Products** table in the **Northwind** database can delete matching rows in other tables that have rows that match the deleted **ProductID** values. A trigger does this by using the **ProductID** foreign key column as a way of locating rows in the **Order Details** table.

Enforce More Complex Data Integrity Than a CHECK Constraint

Unlike CHECK constraints, triggers can reference columns in other tables. For example, you could place an insert trigger on the **Order Details** table that checks the **UnitsInStock** column for that item in the **Products** table. The trigger could determine that when the **UnitsInStock** value is less than 10, that the maximum order amount is three items. This type of check references columns in other tables. Referencing columns in other tables is not permitted with a CHECK constraint.

You can use triggers to enforce complex referential integrity by:

■ Taking action or cascading updates or deletes.

Referential integrity can be defined by using FOREIGN KEY and REFERENCE constraints with the CREATE TABLE statement. Triggers are useful for ensuring appropriate actions when cascading deletions or updates must occur. If constraints exist on the trigger table, they are checked prior to the trigger execution. If constraints are violated, the trigger is not executed.

■ Creating multi-row triggers

When more than one row is inserted, updated, or deleted, you must write a trigger to handle multiple rows.

■ Enforcing referential integrity between databases.

Define Custom Error Messages

Occasionally, your implementation may benefit from custom error messages that indicate the status of an action. By using triggers, you can invoke predefined or dynamic custom error messages when certain conditions occur as a trigger executes.

Maintain Denormalized Data

Triggers can be used to maintain low-level data integrity in denormalized database environments. Maintaining denormalized data is different from cascading in that cascading typically refers to maintaining relationships between primary and foreign key values. Denormalized data is typically contrived, derived, or redundant data values. You must use a trigger if:

■ Referential integrity requires something that is not an exact match, such as maintaining derived data (year-to-date sales) or flagging columns (Y or N to indicate whether a product is available).

■ You require customized messages and complex error messaging.

Note Redundant data and derived data typically require the use of triggers.

Compare Before and After States of Data Under Modification

Most triggers provide the ability to reference the changes that are made to the data by the INSERT, UPDATE, or DELETE statement. This allows you to reference the rows that are being affected by the modification statements inside the trigger.

Note Constraints, rules, and defaults can communicate errors only through standardized system-error messages. If your application requires (or can benefit from) customized messages and more complex error handling, you must use a trigger.

Considerations for Using Triggers

- **Triggers Are Reactive; Constraints Are Proactive**
- **Constraints Are Checked First**
- **Tables Can Have Multiple Triggers for Any Action**
- **Table Owners Can Designate the First and Last Trigger to Fire**
- **You Must Have Permission to Perform All Statements That Define Triggers**
- **Table Owners Cannot Create AFTER Triggers on Views or Temporary Tables**

Consider the following facts and guidelines when you work with triggers:

- Most triggers are reactive; constraints and the INSTEAD OF trigger are proactive.

    Triggers are executed after an INSERT, UPDATE, or DELETE statement is executed on the table in which the trigger is defined. For example, an UPDATE statement updates a row in a table, and then the trigger on that table executes automatically. Constraints are checked before an INSERT, UPDATE, or DELETE statement executes.

- Constraints are checked first.

    If constraints exist on the trigger table, they are checked prior to the trigger execution. If constraints are violated, the trigger does not execute.

- Tables can have multiple triggers for any action.

    SQL Server 2000 allows nesting of several triggers on a single table. A table can have multiple triggers defined for it. Each trigger can be defined for a single action or multiple actions.

- Table owners can designate the first and last trigger to fire.

    When multiple triggers are placed on a table, the table owner can use the **sp_settriggerorder** system stored procedure to specify the first and last triggers to fire. The firing order of the remaining triggers cannot be set.

- You must have permission to perform all trigger-defined statements.

  Only the table owner, members of the **sysadmin** fixed-server role, and members of the **db_owner** and **db_ddladmin** fixed-database roles can create and drop triggers for that table. These permissions cannot be transferred.

  In addition, the trigger creator also must have permission to perform all of the statements on all of the affected tables. If permissions are denied to any portion of the Transact-SQL statements inside the trigger, the entire transaction is rolled back.

- Table owners cannot create AFTER triggers on views or temporary tables. Triggers can, however, reference views and temporary tables.

- Table owners can create INSTEAD OF triggers on views and tables, in which case INSTEAD OF triggers greatly extend the types of updates that a view can support.

- Triggers should not return result sets.

  Triggers contain Transact-SQL statements, in the same way that stored procedures do. Like stored procedures, triggers can contain statements that return a result set. However, including statements that return values in triggers is not recommended because users or developers do not expect to see any result sets when an UPDATE, INSERT, or DELETE statement executes.

- Triggers can handle multi-row actions.

  An INSERT, UPDATE, or DELETE action that invokes a trigger can affect multiple rows. You can choose to:

  - Process all of the rows together, in which case all affected rows must meet the trigger criteria for any action to occur.

  - Allow conditional actions.

    For example, if you want to delete three customers from the **Customers** table, you can define a trigger to ensure that there are no active orders or outstanding invoices for each deleted customer. If one of the three customers has an outstanding invoice, that customer will not be deleted, but the qualifying customers will be deleted.

  To determine whether there are multiple affected rows, use the @@ROWCOUNT system function.

◆ Defining Triggers

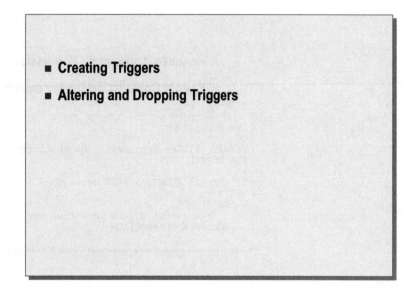

- Creating Triggers
- Altering and Dropping Triggers

This section covers creating, altering, and dropping triggers. It also discusses required permissions and guidelines to follow when defining triggers.

Creating Triggers

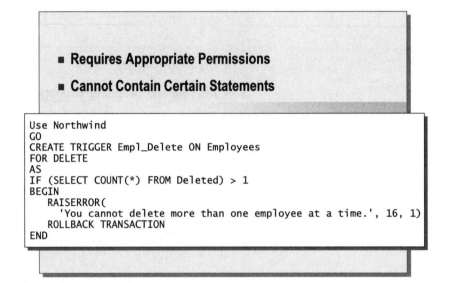

- **Requires Appropriate Permissions**
- **Cannot Contain Certain Statements**

```
Use Northwind
GO
CREATE TRIGGER Empl_Delete ON Employees
FOR DELETE
AS
IF (SELECT COUNT(*) FROM Deleted) > 1
BEGIN
    RAISERROR(
      'You cannot delete more than one employee at a time.', 16, 1)
    ROLLBACK TRANSACTION
END
```

Create triggers by using the CREATE TRIGGER statement. The statement specifies the table on which a trigger is defined, the events for which the trigger executes, and the particular instructions for the trigger.

Syntax

CREATE TRIGGER [*owner.*] *trigger_name*
  ON [*owner.*] *table_name*
  [WITH ENCRYPTION]
  {FOR | AFTER | INSTEAD OF} {INSERT | UPDATE | DELETE}
  AS
  [IF UPDATE (*column_name*)...]
    [{AND | OR} UPDATE (*column_name*)...]
    sql_statements}

When a FOR UPDATE action is specified, the IF UPDATE (*column_name*) clause can be used to focus action on a specific column that is updated.

Both FOR and AFTER are equivalent syntax creating the same type of trigger, which fires after the initiating (INSERT, UPDATE, or DELETE) action.

INSTEAD OF triggers cancel the triggering action and perform a new function instead.

When you create a trigger, information about the trigger is inserted into the **sysobjects** and **syscomments** system tables. If a trigger is created with the same name as an existing trigger, the new trigger will overwrite the original trigger.

Note   SQL Server does not support the addition of user-defined triggers on system tables; therefore, you cannot create triggers on system tables.

Requires Appropriate Permissions

Table owners, and members of the database owner (**db_owner**) and the system administrators (**sysadmin**) roles, have permission to create a trigger.

To avoid situations in which the owner of a view and the owner of the underlying tables differ, it is recommended that the **dbo** user own all objects in a database. Because a user can be a member of multiple roles, always specify the **dbo** user as the owner name when you create the object. Otherwise, the object will be created with your user name as the owner.

Cannot Contain Certain Statements

SQL Server does not allow the following statements to be used in a trigger definition:

- ALTER DATABASE
- CREATE DATABASE
- DISK INIT
- DISK RESIZE
- DROP DATABASE
- LOAD DATABASE
- LOAD LOG
- RECONFIGURE
- RESTORE DATABASE
- RESTORE LOG

To determine the tables with triggers, execute the **sp_depends** <*tablename*> system stored procedure. To view a trigger definition, execute the **sp_helptext** <*triggername*> system stored procedure. To determine the triggers that exist on a specific table and their actions, execute the **sp_helptrigger** <*tablename*> system stored procedure.

Example

The following example creates a trigger on the **Employees** table that prevents users from deleting more than one employee at a time. The trigger fires every time a record or group of records are deleted from the table. The trigger checks the number of records being deleted by querying the **Deleted** table. If more than one record is being deleted, the trigger returns a custom error message and rolls back the transaction.

```
Use Northwind
GO

CREATE TRIGGER Empl_Delete ON NewEmployees
FOR DELETE
AS
IF (SELECT COUNT(*) FROM Deleted) > 1
BEGIN
    RAISERROR(
        'You cannot delete more than one employee at a time.',
        16, 1)
    ROLLBACK TRANSACTION
END
```

The following DELETE statement fires the trigger and prevents the transaction.

```
DELETE FROM Employees WHERE EmployeeID > 6
```

The following DELETE statement fires the trigger and allows the transaction.

```
DELETE FROM Employees WHERE EmployeeID = 6
```

Altering and Dropping Triggers

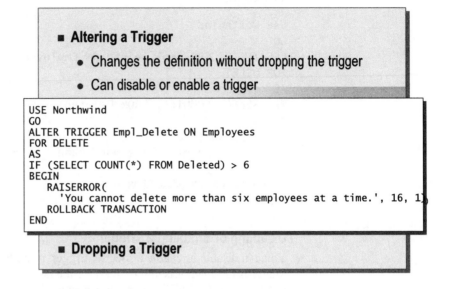

- **Altering a Trigger**
  - Changes the definition without dropping the trigger
  - Can disable or enable a trigger

```
USE Northwind
GO
ALTER TRIGGER Empl_Delete ON Employees
FOR DELETE
AS
IF (SELECT COUNT(*) FROM Deleted) > 6
BEGIN
    RAISERROR(
      'You cannot delete more than six employees at a time.', 16, 1)
    ROLLBACK TRANSACTION
END
```

- **Dropping a Trigger**

You can alter or drop a trigger.

Altering a Trigger

If you must change the definition of an existing trigger, you can alter it without having to drop it.

Changes the Definition Without Dropping the Trigger

The altered definition replaces the definition of the existing trigger with the new definition. Trigger action also can be altered. For example, if you create a trigger for INSERT and then change the action to UPDATE, the altered trigger executes whenever the table is updated.

With delayed name resolution, your trigger can reference tables and views that do not yet exist. If the object does not exist when a trigger is created, you receive a warning message and SQL Server updates the trigger definition immediately.

Syntax

ALTER TRIGGER *trigger_name*
ON *table*
[WITH ENCRYPTION]
{{FOR {[,] [DELETE] [,] [UPDATE] [,][INSERT]}
[NOT FOR REPLICATION]
AS
sql_statement [...*n*] }
|
{FOR {[,] [INSERT] [,] [UPDATE]}
[NOT FOR REPLICATION]
AS
IF UPDATE (*column*)
[{AND | OR} UPDATE (*column*) [,...*n*]]
sql_statement [...*n*] }
}

Example

This example alters the delete trigger created in the previous example. New trigger content is provided, which changes the delete limit from one record to six records.

```
Use Northwind
GO
CREATE TRIGGER Empl_Delete ON Employees
FOR DELETE
AS
IF (SELECT COUNT(*) FROM Deleted) > 6
BEGIN
    RAISERROR(
      'You cannot delete more than six employees at a time.',
      16, 1)
    ROLLBACK TRANSACTION
END
```

Disabling or Enabling a Trigger

You can disable or enable a specific trigger, or all triggers on a table. When a trigger is disabled, it is still defined for the table; however, when an INSERT, UPDATE, or DELETE statement is executed against the table, the actions in the trigger are not performed until the trigger is re-enabled.

You can enable or disable triggers in the ALTER TABLE statement.

Partial Syntax

ALTER TABLE *table*
   {ENABLE | DISABLE} TRIGGER
   {ALL | *trigger_name*[,...*n*]}

Dropping a Trigger

You can remove a trigger by dropping it. Triggers are dropped automatically whenever their associated tables are dropped.

Permission to drop a trigger defaults to the table owner and is non-transferable. However, members of the system administrators (**sysadmin**) and database owner (**db_owner**) roles can drop any object by specifying the owner in the DROP TRIGGER statement.

Syntax

DROP TRIGGER *trigger_name*

◆ How Triggers Work

- How an INSERT Trigger Works
- How a DELETE Trigger Works
- How an UPDATE Trigger Works
- How an INSTEAD OF Trigger Works
- How Nested Triggers Work
- Recursive Triggers

When you design triggers, it is important to understand how they work. This section discusses INSERT, DELETE, UPDATE, INSTEAD OF, nested, and recursive triggers.

How an INSERT Trigger Works

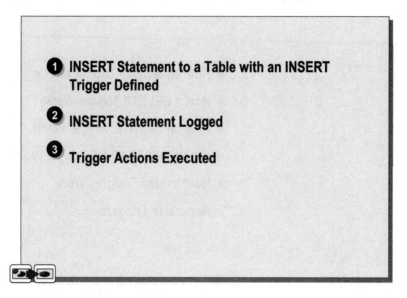

① INSERT Statement to a Table with an INSERT Trigger Defined

② INSERT Statement Logged

③ Trigger Actions Executed

You can define a trigger to execute whenever an INSERT statement inserts data into a table.

When an INSERT trigger is fired, new rows are added to both the trigger table and the **inserted** table. The **inserted** table is a logical table that holds a copy of the rows that have been inserted. The **inserted** table contains the logged insert activity from the INSERT statement. The **inserted** table allows you to reference logged data from the initiating INSERT statement. The trigger can examine the **inserted** table to determine whether, or how, the trigger actions should be carried out. The rows in the **inserted** table are always duplicates of one or more rows in the trigger table.

All data modification activity (INSERT, UPDATE, and DELETE statements) is logged, but the information in the transaction log is unreadable. However, the **inserted** table allows you to reference the logged changes that the INSERT statement caused. Then you can compare the changes to the inserted data in order to verify them or take further action. You also can reference inserted data without having to store the information in variables.

Example

The trigger in this example was created to update a column (**UnitsInStock**) in the **Products** table whenever a product is ordered (whenever a record is inserted into the **Order Details** table). The new value is set to the previous value minus the ordered amount.

```
USE Northwind
CREATE TRIGGER OrdDet_Insert
ON [Order Details]
FOR INSERT
AS
UPDATE P SET
UnitsInStock = (P.UnitsInStock - I.Quantity)
FROM Products AS P INNER JOIN Inserted AS I
ON P.ProductID = I.ProductID
```

How a DELETE Trigger Works

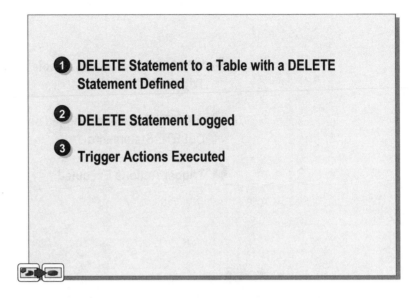

1. **DELETE Statement to a Table with a DELETE Statement Defined**

2. **DELETE Statement Logged**

3. **Trigger Actions Executed**

When a DELETE trigger is fired, deleted rows from the affected table are placed in a special **deleted** table. The **deleted** table is a logical table that holds a copy of the rows that have been deleted. The **deleted** table allows you to reference logged data from the initiating DELETE statement.

Consider the following facts when you use the DELETE trigger:

- When a row is appended to the **deleted** table, it no longer exists in the database table; therefore, the **deleted** table and the database tables have no rows in common.

- Space is allocated from memory to create the **deleted** table. The **deleted** table is always in the cache.

- A trigger that is defined for a DELETE action does not execute for the TRUNCATE TABLE statement because TRUNCATE TABLE is not logged.

Example

The trigger in this example was created to update the **Discontinued** column in the **Products** table whenever a category is deleted (whenever a record is deleted from the **Categories** table). All affected products are marked as 1, indicating they are discontinued.

```
USE Northwind
CREATE TRIGGER Category_Delete
  ON Categories
  FOR DELETE
AS
  UPDATE P SET Discontinued = 1
    FROM Products AS P INNER JOIN deleted AS d
    ON P.CategoryID = d.CategoryID
```

How an UPDATE Trigger Works

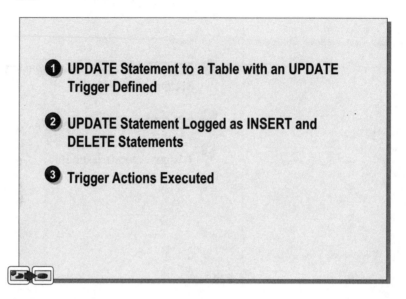

An UPDATE statement can be thought of as two steps: the DELETE step that captures the *before image* of the data, and the INSERT step that captures the *after image* of the data. When an UPDATE statement is executed on a table that has a trigger defined on it, the original rows (before image) are moved into the **deleted** table, and the updated rows (after image) are inserted into the **inserted** table.

The trigger can examine the **deleted** and **inserted** tables, as well as the updated table, to determine whether multiple rows have been updated and how the trigger actions should be carried out.

You can define a trigger to monitor data updates on a specific column by using the IF UPDATE statement. This allows the trigger to isolate activity easily for a specific column. When it detects that the specific column has been updated, it can take proper action, such as raising an error message that says that the column cannot be updated, or by processing a series of statements based on the newly updated column value.

Syntax   IF UPDATE (*<column_name>*)

Example 1

This example prevents a user from modifying the **EmployeeID** column in the **Employees** table.

```
USE Northwind
GO
CREATE TRIGGER Employee_Update
  ON Employees
  FOR UPDATE
AS
IF UPDATE (EmployeeID)
BEGIN TRANSACTION
  RAISERROR ('Transaction cannot be processed.\
  ***** Employee ID number cannot be modified.', 10, 1)
  ROLLBACK TRANSACTION
END
```

How an INSTEAD OF Trigger Works

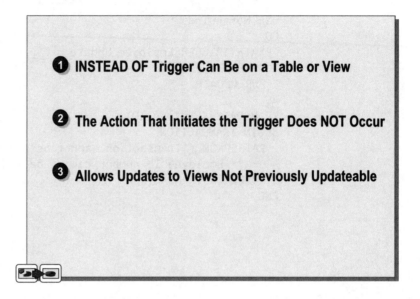

1. INSTEAD OF Trigger Can Be on a Table or View

2. The Action That Initiates the Trigger Does NOT Occur

3. Allows Updates to Views Not Previously Updateable

You can specify an INSTEAD OF trigger on both tables and views. This trigger executes instead of the original triggering action. INSTEAD OF triggers increase the variety of types of updates that you can perform against a view. Each table or view is limited to one INSTEAD OF trigger for each triggering action (INSERT, UPDATE, or DELETE).

You cannot create an INSTEAD OF trigger on views that have the WITH CHECK OPTION defined.

Example

This example creates a table with customers in Germany and a table with customers in Mexico. An INSTEAD OF trigger placed on the view redirects updates to the appropriate underlying table. The insert to the **CustomersGer** table occurs *instead of* the insert to the view.

Create two tables with customer data

```
SELECT * INTO CustomersGer FROM Customers WHERE
Customers.Country = 'Germany'
SELECT * INTO CustomersMex FROM Customers WHERE
Customers.Country = 'Mexico'
GO
```

Create a view on that data

```
CREATE VIEW CustomersView AS
SELECT * FROM CustomersGer
UNION
SELECT * FROM CustomersMex
GO
```

Create an INSTEAD OF trigger on the view

```
CREATE TRIGGER Customers_Update2
ON CustomersView
INSTEAD OF UPDATE AS
DECLARE @Country nvarchar(15)
SET @Country = (SELECT Country FROM Inserted)
IF @Country = 'Germany'
  BEGIN
   UPDATE CustomersGer
    SET CustomersGer.Phone = Inserted.Phone
    FROM CustomersGer JOIN Inserted
    ON CustomersGer.CustomerID = Inserted.CustomerID
  END
ELSE
  IF @Country = 'Mexico'
  BEGIN
   UPDATE CustomersMex
    SET CustomersMex.Phone = Inserted.Phone
    FROM CustomersMex JOIN Inserted
    ON CustomersMex.CustomerID = Inserted.CustomerID
  END
```

Test the trigger by updating the view

```
UPDATE CustomersView SET Phone = ' 030-007xxxx'
  WHERE CustomerID = 'ALFKI'
SELECT CustomerID, Phone FROM CustomersView
  WHERE CustomerID = 'ALFKI'
SELECT CustomerID, Phone FROM CustomersGer
  WHERE CustomerID = 'ALFKI'
```

How Nested Triggers Work

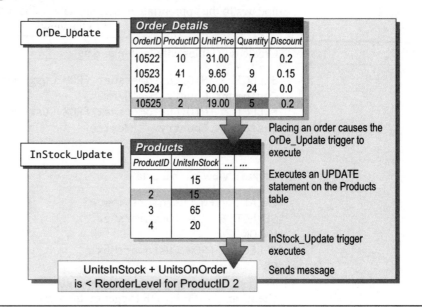

Any trigger can contain an UPDATE, INSERT, or DELETE statement that affects another table. With nesting enabled, a trigger that changes a table can activate a second trigger, which in turn can activate a third trigger, and so on. Nesting is enabled at installation, but you can disable and re-enable it by using the **sp_configure** system stored procedure.

Triggers can be nested up to 32 levels deep. If any trigger in a nested chain sets off an infinite loop, the nesting level is exceeded. The trigger then terminates and rolls back the transaction. You can use nested triggers to perform functions, such as the storage of a backup copy of rows that were affected by a previous trigger. Consider the following facts when you use nested triggers:

- By default, the nested triggers configuration option is on.

- A nested trigger will not fire twice in the same trigger transaction; a trigger does not call itself in response to a second update to the same table within the trigger. For example, if a trigger modifies a table that, in turn, modifies the original trigger table, the trigger does not fire again.

- Because a trigger is a transaction, a failure at any level of a set of nested triggers cancels the entire transaction, and all data modifications are rolled back. Therefore, you should include PRINT statements when you test triggers so that you can determine where the failure occurred.

Checking the Nesting Level

Each time that a nested trigger fires, the nesting level increments. SQL Server supports up to 32 levels of nesting, but you may want to limit the levels of nesting to avoid exceeding the maximum nesting level. You can use the @@NESTLEVEL function to see the current levels of nesting.

Determining Whether to Use Nesting

Nesting is a powerful feature that you can use to maintain data integrity throughout a database. Occasionally, however, you may want to disable nesting. If nesting is disabled, a trigger that modifies another table does not invoke any of the triggers on the second table.

Use the following statement to disable nesting:

Syntax

sp_configure 'nested triggers', 0

You may decide to disable nesting because:

- Nested triggers require a complex and well-planned design. Cascading changes can modify data that you did not intend to affect.

- A data modification at any point in a series of nested triggers sets off the trigger series. Although this offers powerful protection for your data, it can be a problem if your tables must be updated in a specific order.

You can create the same functionality with or without the nesting feature; however, your trigger design will differ substantially. In designing nested triggers, each trigger should initiate only the next data modification —the design should be modular. In designing non-nested triggers, each trigger should initiate all data modifications that you want it to make.

Example

This example shows how placing an order causes the **OrDe_Update** trigger to execute. This trigger executes an UPDATE statement on the **UnitsInStock** column of the **Products** table. When the update occurs, it fires the **Products_Update** trigger and compares the new value of the stock in inventory, plus the stock on order, to the reorder level. If the stock in inventory plus the stock on order falls below the reorder level, a message is sent alerting the buyer to purchase more stock.

```
USE Northwind
GO
CREATE TRIGGER Products_Update
  ON Products
  FOR UPDATE
AS
IF UPDATE (UnitsInStock)
  IF (Products.UnitsInStock + Products.UnitsOnOrder) <
Products.ReorderLevel
BEGIN
  --Send message to the purchasing department
END
```

Recursive Triggers

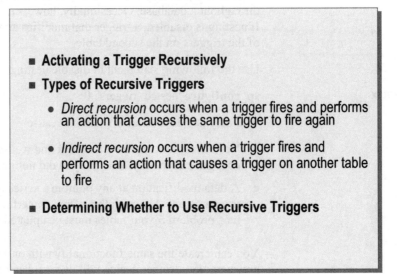

- Activating a Trigger Recursively
- Types of Recursive Triggers
  - *Direct recursion* occurs when a trigger fires and performs an action that causes the same trigger to fire again
  - *Indirect recursion* occurs when a trigger fires and performs an action that causes a trigger on another table to fire
- Determining Whether to Use Recursive Triggers

Any trigger can contain an UPDATE, INSERT, or DELETE statement that affects the same table or another table. With the recursive trigger option enabled, a trigger that changes data in a table can activate itself again, in a recursive execution. The recursive trigger option is disabled by default when a database is created, but you can enable it by using the ALTER DATABASE statement.

Activating a Trigger Recursively

Use the following statement to enable recursive triggers:

Syntax

ALTER DATABASE ClassNorthwind SET RECURSIVE_TRIGGERS ON

sp_dboption *databasename*, 'recursive triggers', True

Note Use the **sp_settriggerorder** system stored procedure to specify a trigger that fires as the first AFTER trigger, or the last AFTER trigger. There is no fixed order in which other triggers, that are defined for a given event, are executed. Each trigger should be self-contained.

If the nested trigger option is off, the recursive trigger option is also disabled, regardless of the recursive trigger setting of the database.

The **inserted** and **deleted** tables for a given trigger contain rows that correspond only to the UPDATE, INSERT, or DELETE statement that last invoked the trigger.

Trigger recursion can occur up to 32 levels deep. If any trigger in a recursive loop sets off an infinite loop, the nesting level is exceeded, and the trigger terminates and rolls back the transaction.

Types of Recursive Triggers

There are two different types of recursion:

- Direct recursion, which occurs when a trigger fires and performs an action that causes the same trigger to fire again.

  For example, an application updates table **T1**, which causes trigger **Trig1** to fire. **Trig1** updates table **T1** again, which causes trigger **Trig1** to fire again.

- Indirect recursion, which occurs when a trigger fires and performs an action that causes a trigger on another table to fire, subsequently causes an update to occur on the original table. This then causes the original trigger to fire again.

  For example, an application updates table **T2**, which causes trigger **Trig2** to fire. **Trig2** updates table **T3**, which causes trigger **Trig3** to fire. **Trig3** in turn updates table **T2**, which causes **Trig2** to fire again.

Determining Whether to Use Recursive Triggers

Recursive triggers are a complex feature that you can use to solve complex relationships, such as self-referencing relationships (also known as *transitive closures*). In these special situations, you may want to enable recursive triggers.

Recursive triggers may be useful when you must maintain:

- The number of reports columns in the **employee** table where the table contains an **employee ID** column and a **manager ID** column.

  For example, assume that two update triggers, **tr_update_employee** and **tr_update_manager**, are defined on the **employee** table. The **tr_update_employee** trigger updates the **employee** table.

  An UPDATE statement fires both **tr_update_employee** and **tr_update_manager** triggers once. In addition, the execution of **tr_update_employee** triggers the execution of **tr_update_employee** again (recursively) and **tr_update_manager**.

- A chart for production scheduling data in which an implied scheduling hierarchy exists.

- An assembly tracking system in which subparts are tracked to parent parts.

Consider the following guidelines before you use recursive triggers:

- Recursive triggers are complex and must be well designed and thoroughly tested. Recursive triggers require controlled looping logic code (termination check). Otherwise, you will exceed the 32-level nesting limit.

- A data modification at any point can set off the trigger series. Although this provides the ability to process complex relationships, it can be a problem if your tables must be updated in a specific order.

You can create similar functionality without the recursive trigger feature; however, your trigger design will differ substantially. In designing recursive triggers, each trigger must contain a conditional check in order to stop recursive processing when the condition becomes false. In designing non-recursive triggers, each trigger must contain the full programming looping structures and checks.

◆ Examples of Triggers

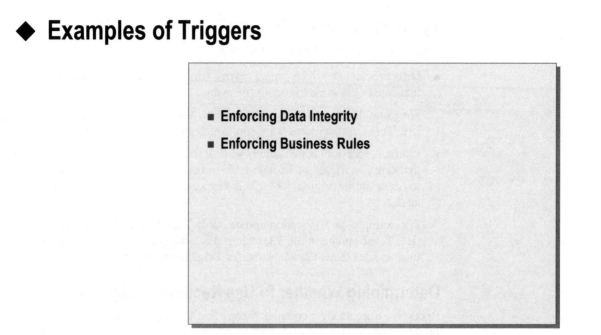

- Enforcing Data Integrity
- Enforcing Business Rules

Triggers enforce data integrity and business rules. You can accomplish some of the actions that triggers perform through the use of constraints, and for certain actions, you should first consider constraints. However, triggers are needed to enforce various degrees of denormalization and to enforce complex business rules.

Enforcing Data Integrity

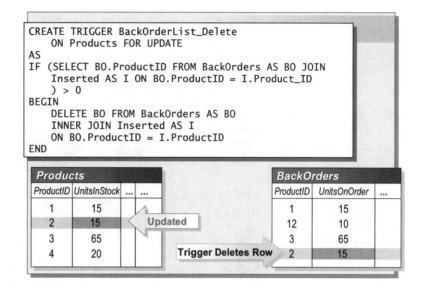

```
CREATE TRIGGER BackOrderList_Delete
    ON Products FOR UPDATE
AS
IF (SELECT BO.ProductID FROM BackOrders AS BO JOIN
    Inserted AS I ON BO.ProductID = I.Product_ID
    ) > 0
BEGIN
    DELETE BO FROM BackOrders AS BO
    INNER JOIN Inserted AS I
    ON BO.ProductID = I.ProductID
END
```

Products			
ProductID	UnitsInStock	...	...
1	15		
2	15		
3	65		
4	20		

Updated

BackOrders		
ProductID	UnitsOnOrder	...
1	15	
12	10	
3	65	
2	15	

Trigger Deletes Row

You can use triggers to maintain data integrity by cascading changes to related tables throughout the database.

Example

The following example shows how a trigger maintains data integrity on a **BackOrders** table. The **BackOrderList_delete** trigger maintains the list of products in the **BackOrders** table. When products are received, the UPDATE trigger on the **Products** table deletes records from a **BackOrders** table.

```
CREATE TRIGGER BackOrderList_Delete
  ON Products FOR UPDATE
AS
IF (SELECT BO.ProductID FROM BackOrders AS BO JOIN
  Inserted AS I ON BO.ProductID = I.Product_ID
  ) > 0
BEGIN
  DELETE BO FROM BackOrders AS BO
  INNER JOIN Inserted AS I
  ON BO.ProductID = I.ProductID
END
```

Enforcing Business Rules

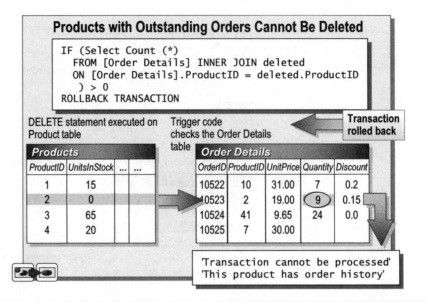

You can use triggers to enforce business rules that are too complex for the CHECK constraint. This includes checking the status of rows in other tables.

For example, you may want to ensure that members' outstanding fines are paid before they are allowed to discontinue membership.

Example

This example creates a trigger that determines whether a product has order history. If it does, the DELETE is rolled back and the trigger returns a custom error message.

```
Use Northwind
GO
CREATE TRIGGER Product_Delete
  ON Products FOR DELETE
AS
IF (Select Count (*)
    FROM [Order Details] INNER JOIN deleted
    ON [Order Details].ProductID = Deleted.ProductID
    ) > 0
BEGIN
    RAISERROR('Transaction cannot be processed.\
            This product has order history.', 16, 1)
    ROLLBACK TRANSACTION
END
```

Performance Considerations

- **Triggers Work Quickly Because the Inserted and Deleted Tables Are in Cache**

- **Execution Time Is Determined by:**
  - Number of tables that are referenced
  - Number of rows that are affected

- **Actions Contained in Triggers Implicitly Are Part of a Transaction**

You should consider the following performance issues when using triggers:

- Triggers work quickly because the **Inserted** and **Deleted** tables are in cache.

  The **Inserted** and **Deleted** tables are always in memory rather than on a disk, because they are logical tables and are usually very small.

- The number of tables referenced and the number of rows affected determines execution time.

  Time that is spent invoking a trigger is minimal. The largest portion of execution time occurs as a result of referencing other tables (which may be either in memory or on a disk) and modifying data, if the trigger definition calls for it.

- Actions contained in triggers are implicitly part of a transaction.

  After a trigger is defined, the user action (INSERT, UPDATE, or DELETE statement) on the table that executes the trigger is always implicitly part of a transaction, along with the trigger itself. If a ROLLBACK TRANSACTION statement is encountered, the whole transaction rolls back. If any statements exist in the trigger script after the ROLLBACK TRANSACTION statement, those statements are executed. Therefore, it may be necessary to use a RETURN clause in an IF statement to prevent the processing of other statements.

Recommended Practices

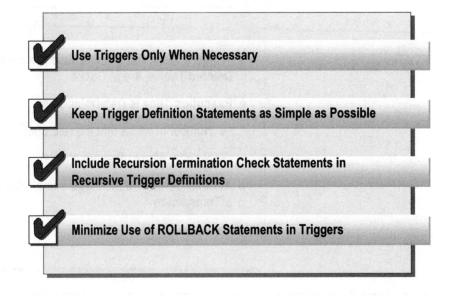

The following recommended practices should help you manage your databases:

- Use triggers only when necessary. Consider a constraint before using a trigger.

- Keep trigger definition statements as simple as possible. Most of the time that is required to process a trigger is spent referencing tables and modifying data. Because triggers are an inherent transaction, locks are maintained until the transaction completes.

- Include recursion-termination check statements in recursive trigger definitions. This prevents the trigger from being stuck in an endless loop.

- Minimize the use of ROLLBACK statements in triggers. When you roll back a trigger, SQL Server must undo all of the actions that it performed up to that point.

Additional information on the following topics is available in SQL Server Books Online.

Topic	Search on
CREATE TRIGGER	"create trigger"
ALTER TRIGGER	"alter trigger"
DROP TRIGGER	"drop trigger"
Creating a trigger	"creating a trigger"
Programming triggers	"programming triggers"

Lab A: Creating Triggers

Objectives

After completing this lab, you will be able to:

- Create triggers to maintain data integrity.
- Create triggers to enforce complex business rules.

Prerequisites

Before working on this lab, you must have:

- Script files for this lab, which are located in C:\Moc\2073A\Labfiles\L11.
- Answer files for this lab, which are located in
  C:\Moc\2073A\Labfiles\L11\Answers.

Lab Setup

To complete this lab, you must have either:

- Completed the prior lab, or
- Executed the C:\Moc\2073A\Batches\Restore11.cmd batch file.

  This command file restores the **ClassNorthwind** database to a state required
  for this lab.

For More Information

If you require help in executing files, search SQL Query Analyzer Help for
"Execute a query".

Other resources that you can use include:

- The **Northwind** database schema.
- Microsoft SQL Server Books Online.

Scenario

The organization of the classroom is meant to simulate that of a worldwide trading firm named Northwind Traders. Its fictitious domain name is nwtraders.msft. The primary DNS server for nwtraders.msft is the instructor computer, which has an Internet Protocol (IP) address of 192.168.x.200 (where x is the assigned classroom number). The name of the instructor computer is London.

The following table provides the user name, computer name, and IP address for each student computer in the fictitious **nwtraders.msft** domain. Find the user name for your computer, and make a note of it.

User name	Computer name	IP address
SQLAdmin1	Vancouver	192.168.x.1
SQLAdmin2	Denver	192.168.x.2
SQLAdmin3	Perth	192.168.x.3
SQLAdmin4	Brisbane	192.168.x.4
SQLAdmin5	Lisbon	192.168.x.5
SQLAdmin6	Bonn	192.168.x.6
SQLAdmin7	Lima	192.168.x.7
SQLAdmin8	Santiago	192.168.x.8
SQLAdmin9	Bangalore	192.168.x.9
SQLAdmin10	Singapore	192.168.x.10
SQLAdmin11	Casablanca	192.168.x.11
SQLAdmin12	Tunis	192.168.x.12
SQLAdmin13	Acapulco	192.168.x.13
SQLAdmin14	Miami	192.168.x.14
SQLAdmin15	Auckland	192.168.x.15
SQLAdmin16	Suva	192.168.x.16
SQLAdmin17	Stockholm	192.168.x.17
SQLAdmin18	Moscow	192.168.x.18
SQLAdmin19	Caracas	192.168.x.19
SQLAdmin20	Montevideo	192.168.x.20
SQLAdmin21	Manila	192.168.x.21
SQLAdmin22	Tokyo	192.168.x.22
SQLAdmin23	Khartoum	192.168.x.23
SQLAdmin24	Nairobi	192.168.x.24

Estimated time to complete this lab: 30 minutes

Exercise 1
Creating Triggers

In this exercise, you will execute a script that creates a trigger. After the trigger is created, you will test it to verify that it works.

▶ **To create a trigger**

In this procedure, you will create a trigger by executing a script file.

1. Log on to the **NWTraders** classroom domain by using the information in the following table.

Option	Value
User name	**SQLAdmin***x* (where *x* corresponds to your computer name as designated in the **nwtraders.msft** classroom domain)
Password	**password**

2. Open SQL Query Analyzer and, if requested, log in to the (local) server with Microsoft Windows® Authentication.

   You have permission to log in to and administer SQL Server because you are logged as **SQLAdmin***x*, which is a member of the Microsoft Windows 2000 local group, Administrators. All members of this group are automatically mapped to the SQL Server **sysadmin** role.

3. In the **DB** list, click **ClassNorthwind**.

4. Open C:\Moc\2073A\Labfiles\L11\OrdDetInsert.sql and review it.

   This script creates a trigger on the **Order Details** table. This trigger updates the **UnitsInStock** column of the **Products** table whenever a row is inserted into the **Order Details** table (whenever an order is received).

5. Execute C:\Moc\2073A\Labfiles\L11\OrdDetInsert.sql.

6. Execute the **sp_helptrigger** system stored procedure on the **Order Details** table in the **ClassNorthwind** database to determine whether the trigger was created.

▶ **To test the trigger**

In this procedure, you will test the trigger that you just created by inserting a row into the **Order Details** table.

1. Execute the following SELECT statement to select a row from the **Products** table to determine the units of a product that are in stock:

```
SELECT * FROM Products WHERE ProductID = 22
```

The **UnitsInStock** column should contain the value of 104. If the **UnitsInStock** column displays a different number, make a note of it.

2. Insert a row into the **Order Details** table ordering 50 units of product 22. Your INSERT statement will be similar to the following:

```
INSERT [Order Details]
(OrderID, ProductID, UnitPrice, Quantity, Discount)
VALUES (11077, 22, 21.00, 50, 0.0)
GO
```

3. Query the **Products** table to verify that the **UnitsInStock** column value for the specific **ProductID** has changed to 54.

Exercise 2
Creating a Trigger for Updating Derived Data

In this exercise, you will create two new tables (without PRIMARY and FOREIGN KEY constraints) and then a trigger on the **NewCategories** table to enforce integrity in the **NewProducts.Discontinued** column. C:\Moc\2073A\Labfiles\L11\Answers\CategoryDelete.sql is a completed script for this exercise.

▶ **To create a trigger that updates derived data**

In this procedure, you will create two new tables called **NewCategories** and **NewProducts**. Neither have the PRIMARY and FOREIGN KEY constraints of the **Categories** and **Products** tables. You will create a trigger on the **NewCategories** table. This trigger updates the **Discontinued** column in the **NewProducts** table whenever a category is deleted (whenever a record is deleted from the **NewCategories** table). All affected products are marked as 1, indicating that they are discontinued. Use C:\Moc\2073A\Labfiles\L11\CategoryDelete.sql and make the appropriate changes.

1. Type and execute the following query to create two new tables called **NewCategories** and **NewProducts**.

```
USE ClassNorthwind
GO
--This creates a NewCategories table
SELECT * INTO NewCategories FROM Categories
--This creates a NewProducts table
SELECT * INTO NewProducts FROM Products
GO
```

2. Type and execute the following query to create a trigger on the **NewCategories** table. This trigger updates the **Discontinued** column of the **NewProducts** table to 1 when a product's parent category is deleted (whenever a row is deleted from the **NewCategories** table).

```
CREATE TRIGGER Category_Delete
    ON NewCategories
    FOR DELETE
AS
    UPDATE P SET Discontinued = 1
    FROM NewProducts AS P INNER JOIN Deleted AS d
    ON P.CategoryID = D.CategoryID
```

3. Type and execute the following SELECT statement that queries the **NewProducts** table to determine the discontinued value of the products in **CategoryID 7**.

```
SELECT ProductID, CategoryID, Discontinued
FROM NewProducts WHERE CategoryID = 7
```

4. Write a DELETE statement that removes a row from the **NewCategories** table, and then verify that the trigger executes correctly.

Are these triggers necessary to maintain data integrity in the **ClassNorthwind** database? Why or why not?

_____

_____

Exercise 3
Creating a Trigger That Maintains a Complex Business Rule

In this exercise, you will create a DELETE trigger on the **NewProducts** table. This trigger determines whether an order history exists in the **Order Details** table before the trigger permits a deletion from the **NewProducts** table.

▶ **To create a trigger for the loan table**

In this procedure, you will use the **NewProducts** table created in the previous exercise. You will create a trigger that determines whether an order history exists for a product that is being deleted. If the product has never been ordered, then the product can be deleted. If the product has a history of orders, then the delete from the product table is rolled back, and the trigger returns a custom error message. C:\Moc\2073A\Labfiles\L11\Answers\BusinessRule.sql is a completed script for this exercise.

1. Create a DELETE trigger on the **NewProducts** table that determines whether an order history exists for a product that is possibly being deleted. If records exist in the **Order Details** table for that product, then display a message and roll back the trigger.

2. Delete product 6 from the **NewProducts** table to test the trigger. Answers\BusinessRule.sql is a completed script for this step.

   Did the trigger fire? Why or why not?

   _____

   _____

Exercise 4
Testing the Firing Order of Constraints and Triggers

In this exercise, you will modify the statement from the previous exercise to test the firing order of constraints and triggers. C:\Moc\2073A\Labfiles\L11\Answers\BusinessRule2.sql is a completed script for this exercise.

▶ **To modify the trigger from the previous exercise**

1. Create a trigger similar to that used in the previous exercise called **Product_Delete2** on the **Products** table.

   Remember that the previous exercise created a DELETE trigger called **Product_Delete** on the **NewProducts** table.

   ```
   CREATE TRIGGER Product_Delete2
     ON Products FOR DELETE
   AS
   IF (Select Count (*)
       FROM [Order Details] INNER JOIN deleted
       ON [Order Details].ProductID = Deleted.ProductID
       ) > 0
   BEGIN
       RAISERROR('Transaction cannot be processed. This Product
   still has a history of orders.', 16, 1)
       ROLLBACK TRANSACTION
   END
   ```

2. Test the trigger.

   Did the trigger fire? Why or why not?

   _____

   _____

Review

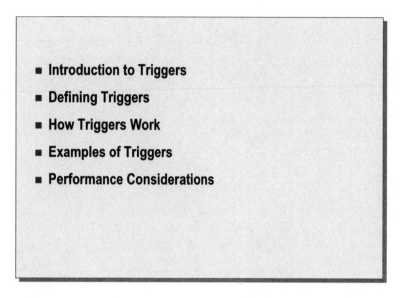

- Introduction to Triggers
- Defining Triggers
- How Triggers Work
- Examples of Triggers
- Performance Considerations

1. If the inventory manager does not provide the **Products.ProductID** column value in the INSERT statement, what characteristics must exist in the column definition?

    _____

    _____

2. If the **Products** table contains a PRIMARY KEY constraint on the **ProductID** column, would a trigger work? Why or why not?

    _____

    _____

3. What must you do to make a trigger work?

_____

_____

Microsoft®
Training &
Certification

Module 12:
Programming Across
Multiple Servers

Contents

Microsoft®

Project Lead: Rich Rose
Instructional Designers: Rich Rose, Cheryl Hoople, Marilyn McGill
Instructional Software Design Engineers: Karl Dehmer, Carl Raebler, Rick Byham
Technical Lead: Karl Dehmer
Subject Matter Experts: Karl Dehmer, Carl Raebler, Rick Byham
Graphic Artist: Kirsten Larson (Independent Contractor)
Editing Manager: Lynette Skinner
Editor: Wendy Cleary
Copy Editor: Edward McKillop (S&T Consulting)
Production Manager: Miracle Davis
Production Coordinator: Jenny Boe
Production Support: Lori Walker (S&T Consulting)
Test Manager: Sid Benavente
Courseware Testing: TestingTesting123
Classroom Automation: Lorrin Smith-Bates
Creative Director, Media/Sim Services: David Mahlmann
Web Development Lead: Lisa Pease
CD Build Specialist: Julie Challenger
Online Support: David Myka (S&T Consulting)
Localization Manager: Rick Terek
Operations Coordinator: John Williams
Manufacturing Support: Laura King; Kathy Hershey
Lead Product Manager, Release Management: Bo Galford
Lead Product Manager, Data Base: Margo Crandall
Group Manager, Courseware Infrastructure: David Bramble
Group Product Manager, Content Development: Dean Murray
General Manager: Robert Stewart

Overview

- **Introduction to Distributed Queries**
- **Executing an Ad Hoc Query on a Remote Data Source**
- **Setting Up a Linked Server Environment**
- **Executing a Query on a Linked Server**
- **Executing a Stored Procedure on a Linked Server**
- **Managing Distributed Transactions**
- **Modifying Data on a Linked Server**
- **Using Partitioned Views**

This module introduces programming across multiple servers. It describes how to execute an ad hoc query on a remote data source. It then describes how to set up a linked server environment, including setting up linked servers and establishing security between servers. The module also presents how to execute linked server and pass-through queries on a linked server, execute stored procedures on a linked server, modify distributed data, and manage distributed transactions. The final section discusses how to use partitioned views to optimize performance.

After completing this module, you will be able to:

- Describe distributed queries.

- Write ad hoc queries that access data that is stored in a remote Microsoft® SQL Server™ 2000 or in an OLE DB data source.

- Set up a linked server environment to access data that is stored in a remote SQL Server 2000 or in an OLE DB data source.

- Write queries that access data from a linked server.

- Execute stored procedures on a remote server or linked server.

- Manage distributed transactions.

- Use distributed transactions to modify distributed data.

- Use partitioned views to increase performance.

Introduction to Distributed Queries

- **Accessing Remote Data**
  - Ad hoc query
  - Linked server query
- **Specifying Where to Process Distributed Queries**
  - Local SQL Server
  - Remote OLE DB data source (pass-through query)
- **Verifying Connection Settings**

Distributed queries access data from multiple heterogeneous data sources stored on a local or remote computer. SQL Server supports distributed queries by using the Microsoft OLE DB Provider.

Distributed queries provide SQL Server users with access to:

- Distributed data stored on multiple computers that are running SQL Server.
- Heterogeneous data stored in various relational and non-relational data sources for which either an OLE DB provider or Open Database Connectivity (ODBC) driver exists.

Accessing Remote Data

You can use two techniques for accessing an OLE DB data source from SQL Server:

- Ad hoc query

  To access remote data when you do not expect to access a data source repeatedly over time, you can write an ad hoc query with the OPENROWSET or OPENDATASOURCE function.

- Linked server query

  To access remote data repeatedly, you can use a linked server and a four-part object name. A linked server is an OLE DB data source that is pre-registered on the local SQL Server so that when it is referenced, the local server knows where to look for the remote data and objects. Using linked servers is an efficient way to provide cross-SQL Server joins and other queries when you know in advance that certain data sources must be available.

Specifying Where to Process Distributed Queries

When you query an OLE DB data source, you can specify whether to process the query locally or on a remote server:

- Local SQL Server

  For linked servers, SQL Server processes distributed queries on the local server by default.

- Remote OLE DB data source

  You can use the OPENQUERY function with linked servers to specify that processing will occur on the remote server. This is called a pass-through query. When you use the OPENROWSET function to execute an ad hoc query on a remote data source, the query is also processed remotely.

Verifying Connection Settings

In any session issuing distributed queries, the ANSI_NULLS and ANSI_WARNINGS options must be on. If you use OBDC or SQL Query Analyzer to issue distributed queries, these options are on by default. If you use the **osql** command line utility, you must explicitly set these options ON.

Executing an Ad Hoc Query on a Remote Data Source

- **Use the OPENROWSET Function When You Do Not Expect to Use the Data Source Repeatedly**

- **Use the OPENROWSET Function to Access Remote Data Without Setting Up a Linked Server**

```
SELECT a.*
FROM OPENROWSET('SQLOLEDB', 'LONDON1';
'newcustomer';'mypassword',
'SELECT ProductID, UnitPrice
FROM Northwind.dbo.Products ORDER BY UnitPrice')
AS a
```

You can access data ad hoc from remote sources by using an OLE DB provider. The OPENROWSET function allows you to connect to and access data from a remote source without setting up a linked server. Use the OPENROWSET function when you do not expect to access a particular data source repeatedly over time.

Syntax

OPENROWSET('*provider_name*'
  {'*data -source*'; '*user_id*' ; '*password*' | '*provider_string*'},
  {[*catalog.*][*schema.*]*object* | '*query*'})

The following table describes the parameters of the OPENROWSET function.

Parameter	Description
provider_name	Unique, friendly name for the OLE DB provider corresponding to this data source.
data_source	Name of the data source as interpreted by the OLE DB provider.
user_id	User name that will be passed to the specified OLE DB provider.
password	Password to be passed to the OLE DB provider.
provider_string	OLE DB provider-specific connection string that identifies a unique data source.
catalog	Catalog or database in which the object resides.
schema	Schema or owner for an object.
object	Unique object name to act upon.
query	String containing a query to be sent to and executed by the provider. If a query is specified rather than a remote object name, the query is executed as a pass-through query.

The following table lists some common OLE DB provider names. See SQL Server Books Online for a more complete listing of OLE DB provider names for various data sources.

Product	Provider name
SQL Server	N'SQLOLEDB'
Microsoft OLE DB Provider for Access (Jet)	'Microsoft.Jet.OLEDB.4.0'
Microsoft OLE DB Provider for Oracle	'MSDAORA' *data_source* is the SQL*Net alias name for the Oracle database to be added as a linked server
OLE DB Provider for ODBC (Using *data_source* parameter)	*provider_name* is 'MSDASQL' *data_source* is 'LocalServer'
OLE DB Provider for ODBC (Using *provider_string* parameter)	*provider_name* is 'MSDASQL' *provider_string* is 'DRIVER={SQL Server} SERVER=*servername* UID=*login*;PWD=*password*;'
Data Transformation Services	DTSPackageDSO
Microsoft Directory Services	ADSDSOObject
Microsoft Indexing Service	MSIDXS

Consider the following facts and guidelines when executing queries by using the OPENROWSET function:

- You must provide catalog and schema names if the data source supports multiple catalogs and schemas (databases and object owners, in the case of SQL Server).

- The *user_id* passed to the OLE DB provider determines the permissions associated with the connection.

- The OPENROWSET function can be used in place of a table name in the FROM clause of a SELECT statement.

Example 1

This example uses the native OLE DB provider for SQL Server to access information in the **Northwind** database on the London1 SQL Server. All connection information as well as the query to be processed is contained in the arguments of the OPENROWSET function. The **newcustomer** user account is used to log in to the remote server.

```
SELECT a.*
FROM OPENROWSET('SQLOLEDB', 'LONDON1'; 'newcustomer';
'mypassword',
'SELECT ProductID, UnitPrice FROM Northwind.dbo.Products
      ORDER BY UnitPrice')
   AS a
```

Example 2

This example uses the OLE DB provider for Microsoft Access (Jet) to access the **Orders** table in the **Northwind** database on a remote Access database.

```
SELECT a.*
FROM OPENROWSET('Microsoft.Jet.OLEDB.4.0'
'C:\MSOffice\Access\Samples\Northwind.mdb';
'newcustomer'; 'mypassword',
Orders)
 AS a
```

Example 3

This example joins the **Orders** table in the **Northwind** database on a remote Access database with the **Customers** table in the **Northwind** database on the local SQL Server.

```
USE Northwind
SELECT cust.* ord.*
FROM  Customers as cust JOIN
OPENROWSET('Microsoft.Jet.OLEDB.4.0'
'C:\MSOffice\Access\Samples\Northwind.mdb'';
'newcustomer'; 'mypassword',
Orders)
 AS ord
On cust.customerid = ord.customerid
```

◆ Setting Up a Linked Server Environment

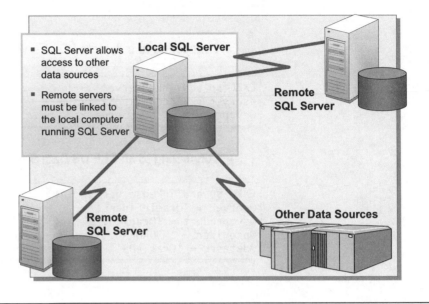

- SQL Server allows access to other data sources
- Remote servers must be linked to the local computer running SQL Server

Local SQL Server

Remote SQL Server

Remote SQL Server

Other Data Sources

To work with data from a remote SQL Server or another OLE DB data source, you must establish a linked server. A linked server is an OLE DB data source that is pre-registered on the local SQL Server so that when it is referenced, the local server knows where to look for the remote data and objects.

Why Use Linked Servers

Linked servers are a way to enable cross-SQL Server joins and other queries when you know in advance that you want certain data sources to be available.

Using a linked server gives you the ability to submit Transact-SQL statements directly to a remote SQL Server. These actions can be performed as part of a distributed transaction. When you use linked servers, consider the following facts and guidelines:

- You can access distributed data that is stored in multiple SQL Servers and heterogeneous data that is stored in various relational and non-relational data sources.

- A source other than SQL Server can be defined as a linked server if an OLE DB provider exists for the source.

- If you regularly access information that resides on another SQL Server computer, you should define that remote server as a linked server on your local SQL Server computer.

- Information about linked servers is stored in the **sysservers** system table.

Setting Up Linked Servers

To set up linked servers, you must first establish a link to a remote data source and then establish security between the servers.

Linking to a Remote Data Source

- ■ **Connecting to a Remote SQL Server**

```
EXEC sp_addlinkedserver
@server = 'AccountingServer',
@svrproduct = 'SQL Server'
```

- ■ **Connecting to an OLE DB Data Source**

```
EXEC sp_addlinkedserver
@server = 'OracleFinance',
@svrproduct = 'Oracle',
@provider = 'MSDAORA',
@datasrc = 'OracleDB'
```

To execute Transact-SQL statements on a remote SQL Server or OLE DB data source, you must establish a link to the server or data source.

You can establish a link to the remote SQL Server by using SQL Server Enterprise Manager or the **sp_addlinkedserver** system stored procedure. The **sp_addlinkedserver** system stored procedure defines a remote SQL Server on the local computer and specifies the OLE DB provider.

Syntax

sp_addlinkedserver [**@server** =] *'server'*
  [, [**@svrproduct** =] *'product_name'*]
  [, [**@provider** =] *'provider_name'*]
  [, [**@datasrc** =] *'data_source'*]
  [, [**@location** =] *'location'*]
  [, [**@provstr** =] *'provider_string'*]
  [, [**@catalog** =] *'catalog'*]

The **sp_addserver** system stored procedure is provided for backward compatibility, but you should use **sp_addlinkedserver** instead.

The following table describes the parameters of the **sp_addlinkedserver** system stored procedure.

Parameter	Description
@server	Name of the linked server to create
@svrproduct	Product name of the OLE DB data source
@provider	The unique, friendly name for the OLE DB provider corresponding to this data source
@datasrc	Name of the data source as interpreted by the OLE DB provider
@location	Location of the database as interpreted by the OLE DB provider

(continued)

Parameter	Description
@provstr	The OLE DB provider-specific connection string that identifies a unique data source
@catalog	The catalog to use when making a connection to the OLE DB provider

Connecting to a Remote SQL Server

If you want to connect to a server that is running SQL Server, the only parameters that you must provide are **@srvproduct** and **@server**. You do not need to specify **@provider, @datasrc, @location, @provstr**, and **@catalog**. The SQL Server OLE DB provider (N'SQLOLEDB') is automatically used.

Example 1

This example adds the **AccountingServer**, a computer running SQL Server, to the list of linked servers that are available from the local SQL Server computer.

```
EXEC sp_addlinkedserver 'AccountingServer', 'SQL Server'
```

Connecting to an OLE DB Data Source

If you want to connect to a data source other than SQL Server, you must specify a **@provider, @datasrc, @location, @provstr**, and **@catalog**, as well as the **@srvproduct** and **@server** parameters when creating a linked server.

Example 2

This example adds the Oracle server OracleFinance to the list of linked servers that are available from the local computer running SQL Server. This example assumes that a SQL*Net alias of 'OracleDB' has been created. This alias is used for the **@datasrc** parameter.

```
EXEC sp_addlinkedserver 'OracleFinance', 'Oracle', 'MSDAORA',
'OracleDB'
```

Establishing Linked Server Security

- **Local Server Must Log In to Remote Server on Behalf of User**

- **If User's Login Account Exists on Both Servers, It Can Be Used to Log In to Remote Server**

- **Map Login Accounts and Passwords Between Servers by Using sp_addlinkedsrvlogin**

- **By Using Security Account Delegation, You Can Connect to Multiple Servers with One Authentication**

- **Without Security Delegation, Map Local Login Account to Login Account on the Linked Server**

You may need to establish security between the local server and a remote server. When you establish security between local and remote SQL Servers, consider the following facts:

- When users log in to the local SQL Server and execute a distributed query, the local SQL Server logs in to the remote SQL Server on behalf of the user.

- If the user's login account and password exist on both the local and remote SQL Servers, the local SQL Server can use the credentials of the user to log in to the remote SQL Server. Establishing security in this manner is useful when both servers are using domain accounts.

- You can map login accounts and passwords between local and remote SQL Servers by using the **sp_addlinkedsrvlogin** system stored procedure. When you map a local account to a remote login account, you do not have to create a login account and password for each user on the remote SQL Server.

  For example, a user can log in to a client application that accesses a local SQL Server. The local SQL Server then accesses the linked server on behalf of the user by using one login account for all end users. The login account on the linked server to which the local login account is mapped has permission to access a specific table.

- It is possible to connect to multiple servers, and with each server change, to retain the authentication credentials of the original client. This is known as *security account delegation*. To use this delegation, all servers must be running Microsoft Windows® 2000 and using providers that employ the Security Support Provider Interface (SSPI). You must also be using the Active Directory™ directory service.

Note For more information about security account delegation, consult the Windows 2000 documentation.

■ If the linked server does not support security account delegation, you must set up a local login mapping from a Windows Authenticated login account to a login account on the linked server. You must establish an account mapping to enable linked server communication.

Syntax

sp_addlinkedsrvlogin [**@rmtsrvname** =] *'rmtsrvname'*
  [, [**@useself** =] *'useself'*]
  [, [**@locallogin** =] *'locallogin'*]
  [, [**@rmtuser** =] *'rmtuser'*]
  [, [**@rmtpassword** =] *'rmtpassword'*

The following table lists the parameters of the **sp_addlinkedsrvlogin** system stored procedure.

Parameter	Description
@rmtsrvname	Name of a linked server to which the login mapping applies.
@useself	Determines whether SQL Server login accounts use their own credentials or the values of the **@rmtuser** and **@rmtpassword** arguments to connect to the server specified by the **@rmtsrvname** argument. A value of TRUE for **@useself** is invalid for a Windows Authenticated login account.
@locallogin	An optional login account on the local server. If used, **@locallogin** must already exist on the local server. If this value is null, then all login accounts on the local SQL Server will be mapped to the account on the remote server specified by **@rmtuser**.
@rmtuser	The optional user name for connection to **@rmtsrvname** when **@useself** is FALSE.
@rmtpassword	The optional password associated with **@rmtuser**.

Example 1

In this example, a user who logs in to the local SQL Server with the **AccountWriter** login account will be able to access remote data on the AccountingServer SQL Server with the credentials of the **rmtAccountWriter** login account.

```
EXEC sp_addlinkedsrvlogin
@rmtsrvname = 'AccountingServer',
@useself = 'false',
@locallogin = 'Accountwriter',
@rmtuser = 'rmtAccountWriter',
@rmtpassword = 'financepass'
```

Example 2

This example establishes security between a local and a linked SQL Server. Any users on the local SQL Server who access remote data on the AccountingServer linked server are logged in to the remote SQL Server with the **AccountingServer/allcustomers** user account.

```
EXEC sp_addlinkedsrvlogin
@rmtsrvname = 'AccountingServer',
@useself = 'false',
@rmtuser= 'allcustomers'
```

Configuring Linked Server Options

- **Collation Compatible**

```
USE master
EXEC sp_serveroption 'AccountingServer',
'collation compatible', true
```

- **Collation Name and Use Remote Collation**
- **Data Access**
- **RPC and RPC out**
- **Lazy Schema Validation**

You can set options for linked servers by using the **sp_serveroption** system stored procedure. Only a member of the **sysadmin** server role can use **sp_serveroption** to set server options.

Syntax

sp_serveroption ['*server*'] [, '*option_name*'] [, '*option_value*']

The following options affect linked servers:

Collation Compatible

This option affects the performance of distributed query execution against linked servers. If this option is set to true, SQL Server assumes that all columns and character sets on the remote server are compatible with the local server-wide character set and collation. This enables SQL Server to send comparisons on character columns to the provider. If this option is not set, SQL Server must return all of the rows to the local server to evaluate comparisons on character columns.

This option should only be set if the data source that corresponds to the linked server has the same character set and sort order as the local server.

Example

This example configures the AccountingServer linked server to be collation compatible with the local SQL Server.

```
USE master
EXEC sp_serveroption 'AccountingServer',
'collation compatible', true
```

Collation Name and Use Remote Collation

The following two options are often used together.

Collation Name   This option specifies the name of the collation used by the remote data source if **use remote collation** is **true** and the data source is not a SQL Server data source. The following conditions apply to this option:

- The name must be one of the collations supported by SQL Server.

- You should use this option when accessing an OLE DB data source, other than SQL Server, that has a collation that matches one of the SQL Server collations.

- The linked server must support a single collation to be used for all columns in that server.

Use Remote Collation   This option determines whether SQL Server will use the collation of a remote column or of a local server:

- If **true**, the collation of remote columns is used for SQL Server data sources, and the collation specified in **collation name** is used for non-SQL Server data sources.

- If **false**, distributed queries will always use the default collation of the local server. The default is **false**.

Data Access

This option enables and disables a linked server for distributed query access. You can only use this for **sysserver** entries that are added by using **sp_addlinkedserver**.

Example

This example configures the AccountingServer remote server for data access and enables its use as a linked server.

```
USE master
EXEC sp_serveroption 'AccountingServer',
'data access', true
```

RPC and RPC out

The RPC option enables remote procedure calls (RPCs) from a given server. The RPC out option enables remote procedure calls to a given server.

Lazy Schema Validation

This option determines whether the schema of remote tables will be checked. If **true**, SQL Server does not check the schema of remote tables at the beginning of the query. Deferring the schema validation can improve performance.

Getting Information About Linked Servers

System stored procedure	Returns
sp_linkedservers	A list of linked servers defined on the local server
sp_catalogs	A list of catalogs and descriptions for a specific linked server
sp_indexes	Index information for the specified remote table
sp_primarykeys	The primary key columns, one row per key column, for the specified table
sp_foreignkeys	The foreign keys defined on the specified remote table
sp_tables_ex	Table information on the tables from the specified linked server
sp_columns_ex	The column information, for all columns or a specified column, for linked table

In addition to using SQL Server Enterprise Manager, you can use the following stored procedures to gather information about linked servers:

sp_linkedservers   This system stored procedure returns a list of linked servers that are defined on the local server.

sp_catalogs   This system stored procedure returns a list of catalogs and descriptions for a specified linked server. For remote SQL Servers, this is a list of available databases.

sp_indexes   This system stored procedure returns index information for the specified remote table.

Syntax

sp_indexes {'*table_server*'} [, '*table_name*'] [, '*table_schema*']
  [, '*table_catalog*'][, '*index*'] [, '*is_unique*']

Example

This example returns all index information from the **Employees** table of the **Northwind** database on the Cairo server.

```
USE master
EXEC sp_indexes 'CAIRO', 'Employees', 'dbo', 'Northwind',
NULL, 0
```

sp_primarykeys   This system stored procedure returns the primary key columns, one row per key column, for the specified table.

sp_foreignkeys   This system stored procedure returns the foreign keys that are defined on the specified remote table.

sp_tables_ex   This system stored procedure is a version of **sp_tables** for use with remote data sources, and it returns table information on the tables from the specified linked server.

Syntax   **sp_tables_ex** {'*table_server*'} [, '*table_name*'] [, '*table_schema*']
[, '*table_catalog*'] [, '*table_type*']

sp_columns_ex   This is a version of **sp_columns** for linked servers. This system stored procedure returns the column information, for all columns or a specified column, for the given linked server table. If a column is specified, only information for that particular column is returned.

Syntax   **sp_columns_ex** {'*table_server*'} [, '*table_name*'] [, '*table_schema*']
[, '*table_catalog*'] [, '*column*']

◆ Executing a Query on a Linked Server

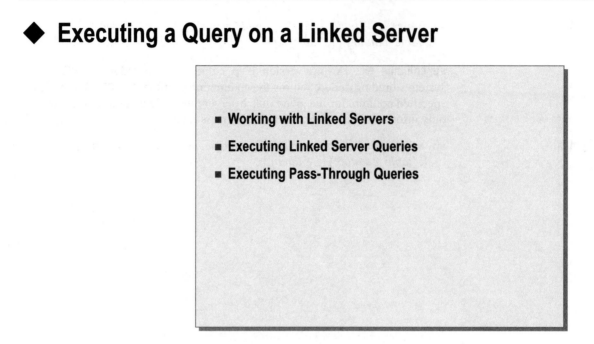

- ■ Working with Linked Servers
- ■ Executing Linked Server Queries
- ■ Executing Pass-Through Queries

SQL Server can process a distributed query locally on the local server, or remotely on a linked server.

Working with Linked Servers

- **How SQL Server Optimizes Remote Queries**
- **Referring to Objects on Linked Servers**
- **Allowed Transact-SQL Statements**
  - SELECT, INSERT, UPDATE, DELETE
- **Disallowed Transact-SQL Statements**
  - CREATE, ALTER, DROP
  - ORDER BY on remote tables containing large objects
  - READTEXT, WRITETEXT, UPDATETEXT

Distributed queries access data from multiple data sources, such as OLE DB providers and other SQL Servers.

How SQL Server Optimizes Remote Queries

SQL Server attempts to delegate distributed query evaluation to the OLE DB providers. SQL Server extracts from the original distributed query those syntactical elements that access only the remote tables in the provider's data source, and then it executes this reduced query against the provider. This process reduces the number of rows returned from the provider and allows the provider to use its indexes to evaluate the query.

Referring to Objects on Linked Servers

When you perform distributed queries, you must refer to the linked objects with four-part names in the following format:
linked-server-name.catalog-name.schema-name.object-name

The following table describes these parameters.

Parameter	Description
linked-server-name	Is the network-wide name of a linked server
catalog-name	Corresponds to a database
schema-name	Is the collection of objects that are owned by a particular user and corresponds to the object owner
object-name	Refers to the table that you want to access

For example, to refer to the **Orders** table that is owned by the **database owner (dbo)** role in the **Northwind** database on the linked server, Corpserver, use the four-part name **corpserver.Northwind.dbo.Orders** in your query.

Allowed Transact-SQL Statements

When you use a linked SQL Server, you can execute the following Transact-SQL statements on linked data:

- SELECT statement with a WHERE clause or a JOIN clause
- INSERT, UPDATE, and DELETE statements

Disallowed Transact-SQL Statements

When you use a linked SQL Server, you cannot:

- Use the CREATE, ALTER, or DROP statements on linked servers.

  Therefore, you cannot execute a CREATE TABLE statement that contains a SELECT INTO statement. However, you can use linked data as the source for tables that are created on the local server with the SELECT INTO statement.

- Include an ORDER BY clause in a SELECT statement if a large object column from a linked table is in the select list of the SELECT statement.

- Use the READTEXT, WRITETEXT, and UPDATETEXT statements.

Executing Linked Server Queries

- **Use Fully Qualified Names to Reference Objects on Linked Servers**

Example 1

```
SELECT CompanyName
FROM AccountingServer.NorthwindRemote.dbo.Suppliers
```

Example 3

```
SELECT CompanyName, Phone
INTO PhoneList
FROM AccountingServer.NorthwindRemote.dbo.Suppliers
```

When you query a linked server, you should reference objects by using the fully qualified four-part object name.

Example 1

This example retrieves the company names from the **Suppliers** table in the **NorthwindRemote** database on the AccountingServer linked server.

```
SELECT CompanyName
FROM AccountingServer.NorthwindRemote.dbo.Suppliers
```

Example 2

This example joins the **Suppliers** table in the **NorthwindRemote** database on a linked server to the **Products** table on the local SQL Server.

```
SELECT ProductName, CompanyName
FROM Products p JOIN
AccountingServer.NorthwindRemote.dbo.Suppliers
ON p.supplierid = s.supplierid
```

Example 3

This example uses a SELECT INTO statement to create and transfer data from a table on a linked SQL Server to a permanent table on the local SQL Server. You must set the SELECT INTO/BULK COPY database option if you want to execute this example.

```
SELECT CompanyName, Phone
INTO PhoneList
FROM AccountingServer.NorthwindRemote.dbo.Suppliers
```

Executing Pass-Through Queries

- Use the OPENQUERY Function to Execute Pass-Through Queries on a Linked Server

- Use the OPENQUERY Function in a SELECT Statement in Place of a Table Name

- Use the Result of an OPENQUERY Function as the Target Table of an INSERT, UPDATE, or DELETE Statement

```
SELECT * FROM OPENQUERY
(AsiaServer, 'SELECT ProductID, Royalty
FROM Northwind.dbo.ProductInfo')
```

When querying a linked server, you can specify that SQL Server perform a pass-through query. Use the OPENQUERY function to execute pass-through queries on a linked server.

Syntax

OPENQUERY (*linked_server*, '*query*')

Consider the following facts when performing pass-through queries with the OPENQUERY function:

- You can use the result of the OPENQUERY function with a SELECT statement in the place of a table name.

- You can use the result of the OPENQUERY function as the target table of an INSERT, UPDATE, or DELETE statement if the OLE DB provider for the data source supports these actions.

Example 1

In this example, the OPENQUERY function is used to process a SELECT statement on the AsiaServer linked server and return the results to the local SQL Server. Assume that AsiaServer has already been established as a linked server and that security has been set up.

```
SELECT * FROM OPENQUERY(AsiaServer, 'SELECT ProductID, Royalty
FROM Northwind.dbo.ProductInfo')
```

Example 2

In this example, the OPENQUERY function is used to delete discontinued products from the **Northwind.Products** table on the AsiaServer linked server. All processing of the DELETE statement occurs on the AsiaServer linked server.

```
DELETE FROM OPENQUERY(AsiaServer, 'Northwind.dbo.Products')
WHERE Discontinued = 1
```

Executing a Stored Procedure on a Linked Server

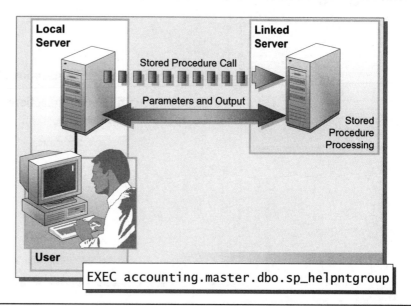

Execution of stored procedures on a linked server allows a client that is connected to one SQL Server to execute a stored procedure on another SQL Server without establishing a client connection to that server.

- The server to which the client is connected accepts the client request and sends the request to the linked server. The EXECUTE statement must contain the name of the linked server as part of its syntax.

- The linked server processes the request and returns any results to the original server, which in turn passes those results to the client.

- Applications on either the client or server can initiate linked stored procedure requests.

Syntax

EXECUTE *servername.dbname.owner. procedure_name*

Example

The following batch executes the **sp_helpntgroup** system stored procedure on the Accounting remote server. The system stored procedure lists the Windows 2000 groups and specifies the databases to which they have access.

```
EXEC accounting.master.dbo.sp_helpntgroup
```

Managing Distributed Transactions

- **Managing Distributed Transactions by Using MS DTC**
- **Managing Distributed Transactions by Using Component Services**

Distributed transactions coordinate activity on multiple resources as a single unit of work. SQL Server supports distributed transactions, allowing users to update multiple SQL Server databases and other sources of data. You can also use Windows 2000 Component Services to coordinate distributed transactions among components.

Managing Distributed Transactions by Using MS DTC

The Microsoft Distributed Transaction Coordinator (MS DTC) coordinates commitment of a distributed transaction across all servers that participate in the transaction. These servers can include SQL Server in addition to middle-tier components.

You can use MS DTC from a SQL Server stored procedure to coordinate transactions across multiple computers running SQL Server or between a SQL Server and linked servers.

You can add remote computers running SQL Server to a distributed transaction. A stored procedure issues a BEGIN DISTRIBUTED TRANSACTION statement, and then it either makes a remote stored procedure call referencing a remote server or executes a distributed query referencing a remote or linked server.

Managing Distributed Transactions by Using Component Services

Use Component Services to deploy and manage distributed transactions. The underlying mechanism is MS DTC. Components in the middle tier can participate in a distributed transaction.

Modifying Data on a Linked Server

- **Distribute Transactions by:**
  - Executing BEGIN DISTRIBUTED TRANSACTION

    -OR-
  - Calling API functions from a client
- **Consider These Facts:**
  - BEGIN DISTRIBUTED TRANSACTION statements cannot be nested
  - ROLLBACK TRANSACTION rolls back entire transaction
  - Savepoints are not supported
  - Set the XACT_ABORT session option

When you want to modify data on a linked server, you must perform a distributed transaction. You can execute a BEGIN DISTRIBUTED TRANSACTION statement or reference the API functions in a client application.

Syntax

BEGIN DISTRIBUTED TRANSACTION [*transaction_name*]

Example

The following example uses a distributed transaction to transfer funds between two bank accounts stored on different servers. A stored procedure named **withdraw** on the local server is used to withdraw funds from a savings account, and a stored procedure named **deposit** on a linked server is used to deposit funds to a checking account. One hundred dollars is withdrawn from account number 1234 on the local server and deposited in the corresponding checking account on the Centralserver linked server. Both the local and linked databases commit or roll back the transaction.

```
SET XACT_ABORT ON
BEGIN DISTRIBUTED TRANSACTION
  EXEC Savingsdb.dbo.withdraw 1234, 100
  EXEC Centralserver.Checkingdb.dbo.deposit 1234, 100
COMMIT TRAN
```

Consider the following facts when you work with distributed transactions:

- BEGIN DISTRIBUTED TRANSACTION statements cannot be nested. SQL Server detects such calls, rejects them, and reports an error.

- A ROLLBACK TRANSACTION statement rolls back the entire distributed transaction.

- Savepoints are not supported. If SQL Server rolls back a distributed transaction, the entire transaction is rolled back to the beginning of the distributed transaction, regardless of any savepoints.

- You must set the XACT_ABORT session option when performing distributed transactions among linked servers. If a Transact-SQL statement fails when the XACT_ABORT session option is set, the entire transaction is rolled back. If this option is not set, only the statement that failed is rolled back, and transaction processing continues.

◆ Using Partitioned Views

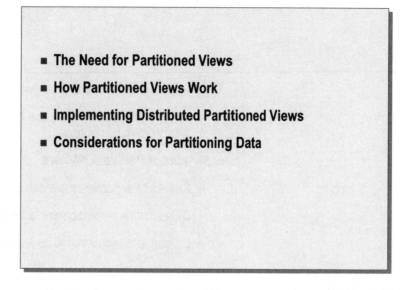

- The Need for Partitioned Views
- How Partitioned Views Work
- Implementing Distributed Partitioned Views
- Considerations for Partitioning Data

Partitioned views can increase performance by distributing what is processed across multiple servers.

The Need for Partitioned Views

- **Scalability**
  - Add more hardware to a single server
  - Divide workload and database across multiple independent computers
- **Benefits of Partitioned Views**
  - Results of separate tables can appear as one table
  - Data location is transparent to the application
  - Database is programmed as a single entity

When workloads increase, it is important to be able to easily add resources.

Scalability

Use scalability to increase the resources of a computer to meet increasing workloads over time. You can achieve scalability by either adding more hardware to a single server or adding multiple independent computers that divide the database. Partitioning the workload across an array is especially suited for e-commerce applications wherein enormous growth will occur.

Benefits of Partitioned Views

You can use views to partition data across multiple databases or instances of SQL Server. The benefits of using partitioned views are as follows:

- The results of separate tables can be combined into one result set that appears to the user as a single table called a *partitioned view*.
- The location of the data is transparent to the application.
- The database is programmed as a single entity.

How Partitioned Views Work

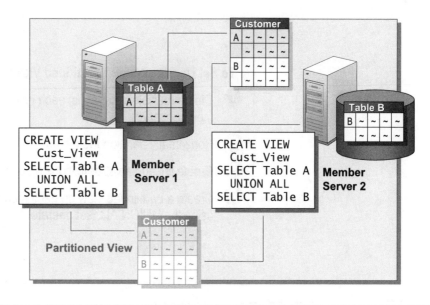

Partitioned views allow the data in a large table to be horizontally partitioned into smaller *member tables*. Each member table has the same format as the original table, but only part of the rows. A server containing a member table is called a *member server*. Each member server contains one member table and a distributed partitioned view.

An application that references the partitioned view on any of the servers gets the same results as would be obtained if a complete copy of the original table were present on each server.

Local and Distributed Partitioned Views

You can implement partitioned views locally on a single server or in a distributed environment on multiple servers. *Local partitioned views* reference member tables on one server. *Distributed partitioned views* reference member tables on multiple servers. You will typically use distributed partitioned views.

In the illustration, the **Customer** table is partitioned by region. Region A is on member server 1, and Region B is on member server 2. A view is created on each server that makes it possible to view the partitioned data as if it were in one table. This view will appear as a virtual table rendition of the original table.

Features Necessary to Implement Partitioned Views

Certain SQL Server features are necessary to implement partitioned views. These features appear in the following table.

Feature	Benefit
Views	Allow user to see all of the partitioned tables as one table
CHECK constraints	Define and enforce the integrity of partitions
Distributed queries	Query and update partitioned data
INSTEAD OF triggers	Manage updates to views

Implementing Distributed Partitioned Views

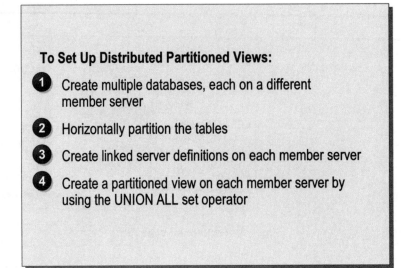

To Set Up Distributed Partitioned Views:

1. Create multiple databases, each on a different member server

2. Horizontally partition the tables

3. Create linked server definitions on each member server

4. Create a partitioned view on each member server by using the UNION ALL set operator

Setting up distributed partitioned views requires four steps.

1. Create multiple databases, each on a different member server running an instance of SQL Server.

2. Horizontally partition the tables by creating tables on each member server.

3. Create linked server definitions on each member server. The linked server definition will be used to send distributed queries to each member server.

4. Create a partitioned view on each member server by using the UNION ALL set operator to combine all of the rows from each member server table.

   Each view should have the same name. This allows queries referencing the distributed partitioned view name to run on any of the member servers.

Considerations for Partitioning Data

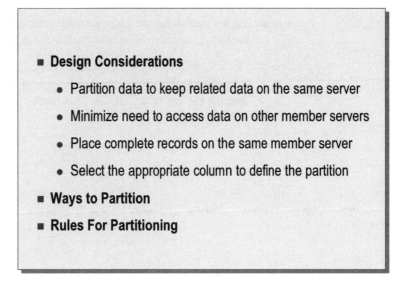

- **Design Considerations**
  - Partition data to keep related data on the same server
  - Minimize need to access data on other member servers
  - Place complete records on the same member server
  - Select the appropriate column to define the partition
- **Ways to Partition**
- **Rules For Partitioning**

Partitioning works well if the tables in the database are naturally divisible into similar partitions where most of the rows accessed by any SQL statement can be found on the same member server.

Design Considerations

Design considerations for partitioning include the following:

- Partition the individual tables in the original database so that most related data is placed together on a member server.

- Minimize any requirements for data on other member servers. Distributed queries should only be needed for 20 percent, or less, of the data.

- Place complete records on the same member server. A partition should allow all rows to be placed on the same member server as all their referencing foreign key rows.

- To evenly distribute the workload, you should define the partition on the column that most evenly distributes the data among the partitioned tables.

  For example, a primary key may be the best method to partition, wherein you specify a range of data for each table. In some cases it may be more beneficial to partition by a non-primary key column such as region.

Ways to Partition

You can use different methods of distributing data in various tables across all the member databases. You should consider:

- Partitioning some tables.

- Making complete copies of other tables in each member database.

- Leaving some tables intact on the original server.

Rules for Partitioning

Some rules for partitioning are:

- Tables must have the same format as the original table. Tables must include the same number of columns, which must have the same attributes.

- Partition ranges cannot overlap.

- You must enforce the partitioned range of values on each member table through the use of a CHECK constraint.

Recommended Practices

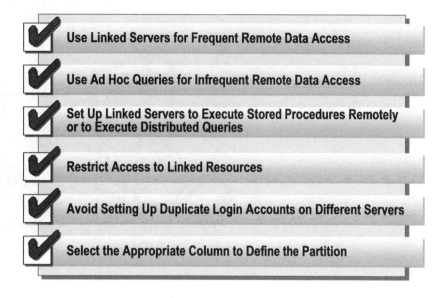

Use Linked Servers for Frequent Remote Data Access

Use Ad Hoc Queries for Infrequent Remote Data Access

Set Up Linked Servers to Execute Stored Procedures Remotely or to Execute Distributed Queries

Restrict Access to Linked Resources

Avoid Setting Up Duplicate Login Accounts on Different Servers

Select the Appropriate Column to Define the Partition

The following recommended practices should help you when you program multiple servers:

- Use linked servers when you expect to access remote data on a regular basis.

- Use ad hoc queries when you do not expect to access a data source repeatedly over time.

- Set up a linked server environment in which to execute either stored procedures remotely or to execute distributed queries.

- Restrict access to linked resources by using application roles or local accounts that are mapped to accounts on the linked server.

- Avoid setting up duplicate login accounts on different servers. Map user accounts on a server to a single account (with appropriate permissions) on the linked server to access data on the linked server.

- Select the appropriate column to define the partition.

Additional information on the following topics is available in SQL Server Books Online.

Topic	Search on
OLE DB providers	"OLE DB providers tested with SQL Server"
Linked servers	**sp_addlinkedserver**
Linked server security	**sp_addlinkedsrvlogin**
Pass-through queries	OPENQUERY
Ad hoc queries	OPENROWSET
Allowed and disallowed Transact-SQL statements and actions	"accessing external data using distributed queries"
Distributed query restrictions	"external data and Transact-SQL"

Lab A: Using Distributed Data

Objectives

After completing this lab, you will be able to:

- Set up a linked server and establish security.
- Query data on a linked server.
- Import data from a linked server.

Prerequisites

Before working on this lab, you must have:

- Script files for this lab, which are located in C:\Moc\2073A\Labfiles\L12.
- Answer files for this lab, which are located in
  C:\Moc\2073A\Labfiles\L12\Answers.

Lab Setup

To complete this lab, you must have either:

- Completed the prior lab, or
- Executed the C:\Moc\2073A\Batches\Restore12.cmd batch file.

  This command file restores the **ClassNorthwind** database to a state required
  for this lab.

For More Information

If you require help with executing files, search SQL Query Analyzer Help for
"Execute a query".

Other resources that you can use include:

- The **Northwind** database schema.

- Microsoft SQL Server Books Online.

Scenario

The organization of the classroom is meant to simulate that of a worldwide trading firm named Northwind Traders. Its fictitious domain name is nwtraders.msft. The primary DNS server for nwtraders.msft is the instructor computer, which has an Internet Protocol (IP) address of 192.168.*x*.200 (where *x* is the assigned classroom number). The name of the instructor computer is London.

The following table provides the user name, computer name, and IP address for each student computer in the fictitious **nwtraders.msft** domain. Find the user name for your computer, and make a note of it.

User name	Computer name	IP address
SQLAdmin1	Vancouver	192.168.*x*.1
SQLAdmin2	Denver	192.168.*x*.2
SQLAdmin3	Perth	192.168.*x*.3
SQLAdmin4	Brisbane	192.168.*x*.4
SQLAdmin5	Lisbon	192.168.*x*.5
SQLAdmin6	Bonn	192.168.*x*.6
SQLAdmin7	Lima	192.168.*x*.7
SQLAdmin8	Santiago	192.168.*x*.8
SQLAdmin9	Bangalore	192.168.*x*.9
SQLAdmin10	Singapore	192.168.*x*.10
SQLAdmin11	Casablanca	192.168.*x*.11
SQLAdmin12	Tunis	192.168.*x*.12
SQLAdmin13	Acapulco	192.168.*x*.13
SQLAdmin14	Miami	192.168.*x*.14
SQLAdmin15	Auckland	192.168.*x*.15
SQLAdmin16	Suva	192.168.*x*.16
SQLAdmin17	Stockholm	192.168.*x*.17
SQLAdmin18	Moscow	192.168.*x*.18
SQLAdmin19	Caracas	192.168.*x*.19
SQLAdmin20	Montevideo	192.168.*x*.20
SQLAdmin21	Manila	192.168.*x*.21
SQLAdmin22	Tokyo	192.168.*x*.22
SQLAdmin23	Khartoum	192.168.*x*.23
SQLAdmin24	Nairobi	192.168.*x*.24

Estimated time to complete this lab: 60 minutes

Exercise 1
Setting Up Linked Servers

In this exercise, you will work with a partner. You will set up your local SQL Server as a remote data source for your partner. You will also set up a link to your partner's SQL Server and manage security for remote data access.

▶ **To create and populate the ProductInfo table on your local server**

In this procedure, you will create a new table in the **ClassNorthwind** database. Your partner will use this table.

1. Log on to the **NWTraders** classroom domain by using the information in the following table.

Option	Value
User name	**SQLAdminx** (where x corresponds to your computer name as designated in the **nwtraders.msft** classroom domain)
Password	**password**

2. Open SQL Query Analyzer and, if requested, log in to the (local) server with Microsoft Windows® Authentication.

   You have permission to log in to and administer SQL Server because you are logged as **SQLAdminx**, which is a member of the Windows 2000 local group, Administrators. All members of this group are automatically mapped to the SQL Server **sysadmin** role.

   Leave this query window open for the remainder of the exercise.

3. Open, review, and execute the Labfiles\L12\RemoteTbl.sql script. This file creates the **ProductInfo** table in the local **ClassNorthwind** database.

▶ **To create login accounts for local and remote users**

In this procedure, you will create two new login accounts: one for your partner to use when your partner links to your SQL Server and one for you to use when you access linked servers.

1. Open SQL Server Enterprise Manager.

2. Open the SQL Server Books Online topics "How to add a SQL Server login (Enterprise Manager)" and "How to grant a SQL Server login access to a database (Enterprise Manager)."

3. Use the procedures in SQL Server Books Online and the information in the following table to create a new login account that remote servers that access information on the local computer will use.

Option	Value
Login name	**NWInfoRemote**
Authentication	SQL Server
Password	**nwpassrmt**
Default database	**ClassNorthwind**
Database access	**ClassNorthwind**
Permit in database role	**public**

4. Create another login account with the following characteristics. This local account will be mapped to the **NWInfoRemote** login account on your partner's SQL Server.

Option	Value
Login name	**NWInfoLocal**
Authentication	SQL Server
Password	**nwpasslocal**
Default database	**ClassNorthwind**
Database access	**ClassNorthwind**
Permit in database role	**public**

▶ **To grant SELECT and INSERT permissions on the ProductInfo table**

In this procedure, you will grant SELECT and INSERT permissions on the **ProductInfo** table on your local computer running SQL Server to the **NWInfoRemote** login account. This allows remote users to read and insert data into the **ProductInfo** table.

1. Open the SQL Server Books Online topic "How to grant permissions on multiple objects to a user, group, or role (Enterprise Manager)."

2. Use the procedure in SQL Server Books Online to grant SELECT and INSERT permissions on the **ClassNorthwind.dbo.ProductInfo** table to the **NWInfoRemote** login account.

▶ **To add the NWInfoLocal login account to the db_datareader role in ClassNorthwind**

In this procedure, you will add the **NWInfoLocal** login account to the **db_datareader** role for the **ClassNorthwind** database. The **db_datareader** role has SELECT permission on all user tables in the database. This role will be used to access the local copy of **ClassNorthwind**.

1. Open the SQL Server Books Online topic, "How to add a member to a SQL Server database role (Enterprise Manager)."

2. Use the procedure in SQL Server Books Online to add the **NWInfoLocal** login account to the **db_datareader** role in the **ClassNorthwind** database.

▶ **To set up a linked server**

In this procedure, you will register your partner's computer as a linked server on your local server.

1. Switch to SQL Query Analyzer.

2. Open the Labfiles\L12\MakeLink.sql script.

3. Modify the script, substituting the name of your partner's SQL Server for *servername*.

4. Execute the script.

▶ **To establish security between your local computer and the linked SQL Server**

In this procedure, you will map a login account on your local computer, running SQL Server, to a login account on your partner's computer running SQL Server.

1. Open the Labfiles\L12\MapToLnk.sql script by using SQL Query Analyzer.

2. Modify the script, substituting the name of your partner's SQL Server for *servername*.

3. Execute the script.

4. Close SQL Query Analyzer.

Exercise 2
Querying Remote Data

In this exercise, you will write and execute queries that access data on the linked server that you set up in the previous exercise. Both you and your partner must complete Exercise 1 before you start this exercise.

▶ **To access remote data on the linked server**

- In this procedure, you will log in to your local SQL Server with security credentials for a local application. You will then write a simple query that returns data from the **ProductInfo** table in the **ClassNorthwind** database on your partner's computer. \L12\Answers\LnkSelect.sql is a completed script for this procedure.

▶ **To access remote data by using a pass-through query**

Because each linked server is using SQL Server Authentication, each server needs to be configured to allow both SQL Server and Windows Authentication.

1. Using SQL Server Enterprise Manager, expand the server group.

2. Right-click your server, and then click **Properties**.

3. Click the **Security** tab.

4. Under **Authentication**, click **SQL Server** and **Windows**.

5. Stop and restart SQL Server.

▶ **To log on to your server by using SQL Server Authentication**

1. On the **Start** menu, point to **Programs**, point to **Microsoft SQL Server**, and then click **Query Analyzer**. Log in to the (local) server with SQL Server Authentication. Connect as **NWInfoLocal** with a password of **nwpasslocal**—you will use this connection for all procedures in this exercise.

2. Write and execute a Transact-SQL statement that returns all columns from the **Northwind.dbo.ProductInfo** table on the linked server (your partner's computer).

▶ **To access remote data by using a pass-through query**

In this procedure, you will write a query that uses the OPENQUERY function to return data from the **ProductInfo** table in the **ClassNorthwind** database on your partner's computer. The query will be processed remotely as a pass-through query. \L12\Answers\PassThru.sql is a completed script for this procedure.

- Write and execute a pass-through query that returns the **ProductID** and **Royalty** columns from the **Northwind.dbo.ProductInfo** table on the linked server (your partner's computer). Use the OPENQUERY function in the FROM clause of the SELECT statement.

▶ **To join local and remote tables**

In this procedure, you will write a query that joins the local copy of **ClassNorthwind.dbo.Products** to the **ClassNorthwind.dbo.ProductInfo** table on your partner's computer. \L12\Answers\LnkJoin.sql is a completed script for this procedure.

- Write and execute a Transact-SQL statement that joins the local copy of **ClassNorthwind.dbo.Products** to the **ClassNorthwind.dbo.ProductInfo** table on the linked server. Join the tables on the **ProductID** column. Include the **ProductName**, **ProductID**, and **ImportTax** columns, and then order the results by **ProductName**.

▶ **To add the NWInfoLocal login account to the database owner role**

In this procedure, you will add the **NWInfoLocal** login account to the **db_owner** role for the **ClassNorthwind** database. As a member of the **db_owner** role, the **NWInfoLocal** login account will have the ability to create new tables in the **ClassNorthwind** database.

1. Open the SQL Server Books Online topic, "How to add a member to a SQL Server database role (Enterprise Manager)."

2. Use the procedure in SQL Server Books Online to add the **NWInfoLocal** login account to the **db_owner** role for the **ClassNorthwind** database.

▶ **To import data from a linked server and create a new local table**

In this procedure, you will create a new table on your local server and populate it with the results of a query on your linked server. \L12\Answers\LnkImport.sql is a completed script for this procedure.

1. Switch to SQL Query Analyzer.

2. Write and execute a Transact-SQL statement that returns the **ProductID** and **Royalty** columns from the **ProductInfo** table on the linked server.

3. Modify the statement to create a new, local, and permanent table named **LocalProdInfo** that contains the results of the query.

4. Examine the contents of **LocalProdInfo**.

► **To execute a stored procedure on a linked server**

In this procedure, you will execute the **Sales by Year** stored procedure on the linked server. \L12\Answers \RmtProc.sql is a completed script for this procedure.

1. Write and execute a Transact-SQL statement that executes the **Sales by Year** stored procedure in the **ClassNorthwind** database on the linked server by using a fully qualified four-part name. Use the information in the following table to write this query.

Parameter	Value
Start_date	'1996'
End_date	'1997'

2. Close all open query windows, and then quit SQL Query Analyzer.

► **To access remote data with an ad hoc query**

In this procedure, you will write an ad hoc query that returns all columns from the **ClassNorthwind.dbo.ProductInfo** table on the remote server. Use the OPENROWSET function to connect to the remote data source. \L12\Answers\Adhoc.sql is a completed script for this procedure.

1. Open SQL Query Analyzer and, if prompted, log in to the (local) server with Windows Authentication.

    You have permission to log in to and administer SQL Server because you are logged as **SQLAdminx**, which is a member of the Windows 2000 local group, Administrators. All members of this group are automatically mapped to the SQL Server **sysadmin** role.

    Because you are not using the **NWInfoLocal** user account, your partner's server cannot be used as a linked server directly from this connection.

2. Write and execute a Transact-SQL statement that returns the **ProductID** and **Royalty** columns from the **ProductInfo** table on your partner's computer. Use the OPENROWSET function to provide connection information. Use the information in the following table to write this query.

Parameter	Value
provider_name	'SQLOLEDB'
data_source	\<Servername\> (your partner's computer name)
User_id	**'nwinforemote'**
Password	**'nwpassrmt'**

3. Close all connections to SQL Query Analyzer.

If Time Permits
Managing Distributed Transactions

In this exercise, you will create a stored procedure to use in distributed transactions. You will confirm that the MS DTC service has been started. You will write and execute Transact-SQL statements inside a distributed transaction to ensure tight data consistency between two SQL Servers.

▶ **To create a stored procedure to use in distributed transactions on your local computer**

In this procedure, you will log in to your local SQL Server as a member of the **sysadmin** role. You will review and execute a script that creates the **DeleteProductInfo** stored procedure and grants EXECUTE permission to the **NWInfoRemote** login account. Later, your partner will use this stored procedure to delete rows from the **ProductInfo** table on your local computer.

Important You and your partner must complete the preceding procedure before continuing with this exercise.

---

1. Open SQL Query Analyzer and, if requested, log in to the (local) server with Windows Authentication.

   You have permission to log in to and administer SQL Server because you are logged as **SQLAdmin*x***, which is a member of the Windows 2000 local group, Administrators. All members of this group are automatically mapped to the SQL Server **sysadmin** role.

2. Open, review, and execute the Labfiles\L12\RemoteSP.sql script. This file creates the **DeleteProductInfo** stored procedure in the local **ClassNorthwind** database and grants EXECUTE permission to the NWInfoRemote user account. Your partner will use this stored procedure to delete rows from the **ProductInfo** table on your local computer.

3. Close SQL Query Analyzer.

▶ **To start the MS DTC service**

In this procedure, you will start the MS DTC service.

1. Open the SQL Server Service Manager.

2. Start the MS DTC service on your local computer if it is not running.

▶ To perform a distributed transaction between the local computer and a linked server

Suppose that ClassNorthwind Traders has two copies of its database, one at each of its warehouses. Any changes to one copy should be made to the other copy.

In this procedure, you will insert data into your local **ProductInfo** table as well as the **ProductInfo** table on your partner's computer as a single transaction. \L12\Answers \DistIns.sql is a completed script for this procedure.

1. On the **Start** menu, point to **Programs**, point to **Microsoft SQL Server**, and then click **Query Analyzer**. Log in to the (local) server with SQL Server Authentication. Connect as **NWInfoLocal** with a password of **nwpasslocal**

2. Write a Transact-SQL statement that inserts a new row into the **ProductInfo** table on your local computer. Select one row in the following table. Your partner should select the remaining row.

Productid	Royalty	Import tax
55	3	.09
55	3	.09

3. Write a Transact-SQL statement that inserts the row that you selected into the **ClassNorthwind.dbo.ProductInfo** table on the linked server (your partner's computer). Use a fully qualified four-part name.

4. Enclose the two statements in a BEGIN DISTRIBUTED TRANSACTION and COMMIT TRANSACTION block and set the XACT_ABORT session option.

5. Execute the transaction.

6. Write and execute queries to confirm that the added row appears in both tables.

▶ **To manage distributed data by using a stored procedure**

In this procedure, you will examine and execute a script that deletes the rows previously added to the **ClassNorthwind.dbo.ProductInfo** tables on the local and linked servers.

1. Open and review the Labfiles\L12\DistDel.sql script by using SQL Query Analyzer. This script deletes the row that you added to the local **ProductInfo** table by using a Transact-SQL statement. A stored procedure deletes the row that you added to the **ProductInfo** table on the linked server. These actions are done as a transaction.

2. Modify the script so that your partner's computer serves as the linked server.

3. Modify the script to delete the **Product_id** that you added in the previous procedure.

4. Execute the modified Labfiles\L12\DistDel.sql script.

5. Examine the output to confirm that the rows were deleted.

Review

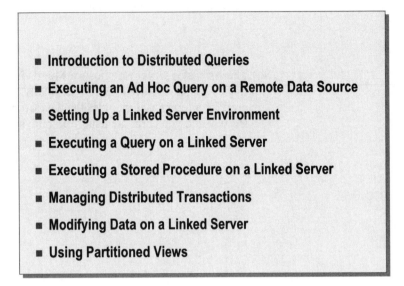

- ■ Introduction to Distributed Queries
- ■ Executing an Ad Hoc Query on a Remote Data Source
- ■ Setting Up a Linked Server Environment
- ■ Executing a Query on a Linked Server
- ■ Executing a Stored Procedure on a Linked Server
- ■ Managing Distributed Transactions
- ■ Modifying Data on a Linked Server
- ■ Using Partitioned Views

You own a mail order business with two warehouse locations, one in the United States and one in Asia. Each warehouse has a SQL Server that hosts a location-specific copy of the inventory database. The servers, named USsales and Asiasales, are connected by a WAN. Your business requires that these databases remain current and synchronized at all times.

1. What method of data distribution should you use to propagate changes from one server to the other?

2. Your office is based in the United States. Each morning, you generate a report that shows the number of units in stock for the ten most frequently sold items from each warehouse. How would you generate this report?

3. Because you often transfer inventory between warehouses, you must update the databases at both locations so that the number of stocked units is always current. How would you do this?

4. The Asiasales server also hosts a Microsoft Access database that contains sales summary information. Occasionally, you want to access this data to produce a report that includes the data from the USsales inventory database. How would you combine data from both sources in your report?

Microsoft®
Training &
Certification

Module 13: Optimizing Query Performance

Contents

Microsoft®

Project Lead: Rich Rose
Instructional Designers: Rich Rose, Cheryl Hoople, Marilyn McGill
Instructional Software Design Engineers: Karl Dehmer, Carl Raebler, Rick Byham
Technical Lead: Karl Dehmer
Subject Matter Experts: Karl Dehmer, Carl Raebler, Rick Byham
Graphic Artist: Kirsten Larson (Independent Contractor)
Editing Manager: Lynette Skinner
Editor: Wendy Cleary
Copy Editor: Edward McKillop (S&T Consulting)
Production Manager: Miracle Davis
Production Coordinator: Jenny Boe
Production Support: Lori Walker (S&T Consulting)
Test Manager: Sid Benavente
Courseware Testing: TestingTesting123
Classroom Automation: Lorrin Smith-Bates
Creative Director, Media/Sim Services: David Mahlmann
Web Development Lead: Lisa Pease
CD Build Specialist: Julie Challenger
Online Support: David Myka (S&T Consulting)
Localization Manager: Rick Terek
Operations Coordinator: John Williams
Manufacturing Support: Laura King; Kathy Hershey
Lead Product Manager, Release Management: Bo Galford
Lead Product Manager, Data Base: Margo Crandall
Group Manager, Courseware Infrastructure: David Bramble
Group Product Manager, Content Development: Dean Murray
General Manager: Robert Stewart

Overview

- **Introduction to the Query Optimizer**
- **Obtaining Execution Plan Information**
- **Using an Index to Cover a Query**
- **Indexing Strategies**
- **Overriding the Query Optimizer**

This module describes how the query optimizer uses indexes and other information to determine the most efficient method of accessing data.

After completing this module, you will be able to:

- Explain the role of the query optimizer and how it works to ensure that queries are optimized.

- Use various methods for obtaining execution plan information so that you can determine how the query optimizer processed a query and validate the most efficient execution plan was generated.

- Create indexes that cover queries.

- Identify indexing strategies that reduce page reads.

- Evaluate when to override the query optimizer.

◆ Introduction to the Query Optimizer

- **Function of the Query Optimizer**
- **How the Query Optimizer Uses Cost-Based Optimization**
- **How the Query Optimizer Works**
- **Query Optimization Phases**
- **Caching the Execution Plan**
- **Setting a Cost Limit**

Knowledge of the role of the query optimizer in optimizing queries prepares you for creating useful indexes, writing efficient queries, and tuning poorly performing queries.

Function of the Query Optimizer

■ **Determines the Most Efficient Execution Plan**

    ● Determining whether indexes exist and evaluating their usefulness

    ● Determining which indexes or columns can be used

    ● Determining how to process joins

    ● Using cost-based evaluation of alternatives

    ● Creating column statistics

■ **Uses Additional Information**

■ **Produces an Execution Plan**

The query optimizer is the component responsible for generating the optimum execution plan for a query.

Determines the Most Efficient Execution Plan

The query optimizer evaluates each Transact-SQL statement and determines the most efficient execution plan.

The query optimizer estimates the input/output (I/O) required to process a query by:

■ Determining whether indexes exist and evaluating their usefulness for a query.

■ Determining which indexes or columns can be used to reduce the number of rows examined by the query. By reducing the number of rows examined, the amount of I/O is reduced, which is the goal of query performance.

■ Determining the most effective strategy for processing join operations, such as in which order to join tables and which join strategy to use.

■ Using cost-based evaluation of alternatives to select the most efficient plan for a given query.

■ Creating column statistics to improve the performance of the query.

Uses Additional Information

The query optimizer uses additional information about the underlying data and storage structures, file size, and file structure types. The query optimizer also uses an assortment from its own internal operations, such as creating temporary indexes or tables in memory, to improve the performance of queries.

Produces an Execution Plan

The query optimizer produces an execution plan that outlines the sequence of steps required to perform a query. The query optimizer optimizes the process of finding, joining, grouping, and ordering rows.

How the Query Optimizer Uses Cost-Based Optimization

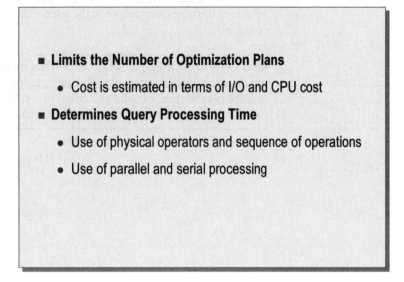

- **Limits the Number of Optimization Plans**
  - Cost is estimated in terms of I/O and CPU cost
- **Determines Query Processing Time**
  - Use of physical operators and sequence of operations
  - Use of parallel and serial processing

The query optimizer is a cost-based optimizer, which means that it evaluates each execution plan by estimating its execution cost.

Note The cost estimates can be only as accurate as the available statistical data about the columns, indexes, and tables.

Limits the Number of Optimization Plans

To execute in a reasonable amount of time, the query optimizer limits the number of optimization plans that it considers. By evaluating sequences of the relational operations required to produce the result set, the query optimizer arrives at an execution plan that has the lowest estimated cost in terms of I/O and CPU resource loss.

Determines Query Processing Time

Query performance is determined by which physical operators the query optimizer uses and the sequence in which the operations are processed. The goal is to reduce:

- The number of rows returned.

- The number of pages read.

- The overall processing time by minimizing I/O and CPU resources used for an execution plan.

When the query optimizer optimizes queries, it does not initiate the execution plan with the lowest resource loss; it chooses the execution plan that returns results in the quickest manner to the user, with a reasonable reduction of resources.

Note   If Microsoft® SQL Server™ 2000 has more than one processor available, the query optimizer may divide the query among them. Long-running queries usually benefit from parallel execution plans, but a parallel query can use more resources overall than processing a query serially.

How the Query Optimizer Works

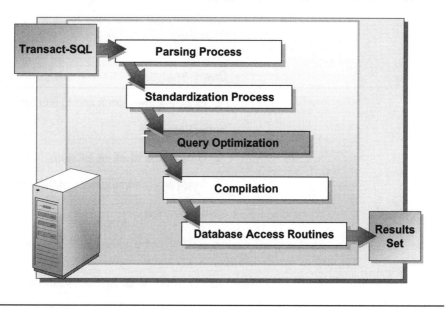

After a query is submitted, several steps occur that transform the original query into a format that the query optimizer can interpret.

Parsing Process

The parsing process checks the incoming query for correct syntax and breaks down the syntax into component parts that the relational database engine can respond to. The output of this step is a parsed query tree.

Standardization Process

The standardization process transforms a query into a useful format for optimization. Any redundant syntax clauses that are detected are removed. Subqueries are standardized if possible. The output of this step is a standardized query tree.

Query Optimization

The process of selecting one execution plan from several possible plans is called *optimization*. Numerous steps are involved in this phase. However, the following steps have the most significant effect on the cost of the execution plan: query analysis, index selection, and join selection.

Compilation

The query is compiled into executable code.

Database Access Routines

The query optimizer determines the best method to access data, by performing a table scan, or by using an available index. The better method is then applied.

Query Optimization Phases

- **Query Analysis**
  - Identifies the search and join criteria of the query
- **Index Selection**
  - Determines whether an index or indexes exist
  - Assesses the usefulness of the index or indexes
- **Join Selection**
  - Evaluates which join strategy to use

The query optimization process consists of three phases. These phases are not discrete processing steps and are only used to conceptually represent the internal activity of the query optimizer.

Query Analysis

The first phase of query optimization is called *query analysis*. In this phase, the query optimizer identifies the search and join criteria of the query. By limiting the search, the query optimizer minimizes the number of rows that are processed. Reducing the number of rows processed reduces the number of index and data pages read.

Index Selection

Index selection is the second phase of query optimization. During this phase, the query optimizer detects whether an index exists for the identified clauses. Then, there is an assessment of the usefulness of the index or indexes. Usefulness of an index is determined by how many rows will be returned. This information is gathered from the index statistics or column statistics. An estimate of the cost of various access methods occurs by means of estimating the logical and physical page reads required to find the qualifying rows.

Join Selection

Join selection is the third phase of query optimization. If there is a multiple-table query or self-join, there is an evaluation of which join strategy to use. The determination of which join strategy to use consists of a consideration of a number of factors: selectivity, density, and memory required to process the query.

Caching the Execution Plan

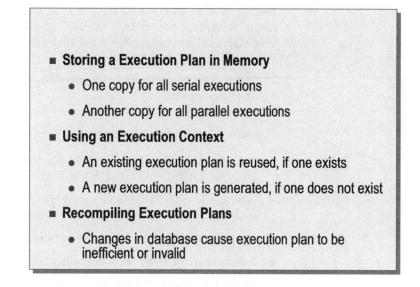

- ■ **Storing a Execution Plan in Memory**
  - One copy for all serial executions
  - Another copy for all parallel executions
- ■ **Using an Execution Context**
  - An existing execution plan is reused, if one exists
  - A new execution plan is generated, if one does not exist
- ■ **Recompiling Execution Plans**
  - Changes in database cause execution plan to be inefficient or invalid

SQL Server has a pool of memory that is used to store execution plans and data buffers. The percentage of the pool allocated to either execution plans or data buffers fluctuates dynamically, depending on the state of the system. The part of the memory pool used to store execution plans is called the *procedure cache*.

Storing a Execution Plan in Memory

The bulk of the execution plan is a reusable, read-only data structure that can be used by any number of users. No user context is stored in the execution plan. There are never more than two copies of the execution plan in memory:

- ■ One copy for all serial executions.
- ■ Another copy for all parallel executions.

  The parallel copy covers all parallel executions, regardless of their degree of parallelism.

Using an Execution Context

Each user executing a query has a data structure that holds the data specific to an execution, such as parameter values. This data structure is called the *execution context*. When a Transact-SQL statement is executed, SQL Server scans the procedure cache for determination of whether an execution plan exists for the same Transact-SQL statement.

- ■ If any existing execution plan exists, SQL Server reuses the execution plan.

  This saves the overhead of recompiling the Transact-SQL statement.

- ■ If no execution plan exists, SQL Server generates a new execution plan for the query.

Recompiling Execution Plans

Certain changes in a database can cause an execution plan to be either inefficient or no longer accurate. When SQL Server detects changes that invalidate an execution plan, it marks the execution plan as invalid. A new execution plan is compiled for the next connection that executes the query.

Important   Performance can be improved by reducing the number of times that a plan is recompiled.

Conditions that invalidate an execution plan include:

- Any structural changes made to a table or view referenced by the query (ALTER TABLE and ALTER VIEW statements).

- New distribution statistics being generated either explicitly from a statement such as UPDATE STATISTICS, or automatically.

- Dropping an index used by the execution plan.

- An explicit call to the **sp_recompile** system stored procedure.

- Large numbers of changes to keys, or INSERT or DELETE statements for a table referenced by the query.

- For tables with triggers, if the number of rows in the inserted or deleted tables grows significantly.

Note   SQL Server uses an aging algorithm to efficiently manage execution plans in cache. It evaluates cost and use of the execution plan.

Setting a Cost Limit

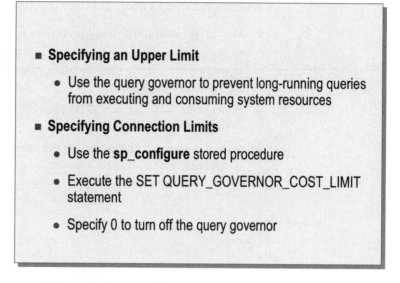

- **Specifying an Upper Limit**
  - Use the query governor to prevent long-running queries from executing and consuming system resources
- **Specifying Connection Limits**
  - Use the **sp_configure** stored procedure
  - Execute the SET QUERY_GOVERNOR_COST_LIMIT statement
  - Specify 0 to turn off the query governor

You may want to control the cost of executing a query by setting a cost limit. The term *query cost* refers to the estimated elapsed time, in seconds, required to execute a query on a specific hardware configuration.

Specifying an Upper Limit

You can use the **query governor cost limit** option to prevent long-running queries from executing and consuming system resources. By default, queries are allowed to execute, no matter how long they take. The query governor uses an estimated cost to prevent queries with a high cost from executing at all.

Although the configuration value is specified in seconds, it does not truly correlate to time, but to the actual estimated cost of the query. You can specify an upper limit of the cost of the query to be executed.

Because the query governor is based on estimated query cost, rather than actual elapsed time, it does not have any run-time overhead. If the estimated cost of a query is greater than the specified cost limit, the query governor statement prevents the query from executing. This is more efficient than letting a query run until some predefined limit is reached, and then stopping the query.

Specifying Connection Limits

You can specify limits for all connections or just the queries for a specific connection. To apply query governor cost limits, you can:

- Use the **sp_configure** stored procedure to apply limits for all connections.

  You can change the query governor cost limit only when **show advanced options** is set to 1. The setting takes effect immediately. You do not have to stop and restart the server.

- Execute the SET QUERY_GOVERNOR_COST_LIMIT statement to apply limits for a specific connection.

- Specify 0 (the default) to turn off the query governor. In this case, all queries are executed with no limits.

◆ Obtaining Execution Plan Information

- ■ **Viewing STATISTICS Statements Output**

- ■ **Viewing SHOWPLAN_ALL and SHOWPLAN_TEXT Output**

- ■ **Graphically Viewing the Execution Plan**

The query optimizer responds to the information that it has available during the determination of the best execution plan. You can obtain information about the execution plan by querying the **sysindexes** table. You can also obtain information by using the STATISTICS statements, the SHOWPLAN statements, and graphically viewing the execution plan.

Viewing STATISTICS Statements Output

Statement	Output Sample
STATISTICS TIME	SQL Server Execution Times: CPU time = 0 ms, elapsed time = 2 ms.

STATISTICS PROFILE	Rows Executes StmtText StmtId...
	--- 	
	47 1 SELECT * FROM [charge] 16
	                 WHERE (([charge_amt]>=@1)
	                          .
	                          .
	                          .

STATISTICS IO	Table 'member'. Scan count 1, logical reads 23, physical reads 0, read-ahead reads 0.

You can use the STATISTICS IO, STATISTICS TIME, and STATISTICS PROFILE statements to get information that can help you diagnose long-running queries. The output from STATISTICS statements provides information about the actual execution plan.

STATISTICS TIME obtains information about the number of milliseconds required to parse, compile, and execute each statement.

STATISTICS PROFILE displays the profile information for a statement. When you execute a query, the output from the SHOWPLAN_ALL statement and two additional columns are included in the result set. The following table shows the additional columns.

Column	Description
Rows	Actual number of rows produced by each operator
Reuse	Actual number of times this operator was told to reuse its data

STATISTICS IO obtains information about the amount of page reads generated by queries. The output from STATISTICS IO includes the values in the following table.

Value	Description	Additional information
Logical reads	Number of pages read from data cache	All pages are accessed in the data cache. If a page is not available in cache, it must be physically read from disk.
Physical reads	Number of pages read from disk	This value is always less than or equal to the value of logical reads. The following is the method for calculating the value of the Cache Hit Ratio: $$Cache\ hit\ ratio = \frac{Logical\ reads\ -\ Physical\ reads}{Logical\ reads}$$
Read-ahead reads	Number of pages placed into cache	A high number for this value means that the value for physical reads is lower, and the cache hit ratio is higher than if read-ahead was not enabled.
Scan count	Number of times the table was accessed	The outer tables of a left join should always have a scan count of 1. For inner tables, the number of logical reads is determined by the scan count multiplied by the number of pages accessed on each scan.

Note The SET statements stay in effect for the session until you specify the OFF option, or until you end the session.

Viewing SHOWPLAN_ALL and SHOWPLAN_TEXT Output

- **Structure of the SHOWPLAN Statement Output**
    - Returns information as a set of rows
    - Forms a hierarchical tree
    - Represents steps taken by the query optimizer
    - Shows estimated values of how a query was optimized, not the actual execution plan
- **Details of the Execution Steps**
- **Difference Between SHOWPLAN_TEXT and SHOWPLAN_ALL Output**

You can use the SET SHOWPLAN_TEXT and SET SHOWPLAN_ALL statements to obtain detailed information about how queries are executed and how many resources are required to process the query.

Structure of the SHOWPLAN Statement Output

The SHOWPLAN statement output:

- Returns information as a set of rows.
- Forms a hierarchical tree.
- Represents steps taken by the query optimizer to execute each statement.
- Shows estimated values of how a query was optimized, not the actual execution plan. The estimated values are based on existing statistics.

Details of the Execution Steps

Each statement reflected in the output contains a single row with the text of the statement, followed by several rows with the details of the execution steps. Details of the execution steps include:

- Which indexes are used with which tables.
- The join order of the tables.
- The chosen update mode.
- Worktables and other strategies.

Difference Between SHOWPLAN_TEXT and SHOWPLAN_ALL Output

The difference between SHOWPLAN_TEXT and SHOWPLAN_ALL output is that the SHOWPLAN_ALL output returns additional information, such as the estimated rows, I/O, CPU, and average row size of the query.

Note   The SET statements stay in effect for the session until you specify the OFF option, or until you end the session.

◆ Graphically Viewing the Execution Plan

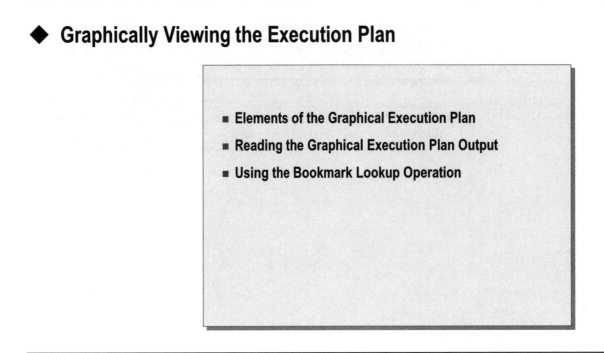

- **Elements of the Graphical Execution Plan**
- **Reading the Graphical Execution Plan Output**
- **Using the Bookmark Lookup Operation**

You can use SQL Query Analyzer to graphically view a color-coded execution plan.

Elements of the Graphical Execution Plan

- Steps Are Units of Work to Process a Query

- Sequence of Steps Is the Order in Which the Steps Are Processed

- Logical Operators Describe Relational Algebraic Operation Used to Process a Statement

- Physical Operators Describe Physical Implementation Algorithm Used to Process a Statement

---

The graphical execution plan, which contains the following elements, uses icons to represent the execution of specific parts of statements and queries:

Steps are units of work used to process a query.

Sequence of steps is the order in which the steps are processed.

Logical operators describe the relational algebraic operation used to process a statement; for example, performing an aggregation. The logical operator typically matches the physical operator. Not all steps used to process a query or update operations involve logical operations.

Physical operators describe the physical implementation algorithm used to process a statement; for example, scanning a clustered index. Each step in the execution of a query or update operation involves a physical operator.

The following table is a partial list of physical operators used to represent the algorithms that the query optimizer uses.

Icon	Physical operator	Operator description
	Bookmark Lookup	Uses a bookmark (row ID or clustering key) to look up the corresponding row in the table or clustered index
	Filter	Scans the input, returning only those rows that satisfy the filter expression that appears in the **argument** column
	Hash Match	Builds a hash table by computing a hash value for each row from its build input
	Index Scan	Retrieves all rows from the nonclustered index specified in the **argument** column
	Index Seek	Uses the seeking ability of indexes to retrieve rows from a nonclustered index
	Merge Join	Performs all types of joins (except self-join and cross join), including UNION operations
	Nested Loops	Searches the inner table for each row of the outer table, typically by using an index
	Sort	Sorts all incoming rows
	Table Scan	Retrieves all rows from the table specified in the **argument** column

Note For the complete listing of icons and more information, search on "graphically displaying the execution plan using SQL Query Analyzer" in SQL Server Books Online.

Reading Graphical Execution Plan Output

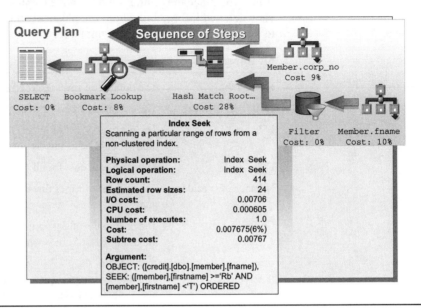

The graphical execution plan output is read from right to left and from top to bottom. Each query in the batch that is analyzed is displayed, including the cost of each query as a percentage of the total cost of the batch.

Each step can have one or many nodes to process. The term *node* refers to an operation that the query optimizer uses, which is represented by an icon.

The execution plan may have multiple nodes for a particular step.

- Each node is related to a parent node.
- All nodes with the same parent are drawn in the same column.
- Arrowheads connect each node to its parent.
- Recursive operations are shown with an iteration symbol.
- Operators are shown as symbols related to a specific parent.
- When the batch contains multiple statements, multiple execution plans are drawn.

Viewing Additional Information

When you place the pointer on each node (represented by an icon), you can view detailed information about the physical and logical operators, in addition to the information in the following table.

Measures	Description
Row count	The number of rows returned by the operator.
Estimated row size	The estimated size of the row returned by the operator.
I/O cost	The estimated cost of all I/O activity for the operation. This value should be as low as possible.
CPU cost	The estimated cost for all CPU activity for the operation.
Number of executes	The number of times that the operation was executed during the query.
Cost	The cost to the query optimizer when executing the operation, including cost of this operation as a percentage of the total cost of the query.
Subtree cost	The total cost to the query optimizer when executing this operation and all operations preceding it in the same subtree.
Argument	The predicates and parameters used by the query.

Using the Bookmark Lookup Operation

- **Analyzing the Query Plan**
  - Typically used after all steps have been processed
- **Retrieving Rows**
  - Row identifiers
  - Clustering Keys
- **Observing the Details**
  - A bookmark label used to find the row
- **Determining When the Bookmark Lookup Operator is Used**
  - Queries containing the IN clause or the OR operator

Bookmark Lookup is an internal operator frequently used by the query optimizer. When the query optimizer identifies records that are possible candidates for the intended result set, it notes the information identifying the row locations (a bookmark) and continues operations that refine the search.

If a row is included in the search, SQL Server uses the row location from the bookmark to find the row by analyzing the query plan, retrieving rows, observing the details, and determining when the Bookmark Lookup operator is used.

Analyzing the Query Plan

In the query plan, the query optimizer typically uses the Bookmark Lookup operator after all other steps have been processed.

Retrieving Rows

The Bookmark Lookup operator retrieves all the qualifying rows by using:

- A row identifier (RID) to find the corresponding row in a heap.
- The clustering key to find the corresponding row in a clustered index.

Observing the Details

In the query plan, details of the Bookmark Lookup operator contain:

- A bookmark label used to find the row in the table or clustered index.
- The table name or clustered index name from which the row is found.
- The WITH PREFETCH clause, if the query optimizer determines that read-ahead is the best way to find bookmarks in the table or clustered index.

Determining When the Bookmark Lookup Operator Is Used

The query optimizer typically uses the Bookmark Lookup operator to process queries containing the IN clause and OR operators in the WHERE clause.

Example

In this example, the **member** table has a nonclustered index on the **member_no** column. The query optimizer uses a Bookmark Lookup operator to retrieve the qualifying rows.

```
USE credit
SELECT *
FROM member
WHERE member_no
IN (4567,8765,4321)
```

◆ Using an Index to Cover a Query

- Introduction to Indexes That Cover a Query

- Locating Data by Using Indexes That Cover a Query

- Identifying Whether an Index Can Be Used to Cover a Query

- Determining Whether an Index Is Used to Cover a Query

- Guidelines for Creating Indexes That Cover a Query

You can create indexes that resolve the query without having to access the data pages. This is a strategy that can improve query performance.

Introduction to Indexes That Cover a Query

- **Only Nonclustered Indexes Cover Queries**
- **Indexes Must Contain All Columns Referenced in the Query**
- **No Data Page Access Is Required**
- **Indexed Views Can Pre-Aggregate Data**
- **Indexes That Cover Queries Retrieve Data Quickly**

When creating indexes, you may want to create an index that covers the most common queries in order to reduce the amount of I/O.

Only Nonclustered Indexes Cover Queries

Indexes that cover queries contain all of the required data of a query in the leaf level of a nonclustered index.

Indexes Must Contain All Columns Referenced in the Query

An index that covers a query must contain all columns that are referenced in the SELECT statement. If a clustered index exists, the fields in the clustering key are in the leaf level of the nonclustered index and contribute to covering the query.

No Data Page Access Is Required

When a query is covered by an index, the query optimizer does not access the data pages, because all of the required data is contained in the index. The amount of I/O is significantly reduced.

Indexed Views Can Pre-Aggregate Data

If an indexed view sums, counts, or averages columns, then the query optimizer can use this view to provide stored values when resolving a query. Indexed views that pre-aggregate data can increase performance dramatically.

Indexes That Cover Queries Retrieve Data Quickly

Creating indexes that cover queries is one of the fastest ways to access to data, especially for a low-selectivity query. When you compare the leaf levels of the clustered and nonclustered indexes, the advantage of having indexes that cover queries are evident.

Index type	Contents of leaf level
Clustered	Entire row (actual data pages)
Nonclustered	Key value

Because key values are typically smaller in size than the actual rows, an index page can store more key values than complete rows. Storing key values requires fewer pages, which reduces the amount of I/O.

◆ Locating Data by Using Indexes That Cover a Query

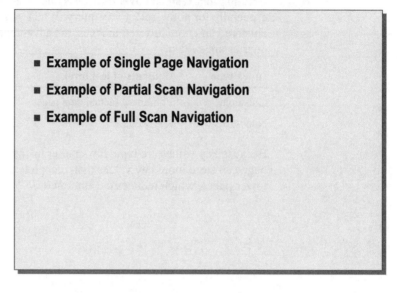

- **Example of Single Page Navigation**
- **Example of Partial Scan Navigation**
- **Example of Full Scan Navigation**

The query optimizer navigates the leaf level in different ways when an index can be used to cover a query. Covering a query can consist of reading a single page, a range of pages, or all of the pages of the leaf level. The data pages are never accessed.

Example of Single Page Navigation

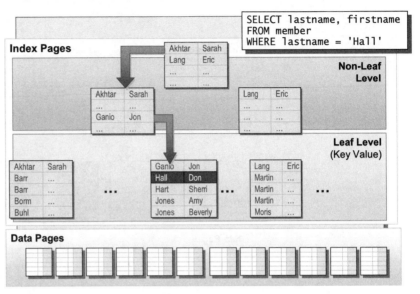

Single page navigation occurs when only one page of the leaf-level pages is read from the non-leaf-level. Reading one page is similar a point query, where the information—a single row or multiple rows—is found on a single page.

Note Single page navigation does not mean that the query can return only one row. A point query can return one row or all of the rows on one page. Either way, all of the data is found on one page.

Example

In this example, a composite, nonclustered index on the **lastname, firstname** columns covers the query.

```
SELECT lastname, firstname
FROM member
WHERE lastname = 'Hall'
```

SQL Server goes through the following steps to retrieve the information:

1. Traverses the index tree comparing the last name Hall to the key values.

2. Continues to traverse the index until it reaches the first page of the leaf level containing the key value Hall.

3. Returns the qualifying rows without accessing the data pages, because the **lastname** and **firstname** key values are contained in the leaf level.

Example of Partial Scan Navigation

A partial scan occurs when a range of pages is read from the leaf level.

Example

In this example, a composite, nonclustered index on the **lastname, firstname** columns covers the query by doing a partial scan of the leaf-level pages.

```
USE credit
SELECT lastname, firstname
FROM member
WHERE lastname BETWEEN 'Funk' AND 'Lang'
```

SQL Server goes through the following steps to retrieve the information:

1. Traverses the index tree.

2. Starts reading leaf-level pages at the page that contains the first occurrence of the last name Funk.

   Data in the leaf level is sorted in ascending order.

3. Reads the range of leaf-level pages through to the last name of Lang.

   At this time, the partial scan is completed.

4. Returns the qualifying rows without accessing the data pages, because the leaf level is scanned for last names between Funk and Lang.

Example of Full Scan Navigation

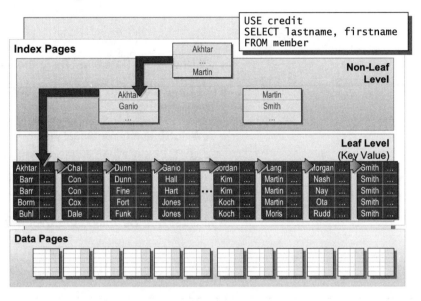

A full scan occurs when all of the pages of the leaf level are read. Similar to a table scan, a full scan occurs when a query does not include a WHERE clause, or when the WHERE clause is not selective.

Example

In this example, a composite, nonclustered index on the **lastname, firstname** columns covers the query by doing a full scan of the leaf-level pages.

```
USE credit
SELECT lastname, firstname
FROM member
```

To retrieve the information, SQL Server:

1. Traverses the index tree.

2. Reads the leaf-level pages, starting with the first page, and scans through all of the leaf-level pages until it reaches the last page in the leaf-level.

3. Returns the qualifying rows without accessing the data pages because the leaf-level is scanned.

Note Scanning the leaf level of an index also is a parallel data scan.
SQL Server uses read-ahead processing to further improve the performance of the query.

Identifying Whether an Index Can Be Used to Cover a Query

- **All Necessary Data Must Be in the Index**

- **A Composite Index Is Useful Even if the First Column Is Not Referenced**

- **A WHERE Is Not Necessary**

- **A Nonclustered Index Can Be Used if It Requires Less I/O Than a Clustered Index Containing a Column Referenced in the WHERE Clause**

- **Indexes Can Be Joined to Cover a Query**

These factors affect the ability of an index to cover a query:

- All necessary data must be in the index. This data includes all referenced columns, whether they are returned in the result set, used for sorting or aggregation, or supplied in the WHERE clause.

- A column in an index can contribute to covering a query even when it is not the first column referenced in a composite index.

   For example, a composite index on **SalesRep**, **Region**, **Amount** (in that order) could cover a query that referenced only **Region** and **SUM(Amount)**.

- A WHERE clause is not necessary. The query optimizer scans the entire leaf level.

- A nonclustered index can be used to cover a query if it requires less I/O than a clustered index containing a column referenced in the WHERE clause.

- Indexes can be joined to cover a query. If some or all tables referenced in a join operation have an index that covers a query, the results are joined together by a special join operation, and the rows are then returned.

Determining Whether an Index Is Used to Cover a Query

- **Observing the Execution Plan Output**
  - Displays the phrase "Scanning a non-clustered index entirely or only a range"
- **Comparing I/O**
  - Nonclustered index
    Total number of levels in the non–leaf level
    Total number of pages that make up the leaf level
    Total number of rows per leaf-level page
    Total number of rows per data page
  - Total number of pages that make up the table

Queries that are covered by an index are not explicitly apparent to users. You can observe the graphical execution plan or compare I/O to determine whether the query optimizer used an index to cover a query.

Observing the Execution Plan Output

You can view the execution plan graphically. If an execution plan output displays the phrase "Scanning a non-clustered index entirely or only a range," the query optimizer was able to cover the query by using an index.

Comparing I/O

You can also view the STATISTICS IO output. When evaluating the cost of an index that covers a query, remember that the query optimizer always attempts to cover the query when evaluating an execution plan.

To help you determine whether the query is covered, you should know the following information about the nonclustered index and table:

- Nonclustered index
  - Total number of levels in the non-leaf level
  - Total number of pages that make up the leaf level
  - Total number of rows per leaf-level page
  - Total number of rows per data page
- Total number of pages that make up the table

Note If you prefer, you can also calculate the size of the leaf level of a nonclustered index rather than using the STATISTICS IO statement. Alternately, you can query **sysindexes** and review the **dpages** column, which will display the size of the leaf level.

Guidelines for Creating Indexes That Cover a Query

- **Add Columns to Indexes**
- **Minimize Index Key Size**
- **Maintain Row-to-Key Size Ratio**

When creating indexes that cover a query, consider the following guidelines:

- Add columns to indexes. You may want to add columns to some indexes that:

  - Cover more than one query.

  - Contribute toward covering some of your more common queries.

  - Are referenced frequently.

  - Do not significantly add to the key size.

- Minimize index key size. When defining the index key (key values), avoid specifying key values that are too wide. Wide rows increase row size, the number of index levels, and the total number of pages. Any performance benefits gained from creating an index that covers queries would be reduced.

- Maintain row-to-key size ratio. If the size of the index key increases relative to the row size, query performance may be affected. An extreme example is if you created a nonclustered index on all of the columns in a table. By doing this, a virtual copy of the table is produced and stored in the leaf level of the nonclustered index in sorted order.

◆ Indexing Strategies

- ■ Evaluating I/O for Queries That Access a Range of Data
- ■ Indexing for Multiple Queries
- ■ Guidelines for Creating Indexes

You can implement indexing strategies to improve query performance.

Evaluating I/O for Queries That Access a Range of Data

```
SELECT charge_no
FROM charge
WHERE charge_amt BETWEEN 20 AND 30
```

Access method	Page I/O
Table scan	10,417
Clustered index on the charge_amt column	1042
Nonclustered index on the charge_amt column	100,273
Composite index on charge_amt, charge_no columns	273

The query optimizer automatically considers multiple execution plans and estimates the needed I/O for each execution plan. It then initiates an execution plan with the least amount of I/O in addition to other considerations. Compare the page I/O among the different access methods that the query optimizer can use.

For example, consider the following query that retrieves a range of data, and then compare the I/O of this query against different methods of accessing data.

```
SELECT charge_no
FROM charge
WHERE charge_amt BETWEEN 20 AND 30
```

Assume the following when comparing the different methods:

- There are 1 million rows, and 96 rows per page.
- The total number of pages is 10,147.
- There is no clustered index.
- 100,000 rows fall within the $20.00 to $30.00 range.
- 367 index rows fit on a nonclustered index leaf page.

Table Scan

Performing a table scan is advantageous for queries where the result set includes a high percentage of a table (low selectivity). Table scans are appropriate when the total page I/O of a query would exceed the number of pages in the table.

When you execute the query that does a table scan, the page I/O is 10,417. Compare the page I/O on a table scan to a nonclustered index on the **charge_amt** column. Performing a table scan is more efficient.

Clustered Index on the charge_amt Column

SQL Server performs the following steps to retrieve the information:

1. Searches clustered index for the minimum value, in this case $20.00.

2. Reads rows starting at $20.00 and stops the search at $30.00.

Because the **charge_amt** column is clustered, the physical order of the data is arranged according to charge amount. All of the data that falls within that range is in sequential order on subsequent pages, making it easy to retrieve data. The page I/O is 1,042 (100,000/96 rows per page).

Nonclustered Index on the charge_amt Column

SQL Server goes through the following steps to retrieve the information:

1. Searches for the range of values in the leaf level of the nonclustered index and retrieves the RID for each row. In this case, 273 leaf-level pages are accessed (100,000/367).

2. Data is retrieved from each page by using the Bookmark Lookup for each qualifying row.

The page I/O is approximately 100,273. To retrieve data by using a nonclustered index on the **charge_amt** column is the least effective method, because SQL Server must read one page for every row—*plus* the leaf level of the index is read to retrieve the RID values. Each data page is read multiple times in cache.

Composite Index on the charge_amt, charge_no Columns

The page I/O is 273 (100,000/367 rows per page). The number of index rows per leaf level averages 367. Because the **charge_amt** and **charge_no** columns are in the index, SQL Server does not search the data pages, which reduces the amount of I/O.

Indexing for Multiple Queries

Example 1

```
USE credit
SELECT charge_no, charge_dt, charge_amt
FROM charge
WHERE statement_no = 19000 AND member_no = 3852
```

Example 2

```
USE credit
SELECT member_no, charge_no, charge_amt
FROM charge
WHERE charge_dt between '07/30/1999'
AND '07/31/1999' AND member_no = 9331
```

To choose the most appropriate index to create, based on an individual query is easier than creating an index for multiple-priority queries. To create indexes to support multiple-priority queries is more complex because the best index for one query may not be the best index for another. The goal is to attain acceptable performance for all of the highest-priority queries by evaluating I/O.

Example Business Scenario

For the following examples, assume that the most common queries requested by users are finding customer charges for a specific statement (Example 1) and finding customer charges for a specific day (Example 2). The first example query is 15 percent of the table. The other query is highly selective, accessing only a few rows.

Example 1

```
USE credit
SELECT charge_no, charge_dt, charge_amt
FROM charge
WHERE statement_no = 19000 AND member_no = 3852
```

Example 2

```
USE credit
SELECT member_no, charge_no, charge_amt
FROM charge
WHERE charge_dt between '07/30/1999' AND '07/31/1999'
 AND member_no = 9331
```

The following table compares the query performance of Examples 1 and 2, based on the possible indexing strategy that you may implement. A clustered index on the **member_no** column is the best strategy.

Type of index	Column	Example 1 query	Example 2 query
Clustered Nonclustered	**member_no** **charge_no**	Very fast. Uses the clustered index.	Very fast. Uses the clustered index.
Clustered Nonclustered	**charge_no** **member_no**	Slower than if a clustered index were created on the **member_no** column.	Slow. The nonclustered index on **member_no** is not efficient with ranges of data.
Clustered Nonclustered, composite	**member_no** **statement_no, member_no**	Very fast. Uses the clustered index.	Very fast. Uses the clustered index.
Clustered Nonclustered, composite	**charge_no** **member_no, charge_dt**	Slower than if a clustered index were created on the **member_no** column.	Fast. A composite index significantly increases performance of the nonclustered index.

Guidelines for Creating Indexes

- ■ **Determine the Priorities of All of the Queries**

- ■ **Determine the Selectivity for Each Portion of the WHERE Clause of Each Query**

- ■ **Determine Whether to Create an Index**

- ■ **Identify the Columns That Should Be Indexed**

- ■ **Determine the Best Column Order of Composite Indexes**

- ■ **Determine What Other Indexes Are Necessary**

- ■ **Test the Performance of the Queries**

Your decision on how many indexes, the type of indexes, and the columns on which to create indexes should be based on a thorough understanding of the data and the needs of users.

To ensure that the indexes that you create are useful to the query optimizer, consider the following guidelines:

- ■ Determine the priorities of all of the queries.

  - • Gain a thorough understanding of the data and how it will be used.

  - • Determine the priority transactions for the database.

- ■ Determine the selectivity for each portion of the WHERE clause of each query.

- ■ Determine whether to create an index.

  There are situations when you will not want to create an index. These include:

  - • If the index is never used by the query optimizer.

  - • If the column values are low in selectivity.

  - • If the column to be indexed is too wide.

- ■ Identify the columns that should be indexed.

  - • Create an index on a column that is used as a join key to improve the performance of the join. This allows the query optimizer the option to use an index rather than perform a table scan.

  - • Evaluate whether the column is searched frequently.

  - • Ensure that the columns referenced in the WHERE clauses of the highest-priority queries are indexed.

- ■ Determine the best column order of composite indexes.

- Determine what other indexes are necessary.

  - Determine the minimum number of indexes that can be created for each table.

  - Balance the performance gain of the index versus the update maintenance.

  - If a query is executed infrequently, you may want to consider creating an index for the duration of a specific activity (when it can provide a significant performance gain) and then dropping it.

- Test the performance of the queries.

  After the indexes are created, test the performance of the highest-priority queries by executing the following statements for each query:

  - SET SHOWPLAN ON

  - SET STATISTICS IO ON

  - SET STATISTICS TIME ON

◆ Overriding the Query Optimizer

- Determining When to Override the Query Optimizer

- Using Hints and SET FORCEPLAN Statement

- Confirming Query Performance After Overriding the Query Optimizer

This section discusses ways to override the query optimizer and how to determine when to do it. When you do override the query optimizer, it is important to test and reconfirm query performance.

Determining When to Override the Query Optimizer

- **Limit Optimizer Hints**
- **Explore Other Alternatives Before Overriding the Query Optimizer by:**
  - Updating statistics
  - Recompiling stored procedures
  - Reviewing the queries or search arguments
  - Evaluating the possibility of building different indexes

If queries do not perform efficiently, you may choose to override the query optimizer by using *optimizer hints*. Optimizer hints are keywords that you include in your query to force a specific optimization operation.

You should limit the use of optimizer hints because they force optimization to become static. Optimizer hints prevent the query optimizer from adjusting to a changing environment. After you use optimizer hints, you must constantly monitor query performance to verify that the query performs optimally.

Before you consider overriding the query optimizer, you should explore all other alternatives by:

- Updating statistics.
- Recompiling stored procedures.
- Reviewing the queries or search arguments to determine whether you should rewrite them.
- Evaluating the possibility of building different indexes.

Using Hints and SET FORCEPLAN Statement

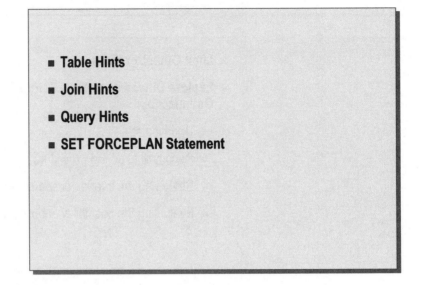

- ■ Table Hints
- ■ Join Hints
- ■ Query Hints
- ■ SET FORCEPLAN Statement

You can override the query optimizer by using hints or the SET FORCEPLAN statement. You can specify a query optimizer hint within SELECT, INSERT, UPDATE, or DELETE statements. There are three types of hints that can be used for overriding the query optimizer.

Table Hints

A *table hint* specifies a table scan, one or more indexes to be used by the query optimizer, or a locking method to be used by the query optimizer with this table and for a statement. When using the table hints, consider the following:

- ■ Each table hint can be specified only once, although you can have multiple table hints

- ■ The WITH clause must be specified next to the table name

Syntax

table_name [[AS] *table_alias*] [WITH (< table_hint > [,...*n*])]

WITH (< table_hint >) ::=
    { INDEX (*index_val* [,...*n*])
      | FASTFIRSTROW
      | HOLDLOCK
      | NOLOCK
      | PAGLOCK
      | READCOMMITTED
      | READPAST
      | READUNCOMMITTED
      | REPEATABLEREAD
      | ROWLOCK
      | SERIALIZABLE
      | TABLOCK
      | TABLOCKX
      | UPDLOCK
      | XLOCK
    }

Join Hints

Join hints enforce a join strategy between two tables. Join hints are specified in a query's FROM clause. When a join hint is specified, the query optimizer automatically enforces the join order for all joined tables in the query, based on the position of the ON keywords.

Syntax

< join_hint > ::=
    { LOOP | HASH | MERGE | REMOTE }

Query Hints

Query hints can control a wide variety of actions. You can specify the query optimizer to use a particular hint for a query by using the OPTION clause. When using the OPTION clause, consider the following facts:

- Each query hint can be specified only once, although you can have multiple query hints.

- The OPTION clause must be specified with the outermost query of the statement.

- The query hint affects all operators in the statement.

- If a UNION is involved in the main query, only the last query involving a UNION operator can have the OPTION clause.

Syntax

[OPTION (< query_hint > [,...n)]
  < query_hint > ::=
    {   { HASH | ORDER } GROUP
    | { CONCAT | HASH | MERGE } UNION
    | { LOOP | MERGE | HASH } JOIN
    | FAST number_rows
    | FORCE ORDER
    | MAXDOP number
    | ROBUST PLAN
    | KEEP PLAN
    | KEEPFIXED PLAN
    | EXPAND VIEWS
    }

SET FORCEPLAN Statement

By using the FROM clause, you can force the query optimizer to join tables in the order in which they are listed. When using the SET FORCEPLAN statement, the query optimizer uses nested loop joins only.

The SET FORCEPLAN statement is a session-level setting.

Syntax

SET FORCEPLAN {ON | OFF}

Note If one or more query hints cause the query optimizer to not generate a valid execution plan, SQL Server cancels the execution and issues error message 8622. You must resubmit the query without specifying any optimizer hints or using the SET FORCEPLAN statement.

Confirming Query Performance After Overriding the Query Optimizer

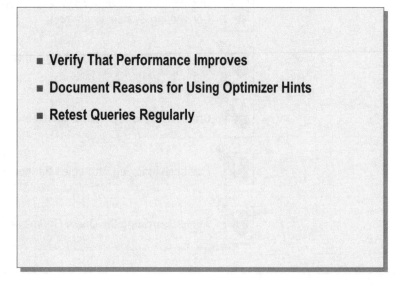

- **Verify That Performance Improves**
- **Document Reasons for Using Optimizer Hints**
- **Retest Queries Regularly**

If you determine that overriding the query optimizer is necessary, verify that performance has improved, document your reasons for overriding the query optimizer, and retest the queries regularly.

Verify That Performance Improves

To verify that the query optimizer hints will improve performance, specify the ON option for the STATISTICS IO and STATISTICS TIME statements and select **Show Execution Plan in Query Analyzer**. In most cases, overriding the query optimizer does not improve performance.

If you are passing input values in a stored procedure, verify that performance is not compromised for *any* of the inputs. Optimizer hints can improve performance for certain input values, but may compromise performance for other input values.

Document Reasons for Using Optimizer Hints

If overriding the query optimizer improves performance, be sure that you document the reasons why. To document your reasons allows you to periodically reevaluate the validity of the optimizer hints. If those reasons change, the optimizer hints may no longer be necessary and may compromise performance.

Retest Queries Regularly

The query optimizer is dynamic and is constantly evaluating the best execution plan as your data changes. If you use optimizer hints, the execution plan becomes static. For this reason, you should consider retesting, on a regular basis, any queries for which you override the query optimizer.

Recommended Practices

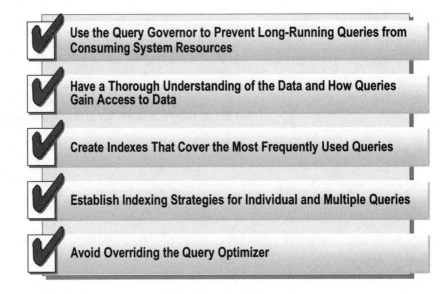

✓	Use the Query Governor to Prevent Long-Running Queries from Consuming System Resources
✓	Have a Thorough Understanding of the Data and How Queries Gain Access to Data
✓	Create Indexes That Cover the Most Frequently Used Queries
✓	Establish Indexing Strategies for Individual and Multiple Queries
✓	Avoid Overriding the Query Optimizer

These recommended practices will help you with indexing strategies that can ensure or improve query performance.

- Use the query governor to prevent long-running queries from executing and consuming system resources. By default, queries are allowed to execute, no matter how long they take. The query governor uses an estimated cost to prevent queries with high cost from executing at all.

- Have a thorough understanding of the data and how queries access it. To know how the query optimizer moves through clustered indexes, nonclustered indexes, and indexes that cover queries, enables design of effective indexes for the queries that your users execute.

- Create indexes that cover the most frequently used queries. When a query is covered by an index, the query optimizer does not access the data pages, because all of the required data is contained in the index. The amount of I/O is significantly reduced.

- Establish indexing strategies for individual and multiple queries. Strive to attain acceptable performance for each of the high-priority queries.

- Avoid overriding the query optimizer. The query optimizer generally selects the most efficient execution plan. If you use optimizer hints, they may become outdated and negatively affect query performance.

Additional information on the following topics is available in SQL Server Books Online.

Topic	Search on
Graphically displaying the execution plan using icons	"graphically displaying the execution plan using SQL Query Analyzer"
Caching the execution plan	"execution plan caching and reuse"
Creating indexes that cover a query	"using indexes on views", "resolving indexes on views"

Lab A: Optimizing Query Performance

Objectives

After completing this lab, you will be able to:

- Use the graphical execution plan to determine how a query is resolved.
- Compare I/O for queries that are covered or not covered by indexes.
- Compare I/O for queries that retrieve a range of data.
- Use optimizer hints to force the use of an index and join method.

Prerequisites

Before working on this lab, you must have:

- Script files for this lab, which are located in C:\Moc\2073A\Labfiles\L13.
- Answer files for this lab, which are located in C:\Moc\2073A\Labfiles\L13\Answers.

Lab Setup

To complete this lab, you must have either:

- Completed the prior lab, or
- Executed the C:\Moc\2073A\Batches\Restore13.cmd batch file.

  This command file restores the **credit** database to a state required for this lab.

- Created the **index_cleanup** stored procedure by running Index_cleanup.sql, which is located in C:\Moc\2073A\Labfiles\L13.

For More Information

If you require help with executing files, search SQL Query Analyzer Help for "Execute a query".

Other resources that you can use include:

- The **credit** database schema.
- SQL Server Books Online.

Scenario

The organization of the classroom is meant to simulate that of a worldwide trading firm named Northwind Traders. Its fictitious domain name is nwtraders.msft. The primary DNS server for nwtraders.msft is the instructor computer, which has an Internet Protocol (IP) address of 192.168.x.200 (where x is the assigned classroom number). The name of the instructor computer is London.

The following table provides the user name, computer name, and IP address for each student computer in the fictitious **nwtraders.msft** domain. Find the user name for your computer, and make a note of it.

User name	Computer name	IP address
SQLAdmin1	Vancouver	192.168.x.1
SQLAdmin2	Denver	192.168.x.2
SQLAdmin3	Perth	192.168.x.3
SQLAdmin4	Brisbane	192.168.x.4
SQLAdmin5	Lisbon	192.168.x.5
SQLAdmin6	Bonn	192.168.x.6
SQLAdmin7	Lima	192.168.x.7
SQLAdmin8	Santiago	192.168.x.8
SQLAdmin9	Bangalore	192.168.x.9
SQLAdmin10	Singapore	192.168.x.10
SQLAdmin11	Casablanca	192.168.x.11
SQLAdmin12	Tunis	192.168.x.12
SQLAdmin13	Acapulco	192.168.x.13
SQLAdmin14	Miami	192.168.x.14
SQLAdmin15	Auckland	192.168.x.15
SQLAdmin16	Suva	192.168.x.16
SQLAdmin17	Stockholm	192.168.x.17
SQLAdmin18	Moscow	192.168.x.18
SQLAdmin19	Caracas	192.168.x.19
SQLAdmin20	Montevideo	192.168.x.20
SQLAdmin21	Manila	192.168.x.21
SQLAdmin22	Tokyo	192.168.x.22
SQLAdmin23	Khartoum	192.168.x.23
SQLAdmin24	Nairobi	192.168.x.24

Estimated time to complete this lab: 45 minutes

Exercise 1
Use the Graphical Execution Plan to Determine How a Query Is Resolved

In this exercise, you will create an index on a computed column and use the graphical execution plan to determine whether the index is useful.

You can open, review, and execute sections of the Indexed_View.sql script file in C:\Moc\SQL2073A\Labfiles\L13, or type and execute the provided Transact-SQL statements.

▶ **To create an indexed view**

In this procedure, you will drop all existing indexes on the **charge** table in the **credit** database and create an indexed view that summarized charges by member.

1. Log on to the **NWTraders** classroom domain by using the information in the following table.

Option	Value
User name	**SQLAdminx** (where *x* corresponds to your computer name as designated in the **nwtraders.msft** classroom domain)
Password	**password**

2. Open SQL Query Analyzer and, if requested, log in to the (local) server with Microsoft Windows® Authentication.

   You have permission to log in to and administer Microsoft SQL Server 2000 because you are logged as **SQLAdminx**, which is a member of the Microsoft Windows 2000 local group, Administrators. All members of this group are automatically mapped to the SQL Server **sysadmin** role.

3. Type and execute this statement to drop existing indexes on the **charge** table in the **credit** database:

```
USE credit
EXEC index_cleanup charge
```

4. Type and execute this statement to create a view on the **charge** table in the **credit** database:

```
CREATE VIEW mem_charges
WITH SCHEMABINDING
AS
SELECT member_no, SUM(charge_amt) AS charge_SUM,
COUNT_BIG(*) AS mem_count
FROM dbo.charge GROUP BY member_no
```

5. Type and execute these two statements to create indexes on the **mem_charges** view:

```
CREATE UNIQUE CLUSTERED INDEX cl_mem_chg ON
mem_charges(member_no)
CREATE NONCLUSTERED INDEX nc_mem_chg_amt ON
mem_charges(charge_SUM)
```

▶ **To view the graphical execution plan.**

In this procedure, you will query the **charge** table and view the query execution plan to determine how the query optimizer obtained the query result.

1. In the Query window, on the **Query** menu, click **Show Execution Plan** to start the graphical execution plan.

2. Type and execute this statement to query the **charge** table:

```
SELECT member_no, SUM(charge_amt) AS Charge_SUM
FROM dbo.charge GROUP BY member_no
```

3. Switch to the **Execution Plan** tab and view the graphical execution plan.

   Did the query optimizer select the **charge** table as the source of the result set? Why or why not?

   _____

   _____

   _____

Exercise 2
Comparing I/O for Queries That Are Covered or Not Covered by Indexes

In this exercise, you will compare the I/O required when clustered and nonclustered indexes are used to retrieve selective data.

You can open, review, and execute sections of the Covered_Queries.sql script file in C:\Moc\SQL2073A\Labfiles\L13, or type and execute the provided Transact-SQL statements.

▶ To create a clustered index

In this procedure, you will drop all existing indexes on the **charge** table and create a clustered index on the **member_no** column of the **charge** table in the **credit** database.

1. Log on to the **NWTraders** classroom domain by using the information in the following table.

Option	Value
User name	**SQLAdmin*x*** (where *x* corresponds to your computer name as designated in the **nwtraders.msft** classroom domain)
Password	**password**

2. Open SQL Query Analyzer and, if prompted, log in to the (local) server with Windows Authentication.

    You have permission to log in to and administer SQL Server because you are logged as **SQLAdmin*x***, which is a member of the Windows 2000 local group, Administrators. All members of this group are automatically mapped to the SQL Server **sysadmin** role.

3. Type and execute this statement to drop existing indexes on the **charge** table:

```
USE credit
EXEC index_cleanup charge
```

4. Type and execute this statement to create a clustered index on the **member_no** column of the **charge** table:

```
CREATE CLUSTERED INDEX charge_member_no_CL
        ON charge(member_no)
```

▶ **To evaluate the difference in execution plans when a query is covered or not covered by an index**

In this procedure, you will execute a query that returns all columns, and you will view the execution plan. Then, you will drop existing clustered indexes and create a nonclustered index, re-execute the query, and evaluate the difference in the execution plan.

1. In SQL Query Analyzer, on the **Query** menu, click **Show Execution Plan**.

2. Type and execute this statement to set the statistics option ON:

```
SET STATISTICS IO ON
```

3. Type and execute this SELECT statement to retrieve all columns for member number 5001:

```
SELECT * FROM charge WHERE member_no = 5001
```

4. Record the statistical information in the following table.

Information	Result
Scan count	
Logical reads	
Execution plan (index or table scan)	
Execution plan (type of index operation)	

5. Type and execute these statements to drop the clustered index and create a nonclustered index on the **member_no** column of the **charge** table:

```
EXEC index_cleanup charge
CREATE NONCLUSTERED INDEX charge_member_no
          ON charge(member_no)
```

6. Re-execute this SELECT statement to retrieve all columns for member number 5001:

```
SELECT * FROM charge WHERE member_no = 5001
```

7. Record the statistical information in the following table.

Information	Result
Scan count	
Logical reads	
Execution plan (index or table scan)	
Execution plan (type of index operation)	

Both queries use an index to locate the records. Why did the nonclustered index require more logical reads?

_____

_____

▶ **To repeat the test with a query that is covered by the nonclustered index**

In this procedure, you will drop existing indexes, create a clustered index on the **member_no** column of the **charge** table, execute a query that is covered by the clustered index, and view the execution plan. Then, you will drop the clustered index, create a nonclustered index on the **member_no** column of the **charge** table, re-execute the query (which is also covered by the nonclustered index), and evaluate the difference in the execution plan.

1. Type and execute these statements to drop existing indexes and create a clustered index on the **member_no** column of the **charge** table:

```
EXEC index_cleanup charge

CREATE CLUSTERED INDEX charge_member_no_CL
        ON charge(member_no)
```

2. Type and execute this SELECT statement to retrieve only the **member_no** column for member number 5001:

```
SELECT member_no FROM charge WHERE member_no = 5001
```

3. Record the statistical information in the following table.

Information	Result
Scan count	
Logical reads	
Execution plan (index or table scan)	
Execution plan (type of index operation)	

4. Type and execute these statements to drop the clustered index and create a nonclustered index on the **member_no** column of the **charge** table:

```
EXEC index_cleanup charge

CREATE NONCLUSTERED INDEX charge_member_no
        ON charge(member_no)
```

5. Re-execute this SELECT statement to retrieve only the **member_no** column for member number 5001:

```
SELECT member_no FROM charge WHERE member_no = 5001
```

Information	Result
Scan count	
Logical reads	
Execution plan (index or table scan)	
Execution plan (type of index operation)	

Did the amount of I/O differ between the two queries executed by using the clustered index, even though one of the queries was covered by the clustered index? Why?

_____

_____

Did the amount of I/O differ between the two queries executed by using the nonclustered index, even though one of the queries was covered by the nonclustered index? Why?

_____

_____

Is the performance of the query covered by the clustered index significantly different from the query covered by the nonclustered index?

_____

_____

Exercise 3
Comparing I/O for Queries That Retrieve a Range of Data

In this exercise, you will compare the I/O required for when clustered and nonclustered indexes are used to retrieve a range of data.

You can open, review, and execute sections of the Range_Queries.sql script file in C:\Moc\SQL2073A\Labfiles\L13, or type and execute the provided Transact-SQL statements.

► **To compare the use of a clustered index and a nonclustered index that covers a query**

In this procedure, you will drop all existing indexes, create a clustered index on the **member_no** column of the **charge** table, execute a query, and view the execution plan. You then will drop existing clustered indexes and create a nonclustered index, re-execute the query, and evaluate the difference in the execution plan.

1. Type and execute these statements to drop existing indexes and create a clustered index on the **member_no** column of the **charge** table:

```
USE credit
EXEC index_cleanup charge

CREATE CLUSTERED INDEX charge_member_no_CL
        ON charge(member_no)
```

2. In the query window, on the **Query** menu, click **Show Execution Plan**.

3. Type and execute this statement to set the statistics option ON:

```
SET STATISTICS IO ON
```

4. Type and execute this SELECT statement to retrieve member numbers 5001 to 6000:

```
SELECT member_no FROM charge WHERE member_no
        BETWEEN 5001 AND 6000
```

5. Record the statistical information in the following table.

Information	Result
Scan count	
Logical reads	
Execution plan (index or table scan)	
Execution plan (type of index operation)	

6. Type and execute these statements to drop the clustered index and create a nonclustered index on the **member_no** column of the **charge** table:

```
EXEC index_cleanup charge

CREATE NONCLUSTERED INDEX charge_member_no
         ON charge(member_no)
```

7. Re-execute this SELECT statement to retrieve member numbers 5001 to 6000:

```
SELECT member_no FROM charge WHERE member_no
         BETWEEN 5001 AND 6000
```

8. Record the statistical information in the following table.

Information	Result
Scan count	
Logical reads	
Execution plan (index or table scan)	
Execution plan (type of index operation)	

9. Compare the statistics output from both queries.

Is the performance of one index significantly greater than the other index in this example? Why?

_____

_____

▶ **To execute a covered query that does not contain a WHERE clause**

In this procedure, you will drop all existing indexes, create a clustered index on the **member_no** column of the **charge** table, execute a query, and view the execution plan. Then, you will drop existing clustered indexes and create a nonclustered index, re-execute the query, and evaluate the difference in the execution plan.

1. Type and execute these statements to drop existing indexes and create a clustered index on the **member_no** column of the **charge** table:

   ```
   EXEC index_cleanup charge

   CREATE CLUSTERED INDEX charge_member_no_CL
           ON charge(member_no)
   ```

2. Type and execute this SELECT statement to retrieve all member numbers:

   ```
   SELECT member_no FROM charge
   ```

3. Record the statistical information in the following table.

Information	Result
Scan count	
Logical reads	
Execution plan (index or table scan)	
Execution plan (type of index operation)	

4. Type and execute these statements to drop the clustered index and create a nonclustered index on the **member_no** column of the **charge** table:

   ```
   EXEC index_cleanup charge

   CREATE NONCLUSTERED INDEX charge_member_no
           ON charge(member_no)
   ```

5. Re-execute this SELECT statement to retrieve all member numbers:

   ```
   SELECT member_no FROM charge
   ```

6. Record the statistical information in the following table.

Information	Result
Scan count	
Logical reads	
Execution plan (index or table scan)	
Execution plan (type of index operation)	

7. Compare the statistics output from both queries.

What is the difference between a table scan and an index scan?

_____

_____

_____

_____

When looking at the statistics output, what is the size (number of pages) of the leaf level of the nonclustered index?

_____

_____

If Time Permits:
Using Optimizer Hints to Force the Use of an Index or Join

In this exercise, you will use optimizer hints to force the query optimizer to use indexes and joins that you specify.

You can open, review, and execute sections of the Hints.sql script file in C:\Moc\SQL2073A\Labfiles\L13, or type and execute the provided Transact-SQL statements.

▶ **To compare execution plans using an index hint**

In this procedure, you will force the query optimizer to use a specific index.

1. Log on to the **NWTraders** classroom domain by using the information in the following table.

Option	Value
User name	**SQLAdmin***x* (where *x* corresponds to your computer name as designated in the **nwtraders.msft** classroom domain)
Password	**password**

2. Open SQL Query Analyzer and, if prompted, log in to the (local) server with Windows Authentication.

   You have permission to log in to and administer SQL Server because you are logged as **SQLAdmin***x*, which is a member of the Windows 2000 local group, Administrators. All members of this group are automatically mapped to the SQL Server **sysadmin** role.

3. Type and execute these statements to drop existing indexes and create a clustered and nonclustered index on the **charge** table in the **credit** database:

   ```
   USE credit
   GO

   EXEC index_cleanup charge
   ```

4. Type and execute this statement to create a clustered index on the **charge_dt** column of the **charge** table:

   ```
   CREATE CLUSTERED INDEX charge_date_CL
      ON charge(charge_dt)
   ```

5. Type and execute this statement to create a nonclustered index on the **member_no** column of the **charge** table:

   ```
   CREATE NONCLUSTERED INDEX charge_member_NC
      ON charge(member_no)
   ```

6. On the **Query** menu, select **Show Execution Plan** to turn on the graphical execution plan.

7. Type and execute this SELECT statement to retrieve rows from the **charge** table where the **member_no** equals 4000:

```
SELECT * FROM charge
WHERE member_no = 4000
```

When looking at the output from the execution plan, what index does the query optimizer use?

8. Type and execute this SELECT statement to retrieve rows from the **charge** table where the **member_no** equals 4000 while using the **charge_date_CL** index.

```
SELECT * FROM charge WITH(INDEX (charge_date_CL))
WHERE member_no = 4000
```

When looking at the output from the execution plan, what index does the query optimizer use?

▶ **To compare the execution plan by using an index hint**

In this procedure, you will see how an index hint forces the query optimizer to provide a different execution plan.

1. Type and execute these statements to drop existing indexes and create a clustered index on the **charge** table in the **credit** database.

```
USE credit
GO

EXEC index_cleanup member
CREATE UNIQUE CLUSTERED INDEX member_no_CL
   ON member(member_no)
```

2. In SQL Query Analyzer, turn on the graphical execution plan, and then, on the **Query** menu, select **Show Execution Plan**.

3. Type and execute this SELECT statement to join the **charge** and **member** tables

```
SELECT m.lastname, SUM(charge_amt)
FROM charge AS c JOIN member AS m
    ON c.member_no = m.member_no
WHERE m.lastname = 'BARR'
GROUP BY m.lastname
```

When looking at the execution plan output, what join method does the query optimizer use?

_____

_____

4. Type and execute this SELECT statement to force the query optimizer to use the hash join method to join the **charge** and **member** tables:

```
SELECT m.lastname, SUM(charge_amt)
FROM charge AS c INNER HASH JOIN member AS m
    ON c.member_no = m.member_no
WHERE m.lastname = 'BARR'
GROUP BY m.lastname
```

When looking at the execution plan output, what join method does the query optimizer use?

_____

_____

Review

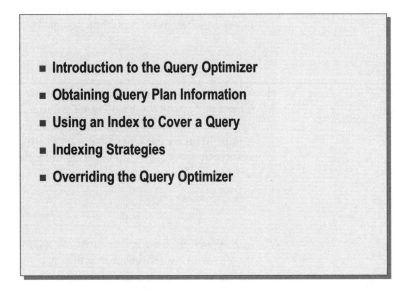

- **Introduction to the Query Optimizer**
- **Obtaining Query Plan Information**
- **Using an Index to Cover a Query**
- **Indexing Strategies**
- **Overriding the Query Optimizer**

1. A financial analyst performs long-running queries that slow down response time for the transaction entry staff. You ask the financial analyst to limit activity, but the financial analyst cannot tell which queries use more resources than others. What can you do to reduce the effect on the transaction query staff?

2. With SQL Profiler, you identify the five worst performing queries. How can you determine the cause of poor query performance? What benefit does each method provide?

3. You have determined that by adding one more index to a table, the index can cover several queries. Having an index that covers a query increases your performance and outweighs the cost of having the additional index. To cover an index, what requirements must you meet?

4. While examining your indexes, you notice that the clustered index of your **Client** table is on the **Last Name** column. You know that you typically look up clients individually by last names. You also know that you frequently group clients by the **Client Representative ID** column for reporting. Should you create a nonclustered index on the **Client Representative ID** column?

5. In July, you used optimizer hints in a query to improve performance. Three months later, you discover that this query again performs poorly. What is the cause?

Course Evaluation

Your evaluation of this course will help Microsoft understand the quality of your learning experience.

At a convenient time between now and the end of the course, please complete a course evaluation, which is available at http://www.metricsthatmatter.com/survey.

Microsoft will keep your evaluation strictly confidential and will use your responses to improve your future learning experience.

Microsoft®
Training &
Certification

Module 14:
Analyzing Queries

Contents

Microsoft®

Project Lead: Rich Rose
Instructional Designers: Rich Rose, Cheryl Hoople, Marilyn McGill
Instructional Software Design Engineers: Karl Dehmer, Carl Raebler, Rick Byham
Technical Lead: Karl Dehmer
Subject Matter Experts: Karl Dehmer, Carl Raebler, Rick Byham
Graphic Artist: Kirsten Larson (Independent Contractor)
Editing Manager: Lynette Skinner
Editor: Wendy Cleary
Copy Editor: Edward McKillop (S&T Consulting)
Production Manager: Miracle Davis
Production Coordinator: Jenny Boe
Production Support: Lori Walker (S&T Consulting)
Test Manager: Sid Benavente
Courseware Testing: TestingTesting123
Classroom Automation: Lorrin Smith-Bates
Creative Director, Media/Sim Services: David Mahlmann
Web Development Lead: Lisa Pease
CD Build Specialist: Julie Challenger
Online Support: David Myka (S&T Consulting)
Localization Manager: Rick Terek
Operations Coordinator: John Williams
Manufacturing Support: Laura King; Kathy Hershey
Lead Product Manager, Release Management: Bo Galford
Lead Product Manager, Data Base: Margo Crandall
Group Manager, Courseware Infrastructure: David Bramble
Group Product Manager, Content Development: Dean Murray
General Manager: Robert Stewart

Overview

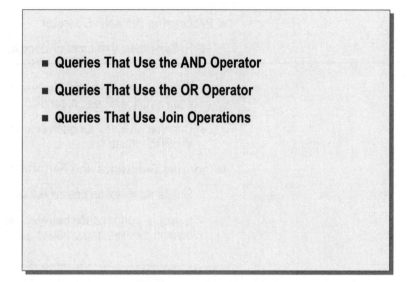

After completing this module, you will be able to:

- Analyze the performance gain of writing efficient queries and creating useful indexes for queries that contain the AND logical operator.

- Analyze the performance gain of writing efficient queries and creating useful indexes for queries that contain the OR logical operator.

- Evaluate how the query optimizer uses different join strategies for query optimization.

Queries That Use the AND Operator

- **Processing the AND Operator**
  - Returns rows that meet all conditions for every criterion specified in the WHERE clause
  - Progressively limits the number of rows returned with each additional search condition
  - Can use an index for each search condition of the WHERE clause
- **Indexing Guidelines and Performance Considerations**
  - Define an index on one highly selective search criterion
  - Evaluate performance between creating multiple, single-column indexes and creating a composite index

How query optimizer processes the AND operator depends on whether indexes exist on some, or all columns referenced in the WHERE clause.

Processing the AND Operator

When a query contains the AND operator, the query optimizer:

- Returns rows that meet all conditions for every criterion specified in the WHERE clause.

- Progressively limits the number of rows returned with each additional search condition.

- Can use an index for each search condition of the WHERE clause.

- Always uses an index if the index is useful.

  If indexes are not useful for any of the columns in the WHERE clause, the query optimizer performs a table scan or clustered index scan.

- May use multiple indexes if they are useful.

  If multiple indexes exist and some indexes are useful for any of the columns in the WHERE clause, the query optimizer determines which combination of indexes to use.

  The execution plan may show that one or most of the indexes were used to process the query. The combination of indexes is determined by the:

  - Selectivity of the search.

  - Type of indexes that exist, such as clustered or nonclustered.

  - Ability to cover the index.

  - Existence of an indexed view.

■ May use only one index even though multiple useful indexes exist.

If the query optimizer finds one index that is highly selective, it uses that index. Then, it uses the filter operation to process the remaining search conditions against the qualifying rows.

Indexing Guidelines and Performance Considerations

The best way to index for queries that contain the AND operator is to have at least one highly selective search criterion and define an index on that column.

You may want to compare the difference in performance when creating multiple, single-column indexes and a composite index. You do not necessarily improve query performance by indexing every column that is part of the AND operator. However, you can benefit from having multiple indexes if the columns referenced by the AND operator are of lower selectivity.

Queries That Use the OR Operator

- ■ **Returns Rows That Meet Any of the Conditions for Every Criterion Specified in the WHERE Clause**

- ■ **Progressively Increases the Number of Rows Returned with Each Additional Search Condition**

- ■ **Can Use One Index or Different Indexes for Each Part of the OR Operator**

- ■ **Always Performs a Table Scan or Clustered Index Scan If One Column Referenced in the OR Operator Does Not Have an Index or If the Index Is Not Useful**

- ■ **Can Use Multiple Indexes**

How the query optimizer processes the OR operator also depends on whether indexes exist on some or all columns referenced in the WHERE clause.

When a query contains the OR operator, the query optimizer:

- ■ Returns rows that meet any of the conditions for every criterion specified in the WHERE clause.

- ■ Progressively increases the number of rows returned with each additional search condition.

- ■ Can use one index that satisfies all parts of the OR operator, or uses different indexes for each part of the OR operator.

- ■ Always performs a table scan or clustered index scan if one column referenced in the OR operator does not have an index, or if the index is not useful.

- ■ If multiple indexes exist and all indexes are useful, the query optimizer:

  - • Searches a table by using an index for each column.

  - • Sorts the qualifying values for each column.

  - • Combines the results.

  - • Retrieves the qualifying rows by using the Bookmark Lookup operation.

Note The query optimizer converts the IN clause to the OR operator.

Lab A: Analyzing Queries That Use the AND and OR Operators

Objectives

After completing this lab, you will be able to:

- Interpret statistical information on a query that uses the AND operator and determine why the query optimizer did or did not use specific indexes.

- Interpret why the query optimizer processes queries that contain a small list of values differently from queries that contain a large list of values.

- Account for the amount of input/output (I/O) used to process a query that contains nested SELECT statements, and explain why the query optimizer selected a specific execution plan.

Prerequisites

Before working on this lab, you must have:

- The **credit** database in Microsoft® SQL Server™ 2000.

- Script files, for this lab, which are located in C:\Moc\2073A\Labfiles\L14.

Lab Setup

To complete this lab, you must have either:

- Completed the prior lab, or

- Executed the C:\Moc\2073A\Batches\Restore14A.cmd batch file.

  This command file restores the **credit** database to a state required for this lab.

For More Information

If you require help with executing files, search SQL Query Analyzer Help for "Execute a query".

Other resources that you can use include:

- The **credit** database schema.

- SQL Server Books Online.

Scenario

The organization of the classroom is meant to simulate that of a worldwide trading firm named Northwind Traders. Its fictitious domain name is nwtraders.msft. The primary DNS server for nwtraders.msft is the instructor computer, which has an Internet Protocol (IP) address of 192.168.*x*.200 (where *x* is the assigned classroom number). The name of the instructor computer is London.

The following table provides the user name, computer name, and IP address for each student computer in the fictitious **nwtraders.msft** domain. Find the user name for your computer, and make a note of it.

User name	Computer name	IP address
SQLAdmin1	Vancouver	192.168.*x*.1
SQLAdmin2	Denver	192.168.*x*.2
SQLAdmin3	Perth	192.168.*x*.3
SQLAdmin4	Brisbane	192.168.*x*.4
SQLAdmin5	Lisbon	192.168.*x*.5
SQLAdmin6	Bonn	192.168.*x*.6
SQLAdmin7	Lima	192.168.*x*.7
SQLAdmin8	Santiago	192.168.*x*.8
SQLAdmin9	Bangalore	192.168.*x*.9
SQLAdmin10	Singapore	192.168.*x*.10
SQLAdmin11	Casablanca	192.168.*x*.11
SQLAdmin12	Tunis	192.168.*x*.12
SQLAdmin13	Acapulco	192.168.*x*.13
SQLAdmin14	Miami	192.168.*x*.14
SQLAdmin15	Auckland	192.168.*x*.15
SQLAdmin16	Suva	192.168.*x*.16
SQLAdmin17	Stockholm	192.168.*x*.17
SQLAdmin18	Moscow	192.168.*x*.18
SQLAdmin19	Caracas	192.168.*x*.19
SQLAdmin20	Montevideo	192.168.*x*.20
SQLAdmin21	Manila	192.168.*x*.21
SQLAdmin22	Tokyo	192.168.*x*.22
SQLAdmin23	Khartoum	192.168.*x*.23
SQLAdmin24	Nairobi	192.168.*x*.24

Estimated time to complete this lab: 60 minutes

Exercise 1
Evaluating Queries That Use Some Indexes

In this exercise, you will create three indexes on the **member** table. You will execute a query that contains three search conditions by using the AND operator and thereby explain why the query optimizer created the type of plan that it did. You will also account for the I/O used to process the query.

You can open, review, and execute sections of the EvalQuery.sql script file in C:\Moc\2073A\Labfiles\L14, or type and execute the provided Transact-SQL statements.

▶ **To create indexes**

In this procedure, you will drop any indexes on the **member** table and create three nonclustered indexes on the **firstname**, **corp_no**, and **member_no** columns.

1. Log on to the **NWTraders** classroom domain by using the information in the following table.

Option	Value
User name	**SQLAdmin***x* (where *x* corresponds to your computer name as designated in the **nwtraders.msft** classroom domain)
Password	**password**

2. Open SQL Query Analyzer and, if requested, log in to the (local) server with Microsoft Windows® Authentication.

   You have permission to log in to and administer SQL Server because you are logged as **SQLAdmin***x*, which is a member of the Microsoft Windows 2000 local group, Administrators. All members of this group are automatically mapped to the SQL Server **sysadmin** role.

3. With SQL Query Analyzer, type and execute this statement to drop existing indexes on the **member** table:

```
USE credit
EXEC index_cleanup member
```

4. Type and execute this statement to create three indexes on the **member** table:

```
USE Credit
CREATE NONCLUSTERED INDEX fname    ON member(firstname)
CREATE NONCLUSTERED INDEX corp_no ON member(corp_no)
CREATE NONCLUSTERED INDEX mem_no  ON member(member_no)
GO
```

Note The **member** table contains 10,000 unique members (rows).

▶ **To execute a query that uses some indexes**

In this procedure, you will set the statistics option to ON, execute a query that contains three search conditions in the WHERE clause (where each column referenced in the WHERE clause has an index created for it), record the statistical information, and observe the results of the execution plan.

1. Type and execute this statement to set the statistics option to ON:

```
SET STATISTICS IO ON
```

2. In the Query window, on the **Query** menu, click **Show Execution Plan**.

3. Type and execute this SELECT statement to retrieve data for members whose first names begin with the letter Q, whose corporate numbers are greater than 450, and whose member numbers are greater than 6000:

```
USE credit
SELECT * FROM member WHERE firstname LIKE 'Q%'
          AND corp_no > 450
          AND member_no > 6000
```

Note   This query is referred to as the *original query* throughout this exercise.

---

4. Record the statistical information in the following table.

Information	Result
Number of rows affected	
Scan count	
Number of logical reads	
Number and name of indexes used to process the query	

5. Click the **Execution Plan** tab to display the execution plan graphically.

6. Examine the execution plan. It will look similar to the illustration that follows.

   Notice the operations used in the execution plan. You will analyze this execution plan throughout this exercise to account for the number of I/O used and the reasons why this execution plan was selected.

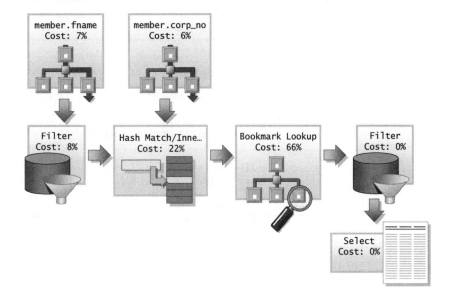

▶ **To account for the I/O used to process the original query**

In this procedure, you will rewrite the original query as three SELECT statements to understand and account for the 15 I/O of the original query. Each statement represents one search condition of the WHERE clause that limits the search. For each statement, you will record statistical information and account for the number of I/O used to process the query.

1. Type and execute this SELECT statement, which includes only the first search condition of the WHERE clause in the original query:

```
USE credit
SELECT firstname FROM member WHERE firstname LIKE 'Q%'
```

2. Record the statistical information in the following table.

Information	Result
Number of rows affected	
Scan count	
Number of logical reads	
Number and name of indexes used to process the query	
Is the query covered by an index?	

3. Type and execute this SELECT statement, which includes only the second search condition of the WHERE clause in the original query:

```
USE credit
SELECT corp_no FROM member WHERE corp_no > 450
```

4. Record the statistical information in the following table.

Information	Result
Number of rows affected	
Scan count	
Number of logical reads	
Number and name of indexes used to process the query	
Is the query covered by an index?	

5. Type and execute this SELECT statement, which includes only the third search condition of the WHERE clause in the original query:

```
USE credit
SELECT member_no FROM member WHERE member_no > 6000
```

6. Record the statistical information in the following table.

Information	Result
Number of rows affected	
Scan count	
Number of logical reads	
Number and name of indexes used to process the query	
Is the query covered by an index?	

7. Compare the statistical information for the original query with the breakdown of each search condition of that query.

Original Query

```
USE credit
SELECT *FROM member WHERE firstname LIKE 'Q%'
          AND corp_no > 450
          AND member_no > 6000
```

Information	Result of original query	Result of query containing first search condition	Result of query containing second search condition	Result of query containing third search condition
Number of rows affected	5	375	316	4000
Scan count	2	1	1	1
Number of logical reads	15	3	3	9
Number and name of indexes used to process the query	2 (**fname** and **corp_no**)	1 (**fname**)	1 (**corp_no**)	1 (**mem_no**)

Note Your statistical information may vary from that presented in the table.

Why did each of the three individual queries use so little I/O?

_____

_____

_____

In the original query, why did the query optimizer not use the index on the **member_no** column?

_____

_____

_____

_____

▶ **To understand the execution plan by combining search conditions**

In this procedure, you will rewrite the original query by combining the search conditions of the WHERE clause that the query optimizer used in the execution plan. You will record the statistical information, and evaluate the execution plan to account for the number of I/O.

1. Type and execute this SELECT statement, which includes the first and second search conditions of the WHERE clause in the original query:

```
USE credit
SELECT firstname FROM member
WHERE firstname LIKE 'Q%' AND corp_no > 450
```

2. Record the statistical information in the following table.

Information	Result
Number of rows affected	
Scan count	
Number of logical reads	
Number and name of indexes used to process the query	
Is the query covered by an index?	

Notice that when you execute the query, the query optimizer uses an index for each search condition.

3. Compare the statistical information for the original query with the query that contains the first and second search conditions.

Original Query

```
USE credit
SELECT * FROM member WHERE firstname LIKE 'Q%'
            AND corp_no > 450
            AND member_no > 6000
```

Information	Result of original query	Result of query containing first and second search conditions
Number of rows affected	5	9
Scan count	2	2
Number of logical reads	15	6
Number and name of indexes used to process the query	2 (**fname** and **corp_no**)	2 (**fname** and **corp_no**)

Note Your statistical information may vary from that presented in the table.

4. Click the **Execution Plan** tab to display the execution plan graphically.

5. Examine the execution plan.

   Why do both queries have a scan count of two?

   _____

   _____

   _____

   _____

   _____

   _____

Exercise 2
Evaluating Queries That Use All Indexes

In this exercise, you will execute queries containing the AND operator against the **member** table and record statistical information. The query used in this exercise is identical to the query used in Exercise 1, except that one search condition has changed from **member_no** > 6500 to **member_no** > 9500. The same three nonclustered indexes exist on the **member** table, which are defined on the **firstname**, **corp_no**, and **member_no** columns.

You will also change the indexing strategy to illustrate how different indexes can reduce your I/O in a query.

You can open, review, and execute the EvalQueryIndex.sql script file in C:\Moc\2073A\Labfiles\L14, or type and execute your own Transact-SQL statements.

▶ **To execute a query that uses all indexes**

In this procedure, you will set the statistics option to ON, execute a query, record the statistical information, and observe the results of the execution plan.

1. Type and execute this SELECT statement to retrieve data for members whose first names begin with the letter Q, whose corporate numbers are greater than 450, and whose member numbers are greater than 9500:

```
USE credit
SELECT * FROM member WHERE firstname LIKE 'Q%'
          AND corp_no > 450
          AND member_no > 9500
```

Note This query is referred to as the *original query* throughout this exercise.

2. Record the statistical information in the following table.

Information	Result
Number of rows affected	
Scan count	
Number of logical reads	
Number and name of indexes used to process the query	

3. Click the **Execution Plan** tab to display the execution plan graphically.

4. Examine the execution plan. It will look similar to the illustration that follows.

    Notice the operations used in the execution plan. You will be analyzing this execution plan throughout this exercise to account for the number of I/O used and the reasons why this execution plan was selected.

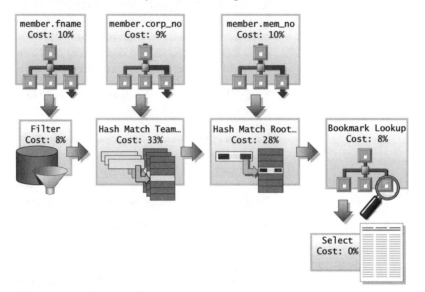

    Does the query optimizer use the index on the **member_no** column? Why?

    _____

    _____

5. Compare the original query in this exercise with the original query in exercise 1.

Original Query

```
USE credit
SELECT * FROM member WHERE firstname LIKE 'Q%'
        AND corp_no > 450
        AND member_no > 9500
```

**Original Query
(exercise 1)**

```
USE credit
SELECT * FROM member WHERE firstname LIKE 'Q%'
        AND corp_no > 450
        AND member_no > 6000
```

    Why does the original query in this exercise use the index defined on the **member_no** column, whereas the original query in Exercise 1 does not?

    _____

    _____

▶ **To account for the I/O used to process the original query**

In this procedure, you will rewrite the original query as three SELECT statements. Each statement will represent one search condition of the WHERE clause that limits the search. For each statement, you will record statistical information. You then will use this information to explain why the query optimizer selects a specific execution plan and to account for the number of I/O.

1. Type and execute this SELECT statement, which includes only the first search condition of the WHERE clause in the original query:

```
USE credit
SELECT firstname FROM member WHERE firstname LIKE 'Q%'
```

2. Record the statistical information in the following table.

Information	Result
Number of rows affected	
Scan count	
Number of logical reads	
Number and name of indexes used to process the query	
Is the query covered by an index?	

3. Type and execute this SELECT statement, which includes only the second search condition of the WHERE clause in the original query:

```
USE credit
SELECT corp_no FROM member WHERE corp_no > 450
```

4. Record the statistical information in the following table.

Information	Result
Number of rows affected	
Scan count	
Number of logical reads	
Number and name of indexes used to process the query	
Is the query covered by an index?	

5. Type and execute this SELECT statement, which includes only the third search condition of the WHERE clause in the original query:

```
USE credit
SELECT member_no FROM member WHERE member_no > 9500
```

6. Record the statistical information in the following table.

Information	Result
Number of rows affected	
Scan count	
Number of logical reads	
Number and name of indexes used to process the query	
Is the query covered by an index?	

7. Compare the statistical information for the original query with the breakdown of each search condition of that query.

Original Query

```
USE credit
SELECT * FROM member WHERE firstname LIKE 'Q%'
            AND corp_no > 450
            AND member_no > 9500
```

Information	Result of original query	Result of query containing first search condition	Result of query containing second search condition	Result of query containing third search condition
Number of rows affected	1	375	316	500
Scan count	3	1	1	1
Number of logical reads	10	3	3	3
Number and name of indexes used to process the query	3 (**fname, corp_no**, and **mem_no**)	1 (**fname**)	1 (**corp_no**)	1 (**mem_no**)

Note   Your statistical information may vary from that presented in the table.

8. Click the **Execution Plan** tab to display the execution plan graphically.

9. Examine the execution plan for the original query.

In the original query, how do you account for the 10 I/O?

_____

_____

_____

_____

▶ **To execute a query against a table with a clustered index**

In this procedure, you will drop the nonclustered index on the **member.member_no** column and create a clustered index on the **member.member_no** column. After you create the index, you will execute the original query and observe the changes in the execution plan and the page I/O.

1. Type and execute this statement to drop the nonclustered index on the **member.member_no** column and create a clustered index:

```
USE credit
DROP INDEX member.mem_no
GO
CREATE CLUSTERED INDEX mem_no_CL ON member(member_no)
GO
```

Note Two nonclustered indexes exist: One is defined on the **corp_no** column, and the other is defined on the **firstname** column.

2. Type and execute the original query against the **member** table with a clustered index on the **member_no** column:

```
USE credit
SELECT * FROM member WHERE firstname LIKE 'Q%'
          AND corp_no > 450
          AND member_no > 9500
```

3. Record the statistical information in the following table.

Information	Result
Number of rows affected	
Scan count	
Number of logical reads	
Number and name of indexes used to process the query	
Is the query covered by an index?	

4. Compare the statistical information of the query against a table that has a clustered index on the **member_no** column with the table that has a nonclustered index on the **member_no** column.

Information	Result of query (clustered index on member_no)	Result of query (nonclustered index on member_no)
Number of rows affected	1	1
Scan count	1	3
Number of logical reads	9	10
Number and name of indexes used to process the query	1 (**mem_no**)	3 (**fname, corp_no**, and **mem_no**)

Note Your statistical information may vary from that presented in the table.

5. Click the **Execution Plan** tab to display the execution plan graphically.

6. Examine the execution plan.

   Has query performance improved with a clustered index on the **member_no** column? Why?

   _____

   _____

   Why does the query optimizer use the clustered index on the **member_no** column?

   _____

   _____

   _____

   _____

Exercise 3
Evaluating Queries That Use the IN Keyword

In this exercise, you will create an index on the **member** table, observe the performance of queries containing the IN keyword, and observe how the execution plan changes as the list of values grows in size. The larger the list, the less efficient the query becomes.

You can open, review, and execute sections of the EvalQueryIN.sql script file in C:\Moc\2073A\Labfiles\L14, or type and execute the provided Transact-SQL statements.

▶ **To execute a query that contains an IN keyword**

In this procedure, you will drop any existing indexes on the **member** table, create an index, execute a query, record the statistical information, and examine the execution plan.

1. Type and execute this statement to drop existing indexes on the **member** table:

```
USE credit
EXEC index_cleanup member
```

2. Type and execute this statement to create a unique, nonclustered index on the **member_no** column of the **member** table:

```
USE credit
CREATE UNIQUE nonclustered INDEX mbr_mem_no
   ON member(member_no)
GO
```

3. Type and execute this statement to set the statistics option to ON:

```
SET STATISTICS IO ON
```

4. Type and execute this SELECT statement to retrieve all data for specific member numbers:

```
USE credit
SELECT * FROM member WHERE member_no
   IN (100,101,102,103,104,105,106,107,108,109,200,201,
       202,203,204,205,206,207,208,209,210,211,212,213,
       214,215,216,217,218,219,220,221,222,223,224,225,
       226,227,228,229,230,231,232)
```

5. Record the statistical information in the following table:

Information	Result
Number of rows affected	
Scan count	
Number of logical reads	
Number and name of indexes used to process the query	
Is the query covered by an index?	

6. Click the **Execution Plan** tab to graphically view the execution plan.

7. Examine the execution plan. It will look similar to the illustration that follows.

   Notice the operations used in the execution plan. You will be analyzing this execution plan throughout this exercise to account for the number of I/O used and the reasons why this execution plan was selected.

   Knowing that the Bookmark Lookup accounts for 43 of the 129 I/O, how do you account for the remaining 86 I/O?

   Tip   STATISTICS I/O shows a scan count of 43.

   _____

   _____

   _____

   _____

   If the query were modified to use an index that covers the query, what step would be eliminated in the execution plan? Why?

   _____

   _____

   _____

What would be the total page I/O for this query, which is covered by an index?

_____

_____

▶ **To show when a query containing a list of values becomes inefficient**

In this procedure, you will execute a query, record the statistical information, and compare the execution plan with that of the preceding query. The query used in this procedure is similar to the previous query, except that the IN list includes one additional value. The additional value in the query causes the query optimizer to process the query in a different way.

1. Type and execute this SELECT statement to retrieve specific member numbers. Notice that this query differs from the original query. There are now 44 values in the IN list:

```
USE credit
SELECT * FROM member WHERE member_no
IN (100,101,102,103,104,105,106,107,108,109,200,201,202,
    203,204,205,206,207,208,209,210,211,212,213,214,215,
    216,217,218,219,220,221,222,223,224,225,226,227,228,
    229,230,231,232,233)
```

2. Record the statistical information in the following table.

Information	Result
Number of rows affected	
Scan count	
Number of logical reads	
Number and name of indexes used to process the query	
Is the query covered by an index?	

3. Compare the statistical information for this query with the statistical information in the previous query.

Previous Query

```
USE credit
SELECT * FROM member WHERE member_no
    IN (100,101,102,103,104,105,106,107,108,109,200,201,
        202,203,204,205,206,207,208,209,210,211,212,213,
        214,215,216,217,218,219,220,221,222,223,224,225,
        226,227,228,229,230,231,232)
```

Query Containing
Additional Value

```
USE credit
SELECT * FROM member WHERE member_no
IN (100,101,102,103,104,105,106,107,108,109,200,201,202,
    203,204,205,206,207,208,209,210,211,212,213,214,215,
    216,217,218,219,220,221,222,223,224,225,226,227,228,
    229,230,231,232,233)
```

Information	Result of previous query	Result of query containing additional value
Number of rows affected	43	44
Scan count	43	1
Number of logical reads	129	145
Number and name of indexes used to process the query	Yes (**mem_no**)	None

4. Click the **Execution Plan** tab to display the execution plan graphically.

5. Examine the execution plan.

    Why did the query optimizer use a different execution plan for the query with the additional value (233) in the list of values?

    _____

    _____

    _____

    _____

    Describe the execution plan for the query containing the additional value (233)?

    _____

    _____

    _____

    _____

Exercise 4
Evaluating Queries That Contain Nested SELECT Statements

In this exercise, you will observe the performance of queries containing nested SELECT statements. You will examine the execution plan of a query that returns a list of values, account for the number of I/O, and explain why the query optimizer selected the specific execution plan.

You can open, review, and execute sections of the EvalQueryNested.sql script file in C:\Moc\2073A\Labfiles\L14, or type and execute the provided Transact-SQL statements.

▶ **To execute a query containing a nested SELECT statement**

In this procedure, you will execute a query that contains a nested SELECT statement that returns a list of values and record the statistical information.

1. Type and execute this SELECT statement to retrieve member data for members whose member numbers are between 100 and 111:

```
USE credit
SELECT * FROM member WHERE member_no
IN (SELECT member_no FROM member WHERE member_no
BETWEEN 100 AND 111)
```

Note This query is referred to as the original query throughout this exercise.

2. Record the statistical information in the following table.

Information	Result
Number of rows affected	
Scan count	
Number of logical reads	
Number and name of indexes used to process the query	

▶ **To account for the I/O used to process the original query**

In this procedure, you will rewrite the original query as two SELECT statements. Each statement represents a step in the execution plan. For each statement, you will record statistical information, explain why the query optimizer selected a specific execution plan, and you then account for the number of I/O.

1. Type and execute this SELECT statement to retrieve member numbers between 100 and 111:

```
USE credit
SELECT member_no FROM member WHERE member_no
      BETWEEN 100 AND 111
```

Note In the original query, this SELECT statement is the first step of the execution plan.

2. Record the statistical information in the following table.

Information	Result
Number of rows affected	
Scan count	
Number of logical reads	

Is an index used to process the query? Is this query covered by an index? Why?

_____

_____

3. Type and execute this SELECT statement to retrieve specific member numbers:

```
USE credit
SELECT member_no FROM member WHERE member_no
IN (100,101,102,103,104,105,106,107,108,109,110,111)
```

Note In the original query, this SELECT statement is the second step of the execution plan.

4. Record the statistical information in the following table.

Information	Result
Number of rows affected	
Scan count	
Number of logical reads	

Is an index used to process the query? Is this query covered by an index?

_____

_____

5. Compare the statistical information for the original query with the breakdown of each step of the execution plan.

Original Query

```
USE credit
SELECT * FROM member WHERE member_no IN
    (SELECT member_no FROM member WHERE member_no
        BETWEEN 100 AND 111)
```

First Step Query

```
USE credit
SELECT member_no FROM member WHERE member_no
        BETWEEN 100 AND 111
```

Second Step Query

```
USE credit
SELECT member_no FROM member WHERE member_no IN
    (100,101,102,103,104,105,106,107,108,109,110,111)
```

Information	Result of original query	Result of query (first step of execution plan)	Result of query (second step of execution plan)
Number of rows affected	12	12	12
Scan count	13	1	12
Number of logical reads	44	2	24

Note Your statistical information may vary from that presented in the table.

6. Click the **Execution Plan** tab to graphically view the execution plan.

7. Execute the original query and examine the execution plan.

   In the original query, explain why the query optimizer created this plan, and specify how much I/O was used by each step in the execution plan.

   _____

   _____

   _____

   _____

   _____

   _____

   _____

   _____

Exercise 5
Evaluating Queries That Contain the OR Operator

In this exercise, you will execute several queries containing the OR operator against the **member** table, which has a nonclustered index on the **member_no** column. You will record the statistical information, compare I/O, and examine the execution plan. You will drop existing indexes, create two indexes, re-execute a query, and compare the execution plan used for the same query executed against a table with partial indexing.

You can open, review, and execute sections of the EvalQueryOR.sql script file in C:\Moc\2073A\Labfiles\L14, or type and execute the provided Transact-SQL statements.

▶ **To execute a query against a table with partial indexing**

In this procedure, you will execute three queries and record and evaluate their statistical information.

1. Drop all indexes on the member table in the **credit** database.

```
USE credit
EXEC index_cleanup member
```

2. Create a unique nonclustered index on the **member_no** column of the **member** table.

```
CREATE UNIQUE nonclustered INDEX mbr_mem_no ON
member(member_no)
```

3. Set statistics I/O to ON.

```
SET STATISTICS IO ON
```

4. Type and execute this SELECT statement to retrieve a member where member number equals 1234, or region number equals 5:

Query 1

```
USE credit
SELECT * FROM member WHERE member_no=1234 OR region_no=5
```

Note A nonclustered index on the **member_no** column of the **member** table exists.

---

5. Record the statistical information in the following table.

Information	Result
Number of rows affected	
Scan count	
Number of logical reads	
Number and name of indexes used to process the query	

6. Type and execute this SELECT statement to retrieve a member where member number equals 1,234, or corporate number equals 410:

Query 2

```
USE credit
SELECT * FROM member WHERE member_no=1234 OR corp_no=410
```

7. Record the statistical information in the following table.

Information	Result
Number of rows affected	
Scan count	
Number of logical reads	
Number and name of indexes used to process the query	

8. Click the **Execution Plan** tab to graphically view the execution plan.

9. Examine the execution plan. It will look similar to the illustration that follows.

Notice the operations used in the execution plan. You will use this execution plan to compare to another execution plan later in the exercise.

10. Type and execute this SELECT statement to retrieve a member where region number equals 5, or corporate number equals 410:

Query 3

```
USE credit
SELECT * FROM member WHERE region_no = 5 OR corp_no = 410
```

11. Record the statistical information in the following table.

Information	Result
Number of rows affected	
Scan count	
Number of logical reads	
Number and name of indexes used to process the query	

12. Compare the statistical information for all three queries.

Query 1

```
USE credit
SELECT * FROM member WHERE member_no=1234 OR region_no=5
```

Query 2

```
USE credit
SELECT * FROM member WHERE member_no=1234 OR corp_no=410
```

Query 3

```
USE credit
SELECT * FROM member WHERE region_no=5 OR corp_no=410
```

Information	Result of query 1	Result of query 2	Result of query 3
Number of rows affected	1,100	7	1,105
Scan count	1	1	1
Number of logical reads	145	145	145
Number and name of indexes used to process the query	None (table scan)	None (table scan)	None (table scan)

Note Your statistical information may vary from that presented in the table.

Do these three execution plans differ? Why?

_____

_____

_____

_____

▶ **To drop existing indexes and create indexes**

In this procedure, you will drop any existing indexes and create two indexes on the **member** table.

1. Type and execute this statement to set the statistics option to OFF:

```
SET STATISTICS IO OFF
```

2. Type and execute this statement to drop existing indexes on the **member** table:

```
USE credit
EXEC index_cleanup member
```

3. Type and execute this statement to create two indexes on the **member** table:

```
USE credit
CREATE UNIQUE nonclustered INDEX mbr_mem_no
   ON member(member_no)
CREATE clustered INDEX mbr_corp_no_CL
   ON member(corp_no)
```

▶ **To execute a query against a table with complete indexing**

In this procedure, you will set the statistics option to ON, re-execute query 2 of this exercise, and record and evaluate the statistical information.

1. Type and execute this statement to set the statistics option to ON:

   ```
   SET STATISTICS IO ON
   ```

2. Re-execute query 2, which retrieves member number 1,234, or corporate number 410.

Query 2

```
USE credit
SELECT * FROM member WHERE member_no=1234 OR corp_no=410
```

3. Record the statistical information in the following table.

Information	Result
Number of rows affected	
Scan count	
Number of logical reads	
Number and name of indexes used to process the query	

4. Compare the statistical information of query 2 against a table with partial indexing with complete indexing.

Query 2

```
USE credit
SELECT * FROM member WHERE member_no=1234 OR corp_no=410
```

Information	Result of query 2 (partial indexing)	Result of query 2 (complete indexing)
Number of rows affected	7	7
Scan count	1	2
Number of logical reads	145	18
Number and name of indexes used to process the query	None (table scan)	Yes (**mbr_mem_no** and **mbr_corp_no_CL**)

5. Click the **Execution Plan** tab to graphically view the execution plan.

6. Examine the execution plan and compare it with the execution plan for the same query executed against a table with partial indexing.

   Why is the execution plan for a table, with complete indexing different from the execution plan, used for the same query executed against a table with partial indexing?

   _____

   _____

   _____

What is the execution plan, and how many I/O does it use?

_____

_____

_____

_____

◆ Queries That Use Join Operations

- Selectivity and Density of a JOIN Clause

- How Joins Are Processed

- How Nested Loop Joins Are Processed

- Multimedia: How Joins Are Processed

- Considerations When Merge Joins Are Used

- How Hash Joins Are Processed

In this section, we will discuss how the query optimizer optimizes queries that use join operations.

Selectivity and Density of a JOIN Clause

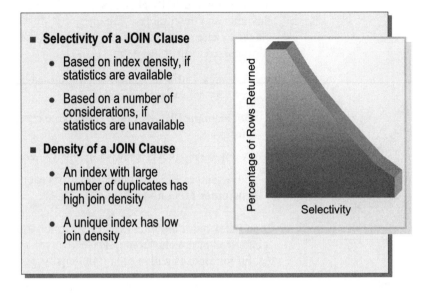

- **Selectivity of a JOIN Clause**
  - Based on index density, if statistics are available
  - Based on a number of considerations, if statistics are unavailable
- **Density of a JOIN Clause**
  - An index with large number of duplicates has high join density
  - A unique index has low join density

(Chart axes: vertical axis — Percentage of Rows Returned; horizontal axis — Selectivity)

The order in which the query optimizer processes joins is determined by the existence of indexes and a WHERE clause, in addition to the selectivity and density of the data.

Selectivity of a JOIN Clause

The selectivity of a JOIN clause is the percentage of rows from one table that are joined to a single row from another. Selectivity is derived from the number of rows that are estimated to be returned, as seen with the WHERE clause.

A low selectivity returns many rows, and a high selectivity returns few rows. The base is the multiple of the rows in both tables after local predicates (WHERE clause) on joined tables and aggregations are applied. This algorithm is different from determining how many rows match a search condition.

How Selectivity of a JOIN Clause Is Determined

You can calculate the selectivity of a JOIN clause by using the density of the data. The query optimizer determines selectivity of a JOIN clause based on the following parameters:

- If statistics are available, join selectivity is based on the density of the index for all of the columns.

- If statistics are unavailable because indexes do not exist, existing indexes are not useful, or if a WHERE clause is not included in the query, the query optimizer processes the query more efficiently by:

  - Applying an appropriate join strategy.

  - Using other physical operators.

  - Building column statistics dynamically.

  - The number of rows in each table of the join.

Density of a JOIN Clause

The density of a JOIN clause is the average percentage of duplicates between the inner and outer tables. The query optimizer uses the density of a JOIN clause to determine which table is processed as the inner table, and which table is processed as the outer table.

- An index with a large number of duplicates has high join density, which is not very selective for joins.

  For example, the **orders_details** table contains many orders for one customer.

- A unique index has a low join density, which is highly selective.

  For example, the **customer** table lists each customer only once. The **customer ID** column is unique.

If an index has a low join density, the query optimizer can access data by using a clustered or nonclustered index. However, only a clustered index is typically useful for indexes with a high join density.

Example

In this example, use the following assumptions to determine how the query optimizer produces a execution plan:

- The **employee** table contains 1,000 rows.

- The **department** table contains 100 rows (unique departments).

- The data is evenly distributed (10 employees per department).

- No indexes or statistics exist.

```
USE credit
SELECT *
FROM department AS dept INNER JOIN employee AS empl
ON dept.deptno = empl.deptno
```

When indexes do not exist on columns that are joined, the query optimizer uses a join strategy that determines which table is the outer table and which table is the inner table. It does this by evaluating the row ratio between tables.

If any search conditions exist in the WHERE clause, the query optimizer may use these conditions first to determine how to join the tables. This determination is based on selectivity.

How Joins Are Processed

```
USE credit
SELECT m.member_no, c.charge_no, c.charge_amt, c.statement_no
FROM member AS m INNER JOIN charge AS c
ON m.member_no = c.member_no
WHERE c.member_no = 5678
```

Unique nonclustered index

member

member_no	...
.	.
.	.
5678	Chen
.	.
.	.

Result

member_no	charge_no	...
5678	30257	
5678	17673	
5678	15259	
5678	16351	
5678	32778	
5678	48897	
5678	60611	
5678	66794	
5678	74396	
5678	76840	
5678	86173	
5678	87902	
5678	99607	

(13 row(s) affected

Nonclustered index

charge

charge_no	member_no	...
.	.	
15259	5678	
.	.	
16351	5678	
.	.	
17673	5678	
.	.	

An understanding of how the query optimizer processes join operations enables you to determine what types of indexes are useful to create.

Joins are processed as pairs. Regardless of how many tables you are combining, joins are always between two tables. The result of these joins is called an *intermediate result*. Intermediate results can then be joined to another table by using any of the join algorithms. For each join, the query optimizer will determine the appropriate join algorithm to use.

When processing join operations, the query optimizer typically:

- Determines the order in which the tables are processed, based on indexes, selectivity, and density.

  Order is not determined by the order of the table referenced in the SELECT statement.

- Identifies which table is the optimal outer table.

- Finds all matching rows in inner table for each qualifying row in the outer table.

Evaluating the Use of Indexes

The selectivity and density of a JOIN clause affects which type of index is most useful for processing the query.

- An index on the column that is specified in the WHERE clause can influence which table is used as the outer table and which join strategy is used. Selectivity determines which table is the inner table.

- The query optimizer automatically considers the use of redundant JOIN clauses and conditions in the WHERE clause.

Example

In this example, there is a unique nonclustered index on the **member_no** column in the **member** table, and a nonclustered index on the **member_no** column in the **charge** table. Both indexes are useful for processing the query.

```
USE credit
SELECT m.member_no, c.charge_no, c.charge_amt, c.statement_no
FROM member AS m INNER JOIN charge AS c
ON m.member_no = c.member_no
WHERE c.member_no = 5678
```

The query optimizer converts the search criteria in the WHERE clause so that the query is processed as:

WHERE m.member_no = 5678

By converting the **member** table to the outer table, the query optimizer limits the search, because the **member** table has only one qualifying row, whereas the **charge** table has many rows.

How Nested Loop Joins Are Processed

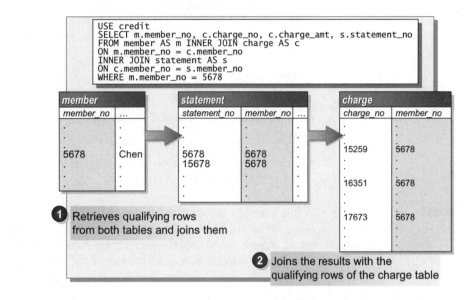

```
USE credit
SELECT m.member_no, c.charge_no, c.charge_amt, s.statement_no
FROM member AS m INNER JOIN charge AS c
ON m.member_no = c.member_no
INNER JOIN statement AS s
ON c.member_no = s.member_no
WHERE m.member_no = 5678
```

If there is a JOIN clause in the query, the query optimizer evaluates the number of tables, indexes, and joins to determine the optimal order, and what join strategy to use. The query optimizer processes nested loop joins as nested iterations.

Defining Nested Iteration

A *nested iteration* is when the query optimizer constructs a set of nested loops, and the result set grows as it progresses through the rows. The query optimizer performs the following steps.

1. Finds a row from the first table.

2. Uses that row to scan the next table.

3. Uses the result of the previous table to scan the next table.

Evaluating Join Combinations

The query optimizer automatically evaluates at least four or more possible join combinations, even if those combinations are not specified in the join predicate. You do not have to add redundant clauses. The query optimizer balances the cost and uses statistics to determine the number of join combinations that it evaluates. Evaluating every possible join combination is inefficient and costly.

Evaluating Cost of Query Performance

When the query optimizer performs a nested join, you should be aware that certain costs are incurred. Nested loop joins are far superior to both merge joins and hash joins when executing small transactions, such as those affecting only a small set of rows. The query optimizer:

- Uses nested loop joins if the outer input is quite small and the inner input is indexed and quite large.

- Uses the smaller input as the outer table.

- Requires that a useful index exist on the join predicate for the inner table.

- Always uses a nested loop join strategy if the join operation uses an operator other than an equality operator.

Example

In this example, the **member** table (10,000 rows) is joined to the **charge** table (100,000 rows), and the **charge** table is joined to the **statement** table (20,000 rows). Nonclustered indexes exist on the **member_no** column in each table. The query optimizer processes the join as the **member** table joined to the **statement** table, and the result of that join is combined with the **charge** table.

```
USE credit
SELECT m.member_no, c.charge_no, c.charge_amt, s.statement_no
FROM member AS m INNER JOIN charge AS c
     ON m.member_no = c.member_no
INNER JOIN statement AS s
     ON c.member_no = s.member_no
WHERE m.member_no = 5678
```

The query optimizer performs the following steps to process the query:

1. Retrieves the qualifying rows from the **member** table and the **statement** table, and then joins the result by using the nested loop join strategy.

2. Retrieves the qualifying rows from the **charge** table, and then joins that result with the results of the first nested loop join by using another nested loop join strategy.

Multimedia: How Merge Joins Are Processed

The columns of the join conditions are used as inputs to process a merge join. SQL Server performs the following steps when using a merge join strategy:

1. Gets the first input values from each input set.

2. Compares input values.

3. Performs a merge algorithm.

   - If the input values are equal, the rows are returned.

   - If the input values are not equal, the lower value is discarded, and the next input value from that input is used for the next comparison.

4. Repeats the process until all of the rows from one of the input sets have been processed.

5. Evaluates any remaining search conditions in the query and returns only rows that qualify.

Note Only one pass per input is done. The merge join operation ends after all of the input values of one input have been evaluated. The remaining values from the other input are not processed.

Considerations When Merge Joins Are Used

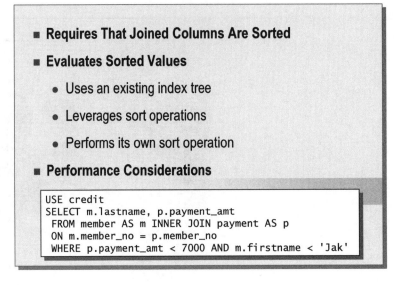

- ■ **Requires That Joined Columns Are Sorted**
- ■ **Evaluates Sorted Values**
  - Uses an existing index tree
  - Leverages sort operations
  - Performs its own sort operation
- ■ **Performance Considerations**

```
USE credit
SELECT m.lastname, p.payment_amt
 FROM member AS m INNER JOIN payment AS p
 ON m.member_no = p.member_no
 WHERE p.payment_amt < 7000 AND m.firstname < 'Jak'
```

A merge uses two sorted inputs and then merges them.

Requires That Joined Columns Are Sorted

If you execute a query with join operations, and the joined columns are in sorted order, the query optimizer processes the query by using a merge join strategy. A merge join is very efficient because the columns are already sorted, and it requires less page I/O.

Evaluates Sorted Values

For the query optimizer to use the merge join, the inputs must be sorted. The query optimizer evaluates sorted values in the following order:

1. Uses an existing index tree (most typical). The query optimizer can use the index tree from a clustered index or a covered nonclustered index.

2. Leverages sort operations that the GROUP BY, ORDER BY, and CUBE clauses use. The sorting operation only has to be performed once.

3. Performs its own sort operation in which a SORT operator is displayed when graphically viewing the execution plan. The query optimizer does this very rarely.

Example 1

In this example, a clustered index exists on the **member_no** column of the **payment** table, and a unique clustered index exists on the **member_no** column of the **member** table. The query optimizer scans the member table and the payment table by using the clustered index for each table. After scanning the contents of each table, the query optimizer performs a merge join between both tables, because both inputs are already sorted from the clustered indexes. This is a merge join/inner join.

```
USE credit
SELECT m.lastname, p.payment_amt
 FROM member AS m INNER JOIN payment AS p
     ON m.member_no = p.member_no
 WHERE p.payment_amt < 7000 AND m.firstname < 'Jak'
```

Example 2

In this example, a unique clustered index exists on the **member_no** column of the **member** table, and the query explicitly specifies an ORDER BY clause on the **member_no** column of the **payment** table.

```
USE credit
SELECT m.lastname, m.firstname, p.payment_dt
  FROM member AS m INNER JOIN payment AS p
     ON m.member_no = p.member_no
  ORDER BY p.member_no
```

Performance Considerations

Consider the following facts about the query optimizer's use of the merge join:

- SQL Server performs a merge join for all types of join operations (except cross join or full join operations), including UNION operations.

- A merge join operation may be a one-to-one, one-to-many, or many-to-many operation.

  If the merge join is a many-to-many operation, SQL Server uses a temporary table to store the rows. If duplicate values from each input exist, one of the inputs rewinds to the start of the duplicates as each duplicate value from the other input is processed.

- Query performance for a merge join is very fast, but the cost can be high if the query optimizer must perform its own sort operation.

  If the data volume is large and the desired data can be obtained presorted from existing Balanced-Tree (B-Tree) indexes, merge join is often the fastest join algorithm.

- A merge join is typically used if the two join inputs have a large amount of data and are sorted on their join columns (for example, if the join inputs were obtained by scanning sorted indexes).

- Merge join operations can only be performed with an equality operator in the join predicate.

How Hash Joins Are Processed

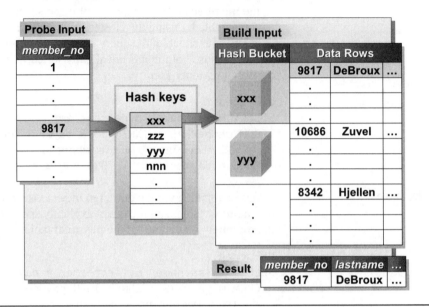

Hashing is a strategy for dividing data into equal sets of a manageable size based on a given property or characteristic. The grouped data can then be used to determine whether a particular data item matches an existing value.

Note Duplicate data or ranges of data are not useful for hash joins because the data is not organized together or in order.

When a Hash Is Join Used

The query optimizer uses a hash join option when it estimates that it is more efficient than processing queries by using a nested loop or merge join. It typically uses a hash join when an index does not exist or when existing indexes are not useful.

Assigns a Build and Probe Input

The query optimizer assigns a *build* and *probe input*. If the query optimizer incorrectly assigns the build and probe input (this may occur because of imprecise density estimates), it reverses them dynamically. The ability to change input roles dynamically is called *role reversal*.

Build input consists of the column values from a table with the lowest number of rows. Build input creates a *hash table* in memory to store these values.

Hash bucket is a storage place in the hash table in which each row of the build input is inserted. Rows from one of the join tables are placed into the hash bucket where the hash key value of the row matches the hash key value of the bucket. Hash buckets are stored as a linked list and only contain the columns that are needed for the query.

A hash table contains hash buckets. The hash table is created from the build input.

Probe input consists of the column values from the table with the most rows. Probe input is what the build input checks to find a match in the hash buckets.

Note The query optimizer uses column or index statistics to help determine which input is the smaller of the two.

Processing a Hash Join

The following list is a simplified description of how the query optimizer processes a hash join. It is not intended to be comprehensive because the algorithm is very complex. SQL Server:

1. Reads the probe input. Each probe input is processed one row at a time.

2. Performs the hash algorithm against each probe input and generates a hash key value.

3. Finds the hash bucket that matches the hash key value.

4. Accesses the hash bucket and looks for the matching row.

5. Returns the row if a match is found.

Performance Considerations

Consider the following facts about the hash joins that the query optimizer uses:

- Similar to merge joins, a hash join is very efficient, because it uses hash buckets, which are like a dynamic index but with less overhead for combining rows.

- Hash joins can be performed for all types of join operations (except cross join operations), including UNION and DIFFERENCE operations.

- A hash operator can remove duplicates and group data, such as SUM (salary) GROUP BY department. The query optimizer uses only one input for both the build and probe roles.

- If join inputs are large and are of similar size, the performance of a hash join operation is similar to a merge join with prior sorting. However, if the size of the join inputs is significantly different, the performance of a hash join is often much faster.

- Hash joins can process large, unsorted, non-indexed inputs efficiently. Hash joins are useful in complex queries because the intermediate results:

  - Are not indexed (unless explicitly saved to disk and then indexed).

  - Are often not sorted for the next operation in the execution plan.

- The query optimizer can identify incorrect estimates and make corrections dynamically to process the query more efficiently.

- A hash join reduces the need for database *denormalization*. Denormalization is typically used to achieve better performance by reducing join operations despite redundancy, such as inconsistent updates. Hash joins give you the option to vertically partition your data as part of your physical database design. Vertical partitioning represents groups of columns from a single table in separate files or indexes.

Note   For additional information on hash joins, search on "understanding hash joins" in SQL Server Books Online.

Lab B: Analyzing Queries That Use Different Join Strategies

Objectives

After completing this lab, you will be able to evaluate how the query optimizer processes a query by using nested loop, merge, and hash join strategies.

Prerequisites

Before working on this lab, you must have:

- Script files, which are located in C:\Moc\2073A\Labfiles\L14.

Lab Setup

To complete this lab, you must have either:

- Completed the prior lab, or

- Executed the C:\Moc\2073A\Batches\Restore14B.cmd batch file.

    This command file restores the **credit** database to a state required for this lab.

For More Information

If you require help in executing files, search SQL Query Analyzer Help for "Execute a query".

Other resources that you can use include:

- The **credit** database schema.

- Microsoft SQL Server Books Online.

Scenario

The organization of the classroom is meant to simulate that of a worldwide trading firm named Northwind Traders. Its fictitious domain name is nwtraders.msft. The primary DNS server for nwtraders.msft is the instructor computer, which has an Internet Protocol (IP) address of 192.168.*x*.200 (where *x* is the assigned classroom number). The name of the instructor computer is London.

The following table provides the user name, computer name, and IP address for each student computer in the fictitious **nwtraders.msft** domain. Find the user name for your computer, and make a note of it.

User name	Computer name	IP address
SQLAdmin1	Vancouver	192.168.*x*.1
SQLAdmin2	Denver	192.168.*x*.2
SQLAdmin3	Perth	192.168.*x*.3
SQLAdmin4	Brisbane	192.168.*x*.4
SQLAdmin5	Lisbon	192.168.*x*.5
SQLAdmin6	Bonn	192.168.*x*.6
SQLAdmin7	Lima	192.168.*x*.7
SQLAdmin8	Santiago	192.168.*x*.8
SQLAdmin9	Bangalore	192.168.*x*.9
SQLAdmin10	Singapore	192.168.*x*.10
SQLAdmin11	Casablanca	192.168.*x*.11
SQLAdmin12	Tunis	192.168.*x*.12
SQLAdmin13	Acapulco	192.168.*x*.13
SQLAdmin14	Miami	192.168.*x*.14
SQLAdmin15	Auckland	192.168.*x*.15
SQLAdmin16	Suva	192.168.*x*.16
SQLAdmin17	Stockholm	192.168.*x*.17
SQLAdmin18	Moscow	192.168.*x*.18
SQLAdmin19	Caracas	192.168.*x*.19
SQLAdmin20	Montevideo	192.168.*x*.20
SQLAdmin21	Manila	192.168.*x*.21
SQLAdmin22	Tokyo	192.168.*x*.22
SQLAdmin23	Khartoum	192.168.*x*.23
SQLAdmin24	Nairobi	192.168.*x*.24

Estimated time to complete this lab: 30 minutes

Exercise 1
Processing Nested Loop Joins

In this exercise, you will create indexes on the **member** and **charge** tables and observe how the query optimizer processes the query by using a nested loop join strategy.

You can open, review, and execute sections of the NestedLoopJoin.sql script file in C:\Moc\2073A\Labfiles\L14, or type and execute the provided Transact-SQL statements.

▶ **To create indexes**

In this procedure, you will create indexes on the **member** and **charge** tables.

1. Log on to the **NWTraders** classroom domain by using the information in the following table.

Option	Value
User name	**SQLAdminx** (where *x* corresponds to your computer name as designated in the **nwtraders.msft** classroom domain)
Password	**password**

2. Open SQL Query Analyzer and, if requested, log in to the (local) server with Microsoft Windows Authentication.

   You have permission to log in to and administer SQL Server because you are logged as **SQLAdminx**, which is a member of the Microsoft Windows 2000 local group, Administrators. All members of this group are automatically mapped to the SQL Server **sysadmin** role.

3. With SQL Query Analyzer, type and execute this statement to drop existing indexes on the **member** and **charge** tables:

```
USE credit
EXEC index_cleanup member
EXEC index_cleanup charge
```

4. Type and execute this statement to create a unique, nonclustered composite index on the **lastname** and **firstname** columns of the **member** table:

```
USE credit
CREATE UNIQUE nonclustered INDEX mbr_name
   ON member(lastname, firstname)
```

5. Type and execute this statement to create a nonclustered index on the **member_no** column of the **charge** table:

```
USE credit
CREATE nonclustered INDEX chg_mem_no
   ON charge(member_no)
```

▶ **To observe how a query is processed by using a nested loop join strategy**

In this procedure, you will set the statistics option to ON, execute a query, and record the statistical information.

1. Type and execute this statement to set the statistics option to ON:

```
SET STATISTICS IO ON
```

2. In the Query window, on the **Query** menu, click **Show Execution Plan**.

3. Type and execute this SELECT statement to retrieve member number, last name, and charge number for members with last name Barr and first name Bos.

```
USE credit
SELECT member.member_no, lastname, charge_no
  FROM member JOIN charge
  ON member.member_no = charge.member_no
  WHERE member.lastname = 'BARR'
      AND firstname = 'BOS'
```

4. Record the statistical information for the **member** table.

Information	Result
Scan count	
Number of logical reads	
Number and name of indexes used to process the query	

5. Record the statistical information for the **charge** table.

Information	Result
Scan count	
Number of logical reads	
Number and name of indexes used to process the query	

Why does the **member** table have three I/O, whereas the **charge** table requires 26 I/O?

_____

_____

6. Click the **Execution Plan** tab to display the execution plan graphically.

7. Examine the execution plan.

   What strategy did the query optimizer use to find the rows in both tables?

   _____

   _____

   _____

   _____

Exercise 2
Processing Merge Joins

In this exercise, you will drop all indexes on the **member** and **charge** tables, execute a query, and evaluate the execution plan. Then, you will create indexes on the **member** and **charge** tables, re-execute a query, and compare page I/O.

You can open, review, and execute sections of the MergeJoin.sql script file in C:\Moc\2073A\Labfiles\L14, or type and execute the provided Transact-SQL statements.

▶ **To observe how the query optimizer processes a query against a table with no indexes**

In this procedure, you will drop all indexes on the **member** and **charge** tables, execute a query, and record the statistical information.

1. Type and execute these statements to drop existing indexes on the **member** and **charge** tables:

```
USE credit
EXEC index_cleanup member
EXEC index_cleanup charge
```

2. With the STATISTICS IO option set to ON, type and execute this SELECT statement to retrieve member number, last name, and charge number for members with the last name Hahn:

```
USE credit
    SELECT member.member_no, lastname, charge_no
    FROM member JOIN charge
    ON member.member_no = charge.member_no
    WHERE member.lastname = 'HAHN'
```

Note This query is referred to as the original query throughout this exercise.

---

3. Record the statistical information for the **member** table.

Information	Result
Scan count	
Number of logical reads	
Number and name of indexes used to process the query	

4. Record the statistical information for the **charge** table.

Information	Result
Scan count	
Number of logical reads	
Number and name of indexes used to process the query	

▶ **To create indexes and evaluate how the query optimizer processes a query against a table with indexes**

In this procedure, you will create indexes on the **member** and **charge** tables, re-execute the original query, and evaluate how the query optimizer processed the query by using a merge join strategy.

1. Type and execute this statement to create a nonclustered, composite index on the **member_no** and **lastname** columns of the **member** table:

```
USE credit
CREATE nonclustered INDEX mbr_name
   ON member(member_no, lastname)
```

2. Type and execute this statement to create a nonclustered, composite index on the **member_no** and **charge_no** columns of the **charge** table:

```
USE credit
CREATE nonclustered INDEX chg_charge_no
   ON charge(member_no, charge_no)
```

3. Re-execute the original query, which retrieves member number, last name, and charge number for members with the last name Hahn.

Original Query

```
USE credit
SELECT member.member_no, lastname, charge_no
  FROM member JOIN charge
  ON member.member_no = charge.member_no
     WHERE member.lastname = 'HAHN'
```

4. Record the statistical information for the **member** table.

Information	Result
Scan count	
Number of logical reads	
Number and name of indexes used to process the query	

5. Record the statistical information for the **charge** table.

Information	Result
Scan count	
Number of logical reads	
Number and name of indexes used to process the query	

6. Compare the statistical information for a query executed against a table with no indexes, and the same query executed against a table with useful indexes.

   Was I/O reduced by adding indexes?

   _____

   _____

7. Click the **Execution Plan** tab to display the execution plan graphically.

8. Examine the execution plan.

   What join strategy did the query optimizer use to process the join?

   _____

   _____

   _____

   _____

   Why did the query optimizer select this strategy?

   _____

   _____

   _____

   _____

Exercise 3
Processing Hash Joins

In this exercise, you will drop all indexes on the **member** and **charge** tables, execute a query, and observe how the query optimizer processes the query by using a hash join strategy.

You can open, review, and execute sections of the HashJoin.sql script file in C:\Moc\2073A\Labfiles\L14, or type and execute the provided Transact-SQL statements.

▶ **To observe how a query is processed by using a hash join strategy**

In this procedure, you will drop all indexes on the **member** and **charge** tables, execute a query, and evaluate how the query optimizer processed the query.

1. Type and execute these statements to drop existing indexes on the **member** and **charge** tables:

```
USE credit
EXEC index_cleanup member
EXEC index_cleanup charge
```

2. Type and execute this SELECT statement to retrieve member number, last name, and charge number for members with the last name Barr and the first name Bos:

```
USE credit
SELECT m.member_no, lastname, charge_no
    FROM member m JOIN charge c
    ON m.member_no = c.member_no
    WHERE m.lastname = 'BARR'
    AND firstname = 'BOS'
```

3. Click the **Execution Plan** tab to display the execution plan graphically.

4. Examine the execution plan.

   What strategy did the query optimizer use to find these rows? Why?

   _____

   _____

   _____

   _____

Recommended Practices

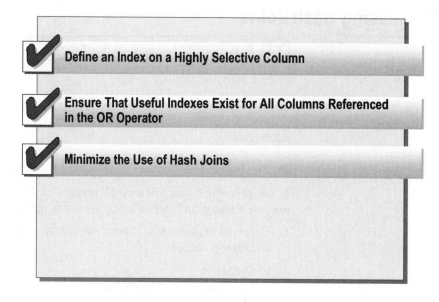

When analyzing queries that use the AND and OR operators or join operations, you should consider the following practices:

- Define an index on a highly selective column. The best way to index for queries that contain the AND operator is to have at least one highly selective search criterion, and define an index on that column.

- Ensure that useful indexes exist for all columns referenced in the OR operator.Minimize the use of hash joins by creating useful indexes and writing efficient queries.

Review

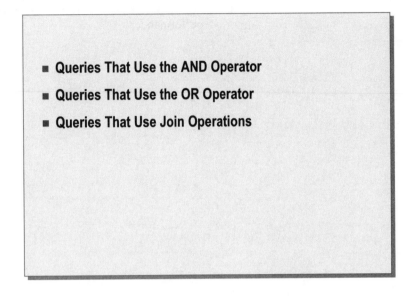

- **Queries That Use the AND Operator**
- **Queries That Use the OR Operator**
- **Queries That Use Join Operations**

1. You are writing queries for an application. You are not sure about the benefits of using multiple restrictions in the WHERE clause by using the AND operator. What are some of the advantages of using multiple AND operators in your queries?

2. A query is performing poorly. The query optimizer currently performs a table scan even though indexes exist on some of the columns referenced in the WHERE clause. What could be causing the poor performance of the following query?

```
SELECT * FROM member
   WHERE lastname = 'GOHAN'
   OR expr_dt < '12/31/1999'
   OR region_no = 7
```

3. One of your queries is performing adequately, but you would like to determine whether you could improve its performance. Currently, the query optimizer performs a hash join operation. What can be done to possibly improve performance?

Microsoft®
Training &
Certification

Module 15: Managing Transactions and Locks

Contents

Microsoft®

Project Lead: Rich Rose
Instructional Designers: Rich Rose, Cheryl Hoople, Marilyn McGill
Instructional Software Design Engineers: Karl Dehmer, Carl Raebler,
Rick Byham
Technical Lead: Karl Dehmer
Subject Matter Experts: Karl Dehmer, Carl Raebler, Rick Byham
Graphic Artist: Kirsten Larson (Independent Contractor)
Editing Manager: Lynette Skinner
Editor: Wendy Cleary
Copy Editor: Edward McKillop (S&T Consulting)
Production Manager: Miracle Davis
Production Coordinator: Jenny Boe
Production Support: Lori Walker (S&T Consulting)
Test Manager: Sid Benavente
Courseware Testing: TestingTesting123
Classroom Automation: Lorrin Smith-Bates
Creative Director, Media/Sim Services: David Mahlmann
Web Development Lead: Lisa Pease
CD Build Specialist: Julie Challenger
Online Support: David Myka (S&T Consulting)
Localization Manager: Rick Terek
Operations Coordinator: John Williams
Manufacturing Support: Laura King; Kathy Hershey
Lead Product Manager, Release Management: Bo Galford
Lead Product Manager, Data Base: Margo Crandall
Group Manager, Courseware Infrastructure: David Bramble
Group Product Manager, Content Development: Dean Murray
General Manager: Robert Stewart

Overview

- **Introduction to Transactions and Locks**
- **Managing Transactions**
- **SQL Server Locking**
- **Managing Locks**

Objectives

After completing this module, you will be able to:

- Describe transaction processing.
- Execute, cancel, or roll back a transaction.
- Identify locking concurrency issues.
- Identify resource items that can be locked and the types of locks.
- Describe lock compatibility.
- Describe how Microsoft® SQL Server™ 2000 uses dynamic locking.
- Set locking options and display locking information.

Introduction to Transactions and Locks

- **Transactions Ensure That Multiple Data Modifications Are Processed Together**
- **Locks Prevent Update Conflicts**
  - Transactions are serializable
  - Locking is automatic
  - Locks allow concurrent use of data
- **Concurrency Control**

Transactions use locking to prevent other users from changing or reading data in a transaction that has not completed. Locking is required in online transaction processing (OLTP) for multiuser systems. SQL Server uses the transaction log to ensure that updates are complete and recoverable.

Transactions

Transactions ensure that multiple data modifications are processed as a unit; this is known as *atomicity*. For example, a banking transaction might credit one account and debit another. Both steps must be completed together. SQL Server supports transaction processing to manage multiple transactions.

Locks

Locks prevent update conflicts. Users cannot read or modify data that other users are in the process of changing. For example, if you want to compute an aggregate and ensure that another transaction does not modify the set of data that is used to compute the aggregate, you can request that the system hold locks on the data. Consider the following facts about locks:

- Locks make possible the serialization of transactions so that only one person at a time can change a data element. For example, locks in an airline reservation system ensure that only one person is assigned a particular seat.

- SQL Server dynamically sets and adjusts the appropriate level of locking during a transaction. It also is possible to manually control how some of the locks are used.

- Locks are necessary for concurrent transactions to allow users to access and update data at the same time. High concurrency means that there are a number of users who are experiencing good response time with little conflict. From the system administrator's perspective, the primary concerns are the number of users, the number of transactions, and the throughput. From the user's perspective, the overriding concern is response time.

Concurrency Control

Concurrency control ensures that modifications that one person makes do not adversely affect modifications that others make. There are two types.

■ Pessimistic concurrency control locks data when data is read in preparation for an update. Other users cannot then perform actions that would alter the underlying data until the user who applied the lock is done with the data. Use pessimistic concurrency where high contention for data exists and the cost of protecting the data with locks is less than the cost of rolling back transactions if concurrency conflicts occur.

■ Optimistic concurrency control does not lock data when data is initially read. Rather, when an update is performed, SQL Server checks to determine whether the underlying data was changed since it initially read it. If so, the user receives an error, the transaction rolls back, and the user must start over. Use optimistic concurrency when low contention for data exists and the cost of occasionally rolling back a transaction is less than the cost of locking data when it is read.

SQL Server supports a wide range of optimistic and pessimistic concurrency control mechanisms. Users specify the type of concurrency control by specifying the transaction isolation level for a connection.

◆ Managing Transactions

- Multimedia Presentation: SQL Server Transactions
- Transaction Recovery and Checkpoints
- Considerations for Using Transactions
- Setting the Implicit Transactions Option
- Restrictions on User-defined Transactions

Multimedia Presentation: SQL Server Transactions

There are two kinds of transactions in SQL Server:

- In an implicit transaction, each Transact-SQL statement, such as INSERT, UPDATE, or DELETE, executes as a transaction.

- In an explicit or user-defined transaction, the statements of the transaction are grouped between a BEGIN TRANSACTION and a COMMIT TRANSACTION clause.

A user can set a savepoint, or marker, within a transaction. A savepoint defines a location to which a transaction can return if part of a transaction is conditionally cancelled. The transaction must then proceed to completion or be rolled back entirely.

SQL Server transactions employ the following syntax.

Syntax   BEGIN TRAN[SACTION] [*transaction_name* | *@tran_name_variable* [WITH MARK ['*description*']]]

The *transaction_name* option specifies a user-defined transaction name. The *tran_name_variable* is the name of a user-defined variable containing a valid transaction name. WITH MARK specifies that the transaction is marked in the transaction log. *Description* is a string that describes the mark that WITH MARK allows for restoring a transaction log to a named mark.

Syntax   SAVE TRAN[SACTION] {savepoint_name | @savepoint_variable}

Syntax   BEGIN DISTRIBUTED TRAN[SACTION]
    [transaction_name | @tran_name_variable]

Syntax   COMMIT [TRAN[SACTION] [*transaction_name* | *@tran_name_variable*]]

Syntax

ROLLBACK [TRAN[SACTION] [*transaction_name* | *@tran_name_variable* | *savepoint_name* | *@savepoint_variable*]]

Example

This example defines a transaction to transfer funds between the checking and savings accounts of one customer.

```
BEGIN TRAN fund_transfer
    EXEC debit_checking 100, 'account1'
    EXEC credit_savings 100, 'account1'
COMMIT TRAN fund_transfer
```

Describing the Transaction Log

Every transaction is recorded in a transaction log to maintain database consistency and to aid in recovery. The log is a storage area that automatically tracks all changes to a database, with the exception of non-logged operations. Modifications are recorded in the log on disk as they are executed, before they are written in the database.

Transaction Recovery and Checkpoints

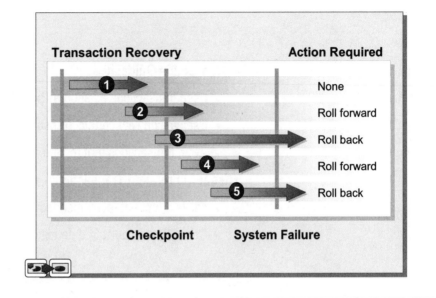

Because the transaction log records all transactions, SQL Server can recover data automatically in the event of a power loss, system software failure, client problem, or a transaction cancellation request.

SQL Server automatically guarantees that all committed transactions are reflected in the database in the event of a failure. It uses the transaction log to roll forward all committed transactions and to roll back any uncommitted transactions. In the slide example:

- Transaction 1 is committed before the checkpoint, so it is reflected in the database.

- Transactions 2 and 4 were committed after the checkpoint, so they must be reconstructed from the log (rolled forward).

- Transactions 3 and 5 were not committed, so SQL Server rolls them back.

Initially, pages are the same in the data cache and on the disk. The following process then occurs:

- Changes appear in the data cache as transactions are committed.

- As the cache becomes full, the changed pages are written to disk.

- When a checkpoint occurs, the cache is written to disk. The disk is once again the same as the cache.

Important   Use a write-caching disk controller with SQL Server only if it was designed for use with a database server. Failure to do so compromises the ability of SQL Server to manage transactions. A write-caching disk controller can make it appear that write-ahead logging is complete, even when it has not.

Considerations for Using Transactions

- **Transaction Guidelines**
  - Keep transactions as short as possible
  - Use caution with certain Transact-SQL statements
  - Avoid transactions that require user interaction
- **Issues in Nesting Transactions**
  - Allowed, but not recommended
  - Use **@@trancount** to determine nesting level

It is usually a good idea to keep transactions short and to avoid nesting transactions.

Transaction Guidelines

Transactions should be as short as possible. Longer transactions increase the likelihood that users will not be able to access locked data. Some methods to keep transactions short include the following:

- To minimize transaction time, use caution when you use certain Transact-SQL statements, such as a WHILE statement or Data Definition Language (DDL) statements.

- Do not require input from users during a transaction. Address issues that require user interaction before you start the transaction. For example, if you are updating a customer record, obtain the necessary information from the user before you begin the transaction.

- INSERT, UPDATE, and DELETE should be the primary statements in a transaction, and they should be written to affect the fewest number of rows. A transaction should never be smaller than a logical unit of work.

- Do not open a transaction while browsing through data, if at all possible. Transactions should not start until all preliminary data analysis has been completed.

- Access the least amount of data possible while in a transaction. This decreases the number of locked rows and reduces contention.

Issues in Nesting Transactions

Consider the following issues regarding nesting transactions:

- It is possible to nest transactions, but nesting does not affect how SQL Server processes the transaction. You should use nesting carefully, if at all, because the failure to commit or roll back a transaction leaves locks in place indefinitely.

  Only the outermost BEGIN...COMMIT statement pair applies. Usually, transaction nesting occurs when stored procedures with BEGIN...COMMIT statement pairs or triggers invoke one another.

- You can use the **@@trancount** global variable to determine whether any open transactions exist and how deeply they are nested:

  - **@@trancount** equals zero when no open transactions exist.

  - A BEGIN TRAN statement increments **@@trancount** by one, and a ROLLBACK TRAN statement sets **@@trancount** to zero.

Note   You also can use the DBCC OPENTRAN statement within your current session to retrieve information on active transactions.

Setting the Implicit Transactions Option

■ **Automatically Starts a Transaction When You Execute Certain Statements**

■ **Nested Transactions Are Not Allowed**

■ **Transaction Must Be Explicitly Completed with COMMIT or ROLLBACK TRANSACTION**

■ **By Default, Setting Is Off**

```
SET IMPLICIT_TRANSACTIONS ON
```

In most cases, it is best to define transactions explicitly with the BEGIN TRANSACTION statement. However, for applications that were originally developed on systems other than SQL Server, the SET IMPLICIT_TRANSACTIONS option can be useful. It sets the implicit transaction mode for a connection.

Syntax

SET IMPLICIT_TRANSACTIONS {ON | OFF}

Consider the following facts when you set implicit transactions:

■ When the implicit transaction mode for a connection is on, executing any of the following statements triggers the start of a transaction:

ALTER TABLE	INSERT
CREATE	OPEN
DELETE	REVOKE
DROP	SELECT
FETCH	TRUNCATE TABLE
GRANT	UPDATE

■ Nested transactions are not allowed. If the connection is already in an open transaction, the statements do not start a new transaction.

■ When the setting is on, the user must commit or roll back the transaction explicitly at the end of the transaction. Otherwise, the transaction and all data changes that it contains are rolled back when the user disconnects.

■ The setting is off by default.

Restrictions on User-defined Transactions

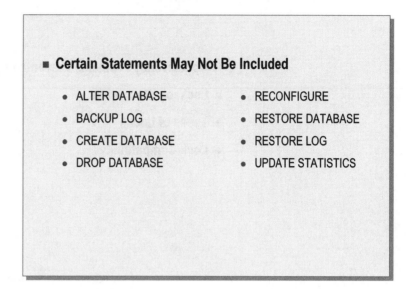

Some restrictions exist on user-defined transactions:

■ Certain statements may not be included inside an explicit transaction. For example, some are long-running operations that you are not likely to use within the context of a transaction. Restricted statements include the following statements:

- ALTER DATABASE

- BACKUP LOG

- CREATE DATABASE

- DROP DATABASE

- RECONFIGURE

- RESTORE DATABASE

- RESTORE LOG

- UPDATE STATISTICS

◆ SQL Server Locking

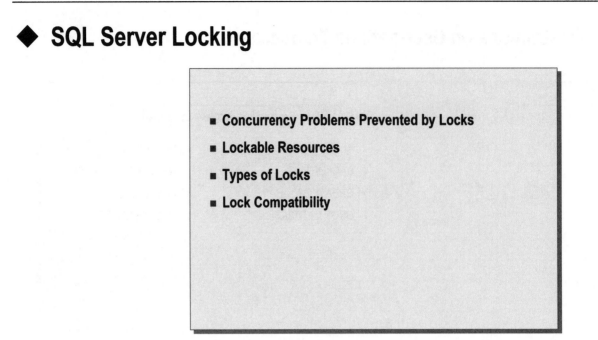

- ■ Concurrency Problems Prevented by Locks
- ■ Lockable Resources
- ■ Types of Locks
- ■ Lock Compatibility

This section describes concurrency issues, the resource items that can be locked, the types of locks that can be placed on those resources, and how locks can be combined.

Concurrency Problems Prevented by Locks

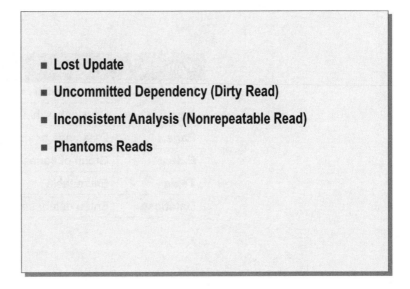

- Lost Update
- Uncommitted Dependency (Dirty Read)
- Inconsistent Analysis (Nonrepeatable Read)
- Phantoms Reads

Locks can prevent the following situations that compromise transaction integrity:

Lost Update   An update can get lost when a transaction overwrites the changes from another transaction. For example, two users can update the same information, but only the last change saved is reflected in the database.

Uncommitted Dependency (Dirty Read)   An uncommitted dependency occurs when a transaction reads uncommitted data from another transaction. The transaction can potentially make changes based on data that is either inaccurate or nonexistent.

Inconsistent Analysis (Nonrepeatable Read)   An inconsistent analysis occurs when a transaction reads the same row more than one time and when, between the two (or more) readings, another transaction modifies that row. Because the row was modified between readings within the same transaction, each reading produces different values, which introduces inconsistency.

For example, an editor reads the same document twice, but between each reading, the writer rewrites the document. When the editor reads the document for the second time, it has completely changed. The original reading is not repeatable, leading to confusion. It would be better if the editor only starts reading the document after the writer has completely finished writing it.

Phantom Reads   Phantom reads can occur when transactions are not isolated from one another. For example, you could perform an update on all records in a region at the same time that another transaction inserts a new record for the region. The next time that the transaction reads the data, an additional record is present.

Lockable Resources

Item	Description
RID	Row identifier
Key	Row lock within an index
Page	Data page or index page
Extent	Group of pages
Table	Entire table
Database	Entire database

For optimal performance, the number of locks that SQL Server maintains must be balanced with the amount of data that each lock holds. To minimize the cost of locking, SQL Server automatically locks resources at a level that is appropriate to the task. SQL Server can lock the following types of items.

Item	Description
RID	A row identifier—used to lock a single row within a table
Key	A row lock within an index—used to protect key ranges in serializable transactions
Page	An 8-KB data page or index page
Extent	A contiguous group of data pages or index pages—used during space allocation
Table	An entire table, including all data and indexes
Database	An entire database—used during the restoration of a database

Types of Locks

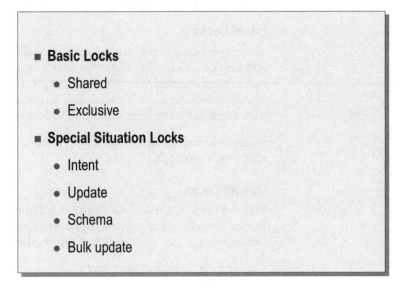

- **Basic Locks**
  - Shared
  - Exclusive
- **Special Situation Locks**
  - Intent
  - Update
  - Schema
  - Bulk update

SQL Server has two main types of locks: basic locks and locks for special situations.

Basic Locks

In general, read operations acquire shared locks, and write operations acquire exclusive locks.

Shared Locks

SQL Server typically uses shared (read) locks for operations that neither change nor update data. If SQL Server has applied a shared lock to a resource, a second transaction also can acquire a shared lock, even though the first transaction has not completed.

Consider the following facts about shared locks:

- They are used for read-only operations; data cannot be modified.
- SQL Server releases shared locks on a record as soon as the next record is read.
- A shared lock will exist until all rows that satisfy the query have been returned to the client.

Exclusive Locks

SQL Server uses exclusive (write) locks for the INSERT, UPDATE, and DELETE data modification statements.

Consider the following facts about exclusive locks:

- Only one transaction can acquire an exclusive lock on a resource.
- A transaction cannot acquire a shared lock on a resource that has an exclusive lock.
- A transaction cannot acquire an exclusive lock on a resource until all shared locks are released.

Special Situation Locks

Depending on the situation, SQL Server may use other types of locks:

Intent Locks

SQL Server uses intent locks internally to minimize locking conflicts. Intent locks establish a locking hierarchy so that other transactions cannot acquire locks at more inclusive levels. For example, if a transaction has an exclusive row-level lock on a specific customer record, the intent lock prevents another transaction from acquiring an exclusive lock at the table-level.

Intent locks include intent share (IS), intent exclusive (IX), and shared with intent exclusive (SIX).

Update Locks

SQL Server uses update locks when it will modify a page at a later point. Before it modifies the page, SQL Server promotes the update page lock to an exclusive page lock to prevent locking conflicts.

Consider the following facts about update locks. Update locks are:

- Acquired during the initial portion of an update operation when the pages are first being read.

- Compatible with shared locks.

Schema Locks

Schema locks ensure that a table or index is not dropped, or its schema modified, when it is referenced by another session.

SQL Server provides two types of schema locks:

- Schema stability (Sch-S), which ensures that a resource is not dropped.

- Schema modification (Sch-M), which ensures that other sessions do not reference a resource that is under modification.

Bulk Update Locks

Bulk update locks allow processes to bulk copy data concurrently into the same table while preventing other processes, that are not bulk-copying data, from accessing the table.

SQL Server uses bulk update locks when either of the following options is specified: the TABLOCK hint or the **table lock on bulk load** option, which is set using the **sp_tableoption** system stored procedure.

Lock Compatibility

- **Locks May or May Not Be Compatible with Other Locks**
- **Examples**
  - Shared locks are compatible with all locks except exclusive
  - Exclusive locks are not compatible with any other locks
  - Update locks are compatible only with shared locks

Locks may or may not be compatible with other locks. Locks have a *compatibility matrix* that shows which locks are compatible with other locks that are obtained on the same resource. The locks in the following table are listed in order from the least restrictive (shared) to the most restrictive (exclusive).

	Existing granted lock					
Requested lock	**IS**	**S**	**U**	**IX**	**SIX**	**X**
Intent shared (IS)	Yes	Yes	Yes	Yes	Yes	No
Shared (S)	Yes	Yes	Yes	No	No	No
Update (U)	Yes	Yes	No	No	No	No
Intent exclusive (IX)	Yes	No	No	Yes	No	No
Shared with intent exclusive (SIX)	Yes	No	No	No	No	No
Exclusive (X)	No	No	No	No	No	No

Note An IX lock is compatible with other IX locks because IX means the intention to update only some of the rows, rather than all of them.

In addition, compatibility for schema locks is as follows:

- The schema modification lock (Sch-M) is incompatible with all locks.
- The schema stability lock (Sch-S) is compatible with all locks except the schema modification lock (Sch-M).

◆ Managing Locks

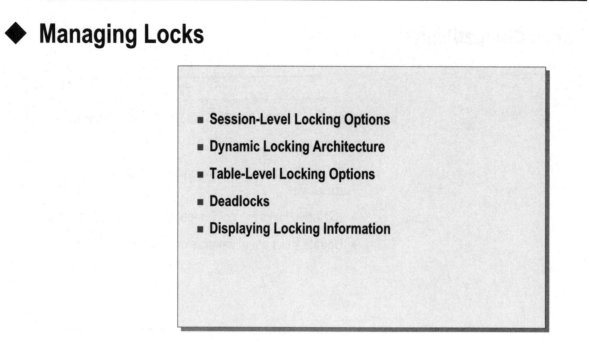

- Session-Level Locking Options
- Dynamic Locking Architecture
- Table-Level Locking Options
- Deadlocks
- Displaying Locking Information

This section describes locking options that you can specify at the session and table levels. It also describes how SQL Server handles deadlocks and how you can view information about locks.

Session-Level Locking Options

- **Transaction Isolation Level**
  - READ COMMITTED (DEFAULT)
  - READ UNCOMMITTED
  - REPEATABLE READ
  - SERIALIZABLE
- **Locking Timeout**
  - Limits time waiting for a locked resource
  - Use SET LOCK_TIMEOUT

SQL Server allows you to control locking options at the session level by setting the transaction isolation level.

Transaction Isolation Level

An *isolation level* protects a specified transaction from other transactions. Use the transaction isolation level to set the isolation level for all transactions during a session. When you set the isolation level, you specify the default locking behavior for all statements in your session.

Setting transaction isolation levels allows programmers to accept increased risk of integrity problems in exchange for greater concurrent access to data. The higher the isolation level, the longer locks are held and the more restrictive these locks are.

You can override a session-level isolation level in individual statements by using lock specification. You also can use the DBCC USEROPTIONS statement to specify transaction isolation for a statement.

Syntax

SET TRANSACTION ISOLATION LEVEL {READ COMMITTED | READ UNCOMMITTED | REPEATABLE READ | SERIALIZABLE}

The following table describes the locking isolation level options.

Option	Description
READ COMMITTED	Directs SQL Server to use shared locks while reading. At this level, you cannot experience dirty reads.
	Directs SQL Server to not issue shared locks and does not honor exclusive locks. You can experience dirty reads.
REPEATABLE READ	Indicates that dirty reads and nonrepeatable reads cannot occur. Read locks are held until the end of the transaction.
SERIALIZABLE	Prevents other users from updating or inserting new rows that match the criteria in the WHERE clause of the transaction. Phantoms cannot occur.

Example

The following example sets the isolation level for the current session to READ UNCOMMITTED and then checks DBCC USEROPTIONS to verify that SQL Server has made the change.

```
SET TRANSACTION ISOLATION LEVEL READ UNCOMMITTED
DBCC USEROPTIONS
```

Result

set option	value
textsize	64512
language	us_english
dateformat	mdy
datefirst	7
.	
.	
.	
isolation level	read uncommitted

(13 row(s) affected)

Note DBCC always prints the following message when it is executed:

```
DBCC execution completed. If DBCC printed error messages, see
your System Administrator.
```

Locking Timeout

With the SET LOCK_TIMEOUT option, it is possible to set the maximum amount of time that SQL Server allows a transaction to wait for the release of a blocked resource.

Syntax

SET LOCK_TIMEOUT *timeout_period*

timeout_period is the number of milliseconds that pass before SQL Server returns a locking error. A value of -1 (the default) indicates no timeout period. After you change it, the new setting is in effect for the remainder of the session.

Example

This example sets the lock timeout period to 180,000 milliseconds.

```
SET LOCK_TIMEOUT 180000
```

To determine the current session value, query the **@@lock_timeout** global variable.

Example

This example displays the current **@@lock_timeout** setting.

```
SELECT @@lock_timeout
```

Result

```
180000

(1 row(s) affected)
```

Dynamic Locking Architecture

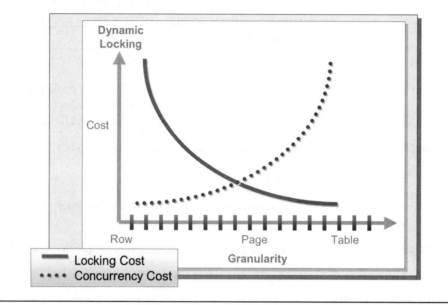

SQL Server uses a dynamic locking architecture to determine the most cost-effective locks. It automatically determines what locks are most appropriate when a query is executed, based on the characteristics of the schema and query.

SQL Server dynamically increases and decreases the granularity and types of locks. The query optimizer usually chooses the correct lock granularity at the time that the execution plan is compiled, thus minimizing the need to escalate locks.

For example, if an update acquires a large number of row-level locks and has locked a significant percentage of a table, the row-level locks are escalated to a table lock. Then the transaction holds the row-level locks, thereby reducing lock overhead.

Dynamic locking has the following advantages:

- Simplified database administration, because database administrators no longer have to be concerned with adjusting lock escalation thresholds

- Increased performance, because SQL Server minimizes system overhead by using locks appropriate to the task

Table-Level Locking Options

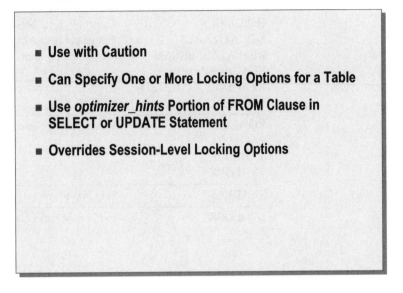

- Use with Caution
- Can Specify One or More Locking Options for a Table
- Use *optimizer_hints* Portion of FROM Clause in SELECT or UPDATE Statement
- Overrides Session-Level Locking Options

Although SQL Server uses dynamic locking architecture to select the best lock for your client, it is possible to specify table-level locking options. A table hint can specify a locking method for the query optimizer to use with a specific table and for a statement.

Note Use table-level locking options only after you thoroughly understand how your application works and have determined that the lock that you request will continue, over time, to be better than that which SQL Server would use.

The following characteristics apply to table-level locking options:

- You can specify one or more locking options for a table.
- Use the *optimizer_hints* portion of the FROM clause in a SELECT or UPDATE statement.
- These locking options override corresponding session-level (transaction isolation level) options that were previously specified with the SET statement.

The following table describes the table-level locking options.

Option	Description
HOLDLOCK SERIALIZABLE REPEATABLEREAD READCOMMITTED READUNCOMMITTED NOLOCK	Control locking behavior for a table and override the locks that would be used to enforce the isolation level of the current transaction
ROWLOCK PAGLOCK TABLOCK TABLOCKX	Specify the size and type of the locks to be used for a table
READPAST	Skip locked rows
UPDLOCK	Use update locks instead of shared locks

Deadlocks

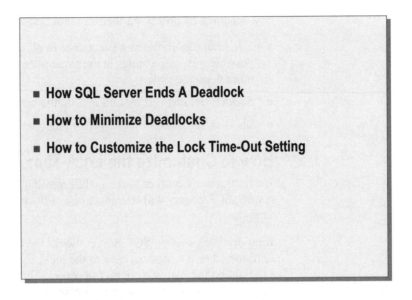

- How SQL Server Ends A Deadlock
- How to Minimize Deadlocks
- How to Customize the Lock Time-Out Setting

A deadlock occurs when two transactions have locks on separate objects and each transaction requests a lock on the other transaction's object. Each transaction must wait for the other to release the lock.

A deadlock can occur when several long-running transactions execute concurrently in the same database. A deadlock also can occur as a result of the order in which the optimizer processes a complex query, such as a join, in which you cannot necessarily control the order of processing.

How SQL Server Ends a Deadlock

SQL Server ends a deadlock by automatically terminating one of the transactions. The process SQL Server uses is in the following list.

1. Rolls back the transaction of the deadlock victim.

   In a deadlock, SQL Server gives priority to the transaction that has been processing the longest; that transaction prevails. SQL Server rolls back the transaction with the least amount of time invested.

2. Notifies the deadlock victim's application (with message number 1205).

3. Cancels the deadlock victim's current request.

4. Allows the other transaction to continue.

Important In a multiuser environment, each client should check regularly for message number 1205, which indicates that the transaction was rolled back. If message 1205 is found, the application should attempt the transaction again.

How to Minimize Deadlocks

While it is not always possible to eliminate deadlocks, you can reduce the risk of a deadlock by observing the following guidelines:

- Use resources in the same sequence in all transactions. For example, if possible, reference tables in the same order in all transactions that reference more than one table.
- Shorten transactions by minimizing the number of steps.
- Shorten transaction times by avoiding queries that affect many rows.

How to Customize the Lock Time-Out Setting

If a transaction becomes locked while waiting for a resource and a deadlock results, SQL Server will terminate one of the participating transactions with no time-out.

If no deadlock occurs, SQL Server blocks the transaction requesting the lock until the other transaction releases the lock. By default, there is no mandatory time-out period that SQL Server observes. The only way to test whether a resource that you want to lock is already locked is to attempt to access the data, which could result in getting locked indefinitely.

The LOCK_TIMEOUT setting allows an application to set a maximum time that a statement waits on a blocked resource before the blocked statement is automatically cancelled. The cancellation does not roll back or cancel the transaction. The application must trap the error to handle the time-out situation and take remedial action, such as resubmitting the transaction or rolling it back.

The KILL command terminates a user process based on the server process ID (spid).

Displaying Locking Information

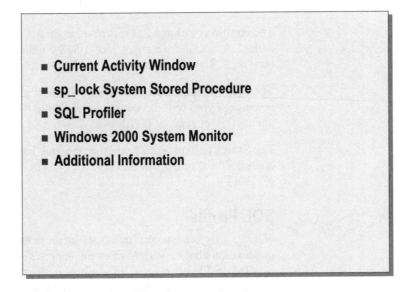

- **Current Activity Window**
- **sp_lock System Stored Procedure**
- **SQL Profiler**
- **Windows 2000 System Monitor**
- **Additional Information**

Typically, you use SQL Server Enterprise Manager or the **sp_lock** system stored procedure to display a report of active locks. You can use SQL Profiler to get information on a specific set of transactions. You can also use Microsoft Windows® 2000 System Monitor to display SQL Server locking histories.

Current Activity Window

Use the Current Activity window in SQL Server Enterprise Manager to display information on current locking activity. You can view server activity by user, detail activity by connection, and locking information by object.

sp_lock System Stored Procedure

The **sp_lock** system stored procedure returns information about active locks in SQL Server.

Syntax

EXECUTE **sp_lock**

Result

A typical result set resembles the following.

spid	dbid	ObjId	IndId	Type	Resource	Mode	Status
12	5	0	0	DB		S	GRANT
12	5	0	0	DB		S	GRANT
12	2	0	0	EXT	1:280	X	GRANT
12	5	0	0	PAG	1:528	IX	GRANT
12	5	981578535	0	RID	1:528:0	X	GRANT
12	1	5575058	0	TAB		IS	GRANT
12	5	981578535	0	TAB		IX	GRANT
13	1	0	0	DB		S	GRANT

The first four columns refer to various IDs: server process ID (spid), database ID (dbid), object ID (ObjId), and the index identification number ID (IndId).

The **Type** column shows the type of resource that is currently locked. Resource types can include: DB (database), EXT (extent), TAB (table), KEY (key), PAG (page), or RID (row identifier).

The **Resource** column has information on the resource type that is being locked. A resource description of 1:528:0 indicates that row number 0, on page number 528, on file 1 has a lock applied to it.

The **Mode** column describes the type of lock that is being applied to the resource. Types of locks can include: shared (S), exclusive (X), intent (I), update (U), or schema (Sch).

The **Status** column shows whether the lock has been obtained (GRANT), is blocking on another process (WAIT), or is in the process of being converted (CNVRT).

SQL Profiler

SQL Profiler is a tool that monitors server activities. You can collect information about a variety of events by creating traces, which provide a detailed profile of server events. You can use this profile to analyze and resolve server resource issues, monitor login attempts and connections, and correct deadlock problems.

Windows 2000 System Monitor

You can view SQL Server locking information with System Monitor. Use the **SQL Server: lock manager** and **SQL Server: locks** objects.

Additional Information

To find information about locks and current server activity, you can query the **syslockinfo, sysprocesses, sysobjects, systables, and syslogins** system tables or you can execute the **sp_who** system stored procedure.

Recommended Practices

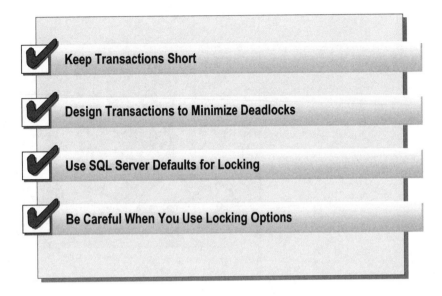

- Keep Transactions Short
- Design Transactions to Minimize Deadlocks
- Use SQL Server Defaults for Locking
- Be Careful When You Use Locking Options

You should consider adopting the following recommended practices when you manage transactions and locks:

- Keep transactions as short as possible, as this reduces the possibility of locking conflicts with other transactions. A transaction should never be smaller than a logical unit of work.

- Design transactions to minimize deadlocks so that transactions do not have to be resubmitted.

- Use SQL Server defaults for locking because the optimizer generally uses the best locks based on the particular transaction and other activity in the database.

- Be careful when you use locking options, and test your transactions to ensure that your locking choices are better than the SQL Server defaults.

Lab A: Managing Transactions and Locks

Objectives

After completing this lab, you will be able to:

- Define transactions with the BEGIN TRANSACTION and COMMIT TRANSACTION statements.

- Determine the number of active transactions by querying the **@@trancount** global variable.

- Use the **sp_lock** system stored procedure and SQL Server Enterprise Manager to view locking information.

- Use the SET TRANSACTION ISOLATION LEVEL statement to control session-level locking behavior.

- Use table-level locking options to control locking behavior for specific tables.

- Use the SET LOCK_TIMEOUT statement to control the maximum amount of time that a statement will wait for a lock to be released.

Prerequisites

Before working on this lab, you must have:

- Script files for this lab, which are located in C:\Moc\2073A\Labfiles\L15.

Lab Setup

To complete this lab, you must have either:

- Completed the prior lab, or

- Executed the C:\Moc\2073A\Batches\Restore15.cmd batch file.

  This command file restores the **ClassNorthwind** database to a state required for this lab.

For More Information

If you require help with executing files, search SQL Query Analyzer Help for "Execute a query".

Other resources that you can use include:

- The **Northwind** database schema.
- SQL Server Books Online.

Scenario

The organization of the classroom is meant to simulate that of a worldwide trading firm named Northwind Traders. Its fictitious domain name is nwtraders.msft. The primary DNS server for nwtraders.msft is the instructor computer, which has an Internet Protocol (IP) address of 192.168.x.200 (where x is the assigned classroom number). The name of the instructor computer is London.

The following table provides the user name, computer name, and IP address for each student computer in the fictitious **nwtraders.msft** domain. Find the user name for your computer, and make a note of it.

User name	Computer name	IP address
SQLAdmin1	Vancouver	192.168.x.1
SQLAdmin2	Denver	192.168.x.2
SQLAdmin3	Perth	192.168.x.3
SQLAdmin4	Brisbane	192.168.x.4
SQLAdmin5	Lisbon	192.168.x.5
SQLAdmin6	Bonn	192.168.x.6
SQLAdmin7	Lima	192.168.x.7
SQLAdmin8	Santiago	192.168.x.8
SQLAdmin9	Bangalore	192.168.x.9
SQLAdmin10	Singapore	192.168.x.10
SQLAdmin11	Casablanca	192.168.x.11
SQLAdmin12	Tunis	192.168.x.12
SQLAdmin13	Acapulco	192.168.x.13
SQLAdmin14	Miami	192.168.x.14
SQLAdmin15	Auckland	192.168.x.15
SQLAdmin16	Suva	192.168.x.16
SQLAdmin17	Stockholm	192.168.x.17
SQLAdmin18	Moscow	192.168.x.18
SQLAdmin19	Caracas	192.168.x.19
SQLAdmin20	Montevideo	192.168.x.20
SQLAdmin21	Manila	192.168.x.21
SQLAdmin22	Tokyo	192.168.x.22
SQLAdmin23	Khartoum	192.168.x.23
SQLAdmin24	Nairobi	192.168.x.24

Estimated time to complete this lab: 60 minutes

Exercise 1
Creating and Executing a Transaction

In this exercise, you will use the BEGIN TRANSACTION and COMMIT TRANSACTION statements to understand the impact of the statements on the way that data is modified. You also will see how SQL Server uses the **@@trancount** global variable to determine whether a transaction is active.

▶ **To create and execute a transaction**

In this procedure, you will use the BEGIN TRANSACTION and COMMIT TRANSACTION statements to control how an UPDATE statement is processed on the **Customers** table.

1. Log on to the **NWTraders** classroom domain by using the information in the following table.

Option	Value
User name	**SQLAdmin***x* (where *x* corresponds to your computer name as designated in the **nwtraders.msft** classroom domain)
Password	**password**

2. Open SQL Query Analyzer and, if prompted, log in to the (local) server with Microsoft Windows® Authentication.

   You have permission to log in to and administer SQL Server because you are logged as **SQLAdmin***x*, which is a member of the Windows 2000 local group, Administrators. All members of this group are automatically mapped to the SQL Server **sysadmin** role.

3. In the **DB** list, click **ClassNorthwind**.

4. Open C:\Moc\2073A\Labfiles\L15\Tran1.sql and review its contents.

   Notice that the BEGIN TRAN statement is followed by an UPDATE statement, but no corresponding COMMIT TRAN or ROLLBACK TRAN statement is present. The SELECT and PRINT statements and the **@@trancount** global variable are used in the script to show the progress of the transaction.

5. Execute the script and review the results.

   At this point, are the changes that were made with the UPDATE statement committed in this transaction? How can you determine this?

   _____

   _____

   Would other transactions be able to query or update the changed data?

   _____

   _____

6. Enter a COMMIT TRANSACTION statement in the query window, and then highlight and execute it to complete the transaction and make the change permanent.

7. Highlight and execute one of the SELECT statements for the **Customers** table to verify that the change has now been completed.

Exercise 2
Rolling Back a Transaction

In this exercise, you will use the ROLLBACK TRANSACTION statement to understand the impact of the way that data is modified within a transaction.

▶ **To use the ROLLBACK TRANSACTION statement**

In this procedure, you will use the BEGIN TRANSACTION and ROLLBACK TRANSACTION statements to control how an UPDATE statement is processed on the **member** table.

1. Open C:\Moc\2073A\Labfiles\L15\Tran2.sql and review its contents.

   Notice that this script is similar to Tran1.sql, but the contact name is different, and a ROLLBACK TRAN statement has been added.

2. Execute the script and review the results.

   Is the change made by the UPDATE statement stored permanently in the database?

   _____

   _____

   Is the transaction complete?

   _____

   _____

Exercise 3
Viewing Locking Information

In this exercise, you will execute multiple transactions simultaneously to determine the impact that such activity has on locking. You will be asked to open multiple connections with SQL Query Analyzer to simulate multiple users sending transactions to SQL Server.

Notice that the scripts used for this exercise do not always include COMMIT TRAN or ROLLBACK TRAN statements. The absence of these statements keeps the transactions open and the associated locks active so that you can view locking information.

▶ To view locking information

In this procedure, you will use the BEGIN TRANSACTION and ROLLBACK TRANSACTION statements to control how an UPDATE statement is processed on the **Customers** table.

1. Start SQL Query Analyzer (connection 1), click **Clear Query Window**.

2. Execute the **sp_lock** system stored procedure and review the output.

3. Start SQL Server Enterprise Manager.

4. In SQL Server Enterprise Manager, in the console tree, expand your server, expand **Management**, and then expand **Current Activity**. Review the information that is displayed in **Process Info**, **Locks / Process ID** and **Locks / Object**.

5. Open a second connection with SQL Query Analyzer (connection 2) and in the **DB** list, click **ClassNorthwind**.

6. Open C:\Moc\2073A\Labfiles\L15\Lock1.sql by using connection 2 and review its contents.

   Notice that a transaction is started with the BEGIN TRAN statement but a corresponding COMMIT TRAN or ROLLBACK TRAN statement to complete the transaction does not exist.

7. Execute \Lock1.sql by using connection 2 and review the results.

8. Switch to connection 1, execute the **sp_lock** system stored procedure, and then review the lock information.

   Identify the different lock types and resources locked by the transaction. Make a note of this information for subsequent use in Exercise 4.

   _____

   _____

9. Switch to SQL Server Enterprise Manager, right-click **Current Activity**, and then click **Refresh**.

10. Review the information in **Current Activity** that is displayed in **Process Info, Locks / Process ID** and **Locks / Object**.

11. Switch to connection 2 and cancel the transaction that you started in step 7 by executing a ROLLBACK TRAN statement.

12. Switch to connection 1 and execute the **sp_lock** system stored procedure.

    You will see that the locks acquired by the transaction in step 6 have now been released.

Exercise 4
Setting Locking Options

In this exercise, you will use some SQL Server locking options to determine how they affect the way that transactions are processed. You will use the connections that you established with SQL Query Analyzer in Exercise 3 to simulate multiple users sending transactions to SQL Server. You also can use the Current Activity window in SQL Server Enterprise Manager to view locking information for this exercise.

▶ **To set the transaction isolation level**

In this procedure, you will use the SET TRANSACTION ISOLATION LEVEL statement to control session-level locking behavior. You will use the connections that you established with SQL Query Analyzer in Exercise 3.

1. Switch to SQL Query Analyzer (connection 2).

2. Open the C:\Moc\2073A\Labfiles\L15\Lock2.sql script file by using connection 2, review its contents, and then execute it.

3. Switch to connection 1, execute the **sp_lock** system stored procedure, and then review the lock information.

   Identify and review the different lock types and resources that are locked by the transaction.

   Did SQL Server use different locks than those that were used in step 8 of Exercise 3? Why or why not?

   _____

   _____

4. Switch to connection 2 and cancel the transaction by executing a ROLLBACK TRAN statement.

▶ **To use locking options for tables**

In this procedure, you will use table-level locking options to control locking behavior.

1. Switch to SQL Query Analyzer (connection 1).

2. Execute the **sp_lock** system stored procedure by using connection 1 and review the output.

3. Switch to SQL Query Analyzer (connection 2).

4. Open the C:\Moc\2073A\Labfiles\L15\Lock3.sql script file by using connection 2 and review its contents.

   Notice that a table locking option has been defined in the FROM clause of the SELECT statement. Also notice that there is no COMMIT TRAN or ROLLBACK TRAN statement in the script.

5. Execute the Lock3.sql script file in connection 2.

6. Switch to connection 1 and execute the **sp_lock** system stored procedure.

   Make a note of the types of locks that are in use and the resources that are locked.

   _____

   _____

7. Open a third connection with SQL Query Analyzer (connection 3) and in the **DB** list, click **ClassNorthwind**.

8. Open the C:\Moc\2073A\Labfiles\L15\Lock1.sql script file by using connection 3 and then execute it.

9. Switch to connection 1 and execute the **sp_lock** system stored procedure.

   Is one transaction unable to execute? If so, why?

   _____

   _____

   How long will a transaction wait on a locked resource?

   _____

   _____

10. Switch to connection 3 and on the toolbar, click **Cancel Query Execution**.

11. Switch to connection 1 and execute the **sp_lock** system stored procedure to verify that the waiting transaction has been cancelled.

▶ **To set the lock timeout period for a transaction**

In this procedure, you will set the lock timeout period so that the transaction will wait to acquire a lock for a specified time.

1. Switch to connection 3 and edit the C:\Moc\2073A\Labfiles\L15\Lock1.sql script file by adding the following statement immediately before the BEGIN TRAN statement:

   SET lock_timeout 500

2. Execute the edited script by using connection 3.

   What happened, and why?

   _____

   _____

3. Close all windows in SQL Query Analyzer.

Review

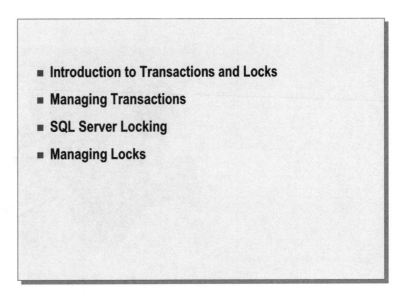

- Introduction to Transactions and Locks
- Managing Transactions
- SQL Server Locking
- Managing Locks

1. You are developing a new order entry system for your company. You expect that the system will be very active because 450 operators take orders from customers 24 hours a day. Should operators process all items that a customer orders during a single phone call in a single transaction?

2. Once a month you are required to perform an update to the **products** table in your order entry system. The **products** table contains millions of items. Each monthly update is expected to affect at least 65 percent of the rows in the table. You can write a single, complex UPDATE statement to perform the update, which typically takes at least 30 minutes to execute. Is this the best way to perform the update?

3. You are receiving calls from users. They say that the response time of the order entry system periodically increases to more than 20 seconds. You have promised them a three-second response time. You suspect that locking conflicts may exist within the system. How would you determine the source of the problem?

Course Evaluation

Your evaluation of this course will help Microsoft understand the quality of your learning experience.

To complete a course evaluation, go to http://www.metricsthatmatter.com/survey.

Microsoft will keep your evaluation strictly confidential and will use your responses to improve your future learning experience.

Notes

Notes